W9-CHX-062

Authorized Self-Study Guide

Interconnecting Cisco Network Devices, Part 2 (ICND2)

Steve McQuerry,
CCIE No. 6108

Cisco Press

800 East 96th Street
Indianapolis, Indiana 46240 USA

Authorized Self-Study Guide
Interconnecting Cisco Network Devices, Part 2 (ICND2)

Steve McQuerry

Copyright© 2008 Cisco Systems, Inc.

Published by:
Cisco Press
800 East 96th Street
Indianapolis, IN 46240 USA

Printed in the United States of America

First Printing February 2008

Library of Congress Cataloging-in-Publication Data:

McQuerry, Steve.

Interconnecting Cisco network devices. Part 2 (ICND2) / Steve McQuerry.

p. cm.

ISBN 978-1-58705-463-1 (hardback)

1. Internetworking (Telecommunication)—Examinations—Study guides. 2. Computer networks—Problems, exercises, etc. 3. Telecommunications engineers—Certification—Examinations—Study guides. I. Title.

TK5105.5.M33992 2008

004.6—dc22

2008000513
ISBN-13: 978-1-58705-463-1
ISBN-10: 1-58705-463-9

Warning and Disclaimer

This book is designed to provide information about the configuration and operation of Cisco routers and switches as described in the Interconnecting Cisco Network Devices 2 (ICND2) course. Every effort has been made to make this book as complete and as accurate as possible, but no warranty or fitness is implied.

The information is provided on an "as is" basis. The authors, Cisco Press, and Cisco Systems, Inc. shall have neither liability nor responsibility to any person or entity with respect to any loss or damages arising from the information contained in this book or from the use of the discs or programs that may accompany it.

The opinions expressed in this book belong to the author and are not necessarily those of Cisco Systems, Inc.

Feedback Information

At Cisco Press, our goal is to create in-depth technical books of the highest quality and value. Each book is crafted with care and precision, undergoing rigorous development that involves the unique expertise of members from the professional technical community.

Readers' feedback is a natural continuation of this process. If you have any comments regarding how we could improve the quality of this book, or otherwise alter it to better suit your needs, you can contact us through email at feedback@ciscopress.com. Please make sure to include the book title and ISBN in your message.

We greatly appreciate your assistance.

Corporate and Government Sales

The publisher offers excellent discounts on this book when ordered in quantity for bulk purchases or special sales, which may include electronic versions and/or custom covers and content particular to your business, training goals, marketing focus, and branding interests. For more information, please contact: **U.S. Corporate and Government Sales** 1-800-382-3419 corpsales@pearsontechgroup.com

For sales outside the United States please contact: **International Sales** international@pearsoned.com

Trademark Acknowledgments

All terms mentioned in this book that are known to be trademarks or service marks have been appropriately capitalized. Cisco Press or Cisco Systems, Inc., cannot attest to the accuracy of this information. Use of a term in this book should not be regarded as affecting the validity of any trademark or service mark.

Publisher	Paul Boger
Associate Publisher	Dave Dusthimer
Cisco Representative	Anthony Wolfenden
Cisco Press Program Manager	Jeff Brady
Executive Editor	Brett Bartow
Managing Editor	Patrick Kanouse
Development Editor	Deadline Driven Publishing
Senior Project Editor	Tonya Simpson
Copy Editors	Gill Editorial Services
	Written Elegance, Inc.
Technical Editors	Tami Day-Orsatti,
	Andrew Whitaker
Editorial Assistant	Vanessa Evans
Book and Cover Designer	Louisa Adair
Composition	ICC Macmillan, Inc.
Indexer	Ken Johnson
Proofreader	Language Logistics, LLC

Americas Headquarters	Asia Pacific Headquarters	Europe Headquarters
Cisco Systems, Inc.	Cisco Systems, Inc.	Cisco Systems International BV
170 West Tasman Drive	168 Robinson Road	Haarlerbergpark
San Jose, CA 95134-1706	#28-01 Capital Tower	Haarlerbergweg 13-19
USA	Singapore 068912	1101 CH Amsterdam
www.cisco.com	www.cisco.com	The Netherlands
Tel: 408 526-4000	Tel: +65 6317 7777	www-europe.cisco.com
800 553-NETS (6387)	Fax: +65 6317 7799	Tel: +31 0 800 020 0791
Fax: 408 527-0883		Fax: +31 0 20 357 1100

Cisco has more than 200 offices worldwide. Addresses, phone numbers, and fax numbers are listed on the Cisco Website at **www.cisco.com/go/offices.**

About the Author

Steve McQuerry, CCIE No. 6108, is a consulting systems engineer with Cisco focused on data center architecture. Steve works with enterprise customers in the Midwestern United States to help them plan their data center architectures. Steve has been an active member of the internetworking community since 1991 and has held multiple certifications from Novell, Microsoft, and Cisco. Before joining Cisco, Steve worked as an independent contractor with Global Knowledge, where he taught and developed coursework around Cisco technologies and certifications.

About the Technical Reviewers

Tami Day-Orsatti, CCSI, CCDP, CCNP, CISSP, MCT, MCSE 2000/2003: Security, is an IT networking and security instructor for T^2 IT Training. She is responsible for the delivery of authorized Cisco, (ISC)^2, and Microsoft classes. She has more than 23 years in the IT industry working with many different types of organizations (private business, city and federal government, and DoD), providing project management and senior-level network and security technical skills in the design and implementation of complex computing environments.

Andrew Whitaker, M.Sc., CISSP, CCVP, CCNP, CCSP, CCNA, CCDA, MCSE, MCTS, CNE, CEI, CEH, ECSA, Security+, A+, Network+, Convergence+, CTP, is the director of Enterprise InfoSec and Networking for Training Camp, an international training company that helps certify thousands of IT professionals each year through its unique accelerated learning model. His expert teaching for Training Camp has garnered coverage by *The Wall Street Journal*, *The Philadelphia Inquirer*, *Certification Magazine*, and *Business Week* magazine. In addition to coauthoring *CCNA Exam Cram*, Andrew coauthored the Cisco Press title *Penetration Testing and Network Defense* and has contributed articles on Cisco certification for CertificationZone. Andrew is currently working on authoring and technical editing other book projects.

Dedications

This work is dedicated to my family. Becky, as the years go by, I love you more. Thank you for your support and understanding. Katie, your work ethic has always amazed me. As you prepare to move into the next phase of your life, remember your goals and keep working hard and you can achieve anything. Logan, you have never believed there was anything you couldn't do. Keep that drive and spirit, and there will be no limit to what you can accomplish. Cameron, you have a keen sense of curiosity that reminds me of myself as a child. Use that thirst for understanding and learning, and you will be successful in all your endeavors.

Acknowledgments

A great number of people go into publishing a work like this, and I would like to take this space to thank everyone who was involved with this project.

Thanks to the ICND course developers. Most of this book is the product of their hard work.

Thanks to the technical editors, Tami and Andrew, for looking over this work and helping maintain its technical integrity.

Thanks to all the real publishing professionals at Cisco Press. This is a group of people with whom I have had the pleasure of working since 1998, and it has been a joy and an honor. Thanks to Brett Bartow for allowing me the opportunity to write for Cisco Press once again, and to Chris Cleveland for gently reminding me how to write again after a three-year break. It's definitely not as easy as riding a bike. Thanks to Ginny Bess for keeping the work flowing and dealing with my bad jokes. Also to Tonya Simpson, Patrick Kanouse, and the rest of the Cisco Press team—you are the best in the industry.

Thanks to my manager at Cisco, Darrin Thomason, for trusting me to keep all my other projects managed while working on this project in my spare time (wait, do we have spare time at Cisco?).

Thanks to my customers, colleagues, and former students. Your questions, comments, and challenges have helped me continue to learn and helped teach me how to pass that information to others.

Thanks to my family, for their patience and understanding during this project and all my projects.

Most importantly, I would like to thank God for giving me the skills, talents, and opportunity to work in such a challenging and exciting profession.

This Book Is Safari Enabled

The Safari™ Enabled icon on the cover of your favorite technology book means that the book is available through Safari Bookshelf. When you buy this book, you get free access to the online edition for 45 days.

Safari Bookshelf is an electronic reference library that lets you easily search thousands of technical books, find code samples, download chapters, and access technical information whenever and wherever you need it.

To gain 45-day Safari Enabled access to this book, follow these steps:

- Go to http://www.ciscopress.com/safarienabled.
- Complete the brief registration form.
- Enter the coupon code IDF8-D9EG-9DFE-SEGX-S6WB.

If you have difficulty registering on Safari Bookshelf or accessing the online edition, please e-mail customer-service@safaribooksonline.com.

Contents at a Glance

Contents

Icons Used in This Book

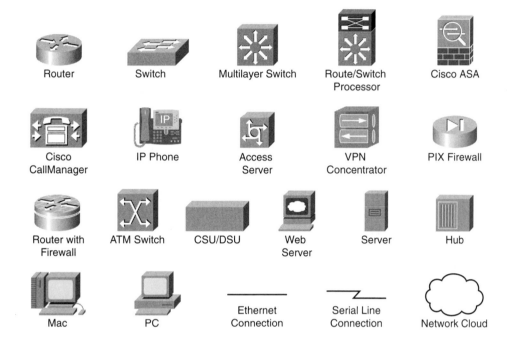

Command Syntax Conventions

The conventions used to present command syntax in this book are the same conventions used in the IOS Command Reference. The Command Reference describes these conventions as follows:

- **Boldface** indicates commands and keywords that are entered literally as shown. In actual configuration examples and output (not general command syntax), boldface indicates commands that are manually input by the user (such as a **show** command).

- *Italics* indicate arguments for which you supply actual values.

- Vertical bars (|) separate alternative, mutually exclusive elements.

- Square brackets [ ] indicate optional elements.

- Braces { } indicate a required choice.

- Braces within brackets [{ }] indicate a required choice within an optional element.

Foreword

Cisco certification self-study guides are excellent self-study resources for networking professionals to maintain and increase internetworking skills, and to prepare for Cisco Career Certification exams. Cisco Career Certifications are recognized worldwide and provide valuable, measurable rewards to networking professionals and their employers.

Cisco Press exam certification guides and preparation materials offer exceptional—and flexible—access to the knowledge and information required to stay current in one's field of expertise, or to gain new skills. Whether used to increase internetworking skills or as a supplement to a formal certification preparation course, these materials offer networking professionals the information and knowledge required to perform on-the-job tasks proficiently.

Developed in conjunction with the Cisco certifications and training team, Cisco Press books are the only self-study books authorized by Cisco, and they offer students a series of exam practice tools and resource materials to help ensure that learners fully grasp the concepts and information presented.

Additional authorized Cisco instructor-led courses, e-learning, labs, and simulations are available exclusively from Cisco Learning Solutions Partners worldwide. To learn more, visit http://www.cisco.com/go/training.

I hope you will find this guide to be an essential part of your exam preparation and professional development, as well as a valuable addition to your personal library.

Drew Rosen
Manager, Learning & Development
Learning@Cisco
December 2007

Introduction

Since the introduction of the personal computer in the early 1970s, businesses have found more uses and applications for technology in the workplace. With the introduction of local-area networks, file sharing, and print sharing in the 1980s, it became obvious that distributed computing was no longer a passing fad. By the 1990s, computers became less expensive, and innovations such as the Internet allowed everyone to connect to computer services worldwide. Computing services have become large and distributed. The days of punch cards and green-bar paper are behind us, and a new generation of computing experts is being asked to keep this distributed technology operational. These experts are destined to have a new set of issues and problems to deal with, the most complex of them being connectivity and compatibility among differing systems and devices.

The primary challenge with data networking today is to link multiple devices' protocols and sites with maximum effectiveness and ease of use for end users. Of course, this must all be accomplished in a cost-effective way. Cisco offers a variety of products to give network managers and analysts the ability to face and solve the challenges of internetworking.

In an effort to ensure that these networking professionals have the knowledge to perform these arduous tasks, Cisco has developed a series of courses and certifications that act as benchmarks for internetworking professionals. These courses help internetworking professionals learn the fundamentals of internetworking technologies along with skills in configuring and installing Cisco products. The certification exams are designed to be a litmus test for the skills required to perform at various levels of internetworking. The Cisco certifications range from the associate level, Cisco Certified Network Associate (CCNA), through the professional level, Cisco Certified Network Professional (CCNP), to the expert level, Cisco Certified Internetwork Expert (CCIE).

The Interconnecting Cisco Network Devices, Part 2 (ICND2) course is one of two recommended training classes for CCNA preparation. As a self-study complement to the course, this book helps to ground individuals in the fundamentals of switches and routed internetworks.
It presents the concepts, commands, and practices required to configure Cisco switches and routers to operate in corporate internetworks. You will be introduced to all the basic concepts and configuration procedures required to build a multiswitch, multirouter, and multigroup internetwork that uses LAN and WAN interfaces for the most commonly used routing and routed protocols. ICND provides the installation and configuration information that network administrators require to install and configure Cisco products.

Interconnecting Cisco Network Devices, Part 2 (ICND2), is the second part of a two-part, introductory-level series and is recommended for individuals who have one to three years of internetworking experience, are familiar with basic internetworking concepts, and have basic experience with the TCP/IP protocol. While the self-study book is designed for those who are pursuing the CCNA certification, it is also useful for network administrators responsible for implementing and managing small- and medium-sized business networks. Network support staff who perform a help-desk role in a medium- or enterprise-sized company will find this a valuable resource. Finally, Cisco customers or channel resellers and network technicians entering the internetworking industry who are new to Cisco products can benefit from the contents of this book.

Goals

The goal of this book is twofold. First, it is intended as a self-study book for the ICND2 test 640-816 and the CCNA test 640-802, which are part of the requirements for the CCNA certification. Like the certification itself, the book should help readers become literate in the use of switches, routers, and the associated protocols and technologies. The second goal is that someone who completes the book and the CCNA certification should be able to use these skills to select, connect, and configure Cisco devices in an internetworking environment. In particular, the book covers the basic steps and processes involved with moving data through the network using routing and Layer 2 switching.

Readers interested in more information about the CCNA certification should consult the Cisco website at http://www.cisco.com/en/US/learning/le3/le2/le0/le9/ learning_certification_type_home.html. To schedule a Cisco certification test, contact Pearson Vue on the web at http://www.PearsonVue.com/cisco or Prometric on the web at http://www.2test.com.

Chapter Organization

This book is divided into eight chapters and an appendix and is designed to be read in order because many chapters build on content from previous chapters.

- Chapter 1, "Review of Cisco IOS for Routers and Switches," provides a review of the Cisco IOS. This is an assumed knowledge for readers, but this chapter provides a brief review of command structure that is used throughout the other chapters of the book.

- Chapter 2, "Medium-Sized Switched Network Construction," explores the operation and configuration of local-area networks, including the challenges associated with these networks, and describes how network devices are used to eliminate these problems focusing on Layer 2 switching.

- Chapter 3, "Medium-Sized Routed Network Construction," describes routing operations. This chapter discusses the differences between link-state and distance vector routing protocols and provides the foundation for Chapters 4 and 5.

- Chapter 4, "Single-Area OSPF Implementation," looks at how to configure OSPF to act as a routing protocol within a network. This chapter describes the operation of the protocol and provides configuration examples for a single area. The chapter also includes troubleshooting steps.

- Chapter 5, "Implementing EIGRP," discusses the EIGRP routing protocol. It describes the operation of the protocol and the configuration requirements. It also includes troubleshooting steps.

- Chapter 6, "Managing Traffic with Access Control Lists," discusses how access control lists are used in Cisco IOS to identify and filter traffic. The chapter discusses the configuration of the lists and provides some practical applications of these lists.

- Chapter 7, "Managing Address Spaces with NAT and IPv6," discusses the limitations of IPv4 address space, specifically that these addresses are running out. The chapter discusses how Network Address Translation (NAT) and Port Address Translation (PAT) are helping conserve addresses and how IPv6 will alleviate this problem. The chapter also discusses the configuration of NAT, PAT, and IPv6.

- Chapter 8, "Extending the Network into the WAN," describes how different sites can be connected across a wide-area network or using the Internet. It discusses VPN and SSL VPN (WebVPN) solutions as well as traditional leased line and Frame Relay connections. The chapter also provides a troubleshooting section.

- The appendix, "Answers to Chapter Review Questions," provides answers to the review questions at the end of each chapter.

Features

This book features actual router and switch output to aid in the discussion of the configuration of these devices. Many notes, tips, and cautions are also spread throughout the text. In addition, you can find many references to standards, documents, books, and websites to help you understand networking concepts. At the end of each chapter, your comprehension and knowledge are tested by review questions prepared by a certified Cisco instructor.

NOTE The operating systems used in this book are Cisco IOS Software Release 12.4 for the routers, and Cisco Catalyst 2960 is based on Cisco IOS Software Release 12.2.

This chapter includes the following sections:

- Chapter Objectives

- Cisco IOS CLI Functions

- Chapter Summary

- Review Questions

CHAPTER 1

Review of Cisco IOS for Routers and Switches

As small networks grow and become more complex, greater functionality and control over network components, delivered through more sophisticated network devices such as switches and routers, become critical. Most Cisco hardware platforms implement Cisco IOS Software, including switches and routers. This software enables network services in Cisco products, including carrying the chosen network protocols and functions, controlling access and prohibiting unauthorized network use, and adding interfaces and capability as needed for network growth. You use the command-line interface of the Cisco IOS Software to enter the configuration details into the Cisco switches and routers that implement the network requirements of an organization. To understand how to configure the more complex protocols and functions of Cisco routers and switches, you need to understand the basics of IOS Software. This chapter briefly reviews some of the key elements of the Cisco IOS Software, provided as an aid for the configuration details in this book. The chapter is in no way intended to be comprehensive and assumes that the reader has Cisco IOS familiarity or has completed the Interconnecting Cisco Network Devices (ICND), Part 1 materials.

If you find this chapter to be lacking or you do not feel comfortable with the commands and content presented here, please refer to *Authorized Self-Study Guide: Interconnecting Cisco Network Devices, Part 1* from Cisco Press.

Chapter Objectives

Upon completing this chapter, you will have reviewed how to configure and manage a Cisco IOS device. This ability includes being able to meet the following objectives:

- Implement a basic switch and router configuration

- Understand the modes and features of Cisco IOS

Cisco IOS Software is implemented on most Cisco hardware platforms, including switches and routers. This software enables network services in Cisco products, including carrying the chosen network protocols and functions, and adding interfaces and capability as needed for network growth.

This chapter is designed as a review of prerequisite knowledge. It is a review of the Cisco IOS command-line interface (CLI) structure and the Cisco IOS commands used to create a basic router and switch configuration. You will use these commands in an introductory lab that will serve as the initial configuration for all the subsequent lab activities.

Cisco IOS CLI Functions

Cisco IOS Software uses a CLI as its traditional console environment to enter commands. This section reviews the functions of the Cisco IOS CLI.

Although Cisco IOS Software is a core technology that extends across many products, its operation details vary depending on the internetworking devices that are involved. To enter commands into the CLI, type or paste the entries within one of the several console configuration modes. In terminal configuration mode, each configuration command entered is parsed as soon as you press the Enter key.

If the syntax has no errors, the command is executed and stored in the running configuration, and it is effective immediately, but the command is not automatically saved to NVRAM.

Cisco IOS Software uses a hierarchy of commands in its configuration-mode structure. Each configuration mode is indicated with a distinctive prompt and supports specific Cisco IOS commands related to a type of operation on the device.

As a security feature, Cisco IOS Software separates the EXEC sessions into the following two access levels:

- **User EXEC:** Allows access to only a limited number of basic monitoring commands.

- **Privileged EXEC:** Allows access to all device commands, such as those used for configuration and management, and can be password-protected to allow only authorized users to access the device.

Configuration Modes of Cisco IOS Software

Depending on the feature being used, there are different configuration modes when working with Cisco IOS Software. Figure 1-1 shows the various Cisco IOS configuration modes employed in this text.

The first method of configuration on a Cisco device is the setup utility, which lets you create a basic initial configuration. For more complex and specific configurations, you can use the CLI to enter terminal configuration mode.

Figure 1-1 *Cisco IOS Configuration Modes*

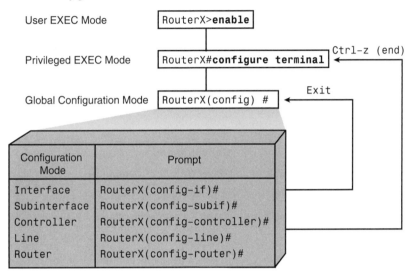

From privileged EXEC mode, you can enter global configuration mode using the **configure terminal** command. From global configuration mode, you can access specific configuration modes, which include, but are not limited to, the following:

- **Interface:** Supports commands that configure operations on a per-interface basis

- **Subinterface:** Supports commands that configure multiple virtual interfaces on a single physical interface

- **Controller:** Supports commands that configure controllers (for example, E1 and T1 controllers)

- **Line:** Supports commands that configure the operation of a terminal line (for example, the console or the vty ports)

- **Router:** Supports commands that configure an IP routing protocol

If you enter the **exit** command, the router backs out one level, eventually logging out. In general, you enter the **exit** command from one of the specific configuration modes to return to global configuration mode. Press Ctrl-Z or enter **end** to leave configuration mode completely and return to the privileged EXEC mode.

Commands that affect the entire device are called *global commands*. The **hostname** and **enable password** commands are examples of global commands.

Commands that point to or indicate a process or interface that will be configured are called *major commands*. When entered, major commands cause the CLI to enter a specific configuration mode. Major commands have no effect unless you immediately enter a subcommand that supplies the configuration entry. For example, the major command **interface serial 0** has no effect unless you follow it with a subcommand that tells what is to be done to that interface.

Table 1-1 provides examples of some major commands and subcommands that go with them.

Table 1-1 *Major Commands and Subcommands*

Major Command	Subcommand
RouterX(config)#**interface serial 0**	RouterX(config-if)#**shutdown**
RouterX(config-if)#**line console 0**	RouterX(config-line)#**password cisco**
RouterX(config-line)#**router rip**	RouterX(config-router)#**network 10.0.0.0**

Notice that entering a major command switches from one configuration mode to another.

NOTE You do not need to return to global configuration mode before entering another configuration mode.

Help Facilities of the Cisco IOS CLI

Cisco IOS Software uses several command-line input help facilities, including context-sensitive help. The following list provides details about the different help facilities of the Cisco IOS CLI.

- **Context-sensitive help:** Provides a list of commands and the arguments associated with a specific command.

- **Console error messages:** Identifies problems with any Cisco IOS commands that are incorrectly entered so that you can alter or correct them.

- **Command history buffer:** Allows recall of long or complex commands or entries for reentry, review, or corrections.

Context-sensitive help eliminates the need for memorization of Cisco IOS commands. At any time during an EXEC session, you can enter a question mark (**?**) to get help. The following two types of context-sensitive help are available:

- **Word help:** Enter the **?** command to get word help for a list of commands that begin with a particular character sequence. Enter the character sequence followed immediately by the question mark. Do not include a space before the question mark. The router displays a list of commands that begin with the characters you entered.

■ **Command syntax help:** Enter the **?** command to get command syntax help for completing a command. Enter a question mark in place of a keyword or argument. Include a space before the question mark. The network device then displays a list of available command options.

Commands Review

This section reviews basic router and switch CLI commands in Cisco IOS Software. Table 1-2 outlines the Cisco IOS CLI commands used on both Cisco routers and switches to create a basic configuration in a small network environment.

Table 1-2 *Cisco IOS CLI Command Review*

Command	Description
banner motd	Configures the Message-of-the-Day banner.
configure terminal	From privileged EXEC mode, enters global configuration mode.
copy running-config startup-config	Saves the running configuration into NVRAM as the startup configuration.
enable	Enters the privileged EXEC mode command interpreter.
enable secret *password*	Sets an enable secret password to enter privilege EXEC.
erase startup-configuration	Erases the startup configuration from memory.
hostname *name*	Assigns the device a hostname.
interface *interface*	Specifies an interface and enters interface configuration mode.
ip address *address mask*	Sets the IP address and mask of the device.
ip default-gateway *address*	Sets the default gateway of the switch.
line console 0	Specifies the console line and enters line configuration mode.
line vty 0 4	Specifies the vty lines and enters line configuration mode.
login	Sets password checking at login.
password *password*	Sets a password on a line.
ping *ip address*	Uses Internet Control Message Protocol (ICMP) echo requests and ICMP echo replies to determine whether a remote host is active.
reload	Reboots the device.
show cdp neighbors	Displays the Cisco Discovery Protocol updates received on each local interface of the device.
show interfaces	Displays information on all the device interfaces.
show running-configuration	Displays the active configuration.
show startup-configuration	Displays the configuration settings of the router NVRAM.
shutdown/no shutdown	Disables or enables an interface.

Summary of Cisco IOS CLI Commands

The key points to remember about Cisco IOS CLI commands are as follows:

■ A basic router or switch configuration includes the provision of hostnames for identification, the provision of passwords for security, and the assignment of IP addresses for connectivity.

■ You use the CLI to enter commands.

■ You use the **configure terminal** command to enter global configuration mode. To exit global configuration mode, you can use the **end** command or press Ctrl-Z.

■ The CLI provides context-sensitive help, console error messages, and a command history buffer.

Chapter Summary

The list that follows summarizes the key points that were discussed in this chapter:

■ The Cisco IOS CLI has hierarchical configuration modes for configuring routers and switches.

■ You will use this interface as a means to implement a basic switched and routed internetwork within the confines of a small network design.

A basic router or switch configuration includes the provision of hostnames for identification, the provision of passwords for security, and the assignment of IP addresses for connectivity.

Review Questions

Use the questions here to review what you learned in this chapter. The correct answers and solutions are found in the appendix, "Answers to Chapter Review Questions."

1. Which access level allows a person to access all router commands and can be password-protected to allow only authorized individuals to access the router?

   a. User EXEC level

   b. Setup EXEC level

   c. Enable EXEC level

   d. Privileged EXEC level

2. How do you instruct a Cisco device to parse and execute an entered command?

   a. Press the Send key.

   b. Press the Enter key.

c. Add a space at the end of the command.

d. Wait five seconds after you enter a command.

3. Which of the following CLI prompts indicates that you are working in privileged EXEC mode?

    a. hostname#

    b. hostname>

    c. hostname-exec>

    d. hostname-config

4. Which of the following commands would you enter in privileged EXEC mode to see a list of the command options?

    a. **?**

    b. **init**

    c. **help**

    d. **login**

5. Which CLI command should you enter to display a list of commands that begin with the letter "c" on a Cisco Catalyst switch?

    a. **c?**

    b. **c ?**

    c. **help c**

    d. **help c***

6. Which CLI command should you enter to display command syntax help so that you can determine how to complete a command that begins with **config**?

    a. **config?**

    b. **config ?**

    c. **help config**

    d. **help config***

7. Which of the following configuration modes should you use to configure a particular port on a switch?

    a. User mode

    b. Global configuration mode

    c. Interface configuration mode

    d. Controller configuration mode

8. Which of the following **show** commands requires you to have privileged EXEC mode access?

   a. **show ip**

   b. **show version**

   c. **show running-config**

   d. **show interfaces**

9. Which of the following statements best describes what the user EXEC mode commands allow you to configure on a Cisco router?

   a. You cannot configure anything; the user mode commands are used to display information.

   b. The user EXEC mode allows you to perform global configuration tasks that affect the entire router.

   c. The user EXEC mode commands allow you to enter a secret password so that you can configure the router.

   d. The user EXEC mode commands allow you to configure interfaces, subinterfaces, lines, and routers.

10. Match each type of help available with the Cisco IOS CLI to its description.

   _____Context-sensitive help

   _____Console error messages

   _____Command history buffer

   a. Provides a list of commands and the arguments associated with a specific command

   b. Allows recall of long or complex commands or entries for reentry, review, or correction

   c. Identifies problems with router commands incorrectly entered so that you can alter or correct them

11. What information does the **show running-config** command provide on a Cisco router?

   a. Current (running) configuration in RAM

   b. System hardware and names of configuration files

   c. Amount of NVRAM used to store the configuration

   d. Version of Cisco IOS Software running on the router

12. Match each router prompt to its configuration mode.

_____Line

_____Router

_____Interface

_____Controller

_____Subinterface

   a. Router(config-if)#

   b. Router(config-line)#

   c. Router(config-subif)#

   d. Router(config-router)#

   e. Router(config-controller)#

13. If you enter a major command on a Cisco router, what happens?

   a. The router returns you to user EXEC mode.

   b. The router returns a list of possible commands.

   c. The router invokes a global configuration command.

   d. The router switches you from one configuration mode to another.

14. Which of the following Cisco IOS commands creates a message to be displayed upon router login?

   a. **hostname** _hostname_

   b. **banner motd** _message_

   c. **hostname interface description**

   d. **description interface description**

15. Which of the following Cisco IOS commands configures serial port in slot 0, port 1 on a modular router?

   a. **serial 0/1 interface**

   b. **interface serial 0 1**

   c. **interface serial 0/1**

   d. **serial 0 1 interface**

This chapter includes the following sections:

CHAPTER 2

Medium-Sized Switched Network Construction

Network administrators must address many factors when expanding a switched network. Cisco provides solutions across its suite of internetworking switches that not only solve many of the immediate problems associated with administrative changes, but also provide scalability, interoperability, increased dedicated throughput, and security.

Chapter Objectives

Upon completing this chapter, you will be able to expand a small-sized, switched LAN to a medium-sized LAN with multiple switches, supporting VLANs, trunking, and a spanning tree. This ability includes being able to meet these objectives:

- Describe how and when to implement and verify VLANs and trunking, and then implement them on the network

- Describe situations in which a spanning tree is used, and implement it on the network

- Describe the application and configuration of inter-VLAN routing for a medium-sized routed network

- Describe situations in which security is required at Layer 2, and implement it on the network

- Identify an approach for troubleshooting and isolating common switched network problems, and offer solutions

Implementing VLANs and Trunks

A VLAN is a logical broadcast domain that can span multiple physical LAN segments. It is used to group end stations that have a common set of requirements, independent of their physical locations. A VLAN has the same attributes as a physical LAN, except that it lets you group end stations even when they are not physically located on the same LAN segment. A VLAN also lets you group ports on a switch so that you can limit unicast, multicast, and broadcast traffic flooding. Flooded traffic that originates from a particular VLAN floods to only the ports belonging to that VLAN.

Understanding VLANs

Understanding how VLANs operate and what the associated protocols are is important for configuring, verifying, and troubleshooting VLANs on Cisco access switches. This section describes VLAN operations and their associated protocols.

A poorly designed network has increased support costs, reduced service availability, security risks, and limited support for new applications and solutions. Less-than-optimal performance affects end users and access to central resources directly. Some of the issues that stem from a poorly designed network include the following:

- **Failure domains:** One of the most important reasons to implement an effective network design is to minimize the extent of problems when they occur. When Layer 2 and Layer 3 boundaries are not clearly defined, failure in one network area can have a far-reaching effect.

- **Broadcast domains:** Broadcasts exist in every network. Many applications and network operations require broadcasts to function properly; therefore, it is not possible to eliminate them completely. In the same way that avoiding failure domains involves clearly defining boundaries, broadcast domains should have clear boundaries and include an optimal number of devices to minimize the negative impact of broadcasts.

- **Large amount of unknown MAC unicast traffic:** Cisco Catalyst switches limit unicast frame forwarding to ports that are associated with the specific unicast address. However, when frames arrive at a destination MAC address that is not recorded in the MAC table, they are flooded out of the switch ports in the same VLAN except for the port that received the frame. This behavior is called *unknown MAC unicast flooding*. Because this type of flooding causes excessive traffic on all the switch ports, network interface cards (NIC) must contend with a larger number of frames on the wire. When data is propagated on a wire for which it was not intended, security can be compromised.

- **Multicast traffic on ports where it is not intended:** IP multicast is a technique that allows IP traffic to be propagated from one source to a multicast group that is identified by a single IP and MAC destination-group address pair. Similar to unicast flooding and broadcasting, multicast frames are flooded out all the switch ports. A proper design allows for the containment of multicast frames while allowing them to be functional.

- **Difficulty in management and support:** A poorly designed network may be disorganized and poorly documented and lack easily identified traffic flows, which can make support, maintenance, and problem resolution time-consuming and arduous tasks.

- **Possible security vulnerabilities:** A switched network that has been designed with little attention to security requirements at the access layer can compromise the integrity of the entire network.

A poorly designed network always has a negative impact and becomes a support and cost burden for any organization. Figure 2-1 shows a network with a single broadcast domain. VLANs can help alleviate some of the problems associated with this design.

Figure 2-1   *Network with Single Broadcast Domain*

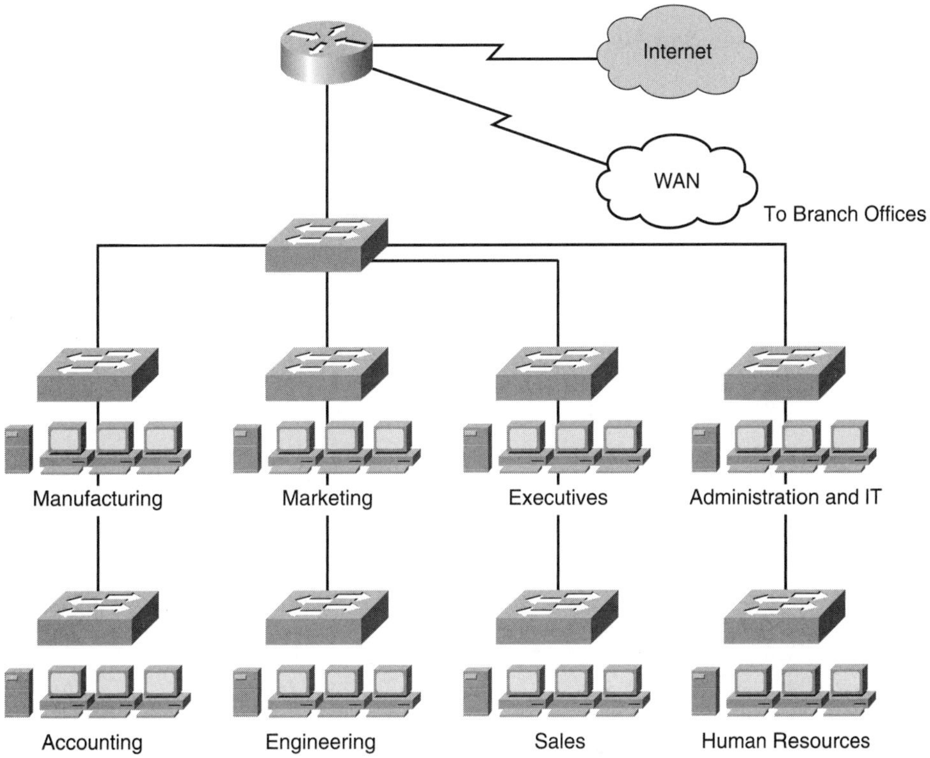

VLAN Overview

A *VLAN* is a logical broadcast domain that can span multiple physical LAN segments. In the switched internetwork, VLANs provide segmentation and organizational flexibility. You can design a VLAN structure that lets you group stations that are segmented logically by functions, project teams, and applications without regard to the physical location of the users. You can assign each switch port to only one VLAN, thereby adding a layer of security. Ports in a VLAN share broadcasts; ports in different VLANs do not. Containing broadcasts in a VLAN improves the overall performance of the network.

In the switched internetwork, VLANs provide segmentation and organizational flexibility. Using VLAN technology, you can group switch ports and their connected users into logically defined communities, such as coworkers in the same department, a cross-functional product team, or diverse user groups sharing the same network application.

A VLAN can exist on a single switch or span multiple switches. VLANs can include stations in a single building or multiple-building infrastructures. This is illustrated in Figure 2-2.

Figure 2-2 *VLANs Can Span Multiple Switches*

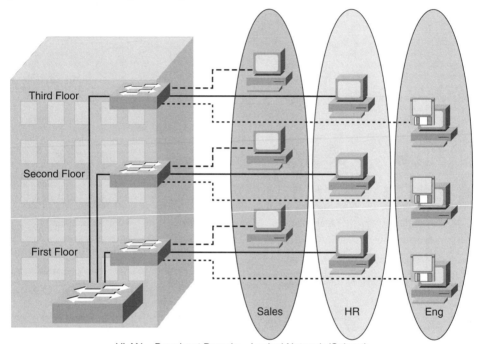

VLAN = Broadcast Domain = Logical Network (Subnet)

Grouping Business Functions into VLANs

Each VLAN in a switched network corresponds to an IP network. So VLAN design must take into consideration the implementation of a hierarchical network-addressing scheme. *Hierarchical network addressing* means that IP network numbers are applied to network segments or VLANs in an orderly fashion that considers the network as a whole. Blocks of contiguous network addresses are reserved for and configured on devices in a specific area of the network.

Some of the benefits of hierarchical addressing include the following:

■ **Ease of management and troubleshooting:** A hierarchical addressing scheme groups network addresses contiguously. Because a hierarchical IP addressing scheme makes problem components easier to locate, network management and troubleshooting are more efficient.

■ **Fewer errors:** Orderly network address assignment can minimize errors and duplicate address assignments.

■ **Reduced routing table entries:** In a hierarchical addressing plan, routing protocols are able to perform route summarization, allowing a single routing table entry to represent a collection of IP network numbers. Route summarization makes routing table entries more manageable and provides these benefits:

— Fewer CPU cycles when recalculating a routing table or sorting through the routing table entries to find a match

— Reduced router memory requirements

— Faster convergence after a change in the network

— Easier troubleshooting

Applying IP Address Space in the Enterprise Network

The Cisco Enterprise Architecture model provides a modular framework for designing and deploying networks. It also provides the ideal structure for overlaying a hierarchical IP addressing scheme. Following are some guidelines:

■ Design the IP addressing scheme so that blocks of 2^n contiguous network numbers (such as 4, 8, 16, 32, 64, and so on) can be assigned to the subnets in a given building distribution and access switch block. This approach lets you summarize each switch block into one large address block.

■ At the building distribution layer, continue to assign network numbers contiguously to the access layer devices.

■ Have a single IP subnet correspond to a single VLAN. Each VLAN is a separate broadcast domain.

■ When possible, subnet at the same binary value on all network numbers to avoid variable-length subnet masks. This approach helps minimize errors and confusion when troubleshooting or configuring new devices and segments.

Figure 2-3 shows how this architectural model is deployed and illustrates IP address allocation between various groups in the enterprise. You will notice that each building has unique subnets. Each of these subnets would be assigned to a single VLAN. Each building has been assigned a range with four IP subnets even though only two departments are shown. The additional subnets could be used from growth.

Figure 2-3 *IP Addressing per VLAN*

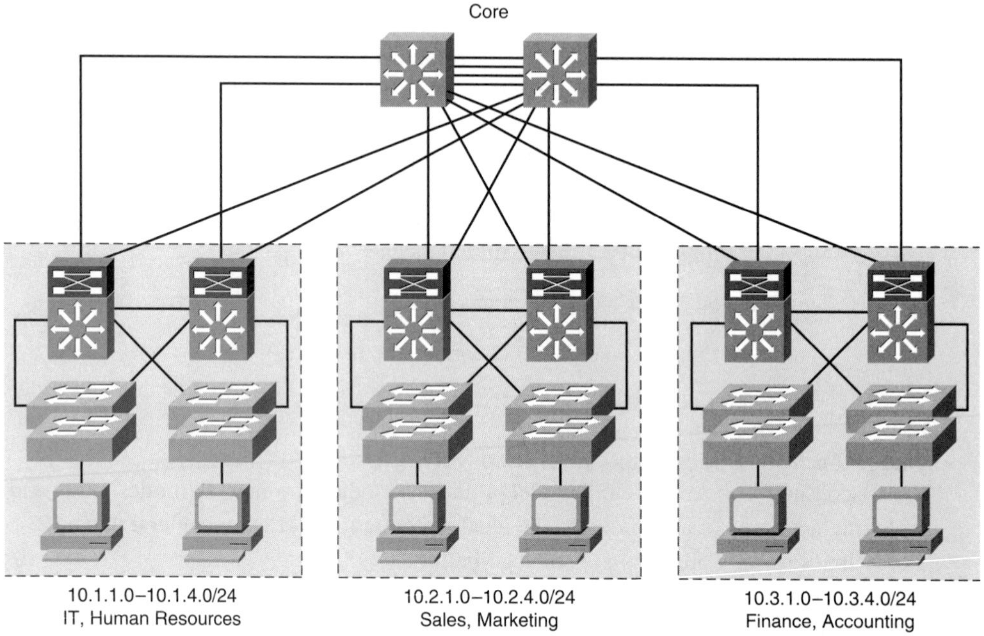

10.1.1.0–10.1.4.0/24
IT, Human Resources

10.2.1.0–10.2.4.0/24
Sales, Marketing

10.3.1.0–10.3.4.0/24
Finance, Accounting

Example: Network Design

A business with approximately 250 employees wants to migrate to the Cisco Enterprise Architecture.

Table 2-1 shows the number of users in each department.

Table 2-1 *Users per Department*

Department	Number of Users	Location
IT	45	Building A
Human Resources	10	Building A
Sales	102	Building B
Marketing	29	Building B
Finance	18	Building C
Accounting	26	Building C

Six VLANs are required to accommodate one VLAN per user community. Following the guidelines of the Cisco Enterprise Architecture, six IP subnets are required.

The business has decided to use network 10.0.0.0 as its base address.

To accommodate future growth, there will be one block of IP addresses per building, as follows:

- Building A is allocated 10.1.0.0/16.

- Building B is allocated 10.2.0.0/16.

- Building C is allocated 10.3.0.0/16.

The sales department is the largest department, requiring a minimum of 102 addresses for its users. A subnet mask of 255.255.255.0 (/24) is chosen, which provides a maximum number of 254 hosts per subnet.

Tables 2-2, 2-3, and 2-4 show the allocation of VLANs and IP subnets in the buildings.

Table 2-2 *Building A: VLANs and IP Subnets*

Department	VLAN	IP Subnet Address
IT	VLAN 11	10.1.1.0/24
Human Resources	VLAN 12	10.1.2.0/24
For future growth		10.1.3.0–10.1.255.0

Table 2-3 *Building B: VLANs and IP Subnets*

Department	VLAN	IP Subnet Address
Sales	VLAN 21	10.2.1.0/24
Marketing	VLAN 22	10.2.2.0/24
For future growth		10.2.3.0–10.2.255.0

Table 2-4 *Building C: VLANs and IP Subnets*

Department	VLAN	IP Subnet Address
Finance	VLAN 31	10.3.1.0/24
Accounting	VLAN 32	10.3.2.0/24
For future growth		10.3.3.0–10.3.255.0

Some of the currently unused VLANs and IP subnets will be used to manage the network devices. If the company decides to implement IP telephony, for example, some of the unused VLANs and IP subnets are allocated to the voice VLANs.

Considering Traffic Source to Destination Paths

When you are designing and implementing networks, a key factor for VLAN deployment is understanding the traffic patterns and the various traffic types. Figure 2-4 displays some common components of a network; this along with the traffic requirements should be a baseline for designing VLANs.

Figure 2-4 *Network Enterprise Components*

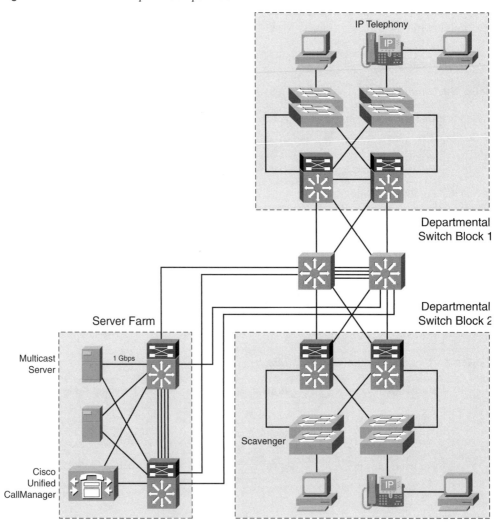

Table 2-5 lists the common types of network traffic that should be considered before placing devices and configuring the VLAN.

Table 2-5   *Traffic Types*

Traffic Type	Description
Network management	Many different types of network management traffic can be present on the network, such as BPDUs[1], CDP[2] updates, SNMP[3] traffic, and RMON[4] traffic. To make network troubleshooting easier, some designers assign a separate VLAN to carry certain types of network management traffic.
IP telephony	There are two types of IP telephony traffic: signaling information between end devices (IP phones and softswitches, such as Cisco Unified CallManager) and the data packets of the voice conversation. Designers often configure the data to and from the IP phones on a separate VLAN designated for voice traffic so that they can apply QoS[5] measures to give high priority to voice traffic.
IP multicast	IP multicast traffic is sent from a particular source address to a multicast group that is identified by a single IP and MAC destination-group address pair. Examples of applications that generate this type of traffic are Cisco IP/TV broadcasts and imaging software used to quickly configure workstations and servers. Multicast traffic can produce a large amount of data streaming across the network. For example, video traffic from online training, security applications, Cisco Meeting Place, and Cisco TelePresence is proliferating on some networks. Switches must be configured to keep this traffic from flooding to devices that have not requested it, and routers must be configured to ensure that multicast traffic is forwarded to the network areas where it is requested.
Normal data	Normal data traffic is typical application traffic that is related to file and print services, e-mail, Internet browsing, database access, and other shared network applications. This data will need to be treated in either the same ways or different ways in different parts of the network, depending on the volume of each type. Examples of this type of traffic are SMB[6], NCP[7], SMTP[8], SQL[9], and HTTP.
Scavenger class	Scavenger class includes all traffic with protocols or patterns that exceed their normal data flows. This type of traffic is used to protect the network from exceptional traffic flows that may be the result of malicious programs executing on end-system PCs. Scavenger class is also used for "less than best effort" traffic, such as peer-to-peer traffic.

[1] BPDUs = bridge protocol data units
[2] CDP = Cisco Discovery Protocol
[3] SNMP = Simple Network Management Protocol
[4] RMON = Remote Monitoring
[5] QoS = quality of service
[6] SMB = Server Message Block
[7] NCP = Netware Core Protocol
[8] SMTP = Simple Mail Transfer Protocol
[9] SQL = Structured Query Language

Voice VLAN Essentials

Some Cisco Catalyst switches offer a unique feature called a *voice VLAN*, which lets you overlay a voice topology onto a data network. You can segment phones into separate logical networks, even though the data and voice infrastructure are physically the same, as illustrated in Figure 2-5.

Figure 2-5   *Voice VLANs*

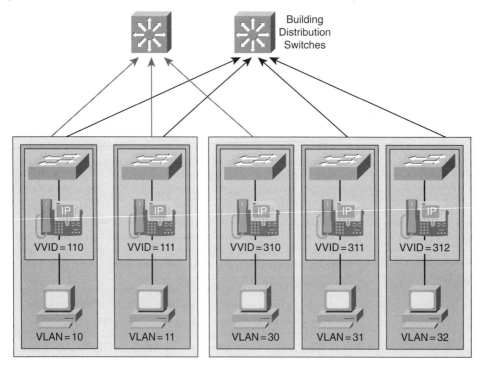

The voice VLAN feature places the phones into their own VLANs without any end-user intervention. The user simply plugs the phone into the switch, and the switch provides the phone with the necessary VLAN information.

Using voice VLANs offers several advantages. Network administrators can seamlessly maintain these VLAN assignments, even if the phones move to new locations. By placing phones into their own VLANs, network administrators gain the advantages of network segmentation and control. Voice VLANs also allow administrators to preserve their existing IP topology for the data end stations and easily assign IP phones to different IP subnets using standards-based DHCP operation.

In addition, with the phones in their own IP subnets and VLANs, network administrators can more easily identify and troubleshoot network problems and create and enforce QoS or security policies.

With the voice VLAN feature, network administrators have all the advantages of the physical infrastructure convergence, while maintaining separate logical topologies for voice and data terminals. This configuration creates the most effective way to manage a multiservice network.

VLAN Operation

A Cisco Catalyst switch operates in a network similar to a traditional bridge. Each VLAN that you configure on the switch implements address learning, forwarding and filtering decisions, and loop avoidance mechanisms as if the VLAN were a separate physical bridge.

The Cisco Catalyst switch implements VLANs by restricting traffic forwarding to destination ports that are in the same VLAN as the originating ports. So when a frame arrives on a switch port, the switch must retransmit the frame to only the ports that belong to the same VLAN. In essence, a VLAN that is operating on a switch limits transmission of unicast, multicast, and broadcast traffic. Traffic originating from a particular VLAN floods to only the other ports in that VLAN.

A port normally carries only the traffic for the single VLAN to which it belongs. For a VLAN to span across multiple switches, a trunk is required to connect two switches. A trunk can carry traffic for multiple VLANs. Figure 2-6 shows a trunk carrying multiple VLANs between two switches.

Figure 2-6   *VLAN Trunk*

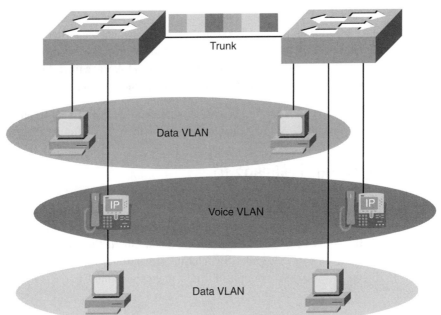

You configure ports that belong to a VLAN with a membership mode that determines to which VLAN they belong. Figure 2-7 displays the various VLAN membership modes.

Figure 2-7 *VLAN Membership Modes*

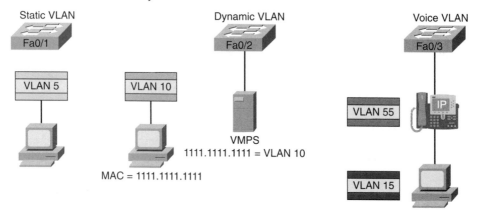

The VLAN membership mode Characteristics of Cisco Catalyst switch ports are as follows:

- **Static VLAN:** An administrator statically configures the assignment of VLANs to ports.

- **Dynamic VLAN:** Cisco Catalyst switches support dynamic VLANs using a VLAN Membership Policy Server (VMPS). Some Cisco Catalyst switches can be designated as the VMPS; you can also designate an external server as the VMPS. The VMPS contains a database that maps MAC addresses to VLAN assignments. When a frame arrives at a dynamic port on the Cisco Catalyst access switch, the switch queries the VMPS server for the VLAN assignment based on the source MAC address of the arriving frame. A dynamic port can belong to only one VLAN at a time. Multiple hosts can be active on a dynamic port only if they belong to the same VLAN.

- **Voice VLAN:** A voice VLAN port is an access port attached to a Cisco IP phone, configured to use one VLAN for voice traffic and another VLAN for data traffic.

Understanding Trunking with 802.1Q

A *trunk* is a point-to-point link between one or more Ethernet switch interfaces and another networking device such as a router or a switch. Ethernet trunks carry the traffic of multiple VLANs over a single link and allow you to extend the VLANs across an entire network. Cisco supports IEEE 802.1Q for FastEthernet and Gigabit Ethernet interfaces. In addition, some Cisco switches support Cisco Inter-Switch Link (ISL) trunks, a prestandard trunking technology. Figure 2-8 shows an example of trunks interconnecting Cisco Catalyst switches.

Figure 2-8 *802.1Q Trunks*

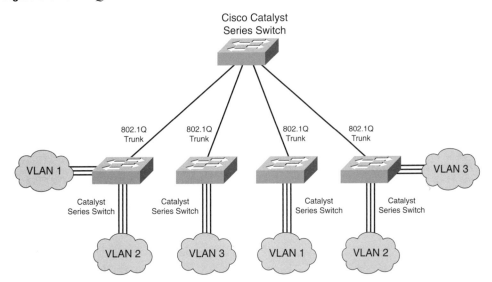

Ethernet trunk interfaces support different trunking modes. You can configure an interface as trunking or nontrunking, or you can have it negotiate trunking with the neighboring interface.

Every 802.1Q port is assigned to a trunk, and all ports on a trunk are in a native VLAN. A native VLAN is used in IEEE 802.1Q to send untagged frames to any non-802.1Q devices that might exist on the segment. Every 802.1Q port is assigned an identifier value that is based on the native VLAN ID (VID) of the port. (The default is VLAN 1.) All untagged frames are assigned to the VLAN specified in this VID parameter.

802.1Q Frame

IEEE 802.1Q uses an internal tagging mechanism that inserts a four-byte tag field into the original Ethernet frame between the Source Address and Type or Length fields. Because 802.1Q alters the frame, the trunking device recomputes the frame check sequence (FCS) on the modified frame.

It is the responsibility of the Ethernet switch to look at the four-byte tag field and determine where to deliver the frame. An Ether Type of 0x8100 indicates to devices that the frame has an 802.1Q tag. A tiny part of the four-byte tag field—three bits to be exact—is used to specify the priority of the frame. The details of this are specified in the IEEE 802.1p standard. The 802.1Q header contains the 802.1p field, so you must have 802.1Q to have 802.1p. Following the priority bit is a single flag to indicate whether the addressing is Token Ring. This is because 802.1Q tagging could also be implemented in a Token Ring environment; the flag will be 0 for an Ethernet frame. The remainder of the tag is used for the VID. Figure 2-9 shows the 802.1Q frame format.

Figure 2-9   *802.1Q Frame Format*

Destination	Source	Length/Ether Type	Data	F̶C̶S̶	Original Frame

Destination	Source	Tag	Length/Ether Type	Data	FCS	Tagged Frame

Ether Type (0x8100)	PRI		VLAN ID

└── Token Ring Encapsulation Flag

802.1Q Native VLAN

An 802.1Q trunk and its associated trunk ports have a native VLAN value. 802.1Q does not tag frames for the native VLAN. Therefore, ordinary stations can read the native untagged frames but cannot read any other frame because the frames are tagged. Figure 2-10 shows a frame from the native VLAN being distributed across the network trunks untagged.

Figure 2-10   *Untagged Frame*

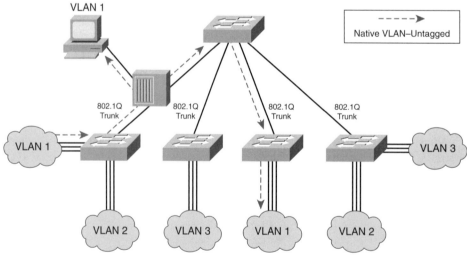

Understanding VLAN Trunking Protocol

VLAN Trunking Protocol (VTP) is a Layer 2 messaging protocol that maintains VLAN configuration consistency by managing the additions, deletions, and name changes of VLANs across networks. VTP minimizes misconfigurations and configuration inconsistencies that can cause problems, such as duplicate VLAN names or incorrect VLAN-type specifications. Figure 2-11 shows how you can use VTP to manage VLANs between switches.

Figure 2-11 *VTP*

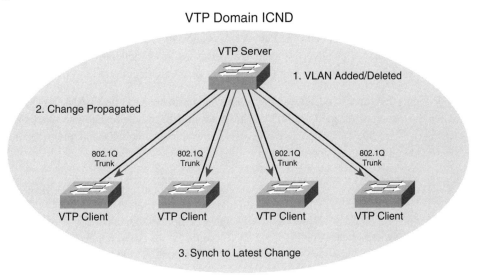

A VTP domain is one switch or several interconnected switches sharing the same VTP environment. You can configure a switch to be in only one VTP domain.

By default, a Cisco Catalyst switch is in the no-management-domain state until it receives an advertisement for a domain over a trunk link or until you configure a management domain. Configurations made to a VTP server are propagated across trunk links to all the connected switches in the network.

VTP Modes

VTP operates in one of three modes: server, transparent, or client. You can complete different tasks depending on the VTP operation mode. The characteristics of the three VTP modes are as follows:

- **Server:** The default VTP mode is server mode, but VLANs are not propagated over the network until a management domain name is specified or learned. When you change (create, modify, or delete) the VLAN configuration on a VTP server, the change is propagated to all switches in the VTP domain. VTP messages are transmitted out of all the trunk connections. A VTP server synchronizes its VLAN database file with other VTP servers and clients.

■ **Transparent:** When you change the VLAN configuration in VTP transparent mode, the change affects only the local switch and does not propagate to other switches in the VTP domain. VTP transparent mode does forward VTP advertisements that it receives within the domain. A VTP transparent device does not synchronize its database with any other device.

■ **Client:** You cannot change the VLAN configuration when in VTP client mode; however, a VTP client can send any VLANs currently listed in its database to other VTP switches. VTP advertisements are forwarded in VTP client mode. A VTP client synchronizes its database with other VTP servers and clients.

VTP clients that run Cisco Catalyst operating systems do not save the VLANs to NVRAM. When the switch is reloaded, the VLANs are not retained, and the revision number is zero. However, Cisco IOS VTP clients save VLANs to the vlan.dat file in flash memory, retaining the VLAN table and revision number.

CAUTION   The **erase startup-config** command does not affect the vlan.dat file on Cisco IOS switches. VTP clients with a higher configuration revision number can overwrite VLANs on a VTP server in the same VTP domain. Delete the vlan.dat file and reload the switch to clear the VTP and VLAN information. See documentation for your specific switch model to determine how to delete the vlan.dat file.

VTP Operation

VTP advertisements are flooded throughout the management domain. VTP advertisements are sent every 5 minutes or whenever VLAN configurations change. Advertisements are transmitted over the default VLAN (VLAN 1) using a multicast frame. A configuration revision number is included in each VTP advertisement. A higher configuration revision number indicates that the VLAN information being advertised is more current than the stored information. Figure 2-12 illustrates this operation.

Figure 2-12   *VTP Operation*

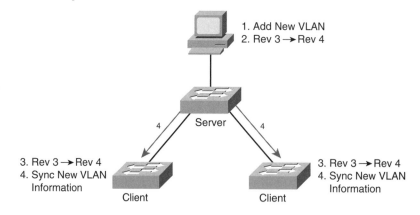

One of the most critical components of VTP is the configuration revision number. Each time a VTP server modifies its VLAN information, the VTP server increments the configuration revision number by one. The server then sends a VTP advertisement with the new configuration revision number. If the configuration revision number being advertised is higher than the number stored on the other switches in the VTP domain, the switches overwrite their VLAN configurations with the new information being advertised.

The configuration revision number in VTP transparent mode is always zero.

NOTE   In the overwrite process, if the VTP server deleted all the VLANs and had the higher revision number, the other devices in the VTP domain would also delete their VLANs.

A device that receives VTP advertisements must check various parameters before incorporating the received VLAN information. First, the management domain name and password in the advertisement must match those configured in the local switch. Next, if the configuration revision number indicates that the message was created after the configuration currently in use, the switch incorporates the advertised VLAN information.

To reset the configuration revision number on some Cisco Catalyst switches, you can change the VTP domain to another name and then change it back. You can also change the VTP mode to transparent and then change it back to client or server.

VTP Pruning

VTP pruning uses VLAN advertisements to determine when a trunk connection is flooding traffic needlessly.

By default, a trunk connection carries traffic for all VLANs in the VTP management domain. In many enterprise networks, not every switch will have ports assigned to every VLAN.

Figure 2-13 shows a switched network with VTP pruning enabled. Only switches 2, 4, and 5 support ports configured in VLAN 3. Switch 5 does not forward the broadcast traffic from host X to switches 1 and 3 because traffic for VLAN 3 has been pruned on the links between switch 5 and switch 1 and switch 3, as indicated in the figure.

VTP pruning increases available bandwidth by restricting flooded traffic to those trunk links that the traffic must use to access the appropriate network devices.

You can enable pruning only on Cisco Catalyst switches that are configured for VTP servers, and not on clients.

Figure 2-13 *VTP Pruning*

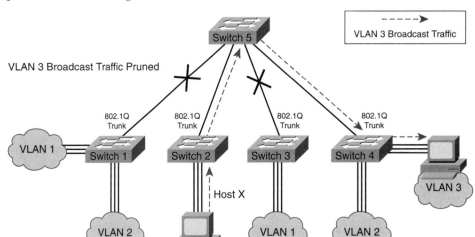

Configuring VLANs and Trunks

By default, all the ports on a Catalyst switch are in VLAN 1. If you want to use VLANs and trunks, you need to configure them on the switches throughout the network. The steps you use to configure and verify VLANs on a switched network include the following:

■ Determine whether to use VTP. If VTP will be used, enable VTP in server, client, or transparent mode.

■ Enable trunking on the inter-switch connections.

■ Create the VLANs on a VTP server and have those VLANs propagate to other switches.

■ Assign switch ports to a VLAN using static or dynamic assignment.

■ Save the VLAN configuration.

VTP Configuration

When creating VLANs, you must decide whether to use VTP in your network. With VTP, you can make configuration changes on one or more switches, and those changes are automatically communicated to all other switches in the same VTP domain.

Default VTP configuration values depend on the switch model and the software version. The default values for Cisco Catalyst switches are as follows:

- **VTP domain name:** Null

- **VTP mode:** Server

- **VTP password:** None

- **VTP pruning:** Enabled/Disabled (OS version specific)

- **VTP version:** Version 1

The VTP domain name can be specified or learned. By default, the domain name is not set. You can set a password for the VTP management domain. However, if you do not assign the same password for each switch in the domain, VTP does not function properly.

VTP pruning eligibility is one VLAN parameter that the VTP protocol advertises. Enabling or disabling VTP pruning on a VTP server propagates the change throughout the management domain.

Use the **vtp** global configuration command to modify the VTP configuration, domain name, interface, and mode:

```
SwitchX# configure terminal
SwitchX(config)# vtp mode [ server | client | transparent ]
SwitchX(config)# vtp domain domain-name
SwitchX(config)# vtp password password
SwitchX(config)# vtp pruning
SwitchX(config)# end
```

Use the **no** form of this command to remove the filename or to return to the default settings. When the VTP mode is transparent, you can save the VTP configuration in the switch configuration file by entering the **copy running-config startup-config** privileged EXEC command.

> **NOTE**   The domain name and password are case sensitive. You cannot remove a domain name after it is assigned; you can only reassign it.

Example: VTP Configuration

Example 2-1 demonstrates the commands that you would enter to configure VTP and display VTP status. The characteristics of the switch in this example are as follows:

- The switch is transparent in the VTP domain.

- The VTP domain name is ICND.

■   Pruning is disabled.

■   The configuration revision is 0.

> **NOTE**   In the output from the **show vtp status** command, "VTP Version" identifies what version of VTP the switch is capable of running, and "VTP V2 Mode" indicates whether VTP Version 2 is being used. If "VTP V2 Mode" shows disabled, VTP Version 1 is being used.

Example 2-1   *Configuring VTP and Displaying VTP Status*

```
SwitchX(config)# vtp domain ICND
Changing VTP domain name to ICND
SwitchX(config)# vtp mode transparent
Setting device to VTP TRANSPARENT mode.
SwitchX(config)# end

SwitchX# show vtp status
VTP Version                   : 2
Configuration Revision        : 0
Maximum VLANs supported locally : 64
Number of existing VLANs      : 17
VTP Operating Mode            : Transparent
VTP Domain Name               : ICND
VTP Pruning Mode              : Disabled
VTP V2 Mode                   : Disabled
VTP Traps Generation          : Disabled
MD5 digest                    : 0x7D 0x6E 0x5E 0x3D 0xAF 0xA0 0x2F 0xAA
Configuration last modified by 10.1.1.4 at 3-3-93 20:08:05
SwitchX#
```

802.1Q Trunking Configuration

The 802.1Q protocol carries traffic for multiple VLANs over a single link on a multivendor network.

802.1Q trunks impose several limitations on the trunking strategy for a network. You should consider the following:

■   Ensure that the native VLAN for an 802.1Q trunk is the same on both ends of the trunk link. If they are different, spanning-tree loops might result.

■   Native VLAN frames are untagged.

Table 2-6 shows how 802.1Q trunking interacts with other switch features.

Table 2-6 *Switch Feature Trunk Interaction*

Switch Feature	Trunk Port Interaction
Secure ports	A trunk port cannot be a secure port.
Port grouping	You can group 802.1Q trunks into EtherChannel port groups, but all trunks in the group must have the same configuration. When you create a group, all ports follow the parameters that are set for the first port you add to the group. If you change the configuration of one of these parameters, the switch propagates the setting that you enter to all ports in the group. The settings include the following: • Allowed VLAN list • STP[1] path cost for each VLAN • STP port priority for each VLAN • STP PortFast setting • Trunk status; if one port in a port group ceases to be a trunk, all ports cease to be trunks

[1] STP = Spanning Tree Protocol

Use the **switchport mode** interface configuration command to set a FastEthernet or Gigabit Ethernet port to trunk mode. Many Cisco Catalyst switches support the Dynamic Trunking Protocol (DTP), which manages automatic trunk negotiation.

Four options for the **switchport mode** command are listed in Table 2-7.

Table 2-7 **switchport mode** *Parameters*

Parameter	Description
trunk	Configures the port into permanent 802.1Q trunk mode and negotiates with the connected device to convert the link to trunk mode.
access	Disables port trunk mode and negotiates with the connected device to convert the link to nontrunk.
dynamic desirable	Triggers the port to negotiate the link from nontrunk to trunk mode. The port negotiates to a trunk port if the connected device is in trunk state, desirable state, or auto state. Otherwise, the port becomes a nontrunk port.
dynamic auto	Enables a port to become a trunk only if the connected device has the state set to trunk or desirable. Otherwise, the port becomes a nontrunk port.

The **switchport nonegotiate** interface command specifies that DTP negotiation packets are not sent on the Layer 2 interface. The switch does not engage in DTP negotiation on this interface. This command is valid only when the interface switchport mode is access or trunk (configured by using the **switchport mode access** or the **switchport mode trunk** interface configuration command). This command returns an error if you attempt to execute it in dynamic (auto or desirable) mode. Use the **no** form of this command to return to the default setting. When you configure a port with the **switchport nonegotiate** command, the port trunks only if the other end of the link is specifically set to trunk. The **switchport nonegotiate** command does not form a trunk link with ports in either dynamic desirable or dynamic auto mode.

Table 2-8 shows the steps to configure a port as an 802.1Q trunk port, beginning in privileged EXEC mode.

Table 2-8   *Configuring a Port as an 802.1Q Trunk Port*

Step	Action	Notes
1	Enter the interface configuration mode and the port to be configured for trunking: SwitchX(config)# **interface** *int_type int_number*	After you enter the **interface** command, the command-line prompt changes from (config) # to (config-if) #.
2	Configure the port as a VLAN trunk: SwitchX(config-if)# **switchport mode trunk**	Enable trunking on the selected interface.

Some Cisco Catalyst switches support only 802.1Q encapsulation, which is configured automatically when trunking is enabled on the interface by using the **switchport mode trunk** command.

To verify a trunk configuration on many Cisco Catalyst switches, use the **show interfaces** *interface* **switchport** or the **show interfaces** *interface* **trunk** command to display the trunk parameters and VLAN information of the port, as demonstrated in Example 2-2.

Example 2-1   *Verifying Trunk Configuration, Parameters, and Port VLAN Information*

```
SwitchX# show interfaces fa0/11 switchport
Name: Fa0/11
Switchport: Enabled
Administrative Mode: trunk
Operational Mode: down
Administrative Trunking Encapsulation: dot1q
Negotiation of Trunking: On
```

Example 2-1   *Verifying Trunk Configuration, Parameters, and Port VLAN Information (Continued)*

```
Access Mode VLAN: 1 (default)
Trunking Native Mode VLAN: 1 (default)


SwitchX# show interfaces fa0/11 trunk

Port        Mode        Encapsulation  Status       Native vlan
Fa0/11      desirable   802.1q         trunking     1


Port        Vlans allowed on trunk
Fa0/11      1-4094


Port        Vlans allowed and active in management domain
Fa0/11      1-13
```

VLAN Creation

Before you create VLANs, you must decide whether to use VTP to maintain global VLAN configuration information for your network.

The maximum number of VLANs is switch dependent. Many access layer Cisco Catalyst switches can support up to 250 user-defined VLANs.

Cisco Catalyst switches have a factory default configuration in which various default VLANs are preconfigured to support various media and protocol types. The default Ethernet VLAN is VLAN 1. Cisco Discovery Protocol and VTP advertisements are sent on VLAN 1.

For you to be able to communicate remotely with the Cisco Catalyst switch for management purposes, the switch must have an IP address. This IP address must be in the management VLAN, which by default is VLAN 1. If VTP is configured, before you can create a VLAN, the switch must be in VTP server mode or VTP transparent mode.

Table 2-9 lists the commands to use when adding a VLAN.

Table 2-9   *Commands to Add VLANs*

Command/Variable	Description
vlan *vlan-id*	ID of the VLAN to be added and configured. For *vlan-id*, the range is 1 to 4094 when the enhanced software image is installed and 1 to 1005 when the standard software image is installed. Do not enter leading zeros. You can enter a single VID, a series of VIDs separated by commas, or a range of VIDs separated by hyphens.
name *vlan-name*	(Optional) Specify the VLAN name, an ASCII string from 1 to 32 characters that must be unique within the administrative domain.

By default, a switch is in VTP server mode so that you can add, change, or delete VLANs. If the switch is set to VTP client mode, you cannot add, change, or delete VLANs.

Use the **vlan** global configuration command to create a VLAN and enter VLAN configuration mode:

```
SwitchX# configure terminal
SwitchX(config)# vlan 2
SwitchX(config-vlan)# name switchlab99
```

Use the **no** form of this command to delete the VLAN.

To add a VLAN to the VLAN database, assign a number and name to the VLAN. VLAN 1 is the factory default VLAN. Normal-range VLANs are identified with a number between 1 and 1001. VLAN numbers 1002 through 1005 are reserved for Token Ring and FDDI VLANs. If the switch is in VTP server or VTP transparent mode, you can add, modify, or remove configurations for VLAN 2 to 1001 in the VLAN database. (VIDs 1 and 1002 to 1005 are automatically created and cannot be removed.)

NOTE   When the switch is in VTP transparent mode and the enhanced software image is installed, you can also create extended-range VLANs (VLANs with IDs from 1006 to 4094), but these VLANs are not saved in the VLAN database.

Configurations for VIDs 1 to 1005 are written to the vlan.dat file (VLAN database). You can display the VLANs by entering the **show vlan** privileged EXEC command. The vlan.dat file is stored in flash memory.

To add an Ethernet VLAN, you must specify at least a VLAN number. If no name is entered for the VLAN, the default is to append the VLAN number to the word **vlan**. For example, VLAN0004 would be the default name for VLAN 4 if no name were specified.

After you configure the VLAN, you should validate the parameters for that VLAN.

Use the **show vlan id** *vlan_number* or the **show vlan name** *vlan-name* command to display information about a particular VLAN, as demonstrated in Example 2-3.

Example 2-3 *Displaying VLAN Information*

```
SwitchX# show vlan id 2

VLAN Name                             Status    Ports
---- -------------------------------- --------- -------------------------------
2    switchlab99                      active    Fa0/2, Fa0/12
```

Example 2-3 *Displaying VLAN Information (Continued)*

```
VLAN Type  SAID       MTU    Parent RingNo BridgeNo Stp  BrdgMode Trans1 Trans2
---- ----- ---------- ----- ------ ------ -------- ---- -------- ------ ------
2    enet  100002     1500  -      -      -        -    -        0      0


.   .   .
SwitchX#
```

Use the **show vlan brief** command to display one line for each VLAN that displays the VLAN name, the status, and the switch ports.

Use the **show vlan** command to display information on all configured VLANs. The **show vlan** command displays the switch ports assigned to each VLAN. Other VLAN parameters that are displayed include the type (the default is Ethernet); the security association ID (SAID), used for the FDDI trunk; the maximum transmission unit (MTU) (the default is 1500 for Ethernet VLAN); the STP; and other parameters used for Token Ring or FDDI VLANs.

VLAN Port Assignment

After creating a VLAN, you can manually assign a port or a number of ports to that VLAN. A port can belong to only one VLAN at a time. When you assign a switch port to a VLAN using this method, it is known as a *static-access port*.

On most Cisco Catalyst switches, you configure the VLAN port assignment from interface configuration mode using the **switchport access** command, as demonstrated in Example 2-4. Use the **vlan** *vlan_number* option to set static-access membership. Use the **dynamic** option to have the VLAN controlled and assigned by a VMPS.

> **NOTE** By default, all ports are members of VLAN 1.

Example 2-4 *Configuring VLAN Port Assignment*

```
SwitchX# configure terminal
SwitchX(config)# interface range fastethernet 0/2 - 4
SwitchX(config-if)# switchport access vlan 2

SwitchX# show vlan

VLAN Name                             Status     Ports
---- -------------------------------- ---------- -----------------------
1    default                          active     Fa0/1
2    switchlab99                      active     Fa0/2, Fa0/3, Fa0/4
```

Use the **show vlan brief** privileged EXEC command to display the VLAN assignment and membership type for all switch ports, as demonstrated in Example 2-5.

Example 2-5 *Displaying VLAN Port Assignment and Membership Type*

```
SwitchX# show vlan brief
VLAN Name                             Status    Ports
---- -------------------------------- --------- -------------------------------
1    default                          active    Fa0/1
2    switchlab99                      active    Fa0/2, Fa0/3, Fa0/4
3    vlan3                            active
4    vlan4                            active
1002 fddi-default                     act/unsup
1003 token-ring-default               act/unsup

VLAN Name                             Status    Ports
---- -------------------------------- --------- -------------------------------
1004 fddinet-default                  act/unsup
1005 trnet-default
```

Alternatively, use the **show interfaces** *interface* **switchport** privileged EXEC command to display the VLAN information for a particular interface, as demonstrated in Example 2-6.

Example 2-6 *Displaying VLAN Information for a Specific Interface*

```
SwitchX# show interfaces fa0/2 switchport
Name: Fa0/2
Switchport: Enabled
Administrative Mode: dynamic auto
Operational Mode: static access
Administrative Trunking Encapsulation: dot1q
Operational Trunking Encapsulation: native
Negotiation of Trunking: On
Access Mode VLAN: 2 (switchlab99)
Trunking Native Mode VLAN: 1 (default)
--- output omitted ----
```

Adds, Moves, and Changes for VLANs

As network topologies, business requirements, and individual assignments change, VLAN requirements also change.

To add, change, or delete VLANs, the switch must be in VTP server or transparent mode. When you make VLAN changes from a switch that is in VTP server mode, the change is automatically propagated to other switches in the VTP domain. VLAN changes made from a switch in VTP transparent mode affect only the local switch; changes are not propagated to the domain.

Adding VLANs and Port Membership

After you create a new VLAN, be sure to make the necessary changes to the VLAN port assignments.

Separate VLANs typically imply separate IP networks. Be sure to plan the new IP addressing scheme and its deployment to stations before moving users to the new VLAN. Separate VLANs also require inter-VLAN routing to permit users in the new VLAN to communicate with other VLANs. Inter-VLAN routing includes setting up the appropriate IP parameters and services, including default gateway and DHCP.

Changing VLANs and Port Membership

To modify VLAN attributes, such as VLAN name, use the **vlan** *vlan-id* global configuration command.

> **NOTE**   You cannot change the VLAN number. To use a different VLAN number, create a new VLAN using a new number and then reassign all ports to this VLAN.

To move a port into a different VLAN, use the same commands that you used to make the original assignments.

You do not need to first remove a port from a VLAN to make this change. After you reassign a port to a new VLAN, that port is automatically removed from its previous VLAN.

Deleting VLANs and Port Membership

When you delete a VLAN from a switch that is in VTP server mode, the VLAN is removed from all switches in the VTP domain. When you delete a VLAN from a switch that is in VTP transparent mode, the VLAN is deleted only on that specific switch. Use the global configuration command **no vlan** *vlan-id* to remove a VLAN.

> **NOTE**   Before deleting a VLAN, be sure to reassign all member ports to a different VLAN. Any ports that are not moved to an active VLAN are unable to communicate with other stations after you delete the VLAN.

To reassign a port to the default VLAN (VLAN 1), use the **no switchport access vlan** command in interface configuration mode.

Summary of Implementing VLANs and Trunks

The following list summarizes the key points that were discussed in this section.

- A poorly designed network has increased support costs, reduced service availability, and limited support for new applications and solutions.

- VLANs provide broadcast segmentation and organizational flexibility.

- Ethernet trunks carry the traffic of multiple VLANs over a single link and allow you to extend VLANs across an entire network.

- VTP is a Layer 2 messaging protocol that maintains VLAN configuration consistency.

Improving Performance with Spanning Tree

Most complex networks include redundant devices to avoid single points of failure. Although a redundant topology eliminates some problems, it can introduce other problems. STP is a Layer 2 link management protocol that provides path redundancy while preventing undesirable loops in a switched network. It is a standard protocol as defined by IEEE 802.1D.

This section identifies the problems caused by redundant switched-network topologies and the functionality of STP to prevent these problems.

Building a Redundant Switched Topology

One of the key characteristics of a well-built communications network is that it is resilient. This means that the network needs to be able to handle a device or link failure. To accomplish this, you will need to select the best interconnection technologies.

Choosing Interconnection Technologies

A number of technologies are available to interconnect devices in a switched network. The interconnection technology that you select depends on the amount of traffic the link must carry. You will likely use a mixture of copper and fiber-optic cabling based on distances, noise immunity requirements, security, and other business requirements. Figure 2-14 illustrates different connectivity for network devices providing services in the enterprise.

Some of the more common interconnection technologies are as follows:

- **FastEthernet (100-Mbps Ethernet):** This LAN specification (IEEE 802.3u) operates at 100 Mbps over twisted-pair cable. The FastEthernet standard raises the speed of Ethernet from 10 Mbps to 100 Mbps with only minimal changes to the existing cable structure. A switch that has ports that function at both 10 Mbps and 100 Mbps can move frames between ports without Layer 2 protocol translation.

- **Gigabit Ethernet:** An extension of the IEEE 802.3 Ethernet standard, Gigabit Ethernet increases speed tenfold over that of FastEthernet, to 1000 Mbps, or 1 Gbps. IEEE 802.3z specifies operations over fiber optics, and IEEE 802.3ab specifies operations over twisted-pair cable.

Figure 2-14 *Interconnectivity at the User Level*

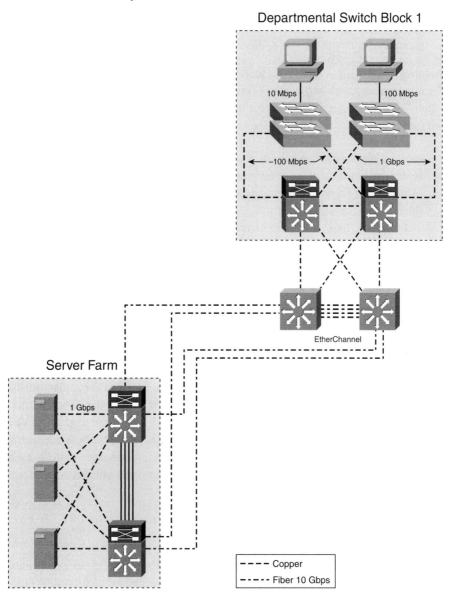

- **10-Gigabit Ethernet:** 10-Gigabit Ethernet was formally ratified as an 802.3 Ethernet standard (IEEE 802.3ae) in June 2002. This technology is the next step for scaling the performance and functionality of an enterprise. With the deployment of Gigabit Ethernet becoming more common, 10-Gigabit Ethernet will become typical for uplinks.

■ **EtherChannel:** This feature provides link aggregation of bandwidth over Layer 2 links between two switches. EtherChannel bundles individual Ethernet ports into a single logical port or link. All interfaces in each EtherChannel bundle must be configured with similar speed, duplex, and VLAN membership.

Determining Equipment and Cabling Needs

The design of any high-performance network has four objectives: security, availability, scalability, and manageability. This list describes the equipment and cabling decisions that you should consider when altering the infrastructure:

■ Replace hubs and legacy switches with new switches at the building access layer. Select equipment with the appropriate port density at the access layer to support the current user base while preparing for growth. Some designers begin by planning for about 30 percent growth. If the budget allows, use modular access switches to accommodate future expansion. Consider planning for the support of inline power and QoS if you think you might implement IP telephony in the future.

■ When building the cable plant from the building access layer to the building distribution layer devices, remember that these links will carry aggregate traffic from the end nodes at the access layer to the building distribution switches. Ensure that these links have adequate bandwidth capability. You can use EtherChannel bundles here to add bandwidth as necessary.

■ At the distribution layer, select switches with adequate performance to handle the load of the current access layer. In addition, plan some port density for adding trunks later to support new access layer devices. The devices at this layer should be multilayer (Layer 2 and Layer 3) switches that support routing between the workgroup VLANs and network resources. Depending on the size of the network, the building distribution layer devices can be fixed chassis or modular. Plan for redundancy in the chassis and in the connections to the access and core layers, as business objectives dictate.

■ The campus backbone equipment must support high-speed data communications between other distribution modules. Be sure to size the backbone for scalability, and plan for redundancy.

Cisco has online tools to help designers make the proper selection of devices and uplink ports based on business and technology needs. Some suggested oversubscription ratios that you can use to plan bandwidth requirements between key devices on a network with average traffic flows are as follows:

■ **Access to distribution layer links:** The oversubscription ratio should be no higher than 20:1. That is, the link can be 1/20 of the total bandwidth available cumulatively to all end devices using that link.

■ **Distribution to core links:** The oversubscription ratio should be no higher than 4:1.

■ **Between core devices:** Little to no oversubscription should be planned here. That is, the links between core devices should be able to carry traffic at the speed represented by the aggregate-number bandwidth of all the distribution uplinks into the core.

> **CAUTION**   These ratios are appropriate for estimating average traffic from access layer, end-user devices. They are not accurate for planning oversubscription from the server farm or edge distribution module. They are also not accurate for planning bandwidth needed on access switches hosting typical user applications with high-bandwidth consumption (for example, nonclient-server databases or multimedia flows to unicast addresses). Using QoS end to end prioritizes the traffic that should be dropped in the event of congestion.

EtherChannel Overview

The increasing deployment of switched Ethernet to the desktop can be attributed to the proliferation of bandwidth-intensive applications. Any-to-any communications of new applications, such as video to the desktop, interactive messaging, and collaborative white-boarding, increase the need for scalable bandwidth. At the same time, mission-critical applications call for resilient network designs. With the wide deployment of faster switched Ethernet links in the campus, organizations either need to aggregate their existing resources or upgrade the speed in their uplinks and core to scale performance across the network backbone.

EtherChannel is a technology that Cisco originally developed as a LAN switch-to-switch technique of inverse multiplexing of multiple FastEthernet or Gigabit Ethernet switch ports into one logical channel. Figure 2-15 shows some common EtherChannel deployment points.

The benefit of EtherChannel is that it is cheaper than higher-speed media while using existing switch ports. The following are advantages of EtherChannel:

■ It enables the creation of a high-bandwidth logical link.

■ It load-shares among the physical links involved.

■ It provides automatic failover.

■ It simplifies subsequent logical configuration. (Configuration is per logical link instead of per physical link.)

Figure 2-15   *EtherChannel*

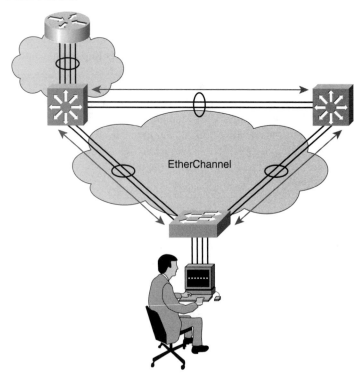

EtherChannel technology provides bandwidth scalability in the campus by offering the following aggregate bandwidth:

- **FastEthernet:** Up to 800 Mbps

- **Gigabit Ethernet:** Up to 8 Gbps

- **10-Gigabit Ethernet:** Up to 80 Gbps

> **NOTE**   Due to the full duplex nature of EtherChannel links, documentation may sometimes duple these numbers indicating the full potential of the link. For example, an 8-port FastEthernet channel operating at full duplex can pass up to 1.6 Gbps of data.

Each of these connection speeds can vary in amounts equal to the speed of the links used (100 Mbps, 1 Gbps, or 10 Gbps). Even in the most bandwidth-demanding situations, EtherChannel technology helps aggregate traffic and keeps oversubscription to a minimum, while providing effective link-resiliency mechanisms.

Redundant Topology

Redundant topology can be accomplished using multiple links, multiple devices, or both. The key is to provide multiple pathways and eliminate a single point of failure. Figure 2-16 shows a simple redundant topology between segment 1 and segment 2.

Figure 2-16 *Redundant Topology*

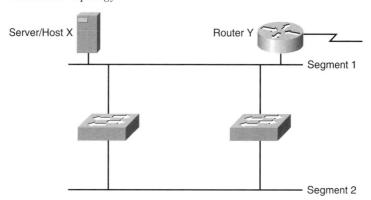

Although redundant designs can eliminate the possibility of a single point of failure causing a loss of function for the entire switched or bridged network, you must consider problems that redundant designs can cause. Some of the problems that can occur with redundant links and devices in switched or bridged networks are as follows:

- **Broadcast storms:** Without some loop-avoidance process in operation, each switch or bridge floods broadcasts endlessly. This situation is commonly called a *broadcast storm*.

- **Multiple frame transmission:** Multiple copies of unicast frames may be delivered to destination stations. Many protocols expect to receive only a single copy of each transmission. Multiple copies of the same frame can cause unrecoverable errors.

- **MAC database instability:** Instability in the content of the MAC address table results from copies of the same frame being received on different ports of the switch. Data forwarding can be impaired when the switch consumes the resources that are coping with instability in the MAC address table.

Layer 2 LAN protocols, such as Ethernet, lack a mechanism to recognize and eliminate endlessly looping frames. Some Layer 3 protocols like IP implement a Time-To-Live (TTL) mechanism that limits the number of times a Layer 3 networking device can retransmit a packet. Lacking such a mechanism, Layer 2 devices continue to retransmit looping traffic indefinitely.

A loop-avoidance mechanism is required to solve each of these problems.

Recognizing Issues of a Redundant Switched Topology

Because of the simple algorithms that a Layer 2 device uses to forward frames, numerous issues must be managed in a redundant topology. Although these issues are managed with technology built into the devices, a failure in these technologies may create network outages. It is important to understand these issues in more detail.

Switch Behavior with Broadcast Frames

Switches handle broadcast and multicast frames differently from the way they handle unicast frames. Because broadcast and multicast frames may be of interest to all stations, the switch or bridge normally floods broadcast and multicast frames to all ports except the originating port. A switch or bridge never learns a broadcast or multicast address because broadcast and multicast addresses never appear as the source address of a frame. This flooding of broadcast and multicast frames can cause a problem in a redundant switched topology. Figure 2-17 shows how a broadcast frame from PC D would be flooded out all ports on the switch.

Figure 2-17   *Broadcast Flooding*

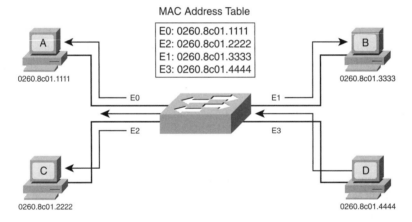

Broadcast Storms

A broadcast storm occurs when each switch on a redundant network floods broadcast frames endlessly. Switches flood broadcast frames to all ports except the port on which the frame was received.

Example: Broadcast Storms

Figure 2-18 illustrates the problem of a broadcast storm.

The following describes the sequence of events that start a broadcast storm:

1. When host X sends a broadcast frame, such as an Address Resolution Protocol (ARP) for its default gateway (Router Y), switch A receives the frame.

Figure 2-18 *Broadcast Storm*

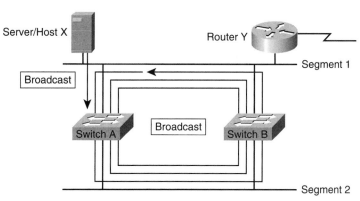

2. Switch A examines the destination address field in the frame and determines that the frame must be flooded onto the lower Ethernet link, segment 2.

3. When this copy of the frame arrives at switch B, the process repeats, and the frame is forwarded to the upper Ethernet segment, which is segment 1, near switch B.

4. Because the original copy of the frame also arrives at switch B from the upper Ethernet link, these frames travel around the loop in both directions, even after the destination station has received a copy of the frame.

A broadcast storm can disrupt normal traffic flow. It can also disrupt all the devices on the switched or bridged network because the CPU in each device on the segment must process the broadcasts; thus, a broadcast storm can lock up the PCs and servers that try to process all the broadcast frames.

A loop avoidance mechanism eliminates this problem by preventing one of the four interfaces from transmitting frames during normal operation, thereby breaking the loop.

Multiple Frame Transmissions

In a redundant topology, multiple copies of the same frame can arrive at the intended host, potentially causing problems with the receiving protocol. Most protocols are not designed to recognize or cope with duplicate transmissions. In general, protocols that use a sequence-numbering mechanism like TCP assume that many transmissions have failed and that the sequence number has recycled. Other protocols attempt to hand the duplicate transmission to the appropriate upper-layer protocol (ULP), with unpredictable results.

Example: Multiple Transmissions

Figure 2-19 illustrates how multiple transmissions can occur.

Figure 2-19 *Multiple Frame Transmissions*

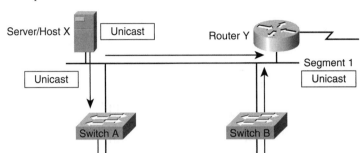

The following describes how multiple copies of the same frame can arrive at the intended host:

1. When host X sends a unicast frame to Router Y, one copy is received over the direct Ethernet connection, segment 1. At more or less the same time, switch A receives a copy of the frame and puts it into its buffers.

2. If switch A examines the destination address field in the frame and finds no entry in the MAC address table for router Y, switch A floods the frame on all ports except the originating port.

3. When switch B receives a copy of the frame through switch A on segment 2, switch B also forwards a copy of the frame to segment 1 if it cannot locate an entry in the MAC address table for Router Y.

4. Router Y receives a copy of the same frame for the second time.

A loop-avoidance mechanism eliminates this problem by preventing one of the four interfaces from transmitting frames during normal operation, thereby breaking the loop.

MAC Database Instability

MAC database instability results when multiple copies of a frame arrive on different ports of a switch. This subtopic describes how MAC database instability can arise and explains what problems can result.

Figure 2-20 illustrates this problem: switch B installs a database entry, mapping the MAC address of host X to port 1. Sometime later, when the copy of the frame transmitted through switch A arrives at port 2 of switch B, switch B removes the first entry and installs an entry that incorrectly maps the MAC address of host X to port 2, which connects to segment 2.

Figure 2-20 *MAC Database Instability*

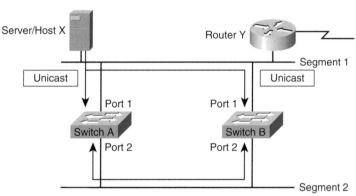

Depending on its internal architecture, the switch in question may or may not cope well with rapid changes in its MAC database. Again, a loop-avoidance mechanism eliminates this problem by preventing one of the four interfaces from transmitting frames during normal operation, thereby breaking the loop.

Resolving Issues with STP

STP provides loop resolution by managing the physical paths to given network segments. STP allows physical path redundancy while preventing the undesirable effects of active loops in the network. STP is an IEEE committee standard defined as 802.1D. Figure 2-21 illustrates how a blocked port would prevent traffic flow between the segments.

Figure 2-21 *Blocking on a Port*

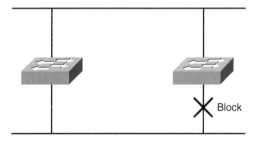

STP behaves as follows:

■ STP forces certain ports into a standby state so that they do not listen to, forward, or flood data frames. The overall effect is that there is only one path to each network segment that is active at any one time.

■ If any of the segments in the network have a connectivity problem, STP reestablishes connectivity by automatically activating a previously inactive path, if one exists.

Figure 2-22 shows the final state of a Layer 2 network after spanning tree has performed the operations to eliminate loops.

Figure 2-22 *Loop Avoidance*

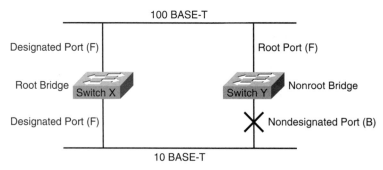

Spanning-Tree Operation

STP performs three steps to provide a loop-free logical network topology:

1. **Elects one root bridge:** STP has a process to elect a root bridge. Only one bridge can act as the root bridge in a given network. On the root bridge, all ports are designated ports. Designated ports are in the forwarding state and are designated to forward traffic for a given segment. When in the forwarding state, a port can send and receive traffic. In Figure 2-22, switch X is elected as the root bridge.

2. **Selects the root port on the nonroot bridge:** STP establishes one root port on each nonroot bridge. The root port is the lowest-cost path from the nonroot bridge to the root bridge. Root ports are in the forwarding state. Spanning-tree path cost is an accumulated cost calculated on the bandwidth. In Figure 2-22, the lowest-cost path to the root bridge from switch Y is through the 100BASE-T FastEthernet link.

3. **Selects the designated port on each segment:** On each segment, STP establishes one designated port. The designated port is selected on the bridge that has the lowest-cost path to the root bridge. Designated ports are in the forwarding state, forwarding traffic for the segment. In Figure 2-22, the designated port for both segments is on the root bridge because the root bridge is directly connected to both segments. The 10BASE-T Ethernet port on switch Y is a nondesignated port because there is only one designated port per segment. Nondesignated ports are normally in the blocking state to logically break the loop topology. When a port is in the blocking state, it is not forwarding data traffic but can still receive traffic.

Switches and bridges running the Spanning Tree Algorithm exchange configuration messages with other switches and bridges at regular intervals (every 2 seconds by default). Switches and bridges exchange these messages using a multicast frame called the BPDU. One of the pieces of information included in the BPDU is the bridge ID (BID).

STP calls for each switch or bridge to be assigned a unique BID. Typically, the BID is composed of a priority value (2 bytes) and the bridge MAC address (6 bytes). The default priority, in accordance with IEEE 802.1D, is 32,768 (1000 0000 0000 0000 in binary, or 0x8000 in hex format), which is the midrange value. The root bridge is the bridge with the lowest BID.

> **NOTE**   A Cisco Catalyst switch uses one of its MAC addresses from a pool of MAC addresses that are assigned either to the backplane or to the supervisor module, depending on the switch model.

Example: Selecting the Root Bridge

In Figure 2-23, both switches use the same default priority. The switch with the lowest MAC address is the root bridge. In the example, switch X is the root bridge, with a BID of 0x8000 (0c00.1111.1111).

Figure 2-23   *Root Bridge Selection*

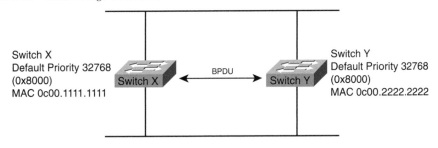

There are five STP port states:

- Blocking

- Listening

- Learning

- Forwarding

- Disabled

When STP is enabled, every bridge in the network goes through the blocking state and the transitory states of listening and learning at power-up. If properly configured, the ports then stabilize to the forwarding or blocking state. Forwarding ports provide the lowest-cost path to the root bridge. During a topology change, a port temporarily implements the listening and learning states.

The disabled state is not strictly part of STP; a network administrator can manually disable a port, or a security or an error condition may disable it. An example of a port that is disabled would be a port that is shut down.

Figure 2-24 shows the flow of spanning-tree port states.

Figure 2-24   *Spanning-Tree Port States*

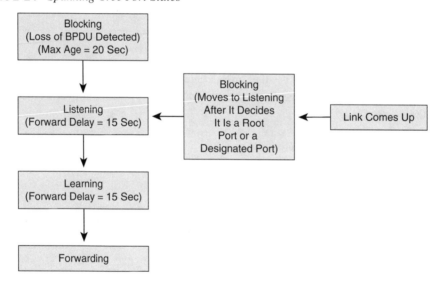

All bridge ports initially start in the blocking state, from which they listen for BPDUs. When the bridge first boots, it functions as if it were the root bridge and transitions to the listening state. An absence of BPDUs for a certain period is called the *maximum age* (max_age), which has a default of 20 seconds. If a port is in the blocking state and does not receive a new BPDU within the max_age, the bridge transitions from the blocking state to the listening state. When a port is in the transitional listening state, it can send and receive BPDUs to determine the active topology. At this point, the switch is not passing user data. During the listening state, the bridge performs these three steps:

1. Selects the root bridge
2. Selects the root ports on the nonroot bridges
3. Selects the designated ports on each segment

The time that it takes for a port to transition from the listening state to the learning state or from the learning state to the forwarding state is called the *forward delay.* The forward delay has a default value of 15 seconds.

The learning state reduces the amount of flooding required when data forwarding begins. If a port is still a designated or root port at the end of the learning state, the port transitions to the forwarding state. In the forwarding state, a port is capable of sending and receiving user data. Ports that are not the designated or root ports transition back to the blocking state.

A port normally transitions from the blocking state to the forwarding state in 30 to 50 seconds. You can tune the spanning-tree timers to adjust the timing, but these timers are meant to be set to the default value. The default values are put in place to give the network enough time to gather all the correct information about the network topology.

Spanning-tree PortFast causes an interface that is configured as a Layer 2 access port to transition immediately from the blocking state to the forwarding state, bypassing the listening and learning states. You can use PortFast on Layer 2 access ports that are connected to a single workstation or server to allow those devices to connect to the network immediately rather than wait for spanning tree to converge. Figure 2-25 shows access ports connected with PortFast enabled.

Figure 2-25 *PortFast*

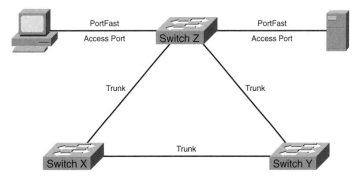

If an interface that is configured with PortFast receives a BPDU, then spanning tree can transition the port to the blocking state. Using a feature called BPDU guard, the port can be disabled completely when it receives a BPDU to prevent any potential loops caused by PortFast.

> **CAUTION** Because the purpose of PortFast is to minimize the time that access ports must wait for spanning tree to converge, you should use it only on access ports. If you enable PortFast on a port connecting to another switch, you risk creating a spanning-tree loop.

Table 2-10 lists the commands used to implement and verify PortFast on an interface.

Table 2-10   *PortFast Commands*

Command	Description
Switch(config-if)#**spanning-tree portfast**	Enables PortFast on a Layer 2 access port and forces it to enter the forwarding state immediately.
Switch(config-if)#**spanning-tree portfast bpdu-guard**	Enables PortFast with BPDU guard. This disables the switch port if a BPDU is ever received, preventing any possibility of a loop.
Switch(config-if)#**no spanning-tree portfast**	Disables PortFast on a Layer 2 access port. PortFast is disabled by default.
Switch(config)#**spanning-tree portfast default**	Globally enables the PortFast feature on all nontrunking ports. When the PortFast feature is enabled, the port changes from a blocking state to a forwarding state without making the intermediate spanning-tree state changes.
Switch#**show running-config interface** *type slot/port*	Indicates whether PortFast has been configured on a port. It can also be used to show if configuration has occurred on an EtherChannel link by specifying *port-channel channel_number* in place of *type slot/port*.

Example: Spanning-Tree Operation

The best way to understand how spanning tree operates is to look at an operation example. Figure 2-26 shows a sample network spanning tree topology and the relevant information used by spanning tree.

Figure 2-26   *Spanning Tree Topology*

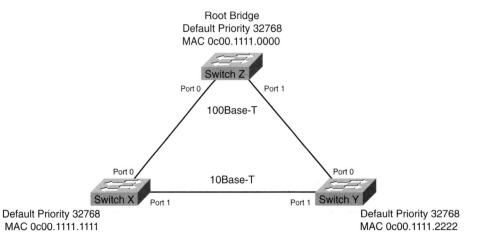

The following describes the STP port states illustrated in Figure 2-26:

■ The root bridge is switch Z, which has the lowest BID.

■ The root port is port 0 on switches X and Y. Port 0 is the lowest-cost path to the root on both switches.

■ The designated ports on switch Z are port 0 and port 1. All ports on the root are designated ports. Port 1 of switch X is a designated port for the segment between switch X and switch Y. Because switch X and switch Y have the same path cost to the root bridge, the designated port is selected to be on switch X because it has a lower BID than switch Y.

■ Port 1 on switch Y is the nondesignated port on the segment and is in the blocking state.

■ All designated and root ports are in the forwarding state.

Example: Spanning-Tree Path Cost

The spanning-tree path cost is an accumulated total path cost based on the bandwidth of all the links in the path. In the figure, some of the path costs specified in the 802.1D specification are shown. The 802.1D specification has been revised; in the older specification, the cost was calculated based on a bandwidth of 1000 Mbps. The calculation of the new specification uses a nonlinear scale to accommodate higher-speed interfaces.

NOTE   Most Cisco Catalyst switches incorporate the revised cost calculations. A key point to remember about STP cost is that lower costs are better.

Table 2-11 describes the spanning-tree path cost calculations based on bandwidth of a link.

Table 2-11   *Spanning-Tree Path Costs*

Link Speed	Cost (Revised IEEE Specification)	Cost (Previous IEEE Specification)
10 Gbps	2	1
1 Gbps	4	1
100 Mbps	19	10
10 Mbps	100	100

When there is a topology change because of a bridge or link failure, spanning tree adjusts the network topology to ensure connectivity by placing blocked ports in the forwarding state.

Example: Spanning-Tree Recalculation

In Figure 2-27, if switch Z (the root bridge) fails and does not send a BPDU to switch Y within the max_age time (default is 20 seconds, which equals 10 missed BPDUs), switch Y detects the missing BPDU from the root bridge. When the max_age timer on switch Y expires before a new BPDU has been received from switch Z, a spanning-tree recalculation is initiated. Switch Y transitions its blocking port (port 1) from the blocking state to the listening state to the learning state, and then finally to the forwarding state.

Figure 2-27 *Spanning-Tree Recalculation*

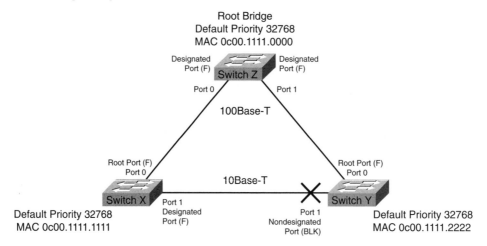

After all the switch and bridge ports have transitioned to either a forwarding state or a blocking state, switch X becomes the root bridge and forwards traffic between the segments.

STP Convergence

Convergence in STP is a state in which all the switch and bridge ports have transitioned to either the forwarding or the blocking state. Convergence is necessary for normal network operations. For a switched or bridged network, a key issue is the time required for convergence when the network topology changes.

Fast convergence is a desirable network feature because it reduces the time that bridge and switch ports are in transitional states and not sending user traffic. The normal convergence time is 30 to 50 seconds for 802.1D STP.

Per VLAN Spanning Tree+

The 802.1D standard defines a Common Spanning Tree (CST) that assumes only one spanning-tree instance for the entire switched network, regardless of the number of VLANs. In a network running CST, these statements are true:

- No load sharing is possible; one uplink must block for all VLANs.

- The CPU is spared; only one instance of spanning tree must be computed.

Per VLAN Spanning Tree Plus (PVST+) defines a spanning-tree protocol that has several spanning-tree instances running for the network, one instance of STP per VLAN. Figure 2-28 shows an example of how you can use PVST+ to forward traffic on all network segments but still maintain STP integrity.

Figure 2-28 *Per VLAN Spanning Tree+*

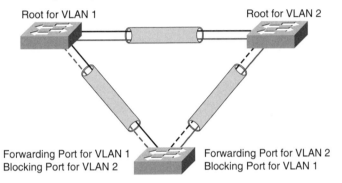

In a network running several spanning-tree instances, these statements are true:

- Optimum load sharing can result.

- One spanning-tree instance for each VLAN maintained can mean a considerable waste of CPU cycles for all the switches in the network (in addition to the bandwidth used for each instance to send its own BPDUs).

PVST+ Operation

In a Cisco PVST+ environment, you can tune the spanning-tree parameters so that half of the VLANs forward on each uplink trunk. To easily achieve this, you configure one switch to be elected the root bridge for half of the total number of VLANs in the network and a second switch to be elected the root bridge for the other half of the VLANs. Providing different STP root switches per VLAN creates a more redundant network.

Spanning-tree operation requires that each switch has a unique BID. In the original 802.1D standard, the BID was composed of the bridge priority and the MAC address of the switch, and all VLANs were represented by a CST. Because PVST+ requires that a separate instance of spanning tree runs for each VLAN, the BID field is required to carry VID information. This is accomplished by reusing a portion of the Priority field as the extended system ID to carry a VID. Figure 2-29 shows how modifying the bridge priority offers this support.

Figure 2-29   *PVST+ VLAN ID*

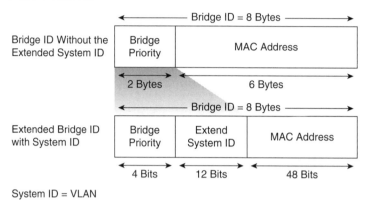

System ID = VLAN

To accommodate the extended system ID, the original 802.1D 16-bit bridge priority field is split into two fields, resulting in these components in the BID:

■ **Bridge priority:** A 4-bit field still used to carry bridge priority. Because of the limited bit count, the priority is conveyed in discreet values in increments of 4096 rather than discreet values in increments of 1, as they would be if the full 16-bit field were available. The default priority, in accordance with IEEE 802.1D, is 32,768, which is the midrange value.

■ **Extended system ID:** A 12-bit field carrying, in this case, the VID for PVST+.

■ **MAC address:** A 6-byte field with the MAC address of a single switch.

By virtue of the MAC address, a BID is always unique. When the priority and extended system ID are prepended to the switch MAC address, each VLAN on the switch can be represented by a unique BID.

If no priority has been configured, every switch will have the same default priority, and the election of the root for each VLAN will be based on the MAC address. This method is a random means of selecting the ideal root bridge; for this reason, it is advisable to assign a lower priority to the switch that should serve as the root bridge. The root bridge should be located in the center of your network traffic flow.

Rapid Spanning Tree Protocol

Rapid Spanning Tree Protocol (RSTP), specified in the IEEE 802.1w standard, supersedes STP as specified in 802.1D, while remaining compatible with STP. RSTP can be seen as an evolution of the 802.1D standard rather than a revolution. The 802.1D terminology remains primarily the same. Most parameters have been left unchanged, so users familiar with 802.1D can configure the new protocol comfortably.

RSTP significantly reduces the time to reconverge the active topology of the network when changes to the physical topology or its configuration parameters occur. RSTP defines the additional port roles of alternate and backup, and it defines port states as discarding, learning, or forwarding.

RSTP selects one switch as the root of a spanning-tree active topology and assigns port roles to individual ports on the switch, depending on whether the ports are part of the active topology.

RSTP provides rapid connectivity following the failure of a switch, a switch port, or a LAN. A new root port and the designated port on the other side of the bridge transition to forwarding through an explicit handshake between them. RSTP allows switch port configuration so that the ports can transition to forwarding directly when the switch reinitializes. Figure 2-30 shows an RSTP topology.

Figure 2-30 *RSTP Topology*

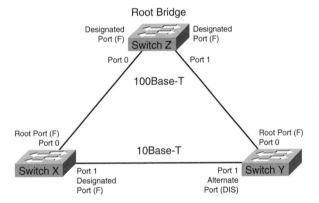

Per VLAN RSTP

The RSTP (802.1w) standard uses CST, which assumes only one spanning-tree instance for the entire switched network, regardless of the number of VLANs. Per VLAN Rapid Spanning Tree Plus (PVRST+) defines a spanning-tree protocol that has one instance of RSTP per VLAN.

Multiple Spanning Tree Protocol

Multiple Spanning Tree Protocol (MSTP), originally defined in IEEE 802.1s and later merged into IEEE 802.1Q-2003, defines a spanning-tree protocol that has several spanning-tree instances running for the network. But unlike PVRST+, which has one instance of RSTP per VLAN, MSTP reduces the switch load by allowing a single instance of spanning tree to run for multiple VLANs.

RSTP Port Roles

RSTP defines the port roles as follows:

- **Root:** A forwarding port elected for the spanning-tree topology.

- **Designated:** A forwarding port elected for every switched LAN segment.

- **Alternate:** An alternate path to the root bridge that is different from the path that the root port takes.

- **Backup:** A backup path that provides a redundant (but less desirable) connection to a segment to which another switch port already connects. Backup ports can exist only where two ports are connected in a loopback by a point-to-point link or bridge with two or more connections to a shared LAN segment.

- **Disabled:** A port that has no role within the operation of spanning tree.

Root and designated port roles include the port in the active topology. Alternate and backup port roles exclude the port from the active topology.

> **NOTE** The Cisco implementation of 802.1D includes some features that are standard in 802.1w. For example, the Cisco implementation of 802.1D determines an alternate root port if it exists.

The port state controls the forwarding and learning processes and provides the values of discarding, learning, and forwarding. Table 2-12 compares STP port states with RSTP port states.

Table 2-12 *Comparing RSTP Port States to STP*

Operational Status	STP Port State	RSTP Port State	Port Included in Active Topology
Enabled	Blocking	Discarding	No
Enabled	Listening	Discarding	No
Enabled	Learning	Learning	Yes
Enabled	Forwarding	Forwarding	Yes
Disabled	Disabled	Discarding	No

In a stable topology, RSTP ensures that every root port and designated port transitions to forwarding, while all alternate ports and backup ports are always in the discarding state.

Configuring RSTP

Cisco Catalyst switches support three types of spanning-tree protocols: PVST+, PVRST+, and MSTP.

■ **PVST+:** Based on the 802.1D standard, this includes Cisco proprietary extensions, such as BackboneFast, UplinkFast, and PortFast, which improve STP convergence time.

■ **PVRST+:** Based on the 802.1w standard, this has a faster convergence than 802.1D.

■ **MSTP (802.1s):** Combines the best aspects of PVST+ and the IEEE standards.

To implement PVRST+, perform these steps:

Step 1   Enable PVRST+.

Step 2   Designate and configure a switch to be the root bridge.

Step 3   Designate and configure a switch to be the secondary (backup) root bridge.

Step 4   Verify the configuration.

Table 2-13 describes the commands that you use to enable and verify PVRST+.

Table 2-13   *PVRST+ Commands*

Command	Description
SwitchX(config)#**spanning-tree mode rapid-pvst**	Sets spanning-tree mode to PVRST+
SwitchX#**show spanning-tree vlan** *vlan-number* **[detail]**	Shows spanning-tree information that is VLAN-based rather than instance-based
SwitchX#**debug spanning-tree pvst+**	Debugs PVST+ events
SwitchX#**debug spanning-tree switch state**	Debugs port state changes Note: Like all debug commands, this command can affect network performance.

Example 2-7 shows how to verify the STP protocol for a given VLAN.

Example 2-7 *STP Protocol Verification*

```
SwitchX#show spanning-tree vlan 30
VLAN0030
Spanning tree enabled protocol rstp
Root ID Priority 24606
Address 00d0.047b.2800
This bridge is the root
Hello Time 2 sec Max Age 20 sec Forward Delay 15 sec
Bridge ID Priority 24606 (priority 24576 sys-id-ext 30)
Address 00d0.047b.2800
Hello Time 2 sec Max Age 20 sec Forward Delay 15 sec
Aging Time 300
Interface Role Sts Cost Prio.Nbr  Type
--------- ----- --- ---  --------  ----
Gi1/1     Desg FWD  4     128.1     P2p
Gi1/2     Desg FWD  4     128.2     P2p
Gi5/1     Desg FWD  4     128.257   P2p
```

In this example, the statement **Spanning tree enabled protocol rstp** indicates that switch X is running PVRST+, the Cisco RSTP implementation.

Switch X is the root bridge for VLAN 30. Its priority of 24606 is derived from the sum of the assigned priority of 24576 and VLAN 30. The MAC address of switch X, which is 00d0.047b.2800, is appended to the priority, 24606, to make up the bridge ID.

As the root bridge for VLAN 30, all the interfaces of switch X are designated ports in the forwarding state.

If all the switches in a network are enabled with the default spanning-tree settings, the switch with the lowest MAC address becomes the root bridge. However, the default root bridge might not be ideal because of traffic patterns, the number of forwarding interfaces, or link types.

Before you configure STP, select a switch to be the root of the spanning tree. This switch does not need to be the most powerful switch, but it should be the most centralized switch on the network. All data flow across the network occurs from the perspective of this switch. The distribution layer switches often serve as the spanning-tree root because these switches typically do not connect to end stations. In addition, moves and changes within the network are less likely to affect these switches.

By increasing the priority (lowering the numerical value) of the preferred switch so that it becomes the root bridge, you force spanning tree to perform a recalculation that reflects a new topology with the preferred switch as the root.

The switch with the lowest BID becomes the root bridge for spanning tree for a VLAN. You can use specific configuration commands to help determine which switch will become the root bridge.

A Cisco Catalyst switch running PVST+ or PVRST+ maintains an instance of spanning tree for each active VLAN that is configured on the switch. A unique BID is associated with each instance. For each VLAN, the switch with the lowest BID becomes the root bridge for that VLAN. Whenever the bridge priority changes, the BID also changes. This change results in the recomputation of the root bridge for the VLAN.

To configure a switch to become the root bridge for a specified VLAN, use the command **spanning-tree vlan** *vlan-ID* **root primary**. With this command, the switch checks the priority of the root switches for the specified VLAN. Because of the extended system ID support, the switch sets its own priority to 24576 for the specified VLAN if this value will cause the switch to become the root for this VLAN. If another switch for the specified VLAN has a priority lower than 24576, then the switch on which you are configuring the **spanning-tree vlan** *vlan-ID* **root primary** command sets its own priority for the specified VLAN to 4096 less than the lowest switch priority.

> **CAUTION**   Spanning-tree commands take effect immediately, so network traffic is interrupted while reconfiguration occurs.

A secondary root is a switch that can become the root bridge for a VLAN if the primary root bridge fails. To configure a switch as the secondary root bridge for the VLAN, use the command **spanning-tree vlan** *vlan-ID* **root secondary**.

With this command, the switch priority is modified from the default value of 32768 to 28672. Assuming that the other bridges in the VLAN retain their default STP priority, this switch becomes the root bridge if the primary root bridge fails. You can execute this command on more than one switch to configure multiple backup root bridges.

Summary of Improving Performance with Spanning Tree

The following summarizes the key points that were discussed in this section.

- A redundant switched topology includes redundantly connected switches and EtherChannel.

- A redundant switched topology causes looping issues such as broadcast storms.

- The 802.1D STP establishes a loop-free network.

- The original STP has been enhanced by PVST+ and RSTP.

Routing Between VLANs

Routing is the process of determining where to send data packets destined for addresses outside of the local network. Routers gather and maintain routing information to enable the transmission and receipt of data packets. For traffic to cross from one VLAN to another, a Layer 3 process is necessary.

This section describes the operation of inter-VLAN routing using a router on a stick.

Understanding Inter-VLAN Routing

Inter-VLAN communication occurs between broadcast domains via a Layer 3 device. In a VLAN environment, frames are switched only between ports within the same broadcast domain. VLANs perform network partitioning and traffic separation at Layer 2. Inter-VLAN communication cannot occur without a Layer 3 device, such as a router. Use IEEE 802.1Q to enable trunking on a router subinterface.

Example: Router on a Stick

Figure 2-31 illustrates a router attached to a core switch. The configuration between a router and a core switch is sometimes referred to as a *router on a stick*.

Figure 2-31   *Router on a Stick*

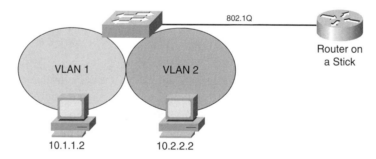

The router can receive packets on one VLAN and forward them to another VLAN. To perform inter-VLAN routing functions, the router must know how to reach all VLANs being interconnected. Each VLAN must have a separate connection on the router, and you must enable 802.1Q trunking on those connections. The router already knows about directly connected networks. The router must learn routes to networks to which it is not directly connected.

To support 802.1Q trunking, you must subdivide the physical FastEthernet interface of the router into multiple, logical, addressable interfaces, one per VLAN. The resulting logical interfaces are called subinterfaces. This is illustrated in Figure 2-32.

Figure 2-32 *Subinterfaces*

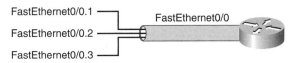

Without this subdivision, you would have to dedicate a separate physical interface to each VLAN.

Example: Subinterfaces

In the figure, the FastEthernet 0/0 interface is divided into multiple subinterfaces: FastEthernet 0/0.1, FastEthernet 0/0.2, and FastEthernet 0/0.3.

Configuring Inter-VLAN Routing

To be able to route between VLANs on a switch, you will need to be able to configure inter-VLAN routing.

In Figure 2-33, the FastEthernet 0/0 interface is divided into multiple subinterfaces: FastEthernet 0/0.1 and FastEthernet 0/0.2. Each subinterface represents the router in each of the VLANs for which it routes.

Figure 2-33 *Inter-VLAN Routing Configuration*

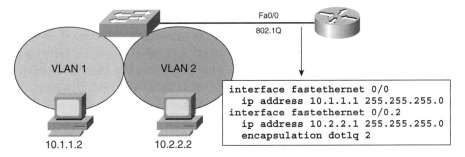

Use the **encapsulation dot1q** *vlan identifier* command (where *vlan identifier* is the VLAN number) on each subinterface to enable 802.1Q encapsulation trunking. The subinterface number does not have to be the same as the dot1Q VLAN number. However, management is easier when the two numbers are the same.

The native VLAN frames in 802.1Q do not carry a tag. Therefore, the native VLAN subinterface is configured with the **encapsulation dot1Q** *vlan identifier* **native** command. Ensure that the VLAN assigned to the native VLAN subinterface matches the native VLAN on the switch it connects to. Each subinterface will have a unique IP address for the VLAN it is associated with. This address will be used as the gateway address for workstations in that VLAN.

Summary of Routing Between VLANs

This list that follows summarizes the key points that were discussed in this section.

- Inter-VLAN routing using a router on a stick utilizes an external router to pass traffic between VLANs.

- A router on a stick is configured with a subinterface for each VLAN and 802.1Q trunk encapsulation.

Securing the Expanded Network

Routers and switches that are internal to an organization often have minimal security configurations, which render them targets for malicious attacks. If an attack is launched at Layer 2 on an internal campus device, the rest of the network can be quickly compromised, often without detection.

This section discusses security features that exist to protect switches and Layer 2 operations.

Overview of Switch Security Concerns

Much industry attention surrounds security attacks from outside the walls of an organization and at the upper Open Systems Interconnection (OSI) layers. Network security often focuses on edge routing devices and the filtering of packets based on Layer 3 and Layer 4 headers, ports, stateful packet inspection, and so on. This focus includes all issues surrounding Layer 3 and above, as traffic makes its way into the campus network from the Internet. Campus access devices and Layer 2 communication are largely unconsidered in most security discussions.

Routers and switches that are internal to an organization and designed to accommodate communication by delivering campus traffic have a default operational mode that forwards all traffic unless it is configured otherwise. Their function as devices that facilitate communication often results in minimal security configuration and renders them targets for malicious attacks. If an attack is launched at Layer 2 on an internal campus device, the rest of the network can be quickly compromised, often without detection. Figure 2-34 shows a trend in the lack of security toward the user access layer.

Figure 2-34 *Security Decreases Near the Access Layer*

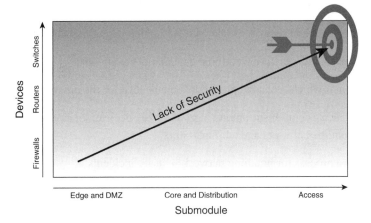

Like Layer 3, where security traditionally has had to be tightened on devices within the campus as malicious activity that compromised this layer has increased, Layer 2 requires that security measures be taken to guard against attacks that are launched by maliciously leveraging normal Layer 2 switch operations. Many security features are available for switches and routers, but you must enable them to make them effective. In the same way that you implement access control lists (ACL) for upper-layer security, you must establish a policy and configure appropriate features to protect against potential malicious acts while maintaining daily network operations.

Network security vulnerabilities include loss of privacy, data theft, impersonation, and loss of data integrity. You should take basic security measures on every network to mitigate adverse effects of user negligence or acts of malicious intent.

Recommended practices dictate that you should follow these general steps whenever placing new equipment in service:

Step 1 Consider or establish organizational security policies.

Step 2 Secure switch devices by securing switch access and switch protocols and mitigating compromises launched through a switch.

You should consider the policies of an organization when determining what level and type of security you want to implement. You must balance the goal of reasonable network security against the administrative overhead that is clearly associated with extremely restrictive security measures.

A well-established security policy has these characteristics:

■ Provides a process for auditing existing network security

■ Provides a general security framework for implementing network security

■ Defines behaviors toward electronic data that is not allowed

■ Determines which tools and procedures are needed for the organization

■ Communicates consensus among a group of key decision makers and defines responsibilities of users and administrators

■ Defines a process for handling network security incidents

■ Enables an enterprise-wide, all-site security implementation and enforcement plan

Securing Switch Devices

You should use your security policy to determine how to configure security on your various network devices. Best practices for securing these devices also exist. Follow these recommended practices for secure switch access:

■ **Set system passwords:** Use the **enable secret** command to set the password that grants privileged access to the Cisco IOS system. Because the **enable secret** command simply implements a Message Digest 5 (MD5) hash on the configured password, that password remains vulnerable to dictionary attacks. Therefore, apply standard practices in selecting a feasible password.

■ **Try to pick passwords that contain both letters and numbers in addition to special characters:** For example, choose "$pecia1$" instead of "specials," in which the "s" has been replaced with "$," and the "l" has been replaced with "1" (one).

■ **Secure access to the console:** Console access requires a minimum level of security both physically and logically. An individual who gains console access to a system is able to recover or reset the system-enable password, thus allowing that person to bypass all other security implemented on that system. Consequently, it is imperative to secure physical access to the console.

■ **Secure access to vty lines:** These are the minimum recommended steps for securing Telnet access:

— Apply a basic ACL for in-band access to all vty lines.

— Configure a line password for all configured vty lines.

— If the installed Cisco IOS Software permits, use the Secure Shell (SSH) protocol instead of Telnet to access the device remotely.

■ **Use SSH:** The SSH protocol and application provide a secure remote connection to a router. Two versions of SSH are available: SSH version 1 (SSHv1) and SSH version 2 (SSHv2). Cisco IOS Software implements SSHv1. It encrypts all traffic, including passwords, between a remote console and a network router across a Telnet session. Because SSH sends no traffic in plaintext, network administrators can conduct remote access sessions that casual observers will not be able to view. The SSH server in the Cisco IOS Software works with publicly and commercially available SSH clients.

■ **Disable the integrated HTTP daemon if not in use:** Although Cisco IOS Software provides an integrated HTTP server for management, it is highly recommended that you disable it to minimize overall exposure. If HTTP access to the switch is required, use basic ACLs to permit access only from trusted subnets.

■ **Configure system-warning banners:** For both legal and administrative purposes, configuring a system-warning banner to display before login is a convenient and effective way to reinforce security and general usage policies. By clearly stating the ownership, usage, access, and protection policies before a login, you provide better support for potential prosecution.

■ **Disable unneeded services:** By default, Cisco devices implement multiple TCP and User Datagram Protocol (UDP) servers to facilitate management and integration into existing environments. For most installations, these services are not required, and disabling them can greatly reduce overall security exposure. These commands disable the services not typically used:

```
no service tcp-small-servers
no service finger
no service config
```

■ **Configure basic logging:** To assist and simplify both problem troubleshooting and security investigations, monitor the switch subsystem information received from the logging facility. View the output in the on-system logging buffer memory. To render the on-system logging useful, increase the default buffer size.

■ **Encrypt passwords:** The configuration file contains many passwords in plaintext. Using the **service password-encryption** command in global configuration mode will provide a simple encryption algorithm to help secure these passwords.

Securing Switch Protocols

Follow these recommended practices to secure the switch protocols:

- **Manage Cisco Discovery Protocol:** Cisco Discovery Protocol does not reveal security-specific information, but it is possible for an attacker to exploit this information in a reconnaissance attack, whereby an attacker learns device and IP address information to launch other types of attacks. You should follow two practical guidelines for Cisco Discovery Protocol:

    — If Cisco Discovery Protocol is not required, or if the device is located in an unsecured environment, disable Cisco Discovery Protocol globally on the device.

    — If Cisco Discovery Protocol is required, disable it on a per-interface basis on ports connected to untrusted networks. Because Cisco Discovery Protocol is a link-level protocol, it is not transient across a network, unless a Layer 2 tunneling mechanism is in place. Limit it to run only between trusted devices and disable it everywhere else. However, Cisco Discovery Protocol is required on any access port where you are attaching a Cisco IP phone to establish a trust relationship.

- **Secure the Spanning-Tree Topology:** It is important to protect the STP process of the switches that form the infrastructure. Inadvertent or malicious introduction of STP BPDUs could overwhelm a device or pose a denial of service (DoS) attack. The first step in stabilizing a spanning-tree installation is to identify the intended root bridge in the design and hard set the STP bridge priority of that bridge to an acceptable root value. Do the same for the designated backup root bridge. These actions protect against inadvertent shifts in STP that are caused by an uncontrolled introduction of a new switch.

    — On some platforms, the BPDU guard feature may be available. If so, enable it on access ports in conjunction with the PortFast feature to protect the network from unwanted BPDU traffic injection. Upon receipt of a BPDU, the BPDU guard feature automatically disables the port.

Mitigating Compromises Launched Through a Switch

Follow these recommended practices to mitigate compromises through a switch:

- **Proactively configure unused router and switch ports:**

    — Execute the **shut** command on all unused ports and interfaces.

— Place all unused ports in a "parking-lot" VLAN, which is dedicated to grouping unused ports until they are proactively placed into service.

— Configure all unused ports as access ports, disallowing automatic trunk negotiation.

- **Consider trunk links:** By default, Cisco Catalyst switches that are running Cisco IOS Software are configured to automatically negotiate trunking capabilities. This situation poses a serious hazard to the infrastructure because an unsecured third-party device can be introduced to the network as a valid infrastructure component. Potential attacks include interception of traffic, redirection of traffic, DoS, and more. To avoid this risk, disable automatic negotiation of trunking and manually enable it on links that require it. Ensure that trunks use a native VLAN that is dedicated exclusively to trunk links. Consider using a password for VTP to prevent someone from adding a switch that could overwrite the VLAN database.

- **Monitor physical device access:** You should closely monitor physical access to the switch to avoid rogue device placement in wiring closets with direct access to switch ports.

- **Ensure access port–based security:** Take specific measures on every access port of every switch placed into service. Ensure that a policy is in place outlining the configuration of unused and used switch ports. For ports that will connect to end devices, you can use a macro called **switchport host**. When you execute this command on a specific switch port, the switch port mode is set to access, spanning-tree PortFast is enabled, and channel grouping is disabled.

NOTE   The **switchport host** macro disables EtherChannel and trunking and enables STP PortFast.

The **switchport host** command is a macro that executes several configuration commands. You cannot revoke the effect of the **switchport host** command by using the **no** form of the command because it does not exist. To return an interface to its default configuration, use the **default interface** *interface-id* global configuration command. This command returns all interface configurations to their defaults.

Describing Port Security

Port security is a feature supported on Cisco Catalyst switches that restricts a switch port to a specific set or number of MAC addresses. The switch can learn these addresses dynamically, or you can configure them statically. Figure 2-35 shows how the switch interacts with port security.

Figure 2-35   *Port Security*

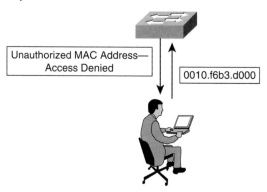

A port that is configured with port security accepts frames only from those addresses that it has learned or that you have configured.

Port security has several implementations:

■ **Dynamic:** You specify how many different MAC addresses are permitted to use a port at one time. You use the dynamic approach when you care only about how many rather than which specific MAC addresses are permitted. Depending on how you configure the switch, these dynamically learned addresses age out after a certain period, and new addresses are learned, up to the maximum that you have defined.

■ **Static:** You statically configure which specific MAC addresses are permitted to use a port. Any source MAC addresses that you do not specifically permit are not allowed to source frames to the port.

■ **A combination of static and dynamic learning:** You can choose to specify some of the permitted MAC addresses and let the switch learn the rest of the permitted MAC addresses. For example, if the number of MAC addresses is limited to four, and you statically configure two MAC addresses, the switch dynamically learns the next two MAC addresses that it receives on that port. Port access is limited to these four addresses: two static and two dynamically learned addresses. The two statically configured addresses do not age out, but the two dynamically learned addresses can, depending on the switch configuration.

■ **Dynamic "sticky learning":** When this feature is configured on an interface, the interface converts dynamically learned addresses to "sticky secure" addresses. This feature adds the dynamically learned addresses to the running configuration as if they were statically configured using the **switchport port-security mac-address** command. "Sticky learned" addresses do not age out.

Scenario for Using Port Security

Imagine five individuals whose laptops are allowed to connect to a specific switch port when they visit an area of the building. You want to restrict switch port access to the MAC addresses of those five laptops and allow no addresses to be learned dynamically on that port.

Process for Configuring Port Security

Table 2-14 describes the process that can achieve the desired results for this scenario.

Table 2-14 *Port Security*

Step	Action	Notes
1.	Port security is configured to allow only five connections on that port, and one entry is configured for each of the five allowed MAC addresses.	This step populates the MAC address table with five entries for that port and allows no additional entries to be learned dynamically.
2.	Allowed frames are processed.	When frames arrive on the switch port, their source MAC address is checked against the MAC address table. If the source MAC address matches an entry in the table for that port, the frames are forwarded to the switch to be processed like any other frames on the switch.
3.	New addresses are not allowed to create new MAC address table entries.	When frames with an unauthorized MAC address arrive on the port, the switch determines that the address is not in the current MAC address table and does not create a dynamic entry for that new MAC address.
4.	The switch takes action in response to unauthorized frames.	The switch disallows access to the port and takes one of these configuration-dependent actions: (a) the entire switch port can be shut down; (b) access can be denied for only that MAC address, and a log error message is generated; (c) access can be denied for that MAC address, but no log message is generated.

NOTE   You cannot apply port security to trunk ports because addresses on trunk links might change frequently. Implementations of port security vary depending on which Cisco Catalyst switch is in use. Check documentation to determine whether and how particular hardware supports this feature.

802.X Port-Based Authentication

The IEEE 802.1X standard defines a port-based access control and authentication protocol that restricts unauthorized workstations from connecting to a LAN through publicly accessible switch ports. The authentication server authenticates each workstation that is connected to a switch port before making available any services offered by the switch or the LAN. Figure 2-36 shows the roles of each device in port-based authentication.

Figure 2-36   *802.1X Port-Based Authentication*

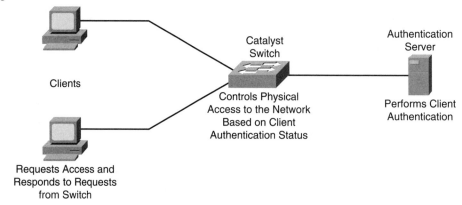

Until the workstation is authenticated, 802.1x access control allows only Extensible Authentication Protocol over LAN (EAPOL) traffic through the port to which the workstation is connected. After authentication succeeds, normal traffic can pass through the port.

With 802.1X port-based authentication, the devices in the network have specific roles, as follows:

- **Client:** The device (workstation) that requests access to the LAN and switch services and responds to requests from the switch. The workstation must be running 802.1X-compliant client software, such as that offered in the Microsoft Windows XP operating system. The port to which the client is attached is the supplicant (client) in the IEEE 802.1X specification.

- **Authentication server:** Performs the actual authentication of the client. The authentication server validates the identity of the client and notifies the switch whether the client is authorized to access the LAN and switch services. Because the switch acts as the proxy, the authentication service is transparent to the client. The RADIUS security system with Extensible Authentication Protocol (EAP) extensions is the only supported authentication server.

> **NOTE**   Whereas the 802.1X standard provides a means for a variety of authentication protocols and servers, RADIUS has become the de-facto standard and is the most common method used with Cisco switches.

■ **Switch (also called the authenticator):** Controls physical access to the network based on the authentication status of the client. The switch acts as an intermediary (proxy) between the client (supplicant) and the authentication server, requesting identifying information from the client, verifying that information with the authentication server, and relaying a response to the client. The switch uses a RADIUS software agent, which is responsible for encapsulating and decapsulating the EAP frames and interacting with the authentication server.

The switch port state determines whether the client is granted access to the network. The port starts in the unauthorized state. While in this state, the port disallows all ingress and egress traffic except for 802.1X protocol packets. When a client is successfully authenticated, the port transitions to the authorized state, allowing all traffic for the client to flow normally.

If the switch requests the client identity (authenticator initiation) and the client does not support 802.1X, the port remains in the unauthorized state, and the client is not granted access to the network.

When an 802.1X-enabled client connects to a port and initiates the authentication process (supplicant initiation) by sending an EAPOL-start frame to a switch that is not running 802.1X, and no response is received, the client begins sending frames as if the port is in the authorized state.

If the client is successfully authenticated (receives an Accept frame from the authentication server), the port state changes to authorized, and all frames from the authenticated client are allowed through the port.

If the authentication fails, the port remains in the unauthorized state, but authentication can be retried. If the authentication server cannot be reached, the switch can retransmit the request. If no response is received from the server after the specified number of attempts, authentication fails, and network access is not granted.

When a client logs out, it sends an EAPOL-logout message, causing the switch port to transition to the unauthorized state.

NOTE   You can find more information on configuring 802.1X port-based authentication in the Cisco CCNP curriculum.

Summary of Securing the Expanded Network

The list that follows summarizes the key points that were discussed in this section.

- Follow recommended practices for securing your switched topology by using passwords, deactivating unused ports, configuring authentication, and using port security.

- To secure a switch device, you must secure access to the switch and the protocols that the switch uses.

Troubleshooting Switched Networks

As the number of switch features grows, so does the possibility that things will go wrong. This section presents recommendations for implementing a functional network. It also addresses some of the common reasons that port connectivity, VLAN configuration, VTP, and STP can fail, as well as what information to look for to identify the source of a problem.

Troubleshooting Switches

There are many ways to troubleshoot a switch. Developing a troubleshooting approach or test plan works much better than using a hit-or-miss approach. Here are some general suggestions to make troubleshooting more effective:

- **Take the time to become familiar with normal switch operation:** The Cisco website (Cisco.com) has a lot of technical information that describes how its switches work. The configuration guides in particular are helpful.

- **For more large multiswitch environments, have an accurate physical and logical map of the network on hand:** A physical map shows how the devices and cables are connected. A logical map shows what segments (VLANs) exist in the network and which routers provide routing services to these segments. A spanning-tree map is also useful for troubleshooting complex issues. Because a switch can create different segments by implementing VLANs, the physical connections alone do not tell the whole story. You must know how the switches are configured to determine which segments (VLANs) exist and how they are logically connected.

- **Have a plan:** Some problems and solutions are obvious; others are not. The symptoms that you see in the network can be the result of problems in another area or layer. Before jumping to conclusions, try to verify in a structured way what is working and what is not. Because networks can be complex, it is helpful to isolate possible problem domains. One way to do this is to use the OSI seven-layer model. For example: Check the physical connections involved (Layer 1), check connectivity issues within the VLAN (Layer 2), check connectivity issues across different VLANs (Layer 3), and so on. Assuming that the switch is configured correctly, many of the problems you encounter will be related to physical layer issues (physical ports and cabling).

- **Do not assume a component is working without first verifying that it is:** If a PC is not able to log into a server across the network, it could be due to any number of things. Do not assume basic components are working correctly without testing them first; someone else might have altered their configurations and not informed you of the change. It usually takes only a minute to verify the basics (for example, that the ports are correctly connected and active), and it can save you valuable time.

Figure 2-37 outlines a basic flow for troubleshooting switch problems that will be used in this section.

Figure 2-37 *Troubleshooting Flow*

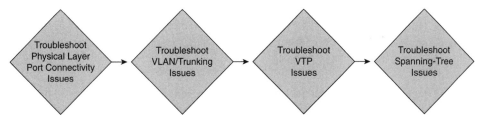

Troubleshooting Port Connectivity

If you are experiencing connectivity problems, the first thing to check is the port. Ports are the foundation of the switched network. If they do not work, nothing works! Some ports have special significance because of their location in the network and the amount of traffic they carry. These include ports that have connections to other switches, routers, and servers. They can be more complicated to troubleshoot because they often take advantage of special features, such as trunking and EtherChannel. However, do not overlook the other ports; they, too, are significant because they connect users in the network. Figure 2-38 shows the flow for troubleshooting port connectivity.

Figure 2-38   *Troubleshooting Port Connectivity*

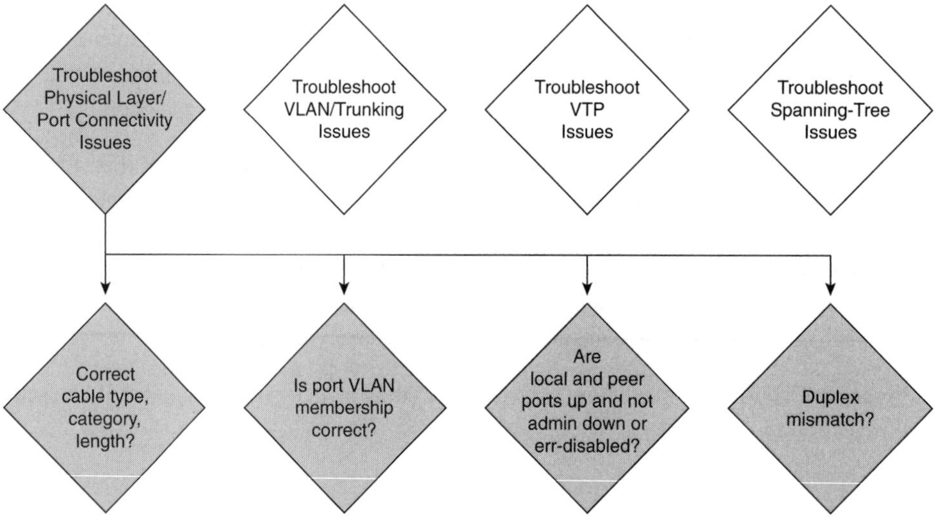

Hardware Issues

Hardware issues can be one of the reasons a switch has connectivity issues. To rule out hardware issues, verify the following:

■ **The port status for both ports involved in the link:** Ensure that neither is shut down. The administrator may have manually shut down one or both ports, or the switch software may have shut down one of the ports because of a configuration error. If one side is shut down and the other is not, the status on the enabled side will be "notconnected" (because it does not sense a neighbor on the other side of the wire). The status on the shutdown side will say something like "disable" or "errDisable" (depending on what actually shuts down the port). The link will not be active unless both ports are enabled.

■ **The type of cable used for the connection:** You should use at least Category 5 cable for 100 Mbps connections, and Category 5e for 1 Gbps or faster. You use a straight-through RJ-45 cable for end stations, routers, or servers to connect to a switch or hub. You use an Ethernet crossover cable for switch-to-switch connections or hub-to-switch connections. The maximum distance for Ethernet, FastEthernet, or Gigabit Ethernet copper wires is 100 meters.

- **A software process disables a port:** A solid orange light on the port indicates that the switch software has shut down the port, either by way of the user interface or by internal processes such as spanning tree BPDU guard; Root Guard, which prevents a port from becoming the root port; or port security violations.

Configuration Issues

Configuration of the port is another possible reason the port may be experiencing connectivity issues. Some of the common configuration issues are as follows:

- **The VLAN to which the port belongs has disappeared:** Each port in a switch belongs to a VLAN. If the VLAN is deleted, then the port becomes inactive.

  The following set of code illustrates that the command **show interface** *interface* will not reveal a problem when a port is configured to be part of a VLAN that does not exist.

```
SwitchX# sh int fa0/2
FastEthernet0/2 is up, line protocol is up (connected)
   Hardware is Fast Ethernet, address is 0017.596d.2a02 (bia 0017.596d.2a02)
   Description: Interface to RouterA F0/0
   MTU 1500 bytes, BW 100000 Kbit, DLY 100 usec,
      reliability 255/255, txload 1/255, rxload 1/255
   Encapsulation ARPA, loopback not set
   Keepalive set (10 sec)
   Full-duplex, 100Mb/s, media type is 10/100BaseTX
```

  However, the command **show interface** *interface* **switchport** does show that the port is inactive and will not be functional until the missing VLAN is replaced.

```
SwitchX# sh int fa0/2 switchport
Name: Fa0/2
Switchport: Enabled
Administrative Mode: static access
Operational Mode: static access
Administrative Trunking Encapsulation: dot1q
Operational Trunking Encapsulation: native
Negotiation of Trunking: Off
Access Mode VLAN: 5 (Inactive)
Trunking Native Mode VLAN: 1 (default)
Administrative Native VLAN tagging: enabled
Voice VLAN: none
```

  Some switches show a steady orange light on each port for which the associated VLAN has disappeared. If many orange lights appear on the switch, do not panic. It may be that all the ports belong to the same VLAN, which was accidentally deleted. When you add the VLAN back into the VLAN table, the ports become active again. A port remembers its assigned VLAN.

■ **Autonegotiation is enabled:** Autonegotiation is an optional function of the FastEthernet (IEEE 802.3u) standard that enables devices to automatically exchange information about speed and duplex abilities over a link. You should not use autonegotiation for ports that support network infrastructure devices, such as switches, routers, or other nontransient end systems, such as servers and printers. Autonegotiating speed and duplex settings is the typical default behavior on switch ports that have this capability. However, you should always configure ports that connect to fixed devices for the correct speed and duplex setting, rather than allow them to autonegotiate these settings. This configuration eliminates any potential negotiation issues and ensures that you always know exactly how the ports should be operating.

Troubleshooting VLANs and Trunking

To effectively troubleshoot switches, you must know how to identify and resolve VLAN performance issues, assuming you have identified and resolved any port connectivity and autonegotiation issues. Figure 2-39 shows the flow for troubleshooting VLANs and trunks.

Figure 2-39 *Troubleshooting VLANs*

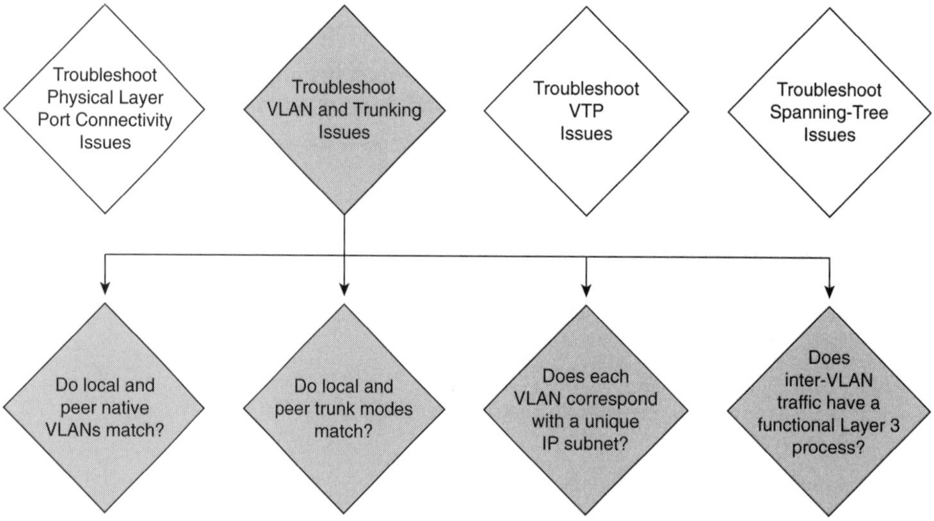

Native VLAN Mismatches

The native VLAN that is configured on each end of an IEEE 802.1Q trunk must be the same. Remember that a switch receiving an untagged frame assigns the frame to the native VLAN of the trunk. If one end of the trunk is configured for native VLAN 1 and the other end is configured for native VLAN 2, a frame sent from VLAN 1 on one side is received on VLAN 2 on the other. VLAN 1 "leaks" into the VLAN 2 segment. There is no reason this behavior would be required, and connectivity issues will occur in the network if a native VLAN mismatch exists.

Trunk Mode Mismatches

You should statically configure trunk links whenever possible. However, Cisco Catalyst switch ports run DTP by default, which tries to automatically negotiate a trunk link. This Cisco proprietary protocol can determine an operational trunking mode and protocol on a switch port when it is connected to another device that is also capable of dynamic trunk negotiation. Table 2-15 outlines DTP mode operations.

Table 2-15 *DTP Mode Examples*

Configuration Parameter	Description
Dynamic Auto	Creates the trunk link based on the DTP request from the neighboring switch. Dynamic Auto does not initiate the negotiation process; therefore, two switches set to Dynamic Auto do not form a trunk link.
Dynamic Desirable	Communicates to the neighboring switch via DTP that the interface would like to become a trunk if the neighboring switch interface is able to.

VLANs and IP Subnets

Each VLAN will correspond to a unique IP subnet. Two devices in the same VLAN should have addresses in the same subnet. With intra-VLAN traffic, the sending device recognizes the destination as local and sends an ARP broadcast to discover the MAC address of the destination.

Two devices in different VLANs should have addresses in different subnets. With inter-VLAN traffic, the sending device recognizes the destination as remote and sends an ARP broadcast for the MAC address of the default gateway.

Inter-VLAN Connectivity

Most of the time, inter-VLAN connectivity issues are the result of user misconfiguration. For example, if you incorrectly configure a router on a stick or Multilayer Switching (Cisco Express Forwarding), then packets from one VLAN may not reach another VLAN. To avoid misconfiguration and to troubleshoot efficiently, you should understand the mechanism used by the Layer 3 forwarding device. If you are sure that the equipment is properly configured, yet hardware switching is not taking place, then a software bug or hardware malfunction may be the cause.

Another type of misconfiguration that affects inter-VLAN routing is misconfiguration on end-user devices such as PCs. A common situation is a misconfigured PC default gateway. Too many PCs having the same default gateway can cause high CPU utilization on the gateway, which affects the forwarding rate.

Troubleshooting VTP

Another important aspect of troubleshooting is the ability to identify and resolve VTP issues, assuming port connectivity and VLAN problems have been identified and resolved. Figure 2-40 shows the flow used for troubleshooting VTP issues.

Figure 2-40   *VTP Troubleshooting*

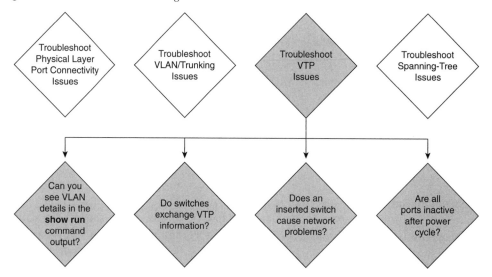

Unable to See VLAN Details in the show run Command Output

VTP client and server systems require VTP updates from other VTP servers to be immediately saved without user intervention. A VLAN database was introduced into Cisco IOS Software as a method to immediately save VTP updates for VTP clients and servers. In some versions of software, this VLAN database is in the form of a separate file in Flash, called the vlan.dat file. You can view VTP and VLAN information that is stored in the vlan.dat file for the VTP client or VTP server if you issue the **show vtp status** command.

VTP server and client mode switches do not save the entire VTP and VLAN configuration to the startup-config file in NVRAM when you issue the **copy running-config startup-config** command on these systems. VTP saves the configuration in the vlan.dat file. This behavior does not apply to systems that run in VTP transparent mode. VTP transparent switches save the entire VTP and VLAN configuration to the startup-config file in NVRAM when you issue the **copy running-config startup-config** command. For example, if you delete the vlan.dat file on a VTP server or client mode switch after you have configured VLANS, and then you reload the switch, VTP is reset to the default settings. (All user-configured VLANs are deleted.) But if you delete the vlan.dat file on a VTP transparent mode switch and then reload the switch, it retains the VTP configuration. This is an example of default VTP configuration.

You can configure normal-range VLANs (2 through 1000) when the switch is in either VTP server or transparent mode. But on the Cisco Catalyst 2960 switch, you can configure extended-range VLANs (1025 through 4094) only on VTP-transparent switches.

Cisco Catalyst Switches Do Not Exchange VTP Information

When Cisco switches do not exchange VTP information, you need to be able to determine why they are not functioning properly. Use the following guidelines to troubleshoot this problem:

- There are several reasons why VTP fails to exchange the VLAN information. Verify these items if switches that run VTP fail to exchange VLAN information.

- VTP information passes only through a trunk port. Ensure that all ports that interconnect switches are configured as trunks and are actually trunking.

- Ensure that the VLANs are active on all the VTP server switches.

- One of the switches must be a VTP server in the VTP domain. All VLAN changes must be done on this switch to have them propagated to the VTP clients.

- The VTP domain name must match, and it is case sensitive. For example, CISCO and cisco are two different domain names.

- Ensure that no password is set between the server and client. If any password is set, ensure that it is the same on both sides. The password is also case sensitive.

- Every switch in the VTP domain must use the same VTP version. VTP version 1 (VTPv1) and VTP version 2 (VTPv2) are not compatible on switches in the same VTP domain. Do not enable VTPv2 unless every switch in the VTP domain supports version 2.

> **NOTE** VTPv2 is disabled by default on VTPv2-capable switches. When you enable VTPv2 on a switch, every VTPv2-capable switch in the VTP domain enables version 2. You can only configure the version on switches in VTP server or transparent mode.

- A switch that is in VTP transparent mode and uses VTPv2 propagates all VTP messages, regardless of the VTP domain that is listed. However, a switch running VTPv1 propagates only VTP messages that have the same VTP domain as the domain that is configured on the local switch. VTP transparent mode switches that are using VTPv1 drop VTP advertisements if they are not in the same VTP domain.

- The extended-range VLANs are not propagated. So you must configure extended-range VLANs manually on each network device.

- The updates from a VTP server are not updated on a client if the client already has a higher VTP revision number. In addition, the client does not propagate the VTP updates to its downstream VTP neighbors if the client has a higher revision number than that which the VTP server sends.

Recently Installed Switch Causes Network Problems

A newly installed switch can cause problems in the network when all the switches in your network are in the same VTP domain, and you add a switch into the network that does not have the default VTP and VLAN configuration.

If the configuration revision number of the switch that you insert into the VTP domain is higher than the configuration revision number on the existing switches of the VTP domain, your recently introduced switch overwrites the VLAN database of the domain with its own VLAN database. This happens whether the switch is a VTP client or a VTP server. A VTP client can erase VLAN information on a VTP server. A typical indication that this has happened is when many of the ports in your network go into an inactive state but continue to be assigned to a nonexistent VLAN.

To prevent this problem from occurring, always ensure that the configuration revision number of all switches that you insert into the VTP domain is lower than the configuration revision number of the switches that are already in the VTP domain. You can accomplish this by changing the VTP mode to transparent and then back to server or client. You can also accomplish it by changing the VTP domain name and then changing it back.

All Ports Inactive After Power Cycle

Switch ports move to the inactive state when they are members of VLANs that do not exist in the VLAN database. A common issue is all the ports moving to this inactive state after a power cycle. Generally, you see this issue when the switch is configured as a VTP client with the uplink trunk port on a VLAN other than VLAN1. Because the switch is in VTP client mode, when the switch resets, it loses its VLAN database and causes the uplink port and any other ports that were not members of VLAN1 to become inactive.

Complete these steps to solve this problem:

Step 1 Temporarily change the VTP mode to transparent.

Step 2 Add the VLAN to which the uplink port is assigned to the VLAN database.

Step 3 Change the VTP mode back to client after the uplink port begins forwarding.

Troubleshooting Spanning Tree

It is also important to know how to identify and resolve spanning-tree issues, assuming port connectivity, VLAN, and VTP problems have been identified and resolved. Figure 2-41 shows the flow for troubleshooting STP.

Figure 2-41 *Troubleshooting STP*

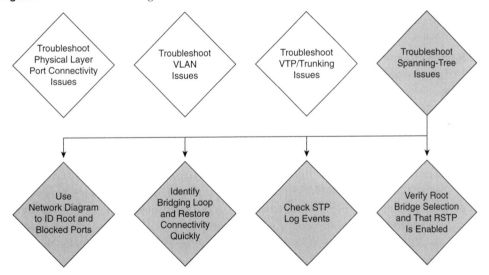

Use the Diagram of the Network

Before you troubleshoot a bridging loop, you must at least be aware of the following:

■   The topology of the bridge network

■   The location of the root bridge

■   The location of the blocked ports and the redundant links

This knowledge is essential for the following reasons:

- Before you can determine what to fix in the network, you must know how the network looks when it is functioning correctly.

- Most of the troubleshooting steps simply use **show** commands to identify error conditions. Knowledge of the network helps you focus on the critical ports on the key devices.

Identify a Bridging Loop

It used to be that a broadcast storm could have a disastrous effect on the network. Today, with high-speed links and devices that provide switching at the hardware level, it is not likely that a single host, such as a server, will bring down a network through broadcasts. The best way to identify a bridging loop is to capture the traffic on a saturated link and verify that you see similar packets multiple times. Realistically, however, if all users in a certain bridge domain have connectivity issues at the same time, you can already suspect a bridging loop. Check the port utilization on your devices to determine whether abnormal values are present.

Restore Connectivity Quickly

Bridging loops have extremely severe consequences on a switched network. Administrators generally do not have time to look for the cause of the loop, and they prefer to restore connectivity as soon as possible. The easy way out in this case is to manually disable every port that provides redundancy in the network.

Disable Ports to Break the Loop

If you can identify the part of the network that is affected most, begin to disable ports in this area. Or, if possible, initially disable ports that should be blocking. Each time you disable a port, check to see if you have restored connectivity in the network. By identifying which disabled port stops the loop, you also identify the redundant path of this port. If this port should have been blocking, you have probably found the link on which the failure appeared.

Log STP Events

If you cannot precisely identify the source of the problem, or if the problem is transient, enable the logging of STP events on the switches of the network that experiences the failure. If you want to limit the number of devices to configure, at least enable this logging on devices that host blocked ports; the transition of a blocked port is what creates a loop.

Issue the privileged EXEC command **debug spanning-tree events** to enable STP debug information. Issue the global configuration mode command **logging buffered** to capture this debug information in the device buffers. You can also try to send the debug output to a syslog device. Unfortunately, when a bridging loop occurs, you seldom maintain connectivity to a syslog server.

Temporarily Disable Unnecessary Features

Disable as many features as possible to help simplify the network structure and ease the identification of the problem. For example, EtherChannel is a feature that requires STP to logically bundle several different links into a single link, so disabling this feature during troubleshooting makes sense. As a rule, make the configuration as simple as possible to ease troubleshooting.

Designate the Root Bridge

Often, information about the location of the spanning-tree root bridge is not available at troubleshooting time. Do not let STP decide which switch becomes the root bridge. For each VLAN, you can usually identify which switch can best serve as the root bridge. Which switch would make the best root bridge depends on the design of the network. Generally, choose a powerful switch in the middle of the network. If you put the root bridge in the center of the network with direct connection to the servers and routers, you generally reduce the average distance from the clients to the servers and routers. For each VLAN, hard code which switches will serve as the root bridge and which will serve as the backup (secondary) root bridge.

Verify the Configuration of RSTP

The 802.1d and PVST+ spanning-tree protocols have convergence times between 30 and 50 seconds. The RSTP and PVRST+ spanning-tree protocols have convergence times within one or two seconds. A slow convergence time may indicate that not all of the switches in your network have been configured with RSTP, which can slow the convergence times globally in your network. Use the **show spanning-tree** command to verify the spanning tree mode.

Summary of Troubleshooting Switched Networks

The list that follows summarizes the key points that were discussed in this section.

- Effective switched-network troubleshooting begins by understanding what makes a network function correctly.

- Hardware issues and port configuration errors can cause port connectivity issues.

- Native VLAN mismatches and trunk mode mismatches can prevent a trunk link from being established.

- Understanding how VTP works is the best defense when troubleshooting VTP problems.

- One of the primary objectives when dealing with an STP failure is to break the loop and restore connectivity as soon as possible.

Chapter Summary

The list that follows summarizes the key points that were discussed in this chapter.

- When expanding a company network, VLANs, VTP, and trunking give a switched network infrastructure segmentation, flexibility, and security.

- The STP and its successor RSTP resolve bridging loops that are an inherent part of redundant switched networks.

- One way to accomplish inter-VLAN routing is to configure a "router on a stick" using subinterfaces and 802.1Q trunking.

- Troubleshooting a switched network requires knowing the characteristics of the underlying protocols, such as VTP, PVRST+, and 802.1Q.

Network administrators must address many aspects of expanding a switched network as their business grows. Cisco provides solutions across its suite of internetworking switches that not only solve many of the immediate problems associated with administrative changes but also provide scalability, interoperability, increased dedicated throughput, and security.

Review Questions

Use the questions here to review what you learned in this chapter. The correct answers and solutions are found in the appendix, "Answers to Chapter Review Questions."

1. Which feature is required for multiple VLANs to span multiple switches?

    a. A trunk to connect the switches

    b. A router to connect the switches

    c. A bridge to connect the switches

    d. A VLAN configured between the switches

2. What does a VMPS map to VLAN assignments?

    a. Host IDs

    b. Usernames

    c. IP addresses

    d. MAC addresses

3. What are two reasons for using 802.1Q? (Choose two.)

    a. To allow switches to share a trunk link with nontrunking clients

    b. To allow clients to see the 802.1Q header

    c. To provide inter-VLAN communications over a bridge

    d. To load-balance traffic between parallel links using STP

    e. To provide trunking between Cisco switches and other vendor switches

4. What primary benefit does VTP offer?

    a. Allows trunking to provide redundancy

    b. Minimizes redundancy on a switched network

    c. Allows you to run several VLANs over a single trunk

    d. Minimizes misconfigurations and configuration inconsistencies

5. How many VTP domains can you configure for a switch?

    a. One

    b. Two

    c. Four

    d. Eight

6. Which command correctly configures a switch for transparent mode in the VTP domain "switchlab"?

    a. **vtp mode trunk on**

    b. **vtp mode transparent**

    c. **vtp domain switchlab**

    d. **vtp domain switchlab transparent**

7.   Which is the default VTP mode on a Cisco Catalyst switch?

   a.   Off

   b.   Client

   c.   Server

   d.   Transparent

8.   Which information does the **show vlan** command display?

   a.   VTP domain parameters

   b.   VMPS server configuration parameters

   c.   Ports that are configured as trunks

   d.   Names of the VLANs and the ports that are assigned to the VLANs

9.   Which command displays the spanning-tree configuration status of the ports on a Cisco Catalyst 2960 Series switch?

   a.   **show vlan**

   b.   **show trunk**

   c.   **show spanning-tree**

   d.   **show spantree config**

10.   When you delete a VLAN from a VTP domain, where should you perform the change?

   a.   On a switch in VTP server mode

   b.   On every switch in VTP client mode

   c.   On a switch in VTP transparent mode

   d.   On every switch, regardless of VTP mode

11.   What precaution should you take when redeploying a switch to a new VTP domain in the network?

   a.   Set a unique VTP password on the switch for security.

   b.   Preconfigure all VLANs in the new VTP domain on the switch.

   c.   Verify that the VTP revision number is lower than the existing domain.

   d.   Configure the switch to VTP transparent mode to minimize impact.

12. Suppose that VTP is not updating the configuration on other switches when the VLAN configuration changes. Which command would you use to determine whether the switch is in VTP transparent mode?

    a. **show trunk**

    b. **show spantree**

    c. **show interfaces**

    d. **show vtp status**

13. Which three frame types are flooded to all ports except the source port on a switch? (Choose three.)

    a. Unicast frames

    b. Multicast frames

    c. Broadcast frames

    d. Frames with a destination address mapped to a given port

    e. Frames with a destination address not yet learned by the switch

    f. Frames with an unknown source address

14. Which term commonly describes the endless flooding or looping of frames?

    a. Flood storm

    b. Loop overload

    c. Broadcast storm

    d. Broadcast overload

15. Which term describes multiple copies of a frame arriving on different ports of a switch?

    a. Flood storm

    b. Multiple frame transmission

    c. MAC database instability

    d. Loop overload

16. When does STP automatically reconfigure switch or bridge ports?

   a. When the network topology changes

   b. When the forward delay timer expires

   c. When an administrator specifies a recalculation

   d. When a new BPDU is not received within the forward delay

17. How does STP provide a loop-free network?

   a. By placing all ports in the blocking state

   b. By placing all bridges in the blocking state

   c. By placing some ports in the blocking state

   d. By placing some bridges in the blocking state

18. Which port is the lowest-cost path from the nonroot bridge to the root bridge?

   a. Root

   b. Blocking

   c. Designated

   d. Nondesignated

19. How does STP select the designated port on a segment?

   a. Lowest-cost path to the root bridge

   b. Highest-cost path to the root bridge

   c. Lowest-cost path to the closest nonroot bridge

   d. Highest-cost path to the closest nonroot bridge

20. Which statement is true of a port in the listening state?

   a. The port is able to check for BPDUs and populate the MAC table.

   b. The port is able to check for BPDUs but not yet populate its MAC table.

   c. The port is able to populate its MAC table but not yet forward user frames.

   d. The port is able to forward user frames but not yet populate its MAC table.

21. Regarding STP, what is the state of a nondesignated port?

    a. Blocking

    b. Learning

    c. Listening

    d. Forwarding

22. Regarding STP, what is the state of a root port?

    a. Blocking

    b. Learning

    c. Listening

    d. Forwarding

23. On which STP bridge are all ports designated ports?

    a. Root bridge

    b. Nonroot bridge

    c. Bridge with the lowest priority

    d. Bridge with the highest bridge ID

24. Which event is required for STP to detect a topology change?

    a. A BPDU is not received within two seconds.

    b. A device does not respond to a handshake message.

    c. The max_age timer has expired without receiving a BPDU.

    d. A device does not respond quickly enough to a handshake request.

25. Which switched network issue does RSTP address?

    a. Network security

    b. Size of network

    c. Redundant topology

    d. Speed of convergence

26. What is the RSTP equivalent of the STP listening state?

   a. Blocking

   b. Listening

   c. Discarding

   d. Forwarding

27. With RSTP, which two port roles are included in the active topology?

   a. Root and alternate

   b. Root and designated

   c. Alternate and backup

   d. Designated and backup

28. Which command correctly assigns a subinterface to VLAN 50 using 802.1Q trunking?

   a. Router(config) # **encapsulation 50 dot1Q**

   b. Router(config) # **encapsulation 802.1Q 50**

   c. Router(config-if) # **encapsulation dot1Q 50**

   d. Router(config-if) # **encapsulation 50 802.1Q**

29. Which command restricts port usage to no more than ten devices?

   a. **switchport secure 10**

   b. **switchport max-mac-count 10**

   c. **switchport port-security maximum 10**

   d. **switchport port-security 10 max-mac**

30. What happens to a switch port when you delete the VLAN to which it belongs?

   a. The port becomes a member of the default VLAN 1.

   b. The port becomes a member of the default VLAN 1 and becomes inactive.

   c. The port remains in the deleted VLAN and becomes inactive.

   d. A VLAN cannot be deleted when ports are assigned to it.

31. What happens when you try to create a trunk link between two switches that have their ports set to dynamic auto?

    a.   The link will become a trunk link.

    b.   The link will become a nontrunked link.

    c.   Both ports will be configured as access ports.

    d.   Both ports will become inactive.

32. Switch A is in VTP client mode and has VLANs 1 through 5 in its VLAN database. Switch B is added to the same VTP domain in VTP server mode and has VLANs 6 through 10 in its VLAN database. How do the VLAN databases of Switch A and Switch B appear after Switch B has been added to the network?

    a.   Both VLAN databases will have VLANs 1 through 10.

    b.   Both VLAN databases will have VLANs 1 through 5.

    c.   Both VLAN databases will have VLANs 6 through 10.

    d.   It depends on which switch has the higher revision number.

This chapter includes the following sections:

- Chapter Objectives

- Reviewing Dynamic Routing

- Implementing Variable-Length Subnet Masks

- Chapter Summary

- Review Questions

CHAPTER 3

Medium-Sized Routed Network Construction

Routing is the process of determining where to send data packets that are destined for addresses outside the local network. Routers gather and maintain routing information to enable the transmission and receipt of these data packets. Routing information takes the form of entries in a routing table, with one entry for each identified route. The router can use a routing protocol to create and maintain the routing table dynamically so that network changes can be accommodated whenever they occur.

It is important to understand dynamic routing and how the various types of routing protocols, such as distance vector and link-state, determine IP routes. It is equally important to understand scalability and convergence constraints with routing protocols.

Classless routing protocols, such as Routing Information Protocol version 2 (RIPv2), Enhanced Interior Gateway Routing Protocol (EIGRP), and Open Shortest Path First (OSPF) scale better than classful routing protocols because they support variable-length subnet masks (VLSM) and route summarization.

To effectively manage an IP network, you must understand the operation of dynamic routing protocols and the impact that they have on an IP network. This chapter describes the operation and limitations of distance vector and link-state routing protocols.

Chapter Objectives

Upon completing this chapter, you will be able to describe the application and limitations of dynamic routing for a medium-sized routed network. This ability includes being able to meet these objectives:

- Describe the purpose and types of dynamic routing protocols

- Describe the operation and implementation of distance vector routing protocols

- Describe the operation and implementation of link-state routing protocols

Reviewing Dynamic Routing

Routers can forward packets over static routes or dynamic routes, based on the router configuration. There are two ways to tell the router how to forward packets to networks that are not directly connected:

■ **Static:** The router learns routes when an administrator manually configures the static route. The administrator must manually update this static route entry whenever an internetwork topology change requires an update. Static routes are user-defined routes that specify the path that packets take when moving between a source and a destination. These administrator-defined routes enable precise control over the routing behavior of the IP internetwork.

■ **Dynamic:** The router dynamically learns routes after an administrator configures a routing protocol that helps determine routes. Unlike the situation with static routes, after the network administrator enables dynamic routing, the routing process automatically updates route knowledge whenever new topology information is received. The router learns and maintains routes to the remote destinations by exchanging routing updates with other routers in the internetwork.

Dynamic routing relies on a routing protocol to disseminate knowledge. A routing protocol defines the rules that a router uses when it communicates with neighboring routers to determine paths to remote networks and maintains those networks in the routing tables. Figure 3-1 illustrates that a router in the network can have knowledge of networks that are not directly connected to an interface on that device. These routes must be configured statically or learned via routing protocols.

Figure 3-1 *Routing Protocols*

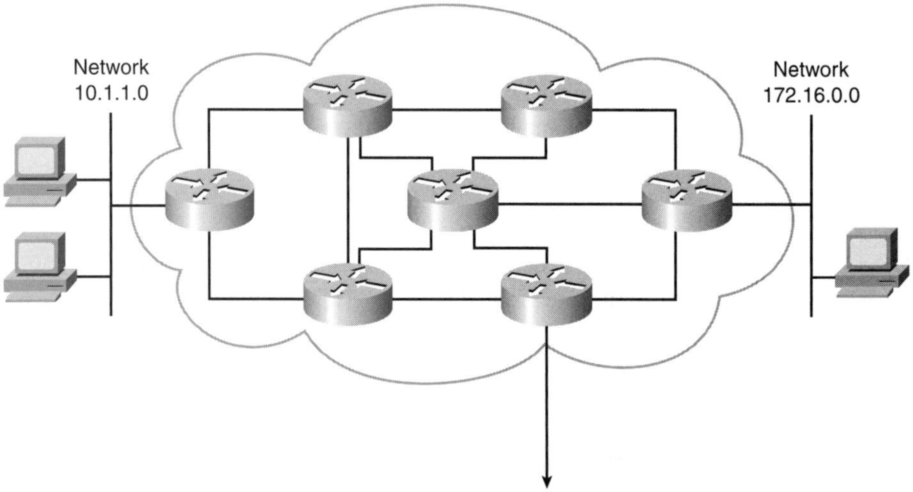

Network Protocol	Destination Network	Exit Interface
EIGRP	10.1.1.0	FA0/1
OSPF	172.16.0.0	FA0/2

The following are the differences between a routed protocol and a routing protocol:

■ **Routed protocol:** Any network protocol that provides enough information in its network layer address to enable a packet to be forwarded from one host to another host based on the addressing scheme, without knowing the entire path from source to destination. Packets generally are conveyed from end system to end system. IP is an example of a routed protocol.

■ **Routing protocol:** Facilitates the exchange of routing information between networks, enabling routers to build routing tables dynamically. Traditional IP routing stays simple because it uses next-hop (next-router) routing, in which the router needs to consider only where it sends the packet and does not need to consider the subsequent path of the packet on the remaining hops (routers). Routing Information Protocol (RIP) is an example of a routing protocol.

Routing protocols describe the following information:

■ How updates are conveyed

■ What knowledge is conveyed

■ When to convey the knowledge

■ How to locate recipients of the updates

You can classify dynamic routing protocols using many different methods. One method to classify a routing protocol is to determine if it is used to route in an autonomous system or between autonomous systems. An *autonomous system* is a collection of networks under a common administration that share a common routing strategy.

There are two types of routing protocols:

■ **Interior Gateway Protocols (IGP):** These routing protocols exchange routing information within an autonomous system. Routing Information Protocol version 2 (RIPv2), Enhanced Interior Gateway Routing (EIGRP), and Open Shortest Path First (OSPF) are examples of IGPs.

■ **Exterior Gateway Protocols (EGP):** These routing protocols are used to route between autonomous systems. Border Gateway Protocol (BGP) is the EGP of choice in networks today.

Figure 3-2 shows the logical separation of where an IGP operates and where an EGP operates.

Figure 3-2 *IGP Versus EGP*

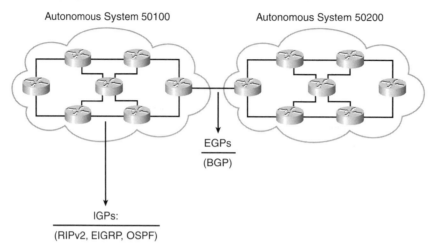

NOTE The Internet Assigned Numbers Authority (IANA) assigns autonomous system numbers for many jurisdictions. Use of IANA numbering is required if your organization plans to use BGP. However, it is good practice to be aware of private versus public autonomous system numbering schema.

Within an autonomous system, most IGP routing can be further classified as conforming to one of the following algorithms:

■ **Distance vector:** The distance vector routing approach determines the direction (vector) and distance (such as hops) to any link in the internetwork.

■ **Link-state:** The link-state approach, which utilizes the shortest path first (SPF) algorithm, creates an abstraction of the exact topology of the entire internetwork, or at least of the partition in which the router is situated.

■ **Advanced distance vector:** The advanced distance vector approach combines aspects of the link-state and distance vector algorithms. This is also sometimes referred to as a hybrid routing protocol.

There is no single best routing algorithm for all internetworks. All routing protocols provide the information differently.

Multiple routes to a destination can exist. When a routing protocol algorithm updates the routing table, the primary objective of the algorithm is to determine the best route to include in the table. Each distance vector routing protocol uses a different routing metric to determine the best route. The algorithm generates a number called the *metric value* for each path through the network. With the exception of BGP, the smaller the metric, the better the path.

Metrics can be calculated based on a single characteristic of a path. More complex metrics can be calculated by combining several path characteristics. The metrics that routing protocols most commonly use are as follows:

■ **Hop count:** The number of times that a packet passes through the output port of one router

■ **Bandwidth:** The data capacity of a link; for instance, normally, a 10-Mbps Ethernet link is preferable to a 64-kbps leased line

■ **Delay:** The length of time that is required to move a packet from source to destination

■ **Load:** The amount of activity on a network resource, such as a router or link

■ **Reliability:** Usually refers to the bit error rate of each network link

■ **Cost:** A configurable value that on Cisco routers is based by default on the bandwidth of the interface

Figure 3-3 shows an example of multiple routes between two hosts and the way different routing protocols compute metrics.

Multiple routing protocols and static routes can be used at the same time. If there are several sources for routing information, an administrative distance value is used to rate the trustworthiness of each routing information source. By specifying administrative distance values, Cisco IOS Software can discriminate between sources of routing information.

An *administrative distance* is an integer from 0 to 255. A routing protocol with a lower administrative distance is more trustworthy than one with a higher administrative distance. As shown in Figure 3-4, if Router A receives a route to network 172.16.0.0 advertised by EIGRP and by OSPF at the same time, Router A would use the administrative distance to determine that EIGRP is more trustworthy.

Figure 3-3 *Routing Protocol Metrics*

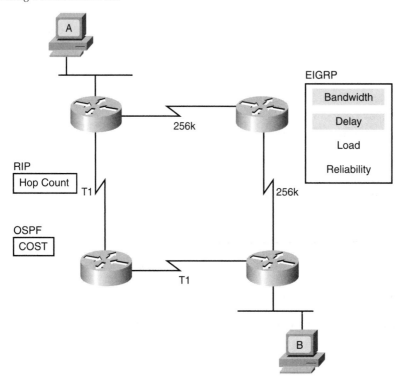

Figure 3-4 *Administrative Distance*

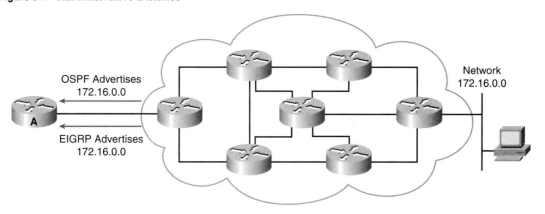

Router A would then add the EIGRP route to the routing table because EIGRP is a more trusted routing source than OSPF. The administrative distance is an arbitrary value that Cisco IOS sets to handle cases when multiple routing protocols send information about the same routes. Table 3-1 shows the default administrative distance for selected routing information sources.

Table 3-1 *Default Administrative Distance Values*

Route Source	Default Distance
Connected network	0
Static route	1
EIGRP	90
OSPF	110
RIPv2	120
External EIGRP	170
Unknown or unbelievable	255 (will not be added to the routing table to pass traffic)

If nondefault values are necessary, you can use Cisco IOS Software to configure administrative distance values on a per-router, per-protocol, and per-route basis.

Understanding Distance Vector Routing Protocols

Distance vector–based routing algorithms (also known as Bellman-Ford-Moore algorithms) pass periodic copies of a routing table from router to router and accumulate distance vectors. (*Distance* means how far, and *vector* means in which direction.) Regular updates between routers communicate topology changes.

Each router receives a routing table from its direct neighbor. For example, in Figure 3-5, Router B receives information from Router A. Router B adds a distance vector metric (such as the number of hops), increasing the distance vector. It then passes the routing table to its other neighbor, Router C. This same step-by-step process occurs in all directions between direct-neighbor routers. (This is also known as *routing by rumor*.)

Figure 3-5 *Distance Vector Protocols*

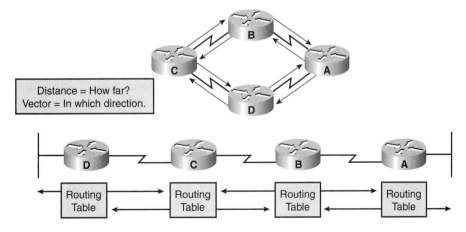

In this way, the algorithm accumulates network distances so that it can maintain a database of internetwork topology information. Distance vector algorithms do not allow a router to know the exact topology of an internetwork.

Route Discovery, Selection, and Maintenance

In Figure 3-6, the interface to each directly connected network is shown as having a distance of 0.

Figure 3-6   *Routing Information Sources*

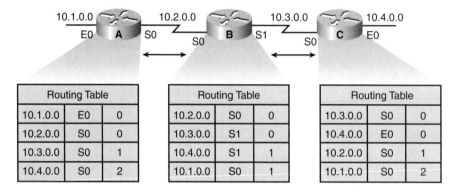

As the distance vector network discovery process proceeds, routers discover the best path to nondirectly connected destination networks based on accumulated metrics from each neighbor.

For example, Router A learns about other networks based on information it receives from Router B. Each of these other network entries in the routing table has an accumulated distance vector to show how far away that network is in the given direction.

When the topology in a distance vector protocol internetwork changes, routing table updates must occur. As with the network discovery process, topology change updates proceed step by step from router to router.

Distance vector algorithms call for each router to send its entire routing table to each of its adjacent or directly connected neighbors. Distance vector routing tables include information about the total path cost (defined by its metric) and the logical address of the first router on the path to each network it knows about.

When a router receives an update from a neighboring router, it compares the update to its own routing table. The router adds the cost of reaching the neighboring router to the path cost reported by the neighbor to establish the new metric. If the router learns about a better route (smaller total metric) to a network from its neighbor, the router updates its own routing table.

For example, if Router B in Figure 3-7 is one unit of cost from Router A, Router B would add 1 to all costs reported by Router A when Router B runs the distance vector processes to update its routing table. This would be maintained by the routers exchanging routing information in a timely manner through some update mechanism.

Figure 3-7 *Maintaining Routes*

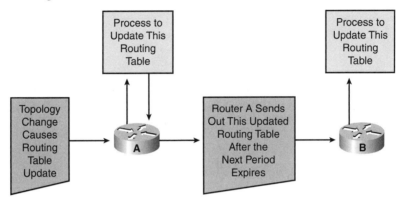

Routing Loops

When you are maintaining the routing information, routing loops can occur if the slow convergence of the internetwork after a topology change causes inconsistent routing entries. The example presented in the next few pages uses a simple network design to convey the concepts. Later in this chapter, you look at how routing loops occur and are corrected in more complex network designs. Figure 3-8 illustrates how each node maintains the distance from itself to each possible destination network.

Figure 3-8 *Maintaining Distance*

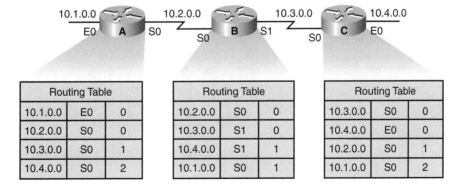

Just before the failure of network 10.4.0.0, shown in Figure 3-9, all routers had consistent knowledge and correct routing tables. The network is said to have *converged*. For this example, the cost function is hop count, so the cost of each link is 1. Router C is directly connected to network 10.4.0.0, with a distance of 0. The path of Router A to network 10.4.0.0 is through Router B, with a hop count of 2.

Figure 3-9 *Slow Convergence Produces Inconsistent Routing*

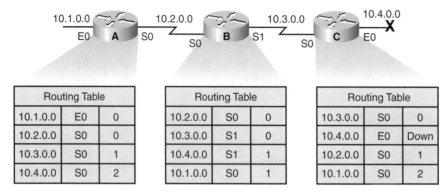

When network 10.4.0.0 fails, Router C detects the failure and stops routing packets out its E0 interface. However, Routers A and B have not yet received notification of the failure. Router A still believes it can access 10.4.0.0 through Router B. The routing table of Router A still reflects a path to network 10.4.0.0 with a distance of 2.

Because the routing table of Router B indicates a path to network 10.4.0.0, Router C believes it has a viable path to network 10.4.0.0 through Router B. Router C updates its routing table to reflect a path to network 10.4.0.0 with a hop count of 2, as illustrated in Figure 3-10.

Figure 3-10 *Inconsistent Path Information Between Routers*

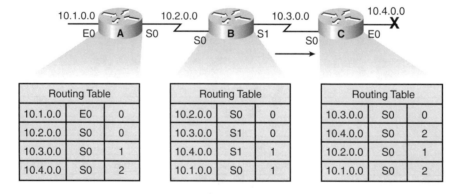

Router B receives a new update from Router C (3 hops). Router A receives the new routing table from Router B, detects the modified distance vector to network 10.4.0.0, and recalculates its own distance vector to 10.4.0.0 as 4, as shown in Figure 3-11.

Figure 3-11 *Inconsistent Data Continues to Propagate*

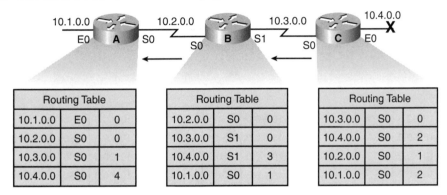

Because Routers A, B, and C conclude that the best path to network 10.4.0.0 is through each other, packets from Router A destined to network 10.4.0.0 continue to bounce between Routers B and C, as illustrated in Figure 3-12.

Figure 3-12 *Routing Loop Exists Because of Erroneous Hop Count*

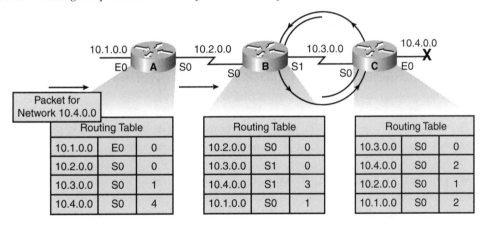

Continuing the example in Figure 3-12, the invalid updates about network 10.4.0.0 continue to loop. Until some other process can stop the looping, the routers update each other inappropriately, considering that network 10.4.0.0 is down.

This condition, called *count-to-infinity*, causes the routing protocol to continually increase its metric and route packets back and forth between the devices, despite the fundamental fact that the destination network, 10.4.0.0, is down. While the routing protocol counts to infinity, the invalid information enables a routing loop to exist, as illustrated in Figure 3-13.

Figure 3-13 *Count-to-Infinity Condition*

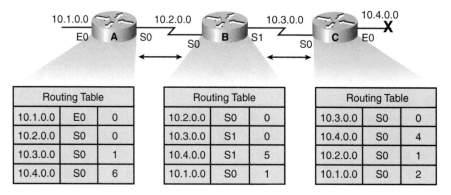

Routing Table		
10.1.0.0	E0	0
10.2.0.0	S0	0
10.3.0.0	S0	1
10.4.0.0	S0	6

Routing Table		
10.2.0.0	S0	0
10.3.0.0	S1	0
10.4.0.0	S1	5
10.1.0.0	S0	1

Routing Table		
10.3.0.0	S0	0
10.4.0.0	S0	4
10.2.0.0	S0	1
10.1.0.0	S0	2

Without countermeasures to stop this process, the distance vector of hop count increments each time the routing update is broadcast to another router. This causes data packets to be sent through the network because of incorrect information in the routing tables. The following sections cover the countermeasures that distance vector routing protocols use to prevent routing loops from running indefinitely.

Troubleshooting Routing Loops with Maximum Metric Settings

IP packets have inherent limits via the Time-To-Live (TTL) value in the IP header. In other words, a router must reduce the TTL field by at least 1 each time it gets the packet. If the TTL value becomes 0, the router discards that packet. However, this does not stop the router from continuing to attempt to send the packet to a network that is down.

To avoid this prolonged problem, distance vector protocols define infinity as some maximum number. This number refers to a routing metric, such as a hop count.

With this approach, the routing protocol permits the routing loop until the metric exceeds its maximum allowed value. Figure 3-14 shows this unreachable value as 16 hops. After the metric value exceeds the maximum, network 10.4.0.0 is considered unreachable.

Figure 3-14 *Maximum Metric*

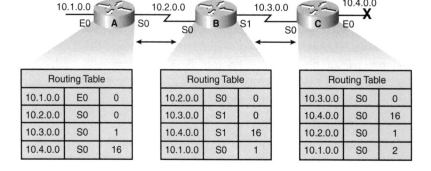

Routing Table		
10.1.0.0	E0	0
10.2.0.0	S0	0
10.3.0.0	S0	1
10.4.0.0	S0	16

Routing Table		
10.2.0.0	S0	0
10.3.0.0	S1	0
10.4.0.0	S1	16
10.1.0.0	S0	1

Routing Table		
10.3.0.0	S0	0
10.4.0.0	S0	16
10.2.0.0	S0	1
10.1.0.0	S0	2

Preventing Routing Loops with Split Horizon

One way to eliminate routing loops and speed up convergence is through the technique called *split horizon*. The split horizon rule is that sending information about a route back in the direction from which the original update came is never useful. For example, Figure 3-15 illustrates the following:

- Router B has access to network 10.4.0.0 through Router C. It makes no sense for Router B to announce to Router C that Router B has access to network 10.4.0.0 through Router C.

- Given that Router B passed the announcement of its route to network 10.4.0.0 to Router A, it makes no sense for Router A to announce its distance from network 10.4.0.0 to Router B.

- Having no alternative path to network 10.4.0.0, Router B concludes that network 10.4.0.0 is inaccessible.

Figure 3-15 *Split Horizon*

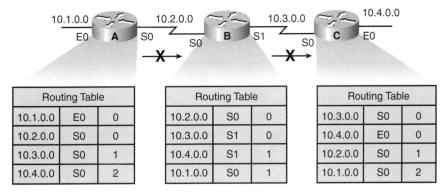

Preventing Routing Loops with Route Poisoning

Another operation complementary to split horizon is a technique called *route poisoning*. Route poisoning attempts to improve convergence time and eliminate routing loops caused by inconsistent updates. With this technique, when a router loses a link, the router advertises the loss of a route to its neighbor device. Route poisoning enables the receiving router to advertise a route back toward the source with a metric higher than the maximum. The advertisement back seems to violate split horizon, but it lets the router know that the update about the down network was received. The router that received the update also sets a table entry that keeps the network state consistent while other routers gradually converge correctly on the topology change. This mechanism allows the router to learn quickly of the down route and to ignore other updates that might be wrong for the hold-down period. This prevents routing loops.

Figure 3-16 illustrates the following example. When network 10.4.0.0 goes down, Router C poisons its link to network 10.4.0.0 by entering a table entry for that link as having infinite cost (that is, being unreachable). By poisoning its route to network 10.4.0.0, Router C is not susceptible to incorrect updates from neighboring routers, which may still have an outdated entry for network 10.4.0.0.

Figure 3-16 *Route Poisoning*

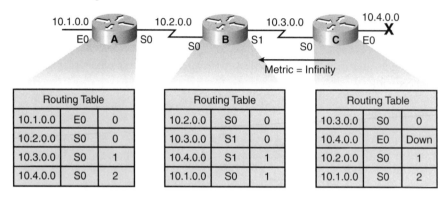

When Router B sees the metric to 10.4.0.0 jump to infinity, it sends an update called a *poison reverse* to Router C, stating that network 10.4.0.0 is inaccessible, as illustrated in Figure 3-17. This is a specific circumstance overriding split horizon, which occurs to make sure that all routers on that segment have received information about the poisoned route.

Figure 3-17 *Poison Reverse*

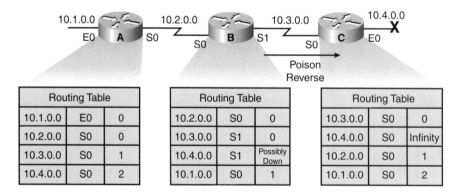

Route Maintenance Using Hold-Down Timers

Hold-down timers prevent regular update messages from inappropriately reinstating a route that might have gone bad. Hold-downs tell routers to hold any changes that might affect routes for some period of time. The hold-down period is usually calculated to be just greater than the time necessary to update the entire network with a routing change.

Hold-down timers perform route maintenance as follows:

1. When a router receives an update from a neighbor indicating that a previously accessible network is now inaccessible, the router marks the route as inaccessible and starts a hold-down timer.

2. If an update arrives from a neighboring router with a better metric than originally recorded for the network, the router marks the network as accessible and removes the hold-down timer.

3. If at any time before the hold-down timer expires, an update is received from a different neighboring router with a poorer metric, the update is ignored. Ignoring an update with a higher metric when a holddown is in effect enables more time for the knowledge of the change to propagate through the entire network.

4. During the hold-down period, routes appear in the routing table as "possibly down."

Figure 3-18 illustrates the hold-down timer process.

Figure 3-18   *Hold-Down Timers*

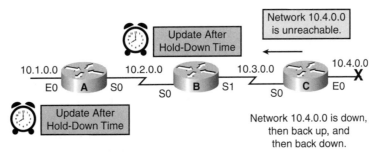

Route Maintenance Using Triggered Updates

In the previous examples, routing loops were caused by erroneous information calculated as a result of inconsistent updates, slow convergence, and timing. If routers wait for their regularly scheduled updates before notifying neighboring routers of network catastrophes, serious problems can occur, such as loops or traffic being dropped.

Normally, new routing tables are sent to neighboring routers on a regular basis. A *triggered update* is a new routing table that is sent immediately, in response to a change. The detecting router immediately sends an update message to adjacent routers, which, in turn, generate triggered updates notifying their adjacent neighbors of the change. This wave propagates throughout the portion of the network that was using the affected link. Figure 3-19 illustrates what takes place when using triggered updates.

Figure 3-19 *Triggered Updates*

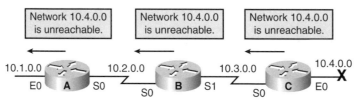

Triggered updates would be sufficient with a guarantee that the wave of updates reached every appropriate router immediately. However, two problems exist:

- Packets containing the update message can be dropped or corrupted by some link in the network.

- The triggered updates do not happen instantaneously. A router that has not yet received the triggered update can issue a regular update at just the wrong time, causing the bad route to be reinserted in a neighbor that had already received the triggered update.

Coupling triggered updates with holddowns is designed to get around these problems.

Route Maintenance Using Hold-Down Timers with Triggered Updates

Because the hold-down rule says that when a route is invalid, no new route with the same or a higher metric will be accepted for the same destination for some period, the triggered update has time to propagate throughout the network.

The troubleshooting solutions presented in the previous sections work together to prevent routing loops in a more complex network design. As depicted in Figure 3-20, the routers have multiple routes to each other. As soon as Router B detects the failure of network 10.4.0.0, Router B removes its route to that network. Router B sends a trigger update to Routers A and D, poisoning the route to network 10.4.0.0 by indicating an infinite metric to that network.

Figure 3-20 *Implementing Multiple Solutions*

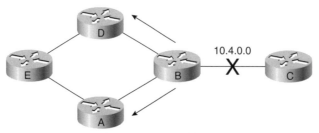

Routers D and A receive the triggered update and set their own hold-down timers, noting that the 10.4.0.0 network is "possibly down." Routers D and A, in turn, send a triggered update to Router E, indicating the possible inaccessibility of network 10.4.0.0. Router E also sets the route to

10.4.0.0 in holddown. Figure 3-21 depicts the way Routers A, D, and E implement hold-down timers.

Figure 3-21   *Route Fails*

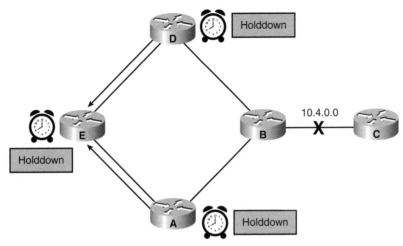

Router A and Router D send a poison reverse to Router B, stating that network 10.4.0.0 is inaccessible. Because Router E received a triggered update from Routers A and D, it sends a poison reverse to Routers A and D. Figure 3-22 illustrates the sending of poison reverse updates.

Figure 3-22   *Route Holddown*

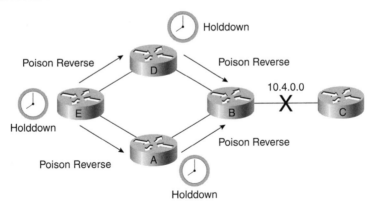

Routers A, D, and E will remain in holddown until one of the following events occurs:

■   The hold-down timer expires.

■   Another update is received, indicating a new route with a better metric.

■   A flush timer, which is the time a route will be held before being removed, removes the route from the routing table.

During the hold-down period, Routers A, D, and E assume that the network status is unchanged from its original state and attempt to route packets to network 10.4.0.0. Figure 3-23 illustrates Router E attempting to forward a packet to network 10.4.0.0. This packet will reach Router B. However, because Router B has no route to network 10.4.0.0, Router B will drop the packet and return an Internet Control Message Protocol (ICMP) network unreachable message.

Figure 3-23 *Packets During Holddown*

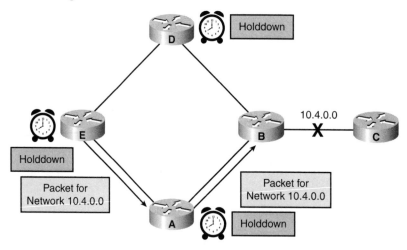

When the 10.4.0.0 network comes back up, Router B sends a trigger update to Routers A and D, notifying them that the link is active. After the hold-down timer expires, Routers A and D add route 10.4.0.0 back to the routing table as accessible, as illustrated in Figure 3-24.

Figure 3-24 *Network Up*

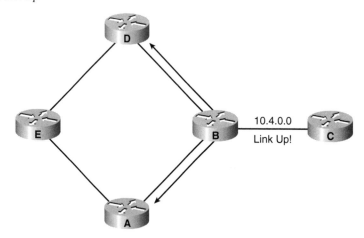

Routers A and D send Router E a routing update stating that network 10.4.0.0 is up, and Router E updates its routing table after the hold-down timer expires, as illustrated in Figure 3-25.

Figure 3-25 *Network Converges*

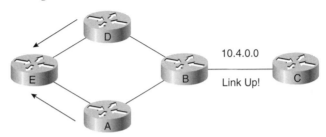

Link-State and Advanced Distance Vector Protocols

In addition to distance vector–based routing, the second basic algorithm used for routing is the link-state algorithm. Link-state protocols build routing tables based on a topology database. This database is built from link-state packets that are passed between all the routers to describe the state of a network. The shortest path first algorithm uses the database to build the routing table. Figure 3-26 shows the components of a link-state protocol.

Figure 3-26 *Link-State Protocols*

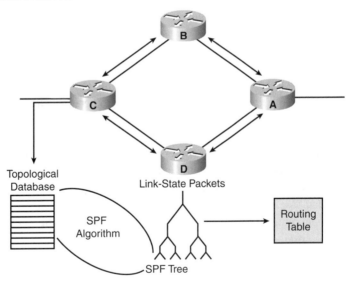

Understanding the operation of link-state routing protocols is critical to being able to enable, verify, and troubleshoot their operation.

Link-state-based routing algorithms—also known as *shortest path first* (SPF) algorithms—maintain a complex database of topology information. Whereas the distance vector algorithm has nonspecific information about distant networks and no knowledge of distant routers, a link-state routing algorithm maintains full knowledge of distant routers and how they interconnect.

Link-state routing uses link-state advertisements (LSA), a topological database, the SPF algorithm, the resulting SPF tree, and, finally, a routing table of paths and ports to each network.

Open Shortest Path First (OSPF) and Intermediate System-to-Intermediate System (IS-IS) are classified as link-state routing protocols. RFC 2328 describes OSPF link-state concepts and operations. Link-state routing protocols collect routing information from all other routers in the network or within a defined area of the internetwork. After all the information is collected, each router, independently of the other routers, calculates its best paths to all destinations in the network. Because each router maintains its own view of the network, it is less likely to propagate incorrect information provided by any one particular neighboring router.

Link-state routing protocols were designed to overcome the limitations of distance vector routing protocols. Link-state routing protocols respond quickly to network changes, send triggered updates only when a network change has occurred, and send periodic updates (known as *link-state refreshes*) at long intervals, such as every 30 minutes. A hello mechanism determines the reachability of neighbors.

When a failure occurs in the network, such as a neighbor becomes unreachable, link-state protocols flood LSAs using a special multicast address throughout an area. Each link-state router takes a copy of the LSA, updates its link-state (topological) database, and forwards the LSA to all neighboring devices. LSAs cause every router within the area to recalculate routes. Because LSAs need to be flooded throughout an area and all routers within that area need to recalculate their routing tables, you should limit the number of link-state routers that can be in an area.

A link is similar to an interface on a router. The state of the link is a description of that interface and of its relationship to its neighboring routers. A description of the interface would include, for example, the IP address of the interface, the mask, the type of network to which it is connected, the routers connected to that network, and so on. The collection of link states forms a link-state, or topological, database. The link-state database is used to calculate the best paths through the network. Link-state routers find the best paths to a destination by applying Dr. Edsger Dijkstra's SPF algorithm against the link-state database to build the SPF tree. The best paths are then selected from the SPF tree and placed in the routing table.

As networks become larger in scale, link-state routing protocols become more attractive for the following reasons:

■ Link-state protocols always send updates when a topology changes.

■ Periodic refresh updates are more infrequent than for distance vector protocols.

■ Networks running link-state routing protocols can be segmented into area hierarchies, limiting the scope of route changes.

■ Networks running link-state routing protocols support classless addressing.

■ Networks running link-state routing protocols support route summarization.

Link-state protocols use a two-layer network hierarchy, as shown in Figure 3-27.

Figure 3-27   *Link-State Network Hierarchy*

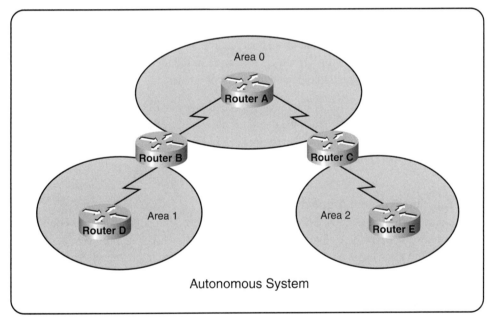

The two-layer network hierarchy contains two primary elements:

■ **Area:** An *area* is a grouping of networks. Areas are logical subdivisions of the autonomous system (AS).

■ **Autonomous system:** An AS consists of a collection of networks under a common administration that share a common routing strategy. An AS, sometimes called a domain, can be logically subdivided into multiple areas.

Within each AS, a contiguous backbone area must be defined. All other nonbackbone areas are connected off the backbone area. The backbone area is the transition area because all other areas communicate through it. For OSPF, the nonbackbone areas can be additionally configured as a stub area, a totally stubby area, a not-so-stubby area (NSSA), or a totally not-so-stubby area to help reduce the link-state database and routing table size.

Routers operating within the two-layer network hierarchy have different routing entities. The terms used to refer to these entities are different for OSPF than IS-IS. Refer to the following examples from Figure 3-27:

- Router A is called the backbone router in OSPF and the L2 router in IS-IS. The backbone, or L2, router provides connectivity between different areas.

- Routers B and C are called area border routers (ABR) in OSPF, and L1/L2 routers in IS-IS. ABR, or L1/L2, routers attach to multiple areas, maintain separate link-state databases for each area to which they are connected, and route traffic destined for or arriving from other areas.

- Routers D and E are called nonbackbone internal routers in OSPF, or L1 routers in IS-IS. Nonbackbone internal, or L1, routers are aware of the topology within their respective areas and maintain identical link-state databases about the areas.

- The ABR, or L1/L2, router will advertise a default route to the nonbackbone internal, or L1, router. The L1 router will use the default route to forward all interarea or interdomain traffic to the ABR, or L1/L2, router. This behavior can be different for OSPF, depending on how the OSPF nonbackbone area is configured (stub area, totally stubby area, or not-so-stubby area).

Link-State Routing Protocol Algorithms

Link-state routing algorithms, known collectively as SPF protocols, maintain a complex database of the network topology. Unlike distance vector protocols, link-state protocols develop and maintain full knowledge of the network routers and how they interconnect. This is achieved through the exchange of link-state packets (LSP) with other routers in a network.

Each router that has exchanged LSPs constructs a topological database using all received LSPs. An SPF algorithm is then used to compute reachability to networked destinations. This information is employed to update the routing table. The process can discover changes in the network topology caused by component failure or network growth.

In fact, the LSP exchange is triggered by an event in the network, instead of running periodically. This can greatly speed up the convergence process because it is unnecessary to wait for a series of timers to expire before the networked routers can begin to converge.

If the network shown in Figure 3-28 uses a link-state routing protocol, connectivity between New York City and San Francisco is not a concern. Depending on the actual protocol employed and the metrics selected, it is highly likely that the routing protocol could discriminate between the two paths to the same destination and try to use the best one.

Figure 3-28 *Link-State Algorithms*

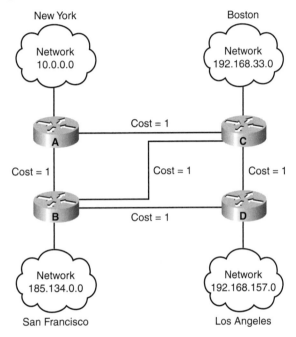

Table 3-2 summarizes the contents of the routing database of each router in the figure.

Table 3-2 *Link-State Routing Database*

Router	Destination	Next Hop	Cost
A	185.134.0.0	B	1
	192.168.33.0	C	1
	192.168.157.0	B	2
	192.168.157.0	C	2
B	10.0.0.0	A	1
	192.168.33.0	C	1
	192.168.157.0	D	1

continues

Table 3-2 *Link-State Routing Database (Continued)*

Router	Destination	Next Hop	Cost
C	10.0.0.0	A	1
	185.134.0.0	B	1
	192.168.157.0	D	1
D	10.0.0.0	B	2
	10.0.0.0	C	2
	185.134.0.0	B	1
	192.168.33.0	C	1

As shown in the table link-state database entries for the New York (Router A) to Los Angeles (Router D) routes, a link-state protocol would remember both routes. Some link-state protocols can even provide a way to assess the performance capabilities of these two routes and bias toward the better-performing one. If the better-performing path, such as the route through Boston (Router C), experienced operational difficulties of any kind, including congestion or component failure, the link-state routing protocol would detect this change and begin forwarding packets through San Francisco (Router B).

Link-state routing might flood the network with LSPs during initial topology discovery and can be both memory- and processor-intensive. This section describes the benefits of link-state routing, the caveats to consider when using it, and the potential problems.

The following list highlights some of the many benefits that link-state routing protocols have over the traditional distance vector algorithms, such as RIP-1 or the now obsolete Interior Gateway Routing Protocol (IGRP):

- Link-state protocols use cost metrics to choose paths through the network. For Cisco IOS devices, the cost metric reflects the capacity of the links on those paths.

- By using triggered, flooded updates, link-state protocols can immediately report changes in the network topology to all routers in the network. This immediate reporting generally leads to fast convergence times.

- Because each router has a complete and synchronized picture of the network, it is difficult for routing loops to occur.

- Because LSPs are sequenced and aged, routers always base their routing decisions on the latest set of information.

- With careful network design, the link-state database sizes can be minimized, leading to smaller SPF calculations and faster convergence.

The link-state approach to dynamic routing can be useful in networks of any size. In a well-designed network, a link-state routing protocol enables your network to gracefully adapt to unexpected topology changes. Using events, such as changes, to drive updates, rather than fixed-interval timers, enables convergence to begin that much more quickly after a topological change.

The overhead of the frequent, time-driven updates of a distance vector routing protocol is also avoided. This makes more bandwidth available for routing traffic rather than for network maintenance, provided you design your network properly.

A side benefit of the bandwidth efficiency of link-state routing protocols is that they facilitate network scalability better than either static routes or distance vector protocols. When compared to the limitations of static routes or distance vector protocols, you can easily see that link-state routing is best in larger, more complex networks, or in networks that must be highly scalable. Initially configuring a link-state protocol in a large network can be challenging, but it is well worth the effort in the long run.

Link-state protocols do, however, have the following limitations:

- They require a topology database, an adjacency database, and a forwarding database, in addition to the routing table. This can require a significant amount of memory in large or complex networks.

- Dijkstra's algorithm requires CPU cycles to calculate the best paths through the network. If the network is large or complex (that is, the SPF calculation is complex), or if the network is unstable (that is, the SPF calculation is running on a regular basis), link-state protocols can use significant CPU power.

- To avoid excessive memory or CPU power, a strict hierarchical network design is required, dividing the network into smaller areas to reduce the size of the topology tables and the length of the SPF calculation. However, this dividing can cause problems because areas must remain contiguous at all times. The routers in an area must always be capable of contacting and receiving LSPs from all other routers in their area. In a multiarea design, an area router must always have a path to the backbone, or it will have no connectivity to the rest of the network. In addition, the backbone area must remain connected at all times to avoid some areas becoming isolated (partitioned).

- The configuration of link-state networks is usually simple, provided that the underlying network architecture has been soundly designed. If the network design is complex, the operation of the link-state protocol might have to be tuned to accommodate it.

- During the initial discovery process, link-state routing protocols can flood the network with LSPs and significantly decrease the capability of the network to transport data because no traffic is passed until after the initial network convergence. This performance compromise is temporary but can be noticeable. Whether this flooding process will noticeably degrade network performance depends on two things: the amount of available bandwidth and the number of routers that must exchange routing information. Flooding in large networks with relatively small links, such as low-bandwidth links, is much more noticeable than a similar exercise on a small network with large links, such as T3s and Ethernet.

■ Link-state routing is both memory- and processor-intensive. Consequently, more fully configured routers are required to support link-state routing than distance vector routing. This increases the cost of the routers that are configured for link-state routing.

The following are some of the benefits of a link-state routing protocol:

■ Troubleshooting is usually easier in link-state networks because every router has a complete copy of the network topology, or at least of its own area of the network. However, interpreting the information stored in the topology, neighbor databases, and routing table requires an understanding of the concepts of link-state routing.

■ Link-state protocols usually scale to larger networks than distance vector protocols, particularly the traditional distance vector protocols such as RIPv1 and IGRP.

You can address and resolve the potential performance impacts of both drawbacks through foresight, planning, and engineering.

Advanced Distance Vector Protocol Algorithm

The advanced distance vector protocol, or hybrid routing protocol, uses distance vectors with more accurate metrics to determine the best paths to destination networks. However, it differs from most distance vector protocols by using topology changes to trigger routing database updates, as opposed to periodic updates.

This routing protocol converges more rapidly, like the link-state protocols. However, it differs from link-state protocols by emphasizing economy in the use of required resources, such as bandwidth, memory, and processor overhead.

An example of an advanced distance vector protocol is the Cisco Enhanced Interior Gateway Routing Protocol (EIGRP).

Summary of Reviewing Routing Operations

The following list summarizes the key points discussed in this section:

■ Dynamic routing requires administrators to configure either a distance vector or a link-state routing protocol.

- Distance vector routing protocols incorporate solutions such as split horizon, route poisoning, and hold-down timers to prevent routing loops.

- Link-state routing protocols scale to large network infrastructures better than distance vector routing protocols, but they require more planning to implement.

Implementing Variable-Length Subnet Masks

Variable-length subnet masks (VLSM) were developed to enable multiple levels of subnetworked IP addresses within a single network. This strategy can be used only when it is supported by the routing protocol in use, such as Routing Information Protocol version 2 (RIPv2), OSPF, and EIGRP. VLSM is a key technology on large, routed networks. Understanding its capabilities is important when planning large networks.

Reviewing Subnets

Prior to working with VLSM, it is important to have a firm grasp on IP subnetting. When you are creating subnets, you must determine the optimal number of subnets and hosts.

Computing Usable Subnetworks and Hosts

Remember that an IP address has 32 bits and comprises two parts: a network ID and a host ID. The length of the network ID and host ID depends on the class of the IP address. The number of hosts available also depends on the class of the IP address.

The default number of bits in the network ID is referred to as the *classful prefix length*. Therefore, a Class C address has a classful prefix length of /24, a Class B address has a classful prefix length of /16, and a Class A address has a classful prefix length of /8. This is illustrated in Figure 3-29.

Figure 3-29 *Classful Prefix Length*

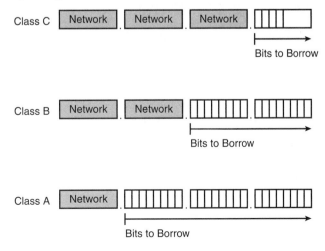

The subnet address is created by taking address bits from the host-number portion of Class A, Class B, and Class C addresses. Usually a network administrator assigns the subnet address locally. Like IP addresses, each subnet address must be unique.

Each time one bit is borrowed from a host field, one less bit remains in the host field that can be used for host numbers, and the number of host addresses that can be assigned per subnet decreases by a power of 2.

When you borrow bits from the host field, note the number of additional subnets that are being created each time one more bit is borrowed. Borrowing two bits creates four possible subnets ($2^2 = 4$). Each time another bit is borrowed from the host field, the number of possible subnets increases by a power of 2, and the number of individual host addresses decreases by a power of 2.

The following are examples of how many subnets are available, based on the number of host bits that you borrow:

- Using 3 bits for the subnet field results in 8 possible subnets ($2^3 = 8$).

- Using 4 bits for the subnet field results in 16 possible subnets ($2^4 = 16$).

- Using 5 bits for the subnet field results in 32 possible subnets ($2^5 = 32$).

- Using 6 bits for the subnet field results in 64 possible subnets ($2^6 = 64$).

In general, you can use the following formula to calculate the number of usable subnets, given the number of subnet bits used:

Number of subnets = 2^s (in which *s* is the number of subnet bits)

For example, you can subnet a network with a private network address of 172.16.0.0/16 so that it provides 100 subnets and maximizes the number of host addresses for each subnet. The following list highlights the steps required to meet these needs:

- How many bits will need to be borrowed?

  — $2^s = 2^7 = 128$ subnets (s = 7 bits)

- What is the new subnet mask?

  — Borrowing 7 host bits = 255.255.254.0 or /23

- What are the first four subnets?

  — 172.16.0.0, 172.16.2.0, 172.16.4.0, and 172.16.6.0

■   What are the ranges of host addresses for the four subnets?

— 172.16.0.1–172.16.1.254

— 172.16.2.1–172.16.3.254

— 172.16.4.1–172.16.5.254

— 172.16.6.1–172.16.7.254

Introducing VLSMs

When an IP network is assigned more than one subnet mask for a given major network, it is considered a network with VLSMs, overcoming the limitation of a fixed number of fixed-size subnetworks imposed by a single subnet mask. Figure 3-30 shows the 172.16.0.0 network with four separate subnet masks.

Figure 3-30   *VLSM Network*

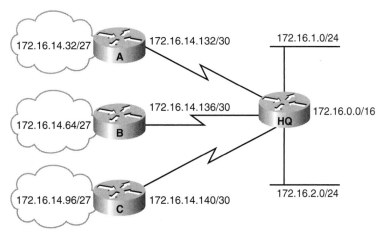

VLSMs provide the capability to include more than one subnet mask within a network and the capability to subnet an already subnetted network address. In addition, VLSM offers the following benefits:

■   **Even more efficient use of IP addresses:** Without the use of VLSMs, companies must implement a single subnet mask within an entire Class A, B, or C network number.

For example, consider the 172.16.0.0/16 network address divided into subnets using /24 masking, and one of the subnetworks in this range, 172.16.14.0/24, further divided into smaller subnets with the /27 masking, as shown in Figure 3-30. These smaller subnets range from 172.16.14.0/27 to 172.16.14.224/27. In the figure, one of these smaller subnets, 172.16.14.128/27, is further divided with the /30 prefix, creating subnets with only two hosts to be used on the WAN links. The /30 subnets range from 172.16.14.128/30 to 172.16.14.156/30. In Figure 3-30, the WAN links used the 172.16.14.132/30, 172.16.14.136/30, and 172.16.14.140/30 subnets out of the range.

■ **Greater capability to use route summarization:** VLSM allows more hierarchical levels within an addressing plan, allowing better route summarization within routing tables. For example, in Figure 3-30, subnet 172.16.14.0/24 summarizes all the addresses that are further subnets of 172.16.14.0, including those from subnet 172.16.14.0/27 and from 172.16.14.128/30.

As already discussed, with VLSMs, you can subnet an already subnetted address. Consider, for example, that you have a subnet address 172.16.32.0/20, and you need to assign addresses to a network that has ten hosts. With this subnet address, however, you have more than 4000 ($2^{12} - 2$ = 4094) host addresses, most of which will be wasted. With VLSMs, you can further subnet the address 172.16.32.0/20 to give you more network addresses and fewer hosts per network. If, for example, you subnet 172.16.32.0/20 to 172.16.32.0/26, you gain 64 (2^6) subnets, each of which could support 62 ($2^6 - 2$) hosts.

Figure 3-31 shows how subnet 172.16.32.0/20 can be divided into smaller subnets.

Figure 3-31 *Calculating VLSM Networks*

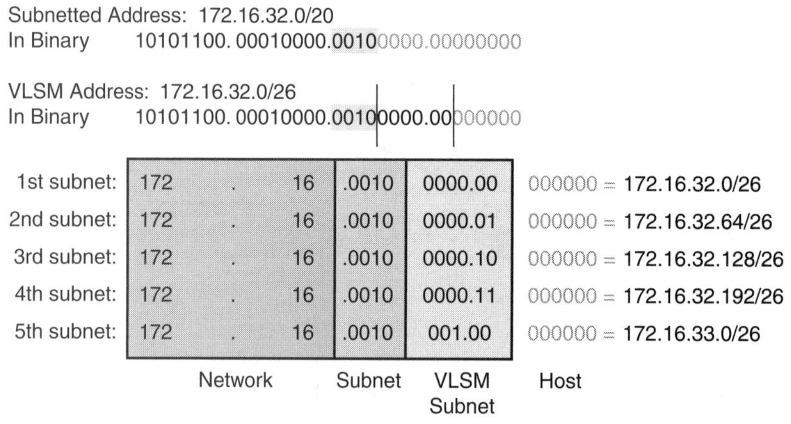

The following procedure shows how to further subnet 172.16.32.0/20 to 172.16.32.0/26:

Step 1   Write 172.16.32.0 in binary form.

Step 2   Draw a vertical line between the twentieth and twenty-first bits, as shown in Figure 3-31. (/20 was the original subnet boundary.)

Step 3   Draw a vertical line between the twenty-sixth and twenty-seventh bits, as shown in the figure. (The original /20 subnet boundary is extended six bits to the right, becoming /26.)

Step 4   Calculate the 64 subnet addresses using the bits between the two vertical lines, from lowest to highest in value. Figure 3-31 shows the first five subnets available.

VLSMs are commonly used to maximize the number of possible addresses available for a network. For example, because point-to-point serial lines require only two host addresses, using a /30 subnet will not waste scarce IP addresses.

In Figure 3-32, the subnet addresses used on the Ethernets are those generated from subdividing the 172.16.32.0/20 subnet into multiple /26 subnets. The figure illustrates where the subnet addresses can be applied, depending on the number of host requirements. For example, the WAN links use subnet addresses with a prefix of /30. This prefix allows for only two hosts: just enough hosts for a point-to-point connection between a pair of routers.

Figure 3-32   *VLSM Example*

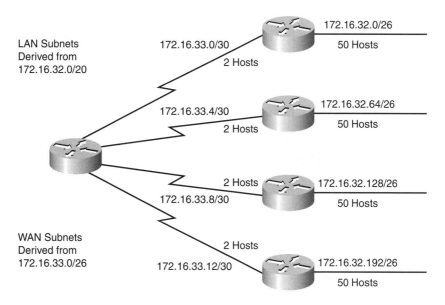

To calculate the subnet addresses used on the WAN links, further subnet one of the unused /26 subnets. In this example, 172.16.33.0/26 is further subnetted with a prefix of /30. This provides four more subnet bits, and therefore 16 (2^4) subnets for the WANs.

> **NOTE** Remember that only subnets that are unused can be further subnetted. In other words, if you use any addresses from a subnet, that subnet cannot be further subnetted. In the example, four subnet numbers are used on the LANs. Another unused subnet, 172.16.33.0/26, is further subnetted for use on the WANs.

Route Summarization with VLSM

In large internetworks, hundreds or even thousands of network addresses can exist. In these environments, it is often not desirable for routers to maintain many routes in their routing table. Route summarization, also called *route aggregation* or *supernetting*, can reduce the number of routes that a router must maintain by representing a series of network numbers in a single summary address. This section describes and provides examples of route summarization, including implementation considerations.

Figure 3-33 shows that Router A can either send three routing update entries or summarize the addresses into a single network number.

Figure 3-33 *VLSM Route Summarization*

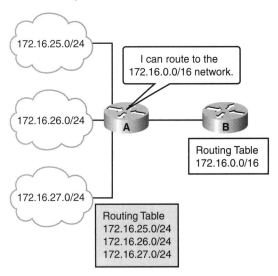

The figure illustrates a summary route based on a full octet: 172.16.25.0/24, 172.16.26.0/24, and 172.16.27.0/24 could be summarized into 172.16.0.0/16.

> **NOTE**   Router A can route to network 172.16.0.0/16, including all subnets of that network. However, if there were other subnets of 172.16.0.0 elsewhere in the network (for example, if 172.16.0.0 were discontiguous), summarizing in this way might not be valid. Discontiguous networks and summarization are discussed later in this chapter.

Another advantage to using route summarization in a large, complex network is that it can isolate topology changes from other routers. That is, if a specific link in the 172.16.27.0/24 domain were "flapping," or going up and down rapidly, the summary route would not change. Therefore, no router external to the domain would need to keep modifying its routing table due to this flapping activity. By summarizing addresses, you also reduce the amount of memory consumed by the routing protocol for table entries.

Route summarization is most effective within a subnetted environment when the network addresses are in contiguous blocks in powers of two. For example, 4, 16, or 512 addresses can be represented by a single routing entry because summary masks are binary masks—just like subnet masks—so summarization must take place on binary boundaries (powers of two).

Routing protocols summarize or aggregate routes based on shared network numbers within the network. Classless routing protocols, such as RIP-2, OSPF, IS-IS, and EIGRP, support route summarization based on subnet addresses, including VLSM addressing. Classful routing protocols, such as RIP-1 and IGRP, automatically summarize routes on the classful network boundary and do not support summarization on any other boundaries.

RFC 1518, "An Architecture for IP Address Allocation with CIDR," describes summarization in full detail.

Suppose a router receives updates for the following routes:

■   172.16.168.0/24

■   172.16.169.0/24

■   172.16.170.0/24

■   172.16.171.0/24

■   172.16.172.0/24

- 172.16.173.0/24

- 172.16.174.0/24

- 172.16.175.0/24

To determine the summary route, the router determines the number of highest-order bits that match in all the addresses. By converting the IP addresses to the binary format, as shown in Figure 3-34, you can determine the number of common bits shared among the IP addresses.

Figure 3-34 *Summarizing Within an Octet*

172.16.168.0/24 =	10101100	00010000	10101	000	00000000
172.16.169.0/24 =	172 .	16 .	10101	001 .	0
172.16.170.0/24 =	172 .	16 .	10101	010 .	0
172.16.171.0/24 =	172 .	16 .	10101	011 .	0
172.16.172.0/24 =	172 .	16 .	10101	100 .	0
172.16.173.0/24 =	172 .	16 .	10101	101 .	0
172.16.174.0/24 =	172 .	16 .	10101	110 .	0
172.16.175.0/24 =	172 .	16 .	10101	111 .	0

Number of Common Bits = 21   Noncommon
Summary: 172.16.168.0/21   Bits = 11

In Figure 3-34, the first 21 bits are in common among the IP addresses. Therefore, the best summary route is 172.16.168.0/21. You can summarize addresses when the number of addresses is a power of two. If the number of addresses is not a power of two, you can divide the addresses into groups and summarize the groups separately.

To allow the router to aggregate the highest number of IP addresses into a single route summary, your IP addressing plan should be hierarchical in nature. This approach is particularly important when using VLSMs.

A VLSM design allows for maximum use of IP addresses, as well as more efficient routing update communication when using hierarchical IP addressing. In Figure 3-35, for example, route summarization occurs at two levels.

- Router C summarizes two routing updates from networks 172.16.32.64/26 and 172.16.32.128/26 into a single update, 172.16.32.0/24.

- Router A receives three different routing updates but summarizes them into a single routing update before propagating it to the corporate network.

Figure 3-35 *Summarizing Addresses in a VLSM-Designed Network*

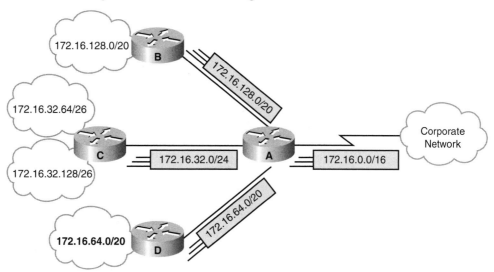

Route summarization reduces memory use on routers and routing protocol network traffic. Requirements for summarization to work correctly are as follows:

■ Multiple IP addresses must share the same highest-order bits.

■ Routing protocols must base their routing decisions on a 32-bit IP address and a prefix length that can be up to 32 bits.

■ Routing protocols must carry the prefix length (subnet mask) with the 32-bit IP address.

Cisco routers manage route summarization in two ways:

■ **Sending route summaries:** Routing protocols, such as RIP and EIGRP, perform automatic route summarization across network boundaries. Specifically, this automatic summarization occurs for those routes whose classful network address differs from the major network address of the interface to which the advertisement is being sent. For OSPF and IS-IS, you must configure manual summarization. For EIGRP and RIP-2, you can disable automatic route summarization and configure manual summarization. Whether routing summarization is automatic or not depends on the routing protocol. It is recommended that you review the documentation for your specific routing protocols. Route summarization is not always a solution. You would not use route summarization if you needed to advertise all networks across a boundary, such as when you have discontiguous networks.

■ **Selecting routes from route summaries:** If more than one entry in the routing table matches a particular destination, the longest prefix match in the routing table is used. Several routes might match one destination, but the longest matching prefix is used.

For example, if a routing table has different paths to 192.16.0.0/16 and to 192.16.5.0/24, packets addressed to 192.16.5.99 would be routed through the 192.16.5.0/24 path because that address has the longest match with the destination address.

Classful routing protocols summarize automatically at network boundaries. This behavior, which cannot be changed with RIP-1 and IGRP, has important results, as follows:

■ Subnets are not advertised to a different major network.

■ Discontiguous subnets are not visible to each other.

In Figure 3-36, RIP-1 does not advertise the 172.16.5.0 255.255.255.0 and 172.16.6.0 255.255.255.0 subnets because RIPv1 cannot advertise subnets; both Router A and Router B advertise 172.16.0.0. This leads to confusion when routing across network 192.168.14.0. In this example, Router C receives routes about 172.16.0.0 from two different directions, so it cannot make a correct routing decision.

Figure 3-36 *Classful Summarization in Discontiguous Networks*

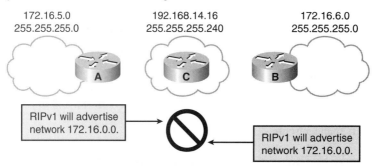

You can resolve this situation by using RIP-2, OSPF, IS-IS, or EIGRP and not using summarization because the subnet routes would be advertised with their actual subnet masks. For example:

> **NOTE**   Cisco IOS Software also provides an IP unnumbered feature that permits discontiguous subnets to be separated by an unnumbered link.

Summary of Implementing Variable-Length Subnet Masks

The following list summarizes the key points discussed in this section:

■ Subnetting lets you efficiently allocate addresses by taking one large broadcast domain and breaking it up into smaller, more manageable broadcast domains.

■ VLSMs let you more efficiently allocate IP addresses by adding multiple layers of the addressing hierarchy.

■ The benefits of route summarization include smaller routing tables and the ability to isolate topology changes.

Chapter Summary

The list that follows summarizes the key points that were discussed in this chapter.

■ Routers gather and maintain routing information to enable the transmission and receipt of packets. Various classes of routing protocols contribute to the different features in each network. The Routing Information Protocol (RIP), the Enhanced Interior Gateway Routing Protocol (EIGRP), and the Open Shortest Path First (OSPF) routing protocol each provide different features and capabilities.

■ A distance vector routing algorithm sends its entire routing table to its neighbors. Link-state routing algorithms maintain a complex database of topology information, which routers use to maintain full awareness of distant routers.

■ OSPF is a classless, link-state routing protocol that is widely deployed in many networks. EIGRP is a classless routing protocol that behaves like a classful routing protocol by default.

■ You can further tune these routing protocols by implementing variable-length subnet masks (VLSMs) and route summarization. It is up to network administrators to be knowledgeable about each protocol so that they can implement the most appropriate routing protocol based on the individual needs of their networks.

Review Questions

Use the questions here to review what you learned in this chapter. The correct answers and solutions are found in the appendix, "Answers to Chapter Review Questions."

1. Which statement most accurately describes static and dynamic routes?

   a. Dynamic routes are manually configured by a network administrator, whereas static routes are automatically learned and adjusted by a routing protocol.

   b. Static routes are manually configured by a network administrator, whereas dynamic routes are automatically learned and adjusted by a routing protocol.

   c. Static routes tell the router how to forward packets to networks that are not directly connected, whereas dynamic routes tell the router how to forward packets to networks that are directly connected.

   d. Dynamic routes tell the router how to forward packets to networks that are not directly connected, whereas static routes tell the router how to forward packets to networks that are directly connected.

2. Which of the following protocols is an example of an Exterior Gateway Protocol?

   a. RIP

   b. BGP

   c. OSPF

   d. EIGRP

3. In which situation is an administrative distance required?

   a. Whenever static routes are defined

   b. Whenever dynamic routing is enabled

   c. When the same route is learned via multiple routing sources

   d. When multiple paths are available to the same destination, and they are all learned via the same routing protocol

4. How does a distance vector router learn about paths for networks that are not directly connected?

   a. From the source router.

   b. From neighboring routers.

   c. From the destination router.

   d. A distance vector router can only learn directly connected networks.

5. What does a distance vector router send to neighboring routers as part of a periodic routing-table update?

   a. The entire routing table

   b. Information about new routes

   c. Information about routes that have changed

   d. Information about routes that no longer exist

6. With distance vector routing, count to infinity can be prevented by setting a maximum for what value?

   a. Metric

   b. Update time

   c. Hold-down time

   d. Administrative distance

7. What does split horizon specify?

   a. That information about a route should not be sent in any direction

   b. That information about a route should not be sent back in the direction from which the original information came

   c. That information about a route should always be sent back in the direction from which the original information came

   d. That information about a route should be sent back only in the direction from which the original information came

8. When a router sets the metric for a down network to the maximum value, what is it doing?

   a. Triggering the route

   b. Poisoning the route

   c. Applying split horizon

   d. Putting the route in holddown

9. If a route for a network is in holddown and an update arrives from a neighboring router with the same metric as was originally recorded for the network, what does the router do?

   a. Ignores the update

   b. Increments the hold-down timer

   c. Marks the network as "accessible" and removes the hold-down timer

   d. Marks the network as "accessible" but keeps the hold-down timer on

10. If a router has a network path in holddown and an update arrives from a neighboring router with a better metric than originally recorded for the network, what two things does it do? (Choose two.)

   a. Removes the holddown

   b. Continues the holddown

   c. Marks the route as "accessible"

   d. Marks the route as "inaccessible"

   e. Marks the route as "possibly down"

11. How can link-state protocols limit the scope of route changes?

   a. By supporting classless addressing

   b. By sending the mask along with the address

   c. By sending only updates of a topology change

   d. By segmenting the network into area hierarchies

12.   What is the purpose of link-state advertisements?

   a.   To construct a topological database

   b.   To specify the cost to reach a destination

   c.   To determine the best path to a destination

   d.   To verify that a neighbor is still functioning

13.   What are two characteristics of OSPF? (Choose two.)

   a.   Hierarchical

   b.   Proprietary

   c.   Open standard

   d.   Similar to RIP

   e.   Distance vector protocol

14.   OSPF routes packets within a single _____.

   a.   Area

   b.   Network

   c.   Segment

   d.   Autonomous system

15.   How many subnets are gained by subnetting 172.17.32.0/20 into multiple /28 subnets?

   a.   16

   b.   32

   c.   256

   d.   1024

16.   How many hosts can be addressed on a subnet that has seven host bits?

   a.   7

   b.   62

   c.   126

   d.   252

17.   How many hosts can be addressed with a prefix of /30?

   a.   1

   b.   2

   c.   4

   d.   30

18. Which subnet mask would be appropriate for a Class C address used for 9 LANs, each with 12 hosts?

   a. 255.255.255.0

   b. 255.255.255.224

   c. 255.255.255.240

   d. 255.255.255.252

19. How can you most effectively summarize the IP range of addresses from 10.1.32.0 to 10.1.35.255?

   a. 10.1.32.0/23

   b. 10.1.32.0/22

   c. 10.1.32.0/21

   d. 10.1.32.0/20

20. How can you most effectively summarize the IP range of addresses from 172.168.12.0/24 to 172.168.13.0/24?

   a. 172.168.12.0/23

   b. 172.168.12.0/22

   c. 172.168.12.0/21

   d. 172.168.12.0/20

This chapter includes the following sections:

- Chapter Objectives

- Introducing OSPF

- Troubleshooting OSPF

- Chapter Summary

- Review Questions

Single-Area OSPF Implementation

This chapter examines Open Shortest Path First (OSPF), which is one of the most commonly used Interior Gateway Protocols (IGPs) in IP networking. OSPF is an open-standard, classless IGP. OSPF is based primarily on RFC 2328 and is designated by the Internet Engineering Task Force (IETF) as one of several IGPs. Because of the complexity and widespread use of OSPF, knowledge of its configuration and maintenance is essential. This chapter describes the function of OSPF and explains how to configure a single-area OSPF network on a Cisco router.

Chapter Objectives

Upon completing this chapter, you will be able to describe the operation and configuration of a single-area OSPF network, including load balancing and authentication. This ability includes being able to meet these objectives:

- Describe the features of OSPF

- Describe how OSPF neighbor adjacencies are established

- Describe the SPF algorithm that OSPF uses

- Configure a single-area OSPF network

- Configure a loopback interface to be used as the router ID

- Verify a single-area OSPF network configuration

- Use the OSPF **debug** commands to troubleshoot OSPF

- Configure load balancing with OSPF

- Configure authentication for OSPF

Introducing OSPF

Open Shortest Path First is a link-state routing protocol. You can think of a *link* as an interface on a router. The state of the link is a description of that interface and of its relationship to its neighboring routers. A description of the interface would include, for example, the IP address of the interface, the subnet mask, the type of network to which it is connected, the routers that are connected to that network, and so on. The collection of all of these link states forms a link-state database.

A router sends link-state advertisement (LSA) packets to advertise its state periodically (every 30 minutes) and immediately when the router state changes. Information about attached interfaces, metrics used, and other variables is included in OSPF LSAs. As OSPF routers accumulate link-state information, they use the shortest path first (SPF) algorithm to calculate the shortest path to each node.

A topological (link-state) database is, essentially, an overall picture of networks in relation to routers. The topological database contains the collection of LSAs received from all routers in the same area. Because routers within the same area share the same information, they have identical topological databases.

OSPF can operate within a hierarchy. The largest entity within the hierarchy is the autonomous system, which is a collection of networks under a common administration that share a common routing strategy. An autonomous system can be divided into a number of areas, which are groups of contiguous networks and attached hosts. Figure 4-1 shows an example of an OSPF hierarchy.

Figure 4-1   *OSPF Hierarchy*

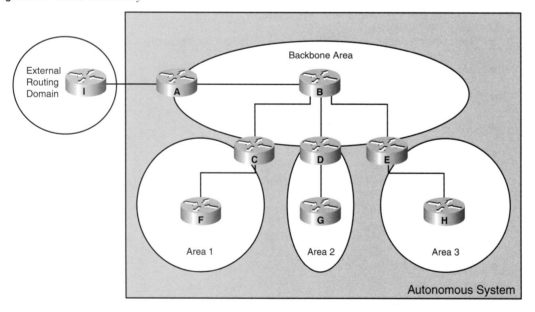

OSPF uses a two-layer network hierarchy that has two primary elements:

- **Autonomous system:** An autonomous system consists of a collection of networks under a common administration that share a common routing strategy. An autonomous system, sometimes called a *domain*, can be logically subdivided into multiple areas.

- **Area:** An *area* is a grouping of contiguous networks. Areas are logical subdivisions of the autonomous system.

Within each autonomous system, a contiguous backbone area must be defined. All other nonbackbone areas are connected off the backbone area. The backbone area is the transition area because all other areas communicate through it. For OSPF, the nonbackbone areas can be additionally configured as stub areas, totally stubby areas, or not-so-stubby areas (NSSA) to help reduce the link-state database and routing table size.

OSPF special areas such as NSSAs, totally stubby, and stub areas are beyond the scope of this text. Routers that operate within the two-layer network hierarchy have different routing entities and different functions in OSPF. The following are some examples based on Figure 4-1:

- Router B is the backbone router. The backbone router provides connectivity between different areas.

- Routers C, D, and E are area border routers (ABR). ABRs attach to multiple areas, maintain separate link-state databases for each area to which they are connected, and route traffic destined for or arriving from other areas.

- Routers F, G, and H are nonbackbone, internal routers. Nonbackbone, internal routers are aware of the topology within their respective areas and maintain identical link-state databases about the areas.

- Depending on the configuration of the OSPF nonbackbone area (stub area, totally stubby area, or NSSA) the ABR advertises a default route to the nonbackbone, internal, router. The nonbackbone, internal router uses the default route to forward all interarea or interdomain traffic to the ABR router.

- Router A is the autonomous system boundary router (ASBR) that connects to an external routing domain, or autonomous system.

- Router I is a router that belongs to another routing domain, or autonomous system.

Establishing OSPF Neighbor Adjacencies

Neighbor OSPF routers must recognize each other on the network before they can share information because OSPF routing depends on the status of the link between two routers. This process is done using the Hello protocol. The Hello protocol establishes and maintains neighbor relationships by ensuring bidirectional (two-way) communication between neighbors. Bidirectional communication occurs when a router recognizes itself listed in the hello packet received from a neighbor. Figure 4-2 illustrates the hello packet.

Figure 4-2 *OSPF Hello*

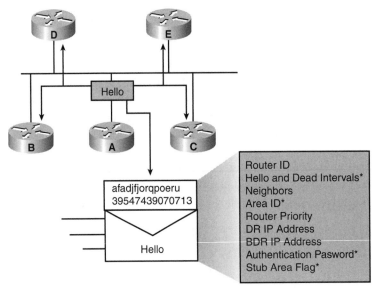

*Entry must match on neighboring routers.

Each interface that is participating in OSPF uses IP multicast address 224.0.0.5 to periodically send hello packets. A hello packet contains the following information:

- **Router ID:** The *router ID* is a 32-bit number that uniquely identifies the router. The highest IP address on an active interface is chosen by default, unless a loopback interface or the router ID is configured; for example, IP address 172.16.12.1 would be chosen over 172.16.1.1. This identification is important in establishing and troubleshooting neighbor relationships and coordinating route exchanges.

- **Hello and dead intervals:** The *hello interval* specifies the frequency in seconds at which a router sends hello packets. The default hello interval on multiaccess networks is 10 seconds. The *dead interval* is the time in seconds that a router waits to hear from a neighbor before declaring the neighboring router out of service. By default, the dead interval is four times the hello interval. These timers must be the same on neighboring routers; otherwise, an adjacency will not be established.

- **Neighbors:** The Neighbors field lists the adjacent routers with established bidirectional communication. This bidirectional communication is indicated when the router recognizes itself listed in the Neighbors field of the hello packet from the neighbor.

- **Area ID:** To communicate, two routers must share a common segment, and their interfaces must belong to the same OSPF area on that segment. The neighbors must also share the same subnet and mask. All these routers will have the same link-state information.

- **Router priority:** The *router priority* is an 8-bit number that indicates the priority of a router. OSPF uses the priority to select a designated router (DR) and a backup DR (BDR).

- **DR and BDR IP addresses:** These are the IP addresses of the DR and BDR for the specific network, if they are known.

NOTE   OSPF DRs and BDRs are discussed in the Cisco Certified Networking Professional (CCNP) curriculum.

- **Authentication password:** If router authentication is enabled, two routers must exchange the same password. OSPF has three types of authentication: Null (no authentication), simple (plain-text passwords), and MD5. Authentication is not required, but if it is enabled, all peer routers must have the same password.

- **Stub area flag:** A stub area is a special area. Designating a stub area is a technique that reduces routing updates by replacing them with a default route. Two routers must agree on the stub area flag in the hello packets.

NOTE   OSPF special areas such as stub areas are discussed in the CCNP curriculum.

SPF Algorithm

The SPF algorithm places each router at the root of a tree and calculates the shortest path to each node, using Dijkstra's algorithm, based on the cumulative cost that is required to reach that destination. LSAs are flooded throughout the area using a reliable algorithm, which ensures that all routers in an area have the same topological database. Each router uses the information in its topological database to calculate a shortest path tree, with itself as the root. The router then uses this tree to route network traffic. Figure 4-3 represents the Router A view of the network, where Router A is the root and calculates pathways assuming this view.

Each router has its own view of the topology, even though all of the routers build a shortest-path tree using the same link-state database.

The cost, or *metric*, of an interface is an indication of the overhead that is required to send packets across a certain interface. The interface cost is inversely proportional to the bandwidth, so a higher bandwidth indicates a lower cost. There is more overhead, higher cost, and more time delays involved in crossing a T1 serial line than in crossing a 10-Mbps Ethernet line.

Figure 4-3 *SPF Algorithm for Route Selection*

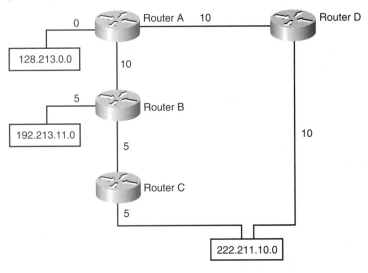

The formula used to calculate OSPF cost is as follows:

cost = reference bandwidth / interface bandwidth (in bps)

The default reference bandwidth is 10^8, which is 100,000,000 or the equivalent of the bandwidth of FastEthernet. Therefore, the default cost of a 10-Mbps Ethernet link will be $10^8 / 10^7 = 10$, and the cost of a T1 link will be $10^8 / 1,544,000 = 64$.

To adjust the reference bandwidth for links with bandwidths greater than FastEthernet, use the **ospf auto-cost reference-bandwidth** *ref-bw* command configured in the OSPF routing process configuration mode.

Configuring and Verifying OSPF

The **router ospf** command uses a process identifier as an argument. The process ID is a unique, arbitrary number that you select to identify the routing process. The process ID does not need to match the OSPF process ID on other OSPF routers.

The **network** command identifies which IP networks on the router are part of the OSPF network. For each network, you must also identify the OSPF area to which the networks belong. The **network** command takes the three arguments listed in Table 4-1. The table defines the parameters of the **network** command.

Table 4-1 **network** *Command Parameters*

router ospf Command Parameters	Description
address	The network, subnet, or interface address.
wildcard-mask	The wildcard mask. This mask identifies the part of the IP address that is to be matched, where 0 is a match and 1 is "don't care." For example, a wildcard mask of 0.0.0.0 indicates a match of all 32 bits in the address.
area-id	The area that is to be associated with the OSPF address range. It can be specified either as a decimal value or in dotted-decimal notation, like an IP address.

Calculating wildcard masks on non-8-bit boundaries can be prone to error. You can avoid calculating wildcard masks by having a network statement that matches the IP address on each interface and uses the 0.0.0.0 mask.

Figure 4-4 shows an example of a single-area OSPF configuration on Router B.

Figure 4-4 *Single-Area OSPF*

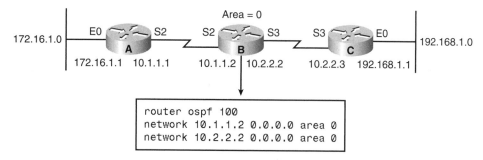

Loopback Interfaces

The OSPF router ID is used to uniquely identify each router in the OSPF network. By default, this ID is selected by the operating system from the configured IP addresses on the router. To modify the OSPF router ID to use a loopback address, first define a loopback interface with the following command:

```
RouterX(config)# interface loopback number
```

The highest IP address, used as the router ID by default, can be overridden by configuring an IP address on a loopback interface. OSPF is more reliable if a loopback interface is configured because the interface is always active and cannot be in a down state like a "real" interface can. For this reason, the loopback address should be used on all key routers. If the loopback address is going to be published with the **network area** command, using a private IP address will save on registered IP address space. Note that a loopback address requires a different subnet for each router, unless the host address is advertised.

Using an address that is not advertised saves real IP address space, but unlike an address that is advertised, the unadvertised address does not appear in the OSPF table and thus cannot be accessed across the network. Therefore, using a private IP address represents a trade-off between the ease of debugging the network and conservation of address space. Figure 4-5 highlights some of the advantages and disadvantages of using advertised and unadvertised loopback addresses.

Figure 4-5 *Loopback Addresses*

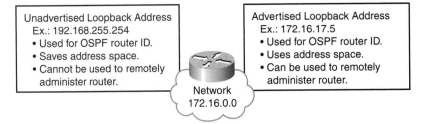

Verifying the OSPF Configuration

You can use any one of a number of **show** commands to display information about an OSPF configuration. The **show ip protocols** command displays parameters about timers, filters, metrics, networks, and other information for the entire router.

The **show ip route** command displays the routes that are known to the router and how they were learned. This command is one of the best ways to determine connectivity between the local router and the rest of the internetwork. Example 4-1 shows the output from the **show ip route** command for a router running OSPF.

Example 4-1 *Displaying Routes Known by Router*

```
RouterX#show ip route

Codes: I - IGRP derived, R - RIP derived, O - OSPF derived,
       C - connected, S - static, E - EGP derived, B - BGP derived,
       * - candidate default route, IA - OSPF inter area route,
       i - IS-IS derived, ia - IS-IS, U - per-user static route,
       o - on-demand routing, M - mobile, P - periodic downloaded static route,
       D - EIGRP, EX - EIGRP external, E1 - OSPF external type 1 route,
       E2 - OSPF external type 2 route, N1 - OSPF NSSA external type 1 route,
       N2 - OSPF NSSA external type 2 route
```

Example 4-1 *Displaying Routes Known by Router (Continued)*

```
Gateway of last resort is 10.119.254.240 to network 10.140.0.0

O 10.110.0.0 [110/5] via 10.119.254.6, 0:01:00, Ethernet2
O IA 10.67.10.0 [110/10] via 10.119.254.244, 0:02:22, Ethernet2
O 10.68.132.0 [110/5] via 10.119.254.6, 0:00:59, Ethernet2
O 10.130.0.0 [110/5] via 10.119.254.6, 0:00:59, Ethernet2
O E2 10.128.0.0 [170/10] via 10.119.254.244, 0:02:22, Ethernet2
```

Table 4-2 describes the significant fields shown in the **show ip route** display.

Table 4-2 *IP Routing Table Fields*

Value	Description
O	This field indicates the learning method that derived the route. It can be one of the following values: **I:** IGRP[1]-derived **R:** RIP[2]-derived **O:** OSPF-derived (the value displayed in the example) **C:** Connected **S:** Static **E:** EGP[3]-derived **B:** BGP[4]-derived **D:** EIGRP[5]-derived **EX:** EIGRP external **i:** IS-IS[6]-derived **ia:** IS-IS **M:** Mobile **P:** Periodic downloaded static route **U:** Per-user static route **o:** On-demand routing

continues

Table 4-2 *IP Routing Table Fields (Continued)*

Value	Description
E2 IA	This field indicates the type of route. It can be one of the following values: ***:** Indicates the last path used when a packet was forwarded. It pertains only to the nonfast-switched packets. However, it does not indicate which path will be used next when forwarding a nonfast-switched packet, except when the paths are equal cost. **IA:** OSPF interarea route **E1:** OSPF external type 1 route **E2:** OSPF external type 2 route (The value displayed in the example.) **L1:** IS-IS level 1 route **L2:** IS-IS level 2 route **N1:** OSPF NSSA external type 1 route **N2:** OSPF NSSA external type 2 route
172.150.0.0	This address indicates the address of the remote network.
[110/5]	The first number in the brackets is the administrative distance of the information source; the second number is the metric for the route.
via 10.119.254.6	This value specifies the address of the next router to the remote network.
0:01:00	This field specifies the last time the route was updated (in hours:minutes:seconds).
Ethernet2	This field specifies the interface through which the specified network can be reached.

[1] IGRP = Interior Gateway Routing Protocol

[2] RIP = Routing Information Protocol

[3] EGP = Exterior Gateway Protocol

[4] BGP = Border Gateway Protocol

[5] EIGRP = Enhanced Interior Gateway Routing Protocol

[6] IS-IS = Intermediate System-to-Intermediate System

Use the **show ip ospf** command to verify the OSPF router ID. This command also displays OSPF timer settings and other statistics, including the number of times the SPF algorithm has been executed. In addition, this command has optional parameters so you can further specify the information that is to be displayed.

Example 4-2 shows the output from this command when it is executed on Router X.

Example 4-2   **show ip ospf** *Command Output*

```
RouterX#show ip ospf
 Routing Process "ospf 50" with ID 10.64.0.2
 Supports only single TOS(TOS0) routes
 Supports opaque LSA
 Supports Link-local Signaling (LLS)
 Supports area transit capability
 Initial SPF schedule delay 5000 msecs
 Minimum hold time between two consecutive SPFs 10000 msecs
 Maximum wait time between two consecutive SPFs 10000 msecs
 Incremental-SPF disabled
 Minimum LSA interval 5 secs
 Minimum LSA arrival 1000 msecs
 LSA group pacing timer 240 secs
 Interface flood pacing timer 33 msecs
 Retransmission pacing timer 66 msecs
 Number of external LSA 0. Checksum Sum 0x000000
 Number of opaque AS LSA 0. Checksum Sum 0x000000
 Number of DCbitless external and opaque AS LSA 0
 Number of DoNotAge external and opaque AS LSA 0
 Number of areas in this router is 1. 1 normal 0 stub 0 nssa
 Number of areas transit capable is 0
 External flood list length 0
    Area BACKBONE(0)
    Area BACKBONE(0)
        Area has no authentication
        SPF algorithm last executed 00:01:25.028 ago
        SPF algorithm executed 7 times
        Area ranges are
        Number of LSA 6. Checksum Sum 0x01FE3E
        Number of opaque link LSA 0. Checksum Sum 0x000000
        Number of DCbitless LSA 0
        Number of indication LSA 0
        Number of DoNotAge LSA 0
        Flood list length 0
```

The **show ip ospf interface** command verifies that interfaces have been configured in the intended areas. If no loopback address is specified, the interface with the highest address is chosen as the router ID. This command also displays the timer intervals, including the hello interval, and shows the neighbor adjacencies. Example 4-3 demonstrates output from the **show ip ospf interface** command.

Example 4-3 show ip ospf interface *Command Output*

```
RouterX#show ip ospf interface ethernet 0

Ethernet 0 is up, line protocol is up
Internet Address 192.168.254.202, Mask 255.255.255.0, Area 0.0.0.0
AS 201, Router ID 192.168.99.1, Network Type BROADCAST, Cost: 10
Transmit Delay is 1 sec, State OTHER, Priority 1
Designated Router id 192.168.254.10, Interface address 192.168.254.10
Backup Designated router id 192.168.254.28, Interface addr 192.168.254.28
Timer intervals configured, Hello 10, Dead 60, Wait 40, Retransmit 5
Hello due in 0:00:05
Neighbor Count is 8, Adjacent neighbor count is 2
  Adjacent with neighbor 192.168.254.28 (Backup Designated Router)
   Adjacent with neighbor 192.168.254.10 (Designated Router)
```

Table 4-3 describes the output for the **show ip ospf interface** command.

Table 4-3 show ip ospf interface Output

Field	Description
Ethernet	Status of physical link and operational status of protocol
Internet Address	Interface IP address, subnet mask, and area address
AS	Autonomous system number (OSPF process ID), router ID, network type, link-state cost
Transmit Delay	Transmit delay, interface state, and router priority
Designated Router	Designated router ID and respective interface IP address
Backup Designated Router	Backup designated router ID and respective interface IP address
Timer Intervals Configured	Configuration of timer intervals
Hello	Number of seconds until the next hello packet is sent out of this interface
Neighbor Count	Count of network neighbors and list of adjacent neighbors

The **show ip ospf neighbor** command displays OSPF neighbor information on a per-interface basis.

Example 4-4 shows output from the **show ip ospf neighbor** command, with a single line of summary information for each neighbor in the output.

Example 4-4 **show ip ospf neighbor** *Command Output*

```
RouterX# show ip ospf neighbor

ID              Pri  State          Dead Time  Address         Interface
10.199.199.137  1    FULL/DR        0:00:31    192.168.80.37   FastEthernet0/0
172.16.48.1     1    FULL/DROTHER   0:00:33    172.16.48.1     FastEthernet0/1
172.16.48.200   1    FULL/DROTHER   0:00:33    172.16.48.200   FastEthernet0/1
10.199.199.137  5    FULL/DR        0:00:33    172.16.48.189   FastEthernet0/1
```

For more specific information about a given neighbor, use the same command, but specify the address of a given neighbor. Example 4-5 shows how to get specific information for the neighbor 190.199.199.137.

Example 4-5 **show ip ospf neighbor** *Command Output for a Specific Neighbor*

```
RouterX#show ip ospf neighbor 10.199.199.137
Neighbor 10.199.199.137, interface address 192.168.80.37
In the area 0.0.0.0 via interface Ethernet0
Neighbor priority is 1, State is FULL
Options 2
Dead timer due in 0:00:32
Link State retransmission due in 0:00:04
Neighbor 10.199.199.137, interface address 172.16.48.189
In the area 0.0.0.0 via interface Fddi0
Neighbor priority is 5, State is FULL
Options 2
Dead timer due in 0:00:32
Link State retransmission due in 0:00:03
```

Table 4-4 describes the significant fields for the **show ip ospf neighbor** command output.

Table 4-4 **show ip ospf neighbor** *Output*

Field	Description
Neighbor	Neighbor router ID.
Interface Address	IP address of the interface.
In the Area	Area and interface through which the OSPF neighbor is known.
Neighbor Priority	Router priority of the neighbor, neighbor state.
State	OSPF state.
State Changes	Number of state changes since the neighbor was created. This value can be reset using the **clear ip ospf counters neighbor** command.
DR	Router ID of the designated router for the interface.
BDR	Router ID of the backup designated router for the interface.

continues

Table 4-4 **show ip ospf neighbor** *Output (Continued)*

Field	Description
Options	Hello packet options field contents. (E-bit only. Possible values are 0 and 2; 2 indicates that the area is not a stub; 0 indicates that the area is a stub.)
LLS Options..., Last OOB-Resync	LLS[1] and OOB[2] link-state database resynchronization performed hours:minutes:seconds ago (Cisco NSF[3] information). The field indicates the last successful OOB resynchronization with the Cisco NSF-capable router.
Dead Timer Due In	Expected time before Cisco IOS Software will declare the neighbor dead.
Neighbor Is Up For	Number of hours:minutes:seconds since the neighbor went into a two-way state.
Index	Neighbor location in the area-wide and autonomous system–wide retransmission queue.
Retransmission Queue Length	Number of elements in the retransmission queue.
Number of Retransmission	Number of times update packets have been re-sent during flooding.
First	Memory location of the flooding details.
Next	Memory location of the flooding details.
Last Retransmission Scan Length	Number of LSAs in the last retransmission packet.
Maximum	Maximum number of LSAs that can be sent in any retransmission packet.
Last Retransmission Scan Time	Time taken to build the last retransmission packet.
Maximum	Maximum time taken to build any retransmission packet.

[1] LLs = link-local signaling

[2] OOB = out-of-band

[3] NSF = nonstop forwarding

Using OSPF debug Commands

The **debug ip ospf events** output shown in Example 4-6 might appear if any of the following situations occur:

■ The IP subnet masks for the routers on the same network do not match.

■ The OSPF hello interval for the router does not match the OSPF hello interval that is configured on a neighbor.

■ The OSPF dead interval for the router does not match the OSPF dead interval that is configured on a neighbor.

If a router that is configured for OSPF routing is not seeing an OSPF neighbor on an attached network, perform the following tasks:

■ Ensure that both routers have been configured with the same IP subnet mask and that the OSPF hello interval and dead intervals match on both routers.

■ Ensure that both neighbors are part of the same area number and area type.

■ Ensure that authentication type and passwords match.

In Example 4-6, which shows output from the **debug ip ospf events** command, the neighbor router and this router are not part of a stub area, denoted by the mismatched E bit. That is, one router is configured for the area to be a transit area, and the other router is configured for the area to be a stub area, as explained in RFC 2328.

Example 4-6 **debug ip ospf events** *Command Output*

```
RouterX#debug ip ospf events

OSPF:hello with invalid timers on interface Ethernet0
hello interval received 10 configured 10
net mask received 255.255.255.0 configured 255.255.255.0
dead interval received 40 configured 30

OSPF: hello packet with mismatched E bit
```

To display information about each OSPF packet that is received, use the **debug ip ospf packet** privileged EXEC command. The **no** form of this command disables the debugging output.

The **debug ip ospf packet** command produces one set of information for each packet that is received. The output varies slightly depending on which authentication is used. The table shows sample output from the **debug ip ospf packet** command when Message Digest 5 (MD5) authentication is used. Example 4-7 shows an OSPF message received and displayed when using this **debug** command.

Example 4-7 **debug ip ospf packet** *Command Output*

```
RouterX# debug ip ospf packet

OSPF: rcv. v:2 t:1 l:48 rid:200.0.0.116
      aid:0.0.0.0 chk:0 aut:2 keyid:1 seq:0x0
```

Table 4-5 describes the significance of the fields in this output.

Table 4-5 **debug ip ospf** *packet Fields*

Field	Description
v:	OSPF version
t:	OSPF packet type; possible packet types are as follows: • Hello • Data description • Link-state request • Link-state update • Link-state acknowledgment
l:	OSPF packet length in bytes
rid:	OSPF router ID
aid:	OSPF area ID
chk:	OSPF checksum
aut:	OSPF authentication type; possible authentication types are as follows: **0:** No authentication **1:** Simple password **2:** MD5
auk:	OSPF authentication key
keyid:	MD5 key ID
seq:	Sequence number

Load Balancing with OSPF

Load balancing is a standard functionality of Cisco IOS Software that is available across all router platforms. It is inherent to the forwarding process in the router, and it enables a router to use multiple paths to a destination when it forwards packets. The number of paths used is limited by the number of entries that the routing protocol puts in the routing table. Four entries is the default in Cisco IOS Software for IP routing protocols except for BGP. BGP has a default of one entry. The maximum number of paths you can configure is 16.

Figure 4-6 shows an example of configuring an OSPF router to load balance across six equal-cost paths.

Figure 4-6 *OSPF Equal-Cost Load Balancing*

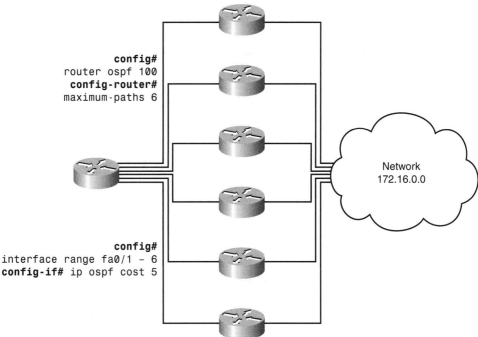

The cost (or metric) of an interface in OSPF indicates the overhead that is required to send packets across a certain interface. The cost of an interface is inversely proportional to its bandwidth. A higher bandwidth indicates a lower cost. By default, Cisco routers calculate the cost of an interface based on the bandwidth. However, you can force the cost of an interface with the command **ip ospf cost** {*value*} in interface configuration mode.

If equal-cost paths exist to the same destination, the Cisco implementation of OSPF can keep track of up to 16 next hops to the same destination in the routing table (which is called *load balancing*). By default, the Cisco router supports up to four equal-cost paths to a destination for OSPF. Use the **maximum-paths** command under the OSPF router process configuration mode to set the number of equal-cost paths in the routing table, as shown in Example 4-8.

Example 4-8 *Setting the Number of Equal-Cost Paths in the Routing Table*

```
RouterX(config)#router ospf 1
RouterX(config-router)#maximum-paths ?
<1-16>  Number of paths
RouterX(config-router)#maximum-paths 3
```

You can use the **show ip route** command to find equal-cost routes. Following is an example of the **show ip route** command output for a specific subnet that has multiple routes available in the routing table. Example 4-9 shows three equal-cost paths to the 194.168.20.0 network.

Example 4-9 *Finding Equal-Cost Routes with the* **show ip route** *Command*

```
RouterX#show ip route 194.168.20.0
 Routing entry for 194.168.20.0/24
  Known via "ospf 1", distance 110, metric 74, type intra area
  Redistributing via ospf 1
  Last update from 10.10.10.1 on Serial1, 00:00:01 ago
  Routing Descriptor Blocks:
  * 20.20.20.1, from 204.204.204.1, 00:00:01 ago, via Serial2
      Route metric is 74, traffic share count is 1
    30.30.30.1, from 204.204.204.1, 00:00:01 ago, via Serial3
      Route metric is 74, traffic share count is 1
    10.10.10.1, from 204.204.204.1, 00:00:01 ago, via Serial1
      Route metric is 74, traffic share count is 1
```

Notice the three routing descriptor blocks. Each block is one available route. Also note the asterisk (*) next to one of the block entries. The asterisk corresponds to the active route that is used for new traffic. The term "new traffic" corresponds to a single packet or an entire flow to a destination, depending on whether the router is performing per-destination or per-packet load balancing.

OSPF Authentication

OSPF neighbor authentication (also called *neighbor router authentication* or *route authentication*) can be configured such that routers can participate in routing based on predefined passwords.

When you configure neighbor authentication on a router, the router authenticates the source of each routing update packet that it receives. This authentication is accomplished by the exchange of an authenticating key (sometimes referred to as a *password*) that is known to both the sending and receiving router.

Types of Authentication

By default, OSPF uses null authentication (Type 0), which means that routing exchanges over a network are not authenticated. OSPF supports two other authentication methods:

■ Plaintext (or simple) password authentication (Type 1)

■ MD5 authentication (Type 2)

OSPF MD5 authentication includes an increasing sequence number in each OSPF packet to protect against replay attacks.

Configuring Plaintext Password Authentication

To configure OSPF plaintext password authentication, complete the following steps:

Step 1   Use the interface level **ip ospf authentication-key** *password* command to assign a password to use with neighboring routers that use the OSPF simple password authentication. The *password* can be any continuous string of characters that can be entered from the keyboard, up to eight characters in length.

> **NOTE**   In Cisco IOS Release 12.4, the router gives a warning message if you try to configure a password longer than eight characters; only the first eight characters are used. Some earlier Cisco IOS Software releases did not provide this warning.

The password that is created by this command is used as a "key" that is inserted directly into the OSPF header when Cisco IOS Software originates routing protocol packets. A separate password can be assigned to each network on a per-interface basis. All neighboring routers on the same network must have the same password to be able to exchange OSPF information.

> **NOTE**   If you do not use the **service password-encryption** command when configuring OSPF authentication, the key is stored as plaintext in the router configuration. If you configure the global **service password-encryption** command, the key is stored and displayed in an encrypted form; when it is displayed, an encryption type of 7 is specified before the encrypted key.

Step 2   Specify the authentication type using the interface level **ip ospf authentication** command. Table 4-6 explains the parameters for this command.

Table 4-6   **ip ospf authentication** *Command Parameters*

Parameter	Description
message-digest	(Optional) Specifies that MD5 authentication will be used.
null	(Optional) No authentication is used. This option is useful for overriding password or MD5 authentication if configured for an area.

For plaintext password authentication, use the **ip ospf authentication** command with no parameters. Before using this command, configure a password for the interface using the **ip ospf authentication-key** command.

The **ip ospf authentication** command was introduced in Cisco IOS
Release 12.0. For backward compatibility, the authentication type for an
area is still supported. If the authentication type is not specified for an
interface, the authentication type for the area is used. (The area default is
null authentication.) To enable authentication for an OSPF area, use the
area *area-id* **authentication** [**message-digest**] router configuration
command. Table 4-7 explains the parameters for this command.

Table 4-7 area authentication *Parameters*

Parameter	Description
area-id	Identifier of the area for which authentication is to be enabled. The identifier can be specified as either a decimal value or an IP address.
message-digest	(Optional) Enables MD5 authentication on the area specified by the *area-id* argument.

Example: Plaintext Password Authentication Configuration

Figure 4-7 shows the network that is used to illustrate the configuration, verification, and
troubleshooting of plaintext password authentication.

Figure 4-7 *Plaintext Password Authentication*

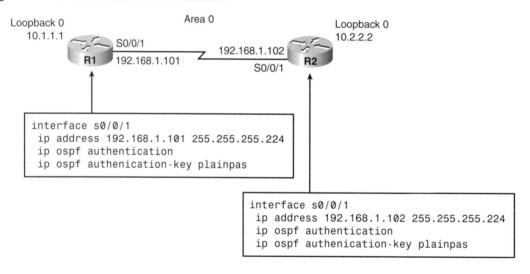

Plaintext password authentication is configured on interface serial 0/0/1 with the **ip ospf
authentication** command. The interface is configured with an authentication key of "plainpas."

Notice that the connecting interfaces on both Router 1 and Router 2 are configured for the same
type of authentication with the same authentication key.

Verifying Plaintext Password Authentication

Example 4-10 shows output from the **show ip ospf neighbor** and **show ip route** commands for a router that was configured with authentication.

Example 4-10   *Verifying Authentication with the **show ip ospf neighbor** and **show ip route** Commands*

```
RouterX#show ip ospf neighbor
Neighbor ID   Pri      State      Dead Time    Address         Interface
10.2.2.2       0       FULL/      00:00:32     192.168.1.102   Serial0/0/1

RouterX#show ip route
<output omitted>
Gateway of last resort is not set
     10.0.0.0/8 is variably subnetted, 2 subnets, 2 masks
O        10.2.2.2/32 [110/782] via 192.168.1.102, 00:01:17, Serial0/0/1
C        10.1.1.0/24 is directly connected, Loopback0
     192.168.1.0/27 is subnetted, 1 subnets
C        192.168.1.96 is directly connected, Serial0/0/1
```

Notice that the neighbor state is FULL, indicating that the two routers have successfully formed an OSPF adjacency. The routing table verifies that the 10.2.2.2 address has been learned via OSPF over the serial connection.

The results of a ping to the Router Y loopback interface address are also displayed to illustrate that the link is working, as shown in Example 4-11.

Example 4-11   *Using **ping** Output to Verify Link Operation*

```
RouterX#ping 10.2.2.2
Type escape sequence to abort.
Sending 5, 100-byte ICMP Echos to 10.2.2.2, timeout is 2 seconds:
!!!!!
Success rate is 100 percent (5/5), round-trip min/avg/max = 28/29/32 ms
```

Summary of OSPF Introduction

The following summarizes the key points that were discussed in this section:

■ OSPF is a classless, link-state routing protocol that uses an area hierarchy for fast convergence.

■ OSPF exchanges hello packets to establish neighbor adjacencies between routers.

■ The SPF algorithm uses a cost metric to determine the best path. Lower costs indicate a better path.

■ The **router ospf** *process-id* command is used to enable OSPF on the router.

- Use a loopback interface to keep the OSPF router ID consistent.

- The **show ip ospf neighbor** command displays OSPF neighbor information on a per-interface basis.

- The commands **debug ip ospf events** and **debug ip ospf packets** can be used to troubleshoot OSPF problems.

- OSPF will load-balance across up to four equal-cost metric paths by default.

- OSPF authentication can be two types: plaintext and MD5.

Troubleshooting OSPF

Because it is a link-state routing protocol, OSPF scales well with a growing network. But this scalability introduces complexity in design, configuration, and maintenance. This section introduces some of the common issues surrounding an OSPF network and offers a flowchart approach to troubleshooting these issues.

Components of Troubleshooting OSPF

Troubleshooting OSPF requires an understanding of the operation of the protocol as well as a specific approach methodology. Figure 4-8 shows the major components of OSPF troubleshooting and the order in which the process flows.

Figure 4-8 *Components of Troubleshooting OSPF*

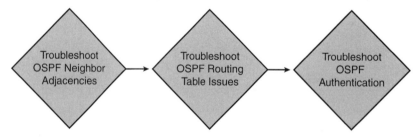

The major components of OSPF troubleshooting include the following:

- OSPF neighbor adjacencies

- The OSPF routing table

- OSPF authentication

Troubleshooting OSPF Neighbor Adjacencies

The first component to troubleshoot and verify is the OSPF neighbor adjacency. Figure 4-9 shows the verification/troubleshooting components for neighbor adjacencies.

Figure 4-9 *Troubleshooting OSPF Neighbor Adjacencies*

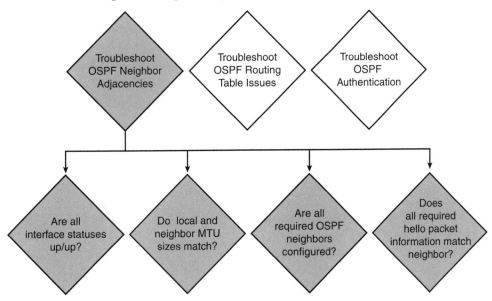

A healthy OSPF neighbor state is "Full." If the OSPF neighbor state remains in any other state, it may indicate a problem. Example 4-12 demonstrates sample output from the **show ip ospf neighbor** command to gather this information.

Example 4-12 *Verifying OSPF Neighbor State*

```
RouterX#show ip ospf neighbor
Neighbor ID      Pri   State      Dead Time    Address       Interface
172.16.31.100    0     Full/  -   00:00:31     10.140.1.1    Serial0/0/0
192.168.1.81     0     Full/  -   00:00:31     10.23.23.2    Serial0/0/1
```

To determine whether a possible Layer 1 or Layer 2 problem exists with a connection, display the status of an interface using the **show ip ospf neighbor** command. "Administratively Down" indicates that the interface is not enabled. If the status of the interface is not up/up, there will be no OSPF neighbor adjacencies. In Example 4-13, serial 0/0/1 is up/up.

Example 4-13   *Verifying Interface Status*

```
RouterX#show ip ospf interface
Serial0/0/1 is up, line protocol is up
  Internet Address 10.23.23.1/24, Area 0
  Process ID 100, Router ID 192.168.1.65, Network Type POINT_TO_POINT, Cost: 1562
```

For OSPF to create an adjacency with a directly connected neighbor router, both routers must agree on the maximum transmission unit (MTU) size. To check the MTU size of an interface, use the **show interface** command. In Example 4-14, the MTU size is 1500 bytes.

Example 4-14   *Verifying Interface MTU Size*

```
RouterX#show ip interface fa0/0
FastEthernet0/0 is up, line protocol is up
  Internet address is 10.2.2.3/24
  Broadcast address is 255.255.255.255
  Address determined by setup command
  MTU is 1500 bytes
  Helper address is not set
  Directed broadcast forwarding is disabled
  Outgoing access list is not set
  Inbound  access list is not set
```

The **network** command that you configure under the OSPF routing process indicates which router interfaces participate in OSPF and determines in which area the interface belongs. If an interface appears under the **show ip ospf interface** command, that interface is running OSPF. In Example 4-15, interfaces serial 0/0/1 and serial 0/0/0 are running OSPF.

Example 4-15   *Verifying Whether an Interface Is Running OSPF*

```
RouterX#show ip ospf interface
Serial0/0/1 is up, line protocol is up
  Internet Address 10.23.23.1/24, Area 0
  Process ID 100, Router ID 192.168.1.65, Network Type POINT_TO_POINT, Cost: 1562
  Transmit Delay is 1 sec, State POINT_TO_POINT,
  Timer intervals configured, Hello 10, Dead 40, Wait 40, Retransmit 5
    oob-resync timeout 40
    Hello due in 00:00:04
  Neighbor Count is 1, Adjacent neighbor count is 1
    Adjacent with neighbor 192.168.1.81
  Suppress hello for 0 neighbor(s)
  Simple password authentication enabled

Serial0/0/0 is up, line protocol is up
  Internet Address 10.140.1.2/24, Area 0
  Process ID 100, Router ID 192.168.1.65, Network Type POINT_TO_POINT, Cost: 1562
  Transmit Delay is 1 sec, State POINT_TO_POINT,
```

OSPF routers exchange hello packets to create neighbor adjacencies. Four items in an OSPF hello packet must match before an OSPF adjacency can occur:

- Area ID

- Hello and dead intervals

- Authentication password

- Stub area flag

To determine whether any of these hello packet options do not match, use the **debug ip ospf adj** command. The output in Example 4-16 illustrates a successful adjacency on the serial 0/0/1 interface.

Example 4-16 *Verifying OSPF Adjacencies*

```
*Feb 17 18:41:51.242: OSPF: Interface Serial0/0/1 going Up
*Feb 17 18:41:51.742: OSPF: Build router LSA for area 0, router ID 10.1.1.1, seq 0x80000013
*Feb 17 18:41:52.242: %LINEPROTO-5-UPDOWN: Line protocol on Interface Serial0/0/1,
  changed state to up
*Feb 17 18:42:01.250: OSPF: 2 Way Communication to 10.2.2.2 on Serial0/0/1, state 2WAY
*Feb 17 18:42:01.250: OSPF: Send DBD to 10.2.2.2 on Serial0/0/1 seq 0x9B6 opt 0x52 flag 0x7
  len 32
*Feb 17 18:42:01.262: OSPF: Rcv DBD from 10.2.2.2 on Serial0/0/1 seq 0x23ED opt0x52 flag 0x7
  len 32  mtu 1500 state EXSTART
*Feb 17 18:42:01.262: OSPF: NBR Negotiation Done. We are the SLAVE
*Feb 17 18:42:01.262: OSPF: Send DBD to 10.2.2.2 on Serial0/0/1 seq 0x23ED opt 0x52 flag 0x2
  len 72
*Feb 17 18:42:01.294: OSPF: Rcv DBD from 10.2.2.2 on Serial0/0/1 seq 0x23EE opt0x52 flag 0x3
  len 72  mtu 1500 state EXCHANGE
*Feb 17 18:42:01.294: OSPF: Send DBD to 10.2.2.2 on Serial0/0/1 seq 0x23EE opt 0x52 flag 0x0
  len 32
*Feb 17 18:42:01.294: OSPF: Database request to 10.2.2.2
*Feb 17 18:42:01.294: OSPF: sent LS REQ packet to 192.168.1.102, length 12
*Feb 17 18:42:01.314: OSPF: Rcv DBD from 10.2.2.2 on Serial0/0/1 seq 0x23EF opt0x52 flag 0x1
  len 32  mtu 1500 state EXCHANGE
*Feb 17 18:42:01.314: OSPF: Exchange Done with 10.2.2.2 on Serial0/0/1
*Feb 17 18:42:01.314: OSPF: Send DBD to 10.2.2.2 on Serial0/0/1 seq 0x23EF opt 0x52 flag 0x0
  len 32
*Feb 17 18:42:01.326: OSPF: Synchronized with 10.2.2.2 on Serial0/0/1, state FULL
*Feb 17 18:42:01.330: %OSPF-5-ADJCHG: Process 10, Nbr 10.2.2.2 on Serial0/0/1
  from LOADING to FULL, Loading Done
*Feb 17 18:42:01.830: OSPF: Build router LSA for area 0, router ID 10.1.1.1, seq 0x80000014
```

Troubleshooting OSPF Routing Tables

After you have verified that the adjacencies are correct, the next step is to troubleshoot/verify the routing tables. Figure 4-10 shows the procedures for verifying the routing tables.

Figure 4-10 *Troubleshooting OSPF Routing Tables*

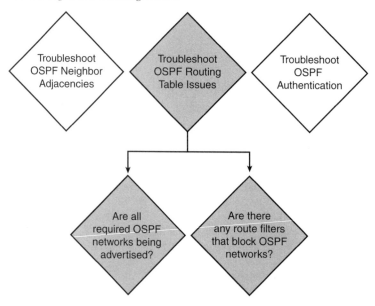

An OSPF route found in the routing table can have a variety of different codes:

- **O:** OSPF intra-area, within the same area, route from a router within the same OSPF area

- **O IA:** OSPF inter-area, from another area in the OSPF network, route from a router in a different OSPF area

- **O E1 or E2:** An external OSPF route from another autonomous system

If you have a single OSPF area, you should not see O IA routes in the routing table. Example 4-17 has both an O IA and an O E2 route.

Example 4-17 *Determining OSPF Route Types*

```
RouterX#show ip route
Codes: C - connected, S - static, R - RIP, M - mobile, B - BGP
       D - EIGRP, EX - EIGRP external, O - OSPF, IA - OSPF inter area
       N1 - OSPF NSSA external type 1, N2 - OSPF NSSA external type 2
       E1 - OSPF external type 1, E2 - OSPF external type 2
       ia - IS-IS inter area, * - candidate default,
         o - ODR, P - periodic downloaded static route
```

Example 4-17 *Determining OSPF Route Types (Continued)*

```
Gateway of last resort is not set
     172.16.0.0/32 is subnetted, 1 subnets
O       172.16.31.100 [110/1563] via 10.140.1.1, 00:03:15, Serial0/0/0
     10.0.0.0/24 is subnetted, 5 subnets
C       10.2.2.0 is directly connected, FastEthernet0/0
O IA      10.1.1.0 [110/1563] via 10.140.1.1, 00:03:15, Serial0/0/0
O       10.140.2.0 [110/3124] via 10.140.1.1, 00:03:15, Serial0/0/0
                   [110/3124] via 10.23.23.2, 00:03:15, Serial0/0/1
     192.168.1.0/24 is variably subnetted, 2 subnets, 2 masks
C       192.168.1.64/28 is directly connected, Loopback0
E2   192.168.1.81/32 [110/1563] via 10.23.23.2, 00:03:17, Serial0/0/1
```

The **network** command that you configure under the OSPF routing process also indicates which networks OSPF advertises.

The **show ip protocols** command indicates whether any route filters have been implemented, which can affect which routes are seen in the routing table. The command, as shown in Example 4-18, also displays the networks that have been configured to be advertised to other OSPF routers.

Example 4-18 *Determining Whether Route Filters Have Been Implemented*

```
RouterX#show ip protocols
Routing Protocol is "ospf 100"
  Outgoing update filter list for all interfaces is not set
  Incoming update filter list for all interfaces is not set
  Router ID 192.168.1.65
  Number of areas in this router is 1. 1 normal 0 stub 0 nssa
  Maximum path: 4
  Routing for Networks:
    10.2.2.3 0.0.0.0 area 0
    10.23.23.1 0.0.0.0 area 0
    10.140.1.2 0.0.0.0 area 0
    192.168.1.65 0.0.0.0 area 0
 Reference bandwidth unit is 100 mbps
  Routing Information Sources:
    Gateway         Distance      Last Update
    192.168.1.81         110      00:04:52
    172.16.31.100        110      00:04:52
  Distance: (default is 110)
```

Troubleshooting Plaintext Password Authentication

If you are using OSPF password authentication, you must also be prepared to troubleshoot any authentication problems that may occur during the adjacency process.

You can use the **debug ip ospf adj** command to display OSPF adjacency-related events. This command is useful when troubleshooting authentication.

If plaintext password authentication is configured on the Router X serial 0/0/1 interface but no authentication is configured on the Router Y serial 0/0/1 interface, the routers will not be able to form an adjacency over that link. The output of the **debug ip ospf adj** command shown in Example 4-19 illustrates that the routers report a mismatch in authentication type; no OSPF packets will be sent between the neighbors.

Example 4-19 *Determining Whether an Authentication Mismatch Exists*

```
RouterX#debug ip ospf adj
*Feb 17 18:51:31.242: OSPF: Rcv pkt from 192.168.1.102, Serial0/0/1 :
  Mismatch Authentication type. Input packet specified type 0, we use type 1

RouterY#debug ip ospf adj
*Feb 17 18:50:43.046: OSPF: Rcv pkt from 192.168.1.101, Serial0/0/1 :
  Mismatch Authentication type. Input packet specified type 1, we use type 0
```

NOTE   The different types of authentication have these codes:

■ Null is type 0

■ Simple password is type 1

■ MD5 is type 2

If plaintext password authentication is configured on the Router X serial 0/0/1 interface and on the router Y serial 0/0/1 interface, but the interfaces are configured with different passwords, the routers will not be able to form an adjacency over that link.

The output of the **debug ip ospf adj** command shown in Example 4-20 illustrates that the routers report a mismatch in authentication key; no OSPF packets will be sent between the neighbors.

Example 4-20 **debug ip ospf adj** *Command Output Confirms an Authentication Mismatch*

```
RouterX#debug ip osp adj
*Feb 17 18:54:01.238: OSPF: Rcv pkt from 192.168.1.102, Serial0/0/1 :
  Mismatch Authentication Key - Clear Text

RouterY#debug ip ospf adj
*Feb 17 18:53:13.050: OSPF: Rcv pkt from 192.168.1.101, Serial0/0/1 :
  Mismatch Authentication Key - Clear Text
```

Summary of Troubleshooting OSPF

Troubleshooting OSPF is an important skill. Most OSPF problems are related to configuration and will most likely show themselves when the routers attempt to form OSPF adjacencies.

The following summarizes the key points that were discussed in this section:

- Troubleshooting OSPF involves looking at neighbor adjacencies, routing tables, and authentication issues.

- Use the **show ip interface** command to verify the MTU of an OSPF interface.

- Use the **show ip ospf interface** command to help troubleshoot whether OSPF is enabled on an interface.

- Use the **debug ip ospf adj** command to troubleshoot OSPF authentication.

Chapter Summary

The Open Shortest Path First (OSPF) protocol is one of the most commonly used Interior Gateway Protocols (IGP) in IP networking. OSPF is a complex, open-standard protocol that is composed of several protocol handshakes, database advertisements, and packet types.

The following summarizes the key points that were discussed in this chapter:

- The routing algorithm of OSPF maintains a complex database of topology information, which routers use to maintain full knowledge of distant routers.

- OSPF is a classless, link-state routing protocol that is widely deployed in many networks.

- OSPF load-balances across four equal metric paths by default on Cisco routers.

- OSPF supports plaintext and MD5 authentication.

- There are several components to troubleshooting OSPF, including OSPF neighbor adjacencies and routing tables.

Review Questions

Use the questions here to review what you learned in this chapter. The correct answers and solutions are found in the appendix, "Answers to Chapter Review Questions."

1. What are two characteristics of OSPF? (Choose two.)

   a. OSPF uses a two-layer hierarchy.

   b. OSPF is a proprietary routing protocol.

    c. OSPF is an open standard.

    d. OSPF is similar to the RIP routing protocol.

    e. OSPF is a distance vector routing protocol.

2. OSPF routes packets within a single _____.

    a. Area

    b. Network

    c. Segment

    d. Autonomous system

3. With OSPF, each router builds its SPF tree using the same link-state information, but each will have a separate _____ of the topology.

    a. State

    b. View

    c. Version

    d. Configuration

4. Which component of the SPF algorithm is inversely proportional to bandwidth?

    a. Link cost

    b. Root cost

    c. Link state

    d. Hop count

5. Which command correctly starts an OSPF routing process using process ID 191?

    a. Router(config)#**router ospf 191**

    b. Router(config)#**network ospf 191**

    c. Router(config-router)#**network ospf 191**

    d. Router(config-router)#**router ospf process-id 191**

6. What is the purpose of the **show ip ospf interface** command?

    a. To display OSPF-related interface information

    b. To display general information about OSPF routing processes

    c. To display OSPF neighbor information on a per-interface basis

    d. To display OSPF neighbor information on a per-interface type basis

7. Which command output includes information about the length of the OSPF packet?

   a. **debug ip ospf events**

   b. **debug ip ospf packet**

   c. **debug ip ospf packet size**

   d. **debug ip ospf mpls traffic-eng advertisements**

8. Which type of authentication does aut:1 indicate in the output from the **debug ip ospf packet** command?

   a. No authentication

   b. Simple password

   c. MD5

   d. 3DES

9. Which OSPF neighbor state indicates that two neighbors have exchanged routes?

   a. Init

   b. Two-way

   c. Loading

   d. Full

This chapter includes the following sections:

- Chapter Objectives

- Implementing EIGRP

- Troubleshooting EIGRP

- Chapter Summary

- Review Questions

CHAPTER 5

Implementing EIGRP

This chapter discusses the features of Enhanced Interior Gateway Routing Protocol (EIGRP), a Cisco routing protocol that is designed to address the shortcomings of both distance vector and link-state routing protocols. The text expands on the underlying technologies in EIGRP, including the path selection process.

Chapter Objectives

Upon completing this chapter, you will be able to configure, verify, and troubleshoot EIGRP. This ability includes being able to meet these objectives:

- Describe the operation and configuration of EIGRP, including load balancing and authentication

- Identify an approach for troubleshooting common EIGRP problems and offer solutions

Implementing EIGRP

EIGRP is an advanced distance vector routing protocol developed by Cisco. EIGRP is suited for many different topologies and media. In a well-designed network, EIGRP scales well and provides extremely quick convergence times with minimal overhead. EIGRP is a popular choice for a routing protocol on Cisco devices.

Introducing EIGRP

EIGRP is a Cisco-proprietary routing protocol that combines the advantages of link-state and distance vector routing protocols. EIGRP is an advanced distance vector or hybrid routing protocol that includes the following features:

- **Rapid convergence:** EIGRP uses the Diffusing Update Algorithm (DUAL) to achieve rapid convergence. A router that uses EIGRP stores all available backup routes for destinations so that it can quickly adapt to alternate routes. If no appropriate route or backup route exists in the local routing table, EIGRP queries its neighbors to discover an alternate route.

- **Reduced bandwidth usage:** EIGRP does not make periodic updates. Instead, it sends partial updates when the path or the metric changes for that route. When path information changes, DUAL sends an update about only that link rather than about the entire table.

- **Multiple network layer support:** EIGRP supports AppleTalk, IP version 4 (IPv4), IP version 6 (IPv6), and Novell Internetwork Packet Exchange (IPX), which use protocol-dependent modules (PDM). PDMs are responsible for protocol requirements that are specific to the network layer.

- **Classless routing:** Because EIGRP is a classless routing protocol, it advertises a routing mask for each destination network. The routing mask feature enables EIGRP to support discontiguous subnetworks and variable-length subnet masks (VLSM).

- **Less overhead:** EIGRP uses multicast and unicast rather than broadcast. As a result, end stations are unaffected by routing updates and requests for topology information.

- **Load balancing:** EIGRP supports unequal metric load balancing, which allows administrators to better distribute traffic flow in their networks.

- **Easy summarization:** EIGRP enables administrators to create summary routes anywhere within the network rather than rely on the traditional distance vector approach of performing classful route summarization only at major network boundaries.

Each EIGRP router maintains a neighbor table. This table includes a list of directly connected EIGRP routers that have an adjacency with this router.

Each EIGRP router maintains a topology table for each routed protocol configuration. The topology table includes route entries for every destination that the router learns. EIGRP chooses the best routes to a destination from the topology table and places these routes in the routing table, as illustrated in Figure 5-1.

Figure 5-1 *EIGRP Tables*

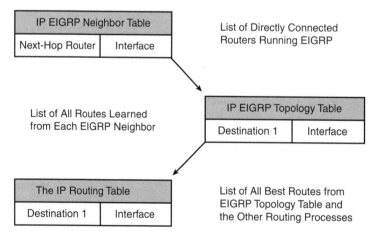

In EIGRP, the best route is called a *successor route* while a backup route is called the *feasible successor*. To determine the best route (successor) and the backup route (feasible successor) to a destination, EIGRP uses the following two parameters:

- **Advertised distance:** The EIGRP metric for an EIGRP neighbor to reach a particular network

- **Feasible distance:** The advertised distance for a particular network learned from an EIGRP neighbor plus the EIGRP metric to reach that neighbor

A router compares all feasible distances to reach a specific network and then selects the lowest feasible distance and places it in the routing table. The feasible distance for the chosen route becomes the EIGRP routing metric to reach that network in the routing table.

The EIGRP topology database contains all the routes that are known to each EIGRP neighbor. Routers A and B send their routing tables to Router C, whose table is displayed in Figure 5-2. Both Routers A and B have pathways to network 10.1.1.0/24, as well as to other networks that are not shown.

Figure 5-2 *Router C EIGRP Tables*

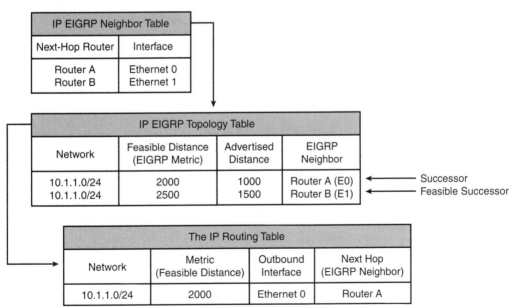

Router C has two entries to reach 10.1.1.0/24 in its topology table. The EIGRP metric for Router C to reach both Routers A and B is 1000. Add this cost (1000) to the respective advertised distance for each router, and the results represent the feasible distances that Router C must travel to reach network 10.1.1.0/24.

Router C chooses the least-cost feasible distance (2000) and installs it in the IP routing table as the best route to reach 10.1.1.0/24. The route with the least-cost feasible distance that is installed in the routing table is called the *successor route*.

Router C then chooses a backup route to the successor called a *feasible successor route*, if one exists. For a route to become a feasible successor, a next-hop router must have an advertised distance that is less than the feasible distance of the current successor route.

If the route through the successor becomes invalid, possibly because of a topology change, or if a neighbor changes the metric, DUAL checks for feasible successors to the destination route. If one is found, DUAL uses it, avoiding the need to recompute the route. If no feasible successor exists, a recomputation must occur to determine the new successor.

Configuring and Verifying EIGRP

Use the **router eigrp** and **network** commands to create an EIGRP routing process. Note that EIGRP requires an autonomous system (AS) number. The AS number does not have to be registered as is the case when routing on the Internet with the Border Gateway Protocol (BGP) routing protocol. However, all routers within an AS must use the same AS number to exchange routing information with each other. Figure 5-3 shows the EIGRP configuration of a simple network.

Figure 5-3 *EIGRP Configuration*

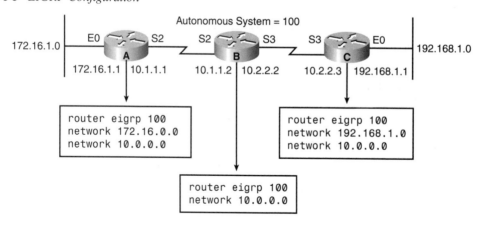

The **network** command defines a major network number to which the router is directly connected. The EIGRP routing process looks for interfaces that have an IP address that belongs to the networks that are specified with the **network** command and begins the EIGRP process on these interfaces.

Table 5-1 applies to the EIGRP configurations on Router A in the EIGRP configuration example.

Table 5-1   *EIGRP Command Example*

Command	Description
router eigrp 100	Enables the EIGRP routing process for AS 100
network 172.16.0.0	Associates network 172.16.0.0 with the EIGRP routing process
network 10.0.0.0	Associates network 10.0.0.0 with the EIGRP routing process

EIGRP sends updates out of the interfaces in networks 10.0.0.0 and 172.16.0.0. The updates include information about networks 10.0.0.0 and 172.16.0.0 and any other networks that EIGRP learns.

EIGRP automatically summarizes routes at the classful boundary. In some cases, you might not want automatic summarization to occur. For example, if you have discontiguous networks, you need to disable automatic summarization to minimize router confusion. Figure 5-4 shows an example of how this summarization can cause advertisements for the 172.16.0.0 network to be sent from both Router A and Router B to Router C.

Figure 5-4   *Autosummarization Causing Discontinuous Subnets*

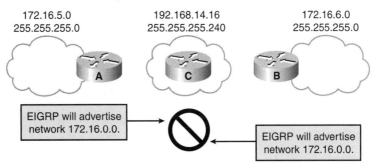

To disable automatic summarization, use the **no auto-summary** command in the EIGRP router configuration mode. When this command is used, both Router A and Router B will advertise the route specific to the subnet of a given interface, as shown in Figure 5-5.

Figure 5-5 *Disabling Autosummarization Corrects Problem*

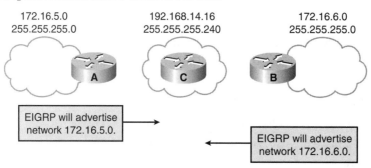

After you enable EIGRP, various commands can be used to display information about how the protocol is operating. The **show ip route eigrp** command displays the current EIGRP entries in the routing table.

The **show ip protocols** command displays the parameters and current state of the active routing protocol process. This command shows the EIGRP AS number. It also displays filtering and redistribution numbers and neighbor and distance information. This also shows the networks that are currently being advertised on the router by the protocol.

Use the **show ip eigrp interfaces** [*type number*] [*as-number*] command to determine on which interfaces EIGRP is active, and to learn information about EIGRP that relates to those interfaces. If you specify an interface by using the *type number* option, only that interface is displayed. Otherwise, all interfaces on which EIGRP is running are displayed. If you specify an AS using the *as-number* option, only the routing process for the specified AS is displayed. Otherwise, all EIGRP processes are displayed. Example 5-1 shows the output of the **show ip eigrp interfaces** command.

Example 5-1 *Determining Router Interface EIGRP Status/Information*

```
RouterX# show ip eigrp interfaces
IP EIGRP interfaces for process 109

                  Xmit Queue    Mean   Pacing Time   Multicast    Pending
Interface  Peers  Un/Reliable   SRTT   Un/Reliable   Flow Timer   Routes
Di0        0      0/0           0      11/434        0            0
Et0        1      0/0           337    0/10          0            0
SE0:1.16   1      0/0           10     1/63          103          0
Tu0        1      0/0           330    0/16          0            0
```

Table 5-2 describes the significant fields generated by the **show ip eigrp interfaces** output.

Table 5-2 **show ip eigrp interfaces** *Output*

Field	Description
Interface	Interface over which EIGRP is configured
Peers	Number of directly connected EIGRP neighbors on the interface
Xmit Queue Un/Reliable	Number of packets remaining in the Unreliable and Reliable queues
Mean SRTT	Average smoothed round-trip time (SRTT) interval (in milliseconds) for all neighbors on the interface
Pacing Time Un/Reliable	Number of milliseconds to wait after transmitting unreliable and reliable packets
Multicast Flow Timer	Number of milliseconds to wait for acknowledgment of a multicast packet by all neighbors before transmitting the next multicast packet
Pending Routes	Number of routes in the packets in the transmit queue waiting to be sent

Use the **show ip eigrp neighbors** command to display the neighbors that were discovered by EIGRP and to determine when neighbors become active and inactive, as demonstrated in Example 5-2. This command is also useful for debugging certain types of transport problems.

Example 5-2 *Displaying Discovered Active/Inactive EIGRP Neighbors*

```
RouterX# show ip eigrp neighbors
IP-EIGRP Neighbors for process 77
Address          Interface    Holdtime     Uptime    Q      Seq   SRTT   RTO
                              (secs)       (h:m:s)   Count  Num   (ms)   (ms)
172.16.81.28     Ethernet1    13           0:00:41   0      11    4      20
172.16.80.28     Ethernet0    14           0:02:01   0      10    12     24
172.16.80.31     Ethernet0    12           0:02:02   0      4     5      20
```

Table 5-3 describes the significant fields for the **show ip eigrp neighbors** command.

Table 5-3 **show ip eigrp neighbors** *Output*

Field	Description
process 77	AS number that is specified with the **router** command.
Address	IP address of the EIGRP peer.
Interface	Interface on which the router is receiving hello packets from the peer.
Holdtime	Length of time (in seconds) that Cisco IOS Software waits to hear from the peer before declaring it down. If the peer is using the default hold time, this number is less than 15. If the peer configures a nondefault hold time, the nondefault hold time is displayed. The hold time would be less than 180 on a sub-T1 multipoint interface.
Uptime	Elapsed time (in hours:minutes:seconds) since the local router first heard from this neighbor.
Q Count	Number of EIGRP packets (update, query, and reply) that the software is waiting to send.
Seq Num	Sequence number of the last update, query, or reply packet that was received from this neighbor.
SRTT	Smooth round-trip time (SRTT). The number of milliseconds that is required for an EIGRP packet to be sent to this neighbor and for the local router to receive an acknowledgment of that packet.
RTO	Retransmission timeout (RTO) (in milliseconds). This is the amount of time the software waits before resending a packet from the retransmission queue to a neighbor.

The **show ip eigrp topology** command displays the EIGRP topology table, the active or passive state of routes, the number of successors, and the feasible distance to the destination, as demonstrated in Example 5-3.

Example 5-3 *Displaying EIGRP Topology Information*

```
RouterX# show ip eigrp topology
IP-EIGRP Topology Table for process 77
Codes: P - Passive, A - Active, U - Update, Q - Query, R - Reply,
       r - Reply status
P 172.16.90.0 255.255.255.0, 2 successors, FD is 46251776
         via 172.16.80.28 (46251776/46226176), Ethernet0
         via 172.16.81.28 (46251776/46226176), Ethernet1
         via 172.16.80.31 (46277376/46251776), Serial0
P 172.16.81.0 255.255.255.0, 2 successors, FD is 307200
         via Connected, Ethernet1
         via 172.16.81.28 (307200/281600), Ethernet1
         via 172.16.80.28 (307200/281600), Ethernet0
         via 172.16.80.31 (332800/307200), Serial0
```

Table 5-4 describes the significant fields for the **show ip eigrp topology** command output.

Table 5-4 **show ip eigrp topology** *Output*

Field	Description
Codes	The state of this topology table entry. Passive and Active refer to the EIGRP state with respect to this destination; Update, Query, and Reply refer to the type of packet that is being sent.
P - Passive	Indicates that no EIGRP computations are being performed for this destination.
A - Active	Indicates that EIGRP computations are being performed for this destination.
U - Update	Indicates that an update packet was sent to this destination.
Q - Query	Indicates that a query packet was sent to this destination.
R - Reply	Indicates that a reply packet was sent to this destination.
r - Reply status	A flag that is set after the software has sent a query and is waiting for a reply.
172.16.90.0	Destination IP network number.
255.255.255.0	Destination subnet mask.
successors	Number of successors. This number corresponds to the number of next hops in the IP routing table. If "successors" is capitalized, the route or next hop is in a transition state.
FD	Feasible distance. The feasible distance is the best metric to reach the destination or the best metric that was known when the route went active. This value is used in the feasibility condition check. If the reported distance of the router (the metric after the slash) is less than the feasible distance, the feasibility condition is met and that path is a feasible successor. After the software determines it has a feasible successor, it does not need to send a query for that destination.
replies	The number of replies that are still outstanding (have not been received) with respect to this destination. This information appears only when the destination is in active state.
state	The exact EIGRP state that this destination is in. It can be the number 0, 1, 2, or 3. This information appears only when the destination is in the active state.
via	The IP address of the peer that told the software about this destination. The first n of these entries, where n is the number of successors, are the current successors. The remaining entries on the list are feasible successors.
(46251776/ 46226176)	The first number is the EIGRP metric that represents the cost to the destination. The second number is the EIGRP metric that this peer advertised.
Ethernet0	The interface from which this information was learned.
Serial0	The interface from which this information was learned.

The **show ip eigrp traffic** command displays the number of packets sent and received, as demonstrated in Example 5-4.

Example 5-4 *Displaying the Number of EIGRP Sent/Received Packets*

```
RouterX# show ip eigrp traffic
IP-EIGRP Traffic Statistics for process 77
  Hellos sent/received: 218/205
  Updates sent/received: 7/23
  Queries sent/received: 2/0
  Replies sent/received: 0/2
  Acks sent/received: 21/14
```

Table 5-5 describes the fields that might be shown in the display.

Table 5-5 **show ip eigrp traffic** *Output*

Field	Description
process 77	The AS number that is specified in the **router** command
Hellos sent/received	The number of hello packets that were sent and received
Updates sent/received	The number of update packets that were sent and received
Queries sent/received	The number of query packets that were sent and received
Replies sent/received	The number of reply packets that were sent and received
Acks sent/received	The number of acknowledgment packets that were sent and received

The **debug ip eigrp** privileged EXEC command helps you analyze the EIGRP packets that an interface sends and receives, as demonstrated in Example 5-5. Because the **debug ip eigrp** command generates a substantial amount of output, use it only when traffic on the network is light.

Example 5-5 *Analyzing Sent/Received EIGRP Packets*

```
RouterX# debug ip eigrp
IP-EIGRP: Processing incoming UPDATE packet
IP-EIGRP: Ext 192.168.3.0 255.255.255.0 M 386560 - 256000 130560 SM 360960 -
256000 104960
IP-EIGRP: Ext 192.168.0.0 255.255.255.0 M 386560 - 256000 130560 SM 360960 -
256000 104960
IP-EIGRP: Ext 192.168.3.0 255.255.255.0 M 386560 - 256000 130560 SM 360960 -
256000 104960
IP-EIGRP: 172.69.43.0 255.255.255.0, - do advertise out Ethernet0/1
IP-EIGRP: Ext 172.69.43.0 255.255.255.0 metric 371200 - 256000 115200
IP-EIGRP: 192.135.246.0 255.255.255.0, - do advertise out Ethernet0/1
IP-EIGRP: Ext 192.135.246.0 255.255.255.0 metric 46310656 - 45714176 596480
IP-EIGRP: 172.69.40.0 255.255.255.0, - do advertise out Ethernet0/1
```

Example 5-5 *Analyzing Sent/Received EIGRP Packets (Continued)*

```
IP-EIGRP: Ext 172.69.40.0 255.255.255.0 metric 2272256 - 1657856 614400
IP-EIGRP: 192.135.245.0 255.255.255.0, - do advertise out Ethernet0/1
IP-EIGRP: Ext 192.135.245.0 255.255.255.0 metric 40622080 - 40000000 622080
IP-EIGRP: 192.135.244.0 255.255.255.0, - do advertise out Ethernet0/1
```

Table 5-6 describes the fields in the sample output from the **debug ip eigrp** command.

Table 5-6 **debug ip eigrp** *Output*

Field	Description
IP-EIGRP	Indicates that this is an IP EIGRP packet.
Ext	Indicates that the following address is an external destination rather than an internal destination, which would be labeled as Int.
do not advertise out	Indicates interfaces out which EIGRP will not advertise the given route. This configuration prevents routing loops (split horizon).
M	Displays the computed metric, which includes the sent metric (SM) and the cost between this router and the neighbor. The first number is the composite metric. The next two numbers are the inverse bandwidth and the delay, respectively.
SM	Displays the metric as reported by the neighbor.

Load Balancing with EIGRP

Typically, networks are configured with multiple paths to a remote network. When these paths are equal or nearly equal, it makes sense to utilize all the available paths. Unlike Layer 2 forwarding, Layer 3 forwarding has the capability to load-balance between multiple paths. That is, the router can send frames out multiple interfaces to reduce the amount of traffic sent to a single network connection. The key to this feature is that the network paths must be of equal cost (or nearly equal for some protocols like EIGRP). EIGRP uses a metric to compute the costs to a given network.

EIGRP Metric

The EIGRP metric can be based on several criteria, but EIGRP uses only two of these criteria by default:

- **Bandwidth:** The smallest bandwidth between source and destination

- **Delay:** The cumulative interface delay in microseconds along the path

The following criteria can be used but are not recommended because they typically result in frequent recalculation of the topology table:

- **Reliability:** This value represents the worst reliability between the source and destination, based on keepalives.

- **Load:** This value represents the worst load on a link between the source and destination, computed based on the packet rate and the configured bandwidth of the interface.

> **NOTE** Although the maximum transmission unit (MTU) is exchanged in EIGRP packets between neighbor routers, MTU is not factored into the EIGRP metric calculation.=

Load Balancing Across Equal Paths

Equal-cost load balancing is the capability of a router to distribute traffic over all its network ports that are the same metric from the destination address. Load balancing increases the use of network segments and increases effective network bandwidth.

For IP, Cisco IOS Software applies load balancing across up to four equal-cost paths by default. With the **maximum-paths** *maximum-path* router configuration command, up to 16 equal-cost routes can be kept in the routing table. If you set the *maximum-path* to 1, you disable load balancing. When a packet is process switched, load balancing over equal-cost paths occurs on a per-packet basis. When packets are fast switched, load balancing over equal-cost paths occurs on a per-destination basis.

> **NOTE** If you test load balancing, do not ping to or from routers that use fast-switching interfaces because these router-generated packets are process switched rather than fast switched and might produce confusing results.

Configuring Load Balancing Across Unequal-Cost Paths

EIGRP can also balance traffic across multiple routes that have different metrics, which is called unequal-cost load balancing. The degree to which EIGRP performs load balancing is controlled with the **variance** command.

The *multiplier* parameter for the **variance** command is a value from 1 to 128, used for load balancing. The default is 1, which indicates that only equal-cost load balancing is being performed. The multiplier defines the range of metric values that are accepted for load balancing by the EIGRP process.

> **NOTE** By default, traffic is distributed proportionately among the links with unequal costs, with respect to the metric.

Example: Variance

In Figure 5-6, a variance of 2 is configured, and the range of the metric values, which are the feasible distances for Router E to get to network 172.16.0.0, is 20 to 45. This range of values determines the feasibility of a potential route.

Figure 5-6 *Variance Example*

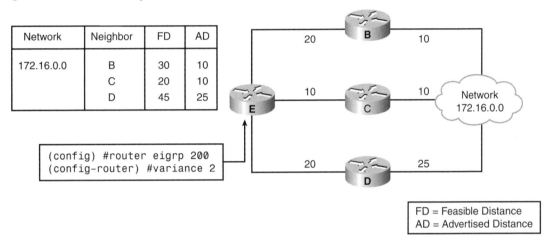

A route is feasible if the next router in the path is closer to the destination than to the current router and if the metric of the alternate path is within the variance. Load balancing can use only feasible paths, and the routing table includes only these paths. The two feasibility conditions are as follows:

■ The local best metric, which is the current feasible distance, must be greater than the best metric (the advertised distance) that is learned from the next router. In other words, the next router in the path must be closer to the destination than to the current router; this criterion prevents routing loops.

■ The metric of the alternate path must be less than the variance multiplied by the local best metric (the current feasible distance).

If both of these conditions are met, the route is determined to be feasible and can be added to the routing table.

In Figure 5-6, three paths to network 172.16.0.0 exist with the following metrics:

■ **Path 1:** 30 (through B)

■ **Path 2:** 20 (through C)

■ **Path 3:** 45 (through D)

By default, the router places only path 2 (through C) in the routing table because it is the least-cost path. To load-balance over paths 1 and 2, use a variance of 2 because 20 * 2 = 40, which is greater than the metric through path 1.

In Figure 5-6, Router E uses Router C as the successor because it has the lowest feasible distance (20). With the **variance 2** command applied to Router E, the path through Router B meets the criteria for load balancing. In this case, the feasible distance through Router B is less than twice the feasible distance for the successor (Router C).

Router D is not considered for load balancing with this variance because the feasible distance through Router D is greater than twice the feasible distance for the successor (Router C). In the example, however, Router D would never be a feasible successor no matter what the variance is. This decision is because the advertised distance of Router D is 25, which is greater than the Router E feasible distance of 20; therefore, to avoid a potential routing loop, Router D is not considered a feasible successor.

EIGRP Authentication

You can configure EIGRP neighbor authentication, also known as neighbor router authentication or route authentication, such that routers can participate in routing based on predefined passwords. By default, no authentication is used for EIGRP packets. EIGRP can be configured to use Message Digest Algorithm 5 (MD5) authentication.

When you configure neighbor authentication on a router, the router authenticates the source of each routing update packet that it receives. For EIGRP MD5 authentication, you must configure an authenticating key and a key ID on both the sending and the receiving router. The key is sometimes referred to as a password.

The MD5 keyed digest in each EIGRP packet prevents the introduction of unauthorized or false routing messages from unapproved sources.

Each key has its own key ID, which the router stores locally. The combination of the key ID and the interface that is associated with the message uniquely identifies the MD5 authentication key in use.

EIGRP enables you to manage keys by using key chains. Each key definition within the key chain can specify a time interval for which that key is activated (its lifetime). Then, during the lifetime of a given key, routing update packets are sent with this activated key. Only one authentication packet is sent, regardless of how many valid keys exist. The software examines the key numbers in order from lowest to highest, and it uses the first valid key that it encounters.

Keys cannot be used during time periods for which they are not activated. Therefore, it is recommended that for a given key chain, key activation times overlap to avoid any period of time for which no key is activated. If a time exists during which no key is activated, neighbor authentication cannot occur, and therefore, routing updates fail.

> **NOTE**   The routers must know the correct time to rotate through keys in synchronization with the other participating routers. This ensures that all the routers are using the same key at the same moment.

Creating a Key Chain

Perform the following steps to create a key chain:

Step 1   Enter the **key chain** command to enter the configuration mode for the key chain. The value provided for the *name-of-chain* parameter for the **key chain** command indicates the name of the authentication key chain from which a key is to be obtained.

Step 2   Use the **key** command to identify a key ID to use, and enter configuration mode for that key. The value provided for the *key-id* parameter of the **key** command indicates the ID number of an authentication key on a key chain. The range of keys is from 0 to 2147483647. The key ID numbers need not be consecutive.

Step 3   Use the **key-string** command to identify the key string (password) for this key. The value provided for the *text* parameter of the **key-string** command indicates the authentication string that is to be used to authenticate sent and received EIGRP packets. The string can contain from 1 to 80 uppercase and lowercase alphanumeric characters. The first character cannot be a number, and the string is case sensitive.

Step 4   Optionally, use **accept-lifetime** to specify the time during which this key is accepted for use on received packets. If you do not enter an **accept-lifetime** command, the time is infinite. Table 5-7 describes the **accept-lifetime** command parameters.

Table 5-7 **accept-lifetime** *Parameters*

Parameter	Description
start-time	Beginning time that the key that is specified by the **key** command is valid for use on received packets. The syntax can be either of the following: hh:mm:ss month date year hh:mm:ss date month year where *hh*: Hours *mm*: Minutes *ss*: Seconds *month*: First three letters of the name of the month *date*: Date (1–31) *year*: Year (four digits) The default start time. The earliest acceptable date is January 1, 1993.
infinite	The key is valid for use on received packets from the *start-time* value on, with no end time.
end-time	The key is valid for use on received packets from the *start-time* value until the *end-time* value. The syntax is the same as that for the *start-time* value. The *end-time* value must be after the *start-time* value. The default end time is infinite.
seconds	Length of time (in seconds) that the key is valid for use on received packets. The range is from 1 to 2147483646.

Step 5   Optionally, specify the time during which this key can be used for sending packets using the **send-lifetime** command. If you do not enter a **send-lifetime** command, the time is infinite. Table 5-8 describes the **send-lifetime** command parameters.

Table 5-8 **send-lifetime** *Parameters*

Parameter	Description
start-time	Beginning time that the key specified by the **key** command is valid to be used for sending packets. The syntax can be either of the following: *hh:mm:ss month date year* *hh:mm:ss date month year* where *hh*: Hours *mm*: Minutes *ss*: Seconds *month*: First three letters of the name of the month *date*: Date (1–31) *year*: Year (four digits) The default start time and the earliest acceptable date is January 1, 1993.
infinite	The key is valid to be used for sending packets from the *start-time* value on.
end-time	The key is valid to be used for sending packets from the *start-time* value until the *end-time* value. The syntax is the same as that for the *start-time* value. The *end-time* value must be after the *start-time* value. The default end time is infinite.
seconds	Length of time (in seconds) that the key is valid to be used for sending packets. The range is from 1 to 2147483646.

NOTE   If the **service password-encryption** command is not used when you are implementing EIGRP authentication, the key string is stored as plain text in the router configuration. If you configure the **service password-encryption** command, the key string is stored and displayed in an encrypted form; when it is displayed, an encryption type of 7 is specified before the encrypted key string.

Configuring MD5 Authentication for EIGRP

To configure MD5 authentication for EIGRP, complete the following steps:

Step 1   Enter configuration mode for the interface on which you want to enable authentication.

Step 2   Use the **ip authentication mode eigrp** *autonomous-system* **md5** command to specify that MD5 authentication is to be used for EIGRP packets. The value provided for the *autonomous-system* parameter of the **ip authentication mode eigrp md5** command indicates the EIGRP AS number in which authentication is to be used.

Step 3   Use the **ip authentication key-chain eigrp** *autonomous-system name-of-chain* command to specify which key chain to use for the authentication of EIGRP packets. Table 5-9 describes the parameters for this command.

Table 5-9   **ip authentication key-chain eigrp** *Parameters*

Parameter	Description
autonomous-system	The EIGRP AS number in which authentication is to be used
name-of-chain	The name of the authentication key chain from which a key is to be obtained

Example: MD5 Authentication Configuration

Figure 5-7 shows an example network used for the configuration of EIGRP MD5 authentication for Router X in Example 5-6.

Figure 5-7   *Network Topology for EIGRP MD5 Configuration Example*

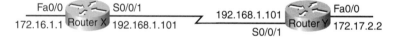

```
Fa0/0          S0/0/1                                    Fa0/0
172.16.1.1  Router X  192.168.1.101    192.168.1.101  Router Y  172.17.2.2
                                       S0/0/1
```

Example 5-6   *Configuring EIGRP MD5 Authentication on Router X*

```
RouterX
<output omitted>
key chain RouterXchain
 key 1
  key-string firstkey
  accept-lifetime 04:00:00 Jan 1 2006 infinite
  send-lifetime 04:00:00 Jan 1 2006 04:01:00 Jan 1 2006
 key 2
  key-string secondkey
  accept-lifetime 04:00:00 Jan 1 2006 infinite
```

Example 5-6   *Configuring EIGRP MD5 Authentication on Router X (Continued)*

```
  send-lifetime 04:00:00 Jan 1 2006 infinite
<output omitted>
!
interface Serial0/0/1
 bandwidth 64
 ip address 192.168.1.101 255.255.255.224
 ip authentication mode eigrp 100 md5
 ip authentication key-chain eigrp 100 RouterXchain
```

MD5 authentication is configured on the Serial 0/0/1 interface with the **ip authentication mode eigrp 100 md5** command. The **ip authentication key-chain eigrp 100 RouterXchain** command specifies that the key chain RouterXchain is to be used for EIGRP AS 100.

The **key chain RouterXchain** command enters configuration mode for the RouterXchain key chain. Two keys are defined. Key 1 is set to "first key" with the **key-string firstkey** command. This key is acceptable for use on packets that are received by Router X from 4:00 a.m. (0400) on January 1, 2006, onward, as specified in the **accept-lifetime 04:00:00 Jan 1 2006 infinite** command. However, the **send-lifetime 04:00:00 Jan 1 2006 04:01:00 Jan 1 2006** command specifies that this key is valid for use only when packets are sent for one minute on January 1, 2006; afterward, it is no longer valid for use in sending packets.

Key 2 is set to "second key" with the **key-string secondkey** command. This key is acceptable for use on packets that are received by Router X from 4:00 a.m. (0400) on January 1, 2006, onward, as specified in the **accept-lifetime 04:00:00 Jan 1 2006 infinite** command. This key can also be used when packets are sent from 4:00 a.m. (0400) on January 1, 2006, onward, as specified in the **send-lifetime 04:00:00 Jan 1 2006 infinite** command.

Therefore, Router X accepts and attempts to verify the MD5 digest of any EIGRP packets with a key ID equal to 1. Router X will also accept a packet with a key ID equal to 2. All other MD5 packets are dropped. Router X sends all EIGRP packets using key 2 because key 1 is no longer valid for use in sending packets.

Example 5-7 shows the configuration of EIGRP MD5 authentication for Router Y in Figure 5-7.

Example 5-7   *Configuring EIGRP MD5 Authentication on Router Y*

```
RouterY
<output omitted>
key chain RouterYchain
 key 1
  key-string firstkey
  accept-lifetime 04:00:00 Jan 1 2006 infinite
  send-lifetime 04:00:00 Jan 1 2006 infinite
```

continues

Example 5-7 *Configuring EIGRP MD5 Authentication on Router Y (Continued)*

```
 key 2
  key-string secondkey
  accept-lifetime 04:00:00 Jan 1 2006 infinite
  send-lifetime 04:00:00 Jan 1 2006 infinite
<output omitted>
!
interface Serial0/0/1
 bandwidth 64
 ip address 192.168.1.102 255.255.255.224
 ip authentication mode eigrp 100 md5
 ip authentication key-chain eigrp 100 RouterYchain
```

MD5 authentication is configured on the Serial 0/0/1 interface with the **ip authentication mode eigrp 100 md5** command. The **ip authentication key-chain eigrp 100 RouterYchain** command specifies that the key chain RouterYchain is to be used for EIGRP AS 100.

The **key chain RouterYchain** command enters configuration mode for the RouterYchain key chain. Two keys are defined. Key 1 is set to "first key" with the **key-string firstkey** command. This key is acceptable for use on packets that are received by Router Y from 4:00 a.m. (0400) on January 1, 2006, onward, as specified in the **accept-lifetime 04:00:00 Jan 1 2006 infinite** command. This key can also be used when packets are sent from 4:00 a.m. (0400) on January 1, 2006, onward, as specified in the **send-lifetime 04:00:00 Jan 1 2006 infinite** command.

Key 2 is set to "second key" with the **key-string secondkey** command. This key is acceptable for use on packets that are received by Router Y from 4:00 a.m. (0400) on January 1, 2006, onward, as specified in the **accept-lifetime 04:00:00 Jan 1 2006 infinite** command. This key can also be used when packets are sent from 4:00 a.m. (0400) on January 1, 2006, onward, as specified in the **send-lifetime 04:00:00 Jan 1 2006 infinite** command.

Therefore, Router Y accepts and attempts to verify the MD5 digest of any EIGRP packets with a key ID equal to 1 or 2. Router Y uses key 1 to send all EIGRP packets because it is the first valid key in the key chain.

Verifying MD5 Authentication

Example 5-8 shows the output of the **show ip eigrp neighbors** and **show ip route** commands on Router X.

Example 5-8 *Verifying EIGRP MD5 Authentication on Router X*

```
RouterX# show ip eigrp neighbors
IP-EIGRP neighbors for process 100
H   Address                 Interface      Hold Uptime    SRTT   RTO  Q  Seq
                                           (sec)          (ms)       Cnt Num
0   192.168.1.102           Se0/0/1          12 00:03:10   17  2280  0  14


RouterX# show ip route
<output omitted>
Gateway of last resort is not set
D    172.17.0.0/16 [90/40514560] via 192.168.1.102, 00:02:22, Serial0/0/1
     172.16.0.0/16 is variably subnetted, 2 subnets, 2 masks
D       172.16.0.0/16 is a summary, 00:31:31, Null0
C       172.16.1.0/24 is directly connected, FastEthernet0/0
     192.168.1.0/24 is variably subnetted, 2 subnets, 2 masks
C       192.168.1.96/27 is directly connected, Serial0/0/1
D       192.168.1.0/24 is a summary, 00:31:31, Null0


RouterX# ping 172.17.2.2
Type escape sequence to abort.
Sending 5, 100-byte ICMP Echos to 172.17.2.2, timeout is 2 seconds:
!!!!!
Success rate is 100 percent (5/5), round-trip min/avg/max = 12/15/16 ms
```

The fact that the neighbor table shows the IP address of Router Y indicates that the two routers have successfully formed an EIGRP adjacency. The routing table verifies that the 172.17.0.0 network has been learned through EIGRP over the serial connection. Therefore, the MD5 authentication for EIGRP must have been successful between Router X and Router Y.

The results of a ping to the Router Y FastEthernet interface address are also displayed to illustrate that the link is working.

Summary of Implementing EIGRP

The following summarizes the key points that were discussed in the previous sections:

- EIGRP is a classless, advanced distance vector routing protocol that runs the DUAL algorithm.

- EIGRP requires you to configure an autonomous system number that must match on all routers to exchange routes.

- EIGRP is capable of load balancing across unequal-cost paths.

- EIGRP supports MD5 authentication to protect against unauthorized, rogue routers entering your network.

Troubleshooting EIGRP

As an advanced distance vector routing protocol, EIGRP scales well with a growing network. However, this scalability introduces complexity in design, configuration, and maintenance. This section introduces some of the common issues surrounding an EIGRP network and a flowchart approach to troubleshooting these issues.

Components of Troubleshooting EIGRP

When troubleshooting any network protocol, it is important to follow a defined flow or methodology. The main aspect of troubleshooting routing protocols involves ensuring that communication exists between the routers. The following sections describe the basic components of troubleshooting a network that is running EIGRP. Figure 5-8 shows an example of the flow used for diagnosing EIGRP problems.

Figure 5-8 *EIGRP Troubleshooting*

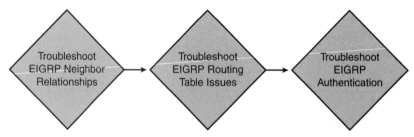

The major components of EIGRP troubleshooting include the following items:

■ EIGRP neighbor relationships

■ EIGRP routes in the routing table

■ EIGRP authentication

Troubleshooting EIGRP Neighbor Relationships

The first step in the flow is to troubleshoot neighbor relationships. Figure 5-9 shows the steps for troubleshooting these issues.

Figure 5-9 *Troubleshooting EIGRP Neighbor Issues*

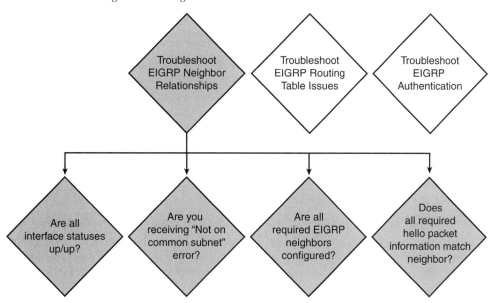

Example 5-9 shows output from the **show ip eigrp neighbors** command, which indicates that a successful neighbor relationship exists with two routers.

Example 5-9 *Confirming EIGRP Neighbor Relationships*

```
RouterX# show ip eigrp neighbors
IP-EIGRP neighbors for process 100
H    Address          Interface       Hold Uptime    SRTT  RTO  Q    Seq
                                       (sec)          (ms)       Cnt  Num
1    10.23.23.2       Se0/0/1         13 00:02:26    29    2280 0    15
0    10.140.1.1       Se0/0/0         10 00:28:26    24    2280 0    25
```

For EIGRP routers to form a neighbor relationship, both routers must share a directly connected IP subnet. A log message that displays that EIGRP neighbors are "not on common subnet" indicates that an improper IP address exists on one of the two EIGRP neighbor interfaces. Use the **show interface** *interface* command to verify the IP addresses.

In the output in Example 5-10, the interface address is 10.2.2.3/24.

Example 5-10 *Confirming EIGRP Neighbor IP Address*

```
RouterX# show ip interface fa0/0
FastEthernet0/0 is up, line protocol is up
  Internet address is 10.2.2.3/24
  Broadcast address is 255.255.255.255
  Address determined by setup command
  MTU is 1500 bytes
  Helper address is not set
  Directed broadcast forwarding is disabled
  Outgoing access list is not set
  Inbound  access list is not set
```

The **network** command that is configured under the EIGRP routing process indicates which router interfaces will participate in EIGRP. The "Routing for Networks" section of the **show ip protocols** command indicates that the networks have been configured; any interfaces in those networks participate in EIGRP. In the output of Example 5-11, EIGRP is running on any interfaces that have an IP address on the 10.0.0.0 and 192.168.1.0 networks.

Example 5-11 *Confirming Router Interface Participation in EIGRP Routing*

```
RouterX# show ip protocols
Routing Protocol is "eigrp 100"
  Outgoing update filter list for all interfaces is not set
  Incoming update filter list for all interfaces is not set
  Default networks flagged in outgoing updates
  Default networks accepted from incoming updates
  EIGRP metric weight K1=1, K2=0, K3=1, K4=0, K5=0
  EIGRP maximum hopcount 100
  EIGRP maximum metric variance 1
  Redistributing: eigrp 100
--output omitted --
  Maximum path: 4
  Routing for Networks:
    10.0.0.0
    192.168.1.0
  Routing Information Sources:
    Gateway         Distance      Last Update
    (this router)         90      00:01:08
    10.140.1.1            90      00:01:08
  Distance: internal 90 external 170
```

The **show ip eigrp interfaces** command can quickly indicate on which interfaces EIGRP is enabled and show how many neighbors can be found on each interface. In the output in

Example 5-12, no peers currently exist on the FastEthernet 0/0 interface, and one peer exists on the Serial 0/0/0 interface.

Example 5-12 *Confirming EIGRP Status and Neighbors on an Interface*

```
RouterX# show ip eigrp interfaces
IP-EIGRP interfaces for process 100

              Xmit Queue   Mean   Pacing Time   Multicast    Pending
Int    Peers  Un/Reliable  SRTT   Un/Reliable   Flow Timer   Routes
Fa0/0    0       0/0         0        0/1            0           0
Se0/0/0  1       0/0        38       10/380         552          0
```

EIGRP routers create a neighbor relationship by exchanging hello packets. Certain fields in the hello packets must match before an EIGRP neighbor relationship is established:

■ EIGRP autonomous system (AS) number

■ EIGRP K values

> **NOTE** EIGRP K values are used in the EIGRP best-path selection process and are discussed in the Cisco CCNP curriculum.

You can use the **debug eigrp packets** command to troubleshoot when hello packet information does not match. In Example 5-13, a K value mismatch exists.

Example 5-13 *Verifying EIGRP Hello Packet Mismatches*

```
RouterX# debug eigrp packets

Mismatched adjacency values
01:39:13: EIGRP: Received HELLO on Serial0/0 nbr 10.1.2.2
01:39:13:AS 100, Flags 0x0, Seq 0/0 idbQ 0/0 iidbQ un/rely 0/0 peerQ un/rely 0/0
01:39:13:        K-value mismatch
```

Troubleshooting EIGRP Routing Tables

If the neighbor relationships are established, routes can be exchanged. If they are not being exchanged, the next step is to troubleshoot EIGRP routing table issues. Figure 5-10 shows the steps involved in troubleshooting these problems.

Figure 5-10 *Troubleshooting EIGRP Routing Tables*

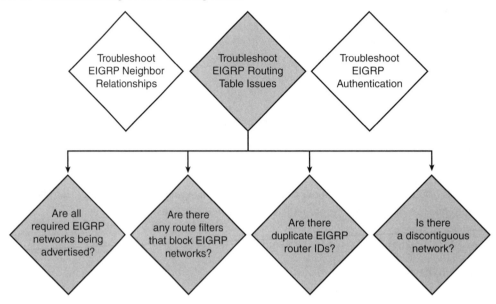

EIGRP routes that appear with a "D" in the routing table indicate that they are intra-AS routes, and those with **"D EX"** indicate that they are external AS routes. No EIGRP routes in the routing table can indicate that a Layer 1 or 2 issue or an EIGRP neighbor problem exists.

In the output in Example 5-14, the 172.16.31.0/24 network is an intra-AS route, and 10.3.3.0/24 is a route that was redistributed into EIGRP.

Example 5-14 *Confirming EIGRP Intra-AS and Redistributed Routes*

```
RouterX# show ip route
Codes: C - connected, S - static, R - RIP, M - mobile, B - BGP
       D - EIGRP, EX - EIGRP external, O - OSPF, IA - OSPF inter area
       N1 - OSPF NSSA external type 1, N2 - OSPF NSSA external type 2
       E1 - OSPF external type 1, E2 - OSPF external type 2

Gateway of last resort is not set

     172.16.0.0/16 is variably subnetted, 2 subnets, 2 masks
D       172.16.31.0/24 [90/40640000] via 10.140.1.1, 00:01:09, Serial0/0/0
O       172.16.31.100/32 [110/1563] via 10.140.1.1, 00:26:55, Serial0/0/0
     10.0.0.0/8 is variably subnetted, 7 subnets, 2 masks
C       10.23.23.0/24 is directly connected, Serial0/0/1
D EX    10.3.3.0/24 [170/40514560] via 10.23.23.2, 00:01:09, Serial0/0/1
C       10.2.2.0/24 is directly connected, FastEthernet0/0
```

The **show ip eigrp topology** command displays the EIGRP router ID. The EIGRP router ID comes from the highest IP address assigned to a loopback interface. If no loopback interfaces are configured, the highest IP address assigned to any other active interface is chosen as the router ID. No two EIGRP routers can have the same EIGRP router ID. If they do, you will experience problems exchanging routes between the two routers with equal router IDs.

In the output in Example 5-15, the router ID is 192.168.1.65.

Example 5-15 *Displaying EIGRP Router IDs*

```
RouterX# show ip eigrp topology
IP-EIGRP Topology Table for AS(100)/ID(192.168.1.65)

Codes: P - Passive, A - Active, U - Update, Q - Query, R - Reply,
       r - reply Status, s - sia Status

P 10.1.1.0/24, 1 successors, FD is 40514560
        via 10.140.1.1 (40514560/28160), Serial0/0/0
P 10.2.2.0/24, 1 successors, FD is 28160
        via Connected, FastEthernet0/0
P 10.3.3.0/24, 1 successors, FD is 40514560
        via 10.23.23.2 (40514560/28160), Serial0/0/1
P 10.23.23.0/24, 1 successors, FD is 40512000
        via Connected, Serial0/0/1
P 192.168.1.64/28, 1 successors, FD is 128256
        via Connected, Loopback0
P 192.168.1.0/24, 1 successors, FD is 40640000
        via 10.23.23.2 (40640000/128256), Serial0/0/1
P 10.140.2.0/24, 2 successors, FD is 41024000
        via 10.23.23.2 (41024000/40512000), Serial0/0/1
        via 10.140.1.1 (41024000/40512000), Serial0/0/0
P 10.140.1.0/24, 1 successors, FD is 40512000
        via Connected, Serial0/0/0
P 172.16.31.0/24, 1 successors, FD is 40640000
```

EIGRP routes that are found in the topology table but not in the routing table can indicate an issue that requires help from Cisco Technical Assistance Center (TAC) to diagnose the problem.

Route filtering enables routes to be filtered from an EIGRP routing advertisement as they come in from a neighbor or as they are sent out to a neighbor. These filters can cause routes to be missing from the routing table. The **show ip protocols** command shows whether any filter lists are applied to EIGRP.

NOTE   Filtering routing information is covered in the CCNP course materials.

By default, EIGRP is classful and performs automatic network summarization. Automatic network summarization causes connectivity issues in discontiguous networks. The **show ip protocols** command confirms whether automatic network summarization is in effect.

In the sample output in Example 5-16, no filter lists are applied to EIGRP AS 100, and automatic network summarization is in effect.

Example 5-16   *Confirming EIGRP Automatic Network Summarization*

```
RouterX# show ip protocols
Routing Protocol is "eigrp 100"
  Outgoing update filter list for all interfaces is not set
  Incoming update filter list for all interfaces is not set
  Default networks flagged in outgoing updates
  Default networks accepted from incoming updates
  EIGRP metric weight K1=1, K2=0, K3=1, K4=0, K5=0
  EIGRP maximum hopcount 100
  EIGRP maximum metric variance 1
  Redistributing: eigrp 100
  EIGRP NSF-aware route hold timer is 240s
  Automatic network summarization is in effect
  Automatic address summarization:
    192.168.1.0/24 for FastEthernet0/0, Serial0/0/0, Serial0/0/1
      Summarizing with metric 128256
    10.0.0.0/8 for Loopback0
      Summarizing with metric 28160
  Maximum path: 4
```

Troubleshooting EIGRP Authentication

The last step in the flowchart in Figure 5-8 is to troubleshoot EIGRP authentication problems, if configured. This is accomplished by verifying that EIGRP authentication is successful.

Example: Successful MD5 Authentication

The output of the **debug eigrp packets** command on Router X, shown in Example 5-17, illustrates that Router X is receiving EIGRP packets with MD5 authentication and a key ID equal to 1 from Router Y.

Example 5-17   *Confirming MD5 Authentication on Router X*

```
RouterX# debug eigrp packets
EIGRP Packets debugging is on
    (UPDATE, REQUEST, QUERY, REPLY, HELLO, IPXSAP, PROBE, ACK, STUB, SIAQUERY, SIAREPLY)
*Jan 21 16:38:51.745: EIGRP: received packet with MD5 authentication, key id = 1
*Jan 21 16:38:51.745: EIGRP: Received HELLO on Serial0/0/1 nbr 192.168.1.102
*Jan 21 16:38:51.745:   AS 100, Flags 0x0, Seq 0/0 idbQ 0/0 iidbQ un/rely 0/0 peerQ
  un/rely 0/0
```

Similarly, the output of the **debug eigrp packets** command on Router Y, shown in Example 5-18, illustrates that Router Y is receiving EIGRP packets with MD5 authentication and a key ID equal to 2 from Router X.

Example 5-18 *Confirming MD5 Authentication on Router Y*

```
RouterY# debug eigrp packets
EIGRP Packets debugging is on
    (UPDATE, REQUEST, QUERY, REPLY, HELLO, IPXSAP, PROBE, ACK, STUB, SIAQUERY,
SIAREPLY)
RouterY#
*Jan 21 16:38:38.321: EIGRP: received packet with MD5 authentication, key id = 2
*Jan 21 16:38:38.321: EIGRP: Received HELLO on Serial0/0/1 nbr 192.168.1.101
*Jan 21 16:38:38.321:   AS 100, Flags 0x0, Seq 0/0 idbQ 0/0 iidbQ un/rely 0/0 peerQ
 un/rely 0/0
```

Example: Troubleshooting MD5 Authentication Problems

In the example, the key string for key 2 of Router X, the one that is used when EIGRP packets are sent, is changed to be different from the key string that Router Y is expecting.

The output of the **debug eigrp packets** command on Router Y, shown in Example 5-19, illustrates that Router Y is receiving EIGRP packets with MD5 authentication and a key ID equal to 2 from Router X, but that an authentication mismatch exists. The EIGRP packets from Router X are ignored, and the neighbor relationship is declared to be down. The output of the **show ip eigrp neighbors** command should confirm that Router Y has no EIGRP neighbors.

Example 5-19 *MD5 Authentication Mismatch*

```
RouterY# debug eigrp packets
EIGRP Packets debugging is on
    (UPDATE, REQUEST, QUERY, REPLY, HELLO, IPXSAP, PROBE, ACK, STUB, SIAQUERY, SIAREPLY)
RouterY#
*Jan 21 16:50:18.749: EIGRP: pkt key id = 2, authentication mismatch
*Jan 21 16:50:18.749: EIGRP: Serial0/0/1: ignored packet from 192.168.1.101, opc
ode = 5 (invalid authentication)
*Jan 21 16:50:18.749: EIGRP: Dropping peer, invalid authentication
*Jan 21 16:50:18.749: EIGRP: Sending HELLO on Serial0/0/1
*Jan 21 16:50:18.749:   AS 100, Flags 0x0, Seq 0/0 idbQ 0/0 iidbQ un/rely 0/0
*Jan 21 16:50:18.753: %DUAL-5-NBRCHANGE: IP-EIGRP(0) 100: Neighbor 192.168.1.101
 (Serial0/0/1) is down: Auth failure

RouterY# show ip eigrp neighbors
IP-EIGRP neighbors for process 100
RouterY#
```

The two routers keep trying to reestablish their neighbor relationship. Because of the different keys that are used by each router in this scenario, Router X authenticates the hello messages that are sent by Router Y using key 1. However, when Router X sends a hello message back to Router Y using key 2, an authentication mismatch will occur. From the perspective of Router X, the relationship appears to be up for a while, but then it times out, as illustrated by the messages that were received on Router X, shown in Example 5-20. The output of the **show ip eigrp neighbors** command on Router X also illustrates that Router X does have Router Y in its neighbor table for a short time.

Example 5-20   *Confirming MD5 Authentication*

```
RouterX# debug eigrp packets
*Jan 21 16:54:09.821: %DUAL-5-NBRCHANGE: IP-EIGRP(0) 100: Neighbor 192.168.1.102 (Serial0/
  0/1) is down: retry limit exceeded
*Jan 21 16:54:11.745: %DUAL-5-NBRCHANGE: IP-EIGRP(0) 100: Neighbor 192.168.1.102 (Serial0/
  0/1) is up: new adjacency
RouterX# show ip eigrp neighbors
H Address     Interface  Hold Uptime SRTT RTO Q Seq
                                    (sec)        (ms)        Cnt Num
0   192.168.1.102  Se0/0/1         13 00:00:38    1    5000  1   0
```

Summary of Troubleshooting EIGRP

The following summarizes the key points that were discussed in this section:

- Troubleshooting EIGRP includes several aspects, such as resolving neighbor relationships, routing table issues, and authentication problems.

- Issues that can cause EIGRP neighbor problems include incorrect network commands and hello packet information mismatches. Use the **show ip eigrp neighbors** command to help troubleshoot these issues.

- Missing EIGRP routes from the routing table can be because of route filtering or automatic summarization in discontiguous networks. Use the **show ip route** command to help troubleshoot these issues.

- The **debug eigrp packets** command can help you troubleshoot MD5 authentication problems.

Chapter Summary

Enhanced Interior Gateway Routing Protocol (EIGRP) is a Cisco routing protocol that is designed to address the shortcomings of both distance vector and link-state routing protocols. This chapter expanded on the underlying technologies within EIGRP, including the path selection process, changes in topology, load balancing, authentication, and troubleshooting common problems.

The following summarizes the key points that were discussed in this chapter:

- EIGRP is a classless routing protocol that supports VLSM.

- Path selection is based on several factors.

- EIGRP keeps a next-best alternative path, called a feasible successor, for fast convergence.

- EIGRP supports unequal-cost load balancing.

- EIGRP uses MD5 authentication for router authenticity.

- Troubleshooting EIGRP requires resolving link, neighbor, redistribution, and routing issues.

- The following commands help you troubleshoot EIGRP issues: **show ip eigrp neighbor**, **show ip eigrp topology**, **show ip eigrp interface**, and **show ip route**.

Review Questions

Use the questions here to review what you learned in this chapter. The correct answers and solutions are found in the appendix, "Answers to Chapter Review Questions."

1. How do you minimize the bandwidth requirement for EIGRP packets?

   a. By propagating only data packets

   b. By propagating only hello packets

   c. By propagating only routing table changes and hello packets

   d. By propagating the entire routing table only to those routers that are affected by a topology change

2. Which command correctly specifies that network 10.0.0.0 is directly connected to a router that is running EIGRP?

   a. Router(config)# **network 10.0.0.0**

   b. Router(config)# **router eigrp 10.0.0.0**

   c. Router(config-router)# **network 10.0.0.0**

   d. Router(config-router)# **router eigrp 10.0.0.0**

3. Which command displays the amount of time since the router heard from an EIGRP neighbor?

   a. **show ip eigrp traffic**

   b. **show ip eigrp topology**

   c. **show ip eigrp interfaces**

   d. **show ip eigrp neighbors**

4. Which command must you configure for EIGRP to pass the subnet mask with the route?

    a. ip classless

    b. no auto-summary

    c. no summary

    d. ip subnet vlsm

5. Which command displays whether route filtering has been enabled?

    a. show interface

    b. show access-list

    c. show ip protocols

    d. show route-filter

6. Which form of authentication does EIGRP support?

    a. Plain text

    b. 3DES

    c. MD5

    d. Both A and C

7. What does the EIGRP message "neighbor not on common subnet" mean?

    a. Duplicate EIGRP router IDs exist.

    b. The two adjacent neighbor interfaces do not have addresses in the same IP network.

    c. The MTU sizes on the two adjacent neighbor routers do not match.

This chapter includes the following sections:

- Chapter Objectives

- Access Control List Operation

- Configuring ACLs

- Troubleshooting ACLs

- Chapter Summary

- Review Questions

CHAPTER 6

Managing Traffic with Access Control Lists

Standard and extended Cisco IOS access control lists (ACLs) can be used to classify IP packets. Using ACLs, you can apply a number of features, such as encryption, policy-based routing, quality of service (QoS), dial-on-demand routing (DDR), Network Address Translation (NAT), and Port Address Translation (PAT), to the classified packets.

You can also configure standard and extended Cisco IOS ACLs on router interfaces for access control (security) to control the type of traffic that is permitted through a given router. Cisco IOS features are applied on interfaces for specific directions (inbound versus outbound). This chapter describes the operation of different types of ACLs and shows you how to configure IP version 4 (IPv4) ACLs.

Chapter Objectives

Upon completing this chapter, you will be able to determine how to apply ACLs based on network requirements and configure, verify, and troubleshoot ACLs on a medium-sized network. This ability includes being able to meet these objectives:

■ Describe the different types of IPv4 ACLs

■ Configure and troubleshoot standard and extended, numbered and named IPv4 ACLs

Access Control List Operation

Understanding the uses of access control lists (ACL) enables you to determine how to implement them on your Cisco network. ACLs can provide an important network security feature and filter packets on inbound and outbound router interfaces.

This section describes some of the applications for ACLs on Cisco networks, identifies the different types of ACLs that can be implemented, and explains how Cisco IOS Software processes ACLs.

Understanding ACLs

To be able to configure and implement ACLs, you need to understand the capacity in which they are used. Cisco devices use ACLs in two primary functions: classification and filtering. The following explains each of these functions:

- **Classification:** Routers also use ACLs to identify particular traffic. After an ACL has identified and classified traffic, you can configure the router with instructions on how to handle that traffic. For example, you can use an ACL to identify the executive subnet as the traffic source and then give that traffic priority over other types of traffic on a congested WAN link.

- **Filtering:** As the number of router connections to outside networks increase and the use of the Internet increases, access control presents new challenges. Network administrators face the dilemma of how to deny unwanted traffic while allowing appropriate access. For example, you can use an ACL as a filter to keep the rest of your network from accessing sensitive data on the finance subnet.

Through classification and filtering, ACLs provide a powerful toolset in Cisco IOS. Consider the network diagram in Figure 6-1. Using ACLs, administrators have the tools to block traffic from the Internet, provide controlled access to manage Cisco IOS devices, and provide address translation for private addresses such as the 172.16.0.0 network.

Figure 6-1 *ACLs Provide Control*

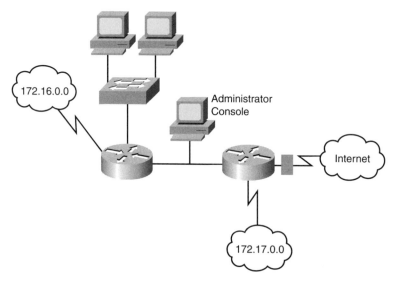

Filtering is the function of ACLs that people identify most readily. ACLs offer an important tool for controlling traffic on the network. Packet filtering helps control packet movement through the network. Figure 6-2 shows an example of ACLs filtering traffic transmission in and out of a physical interface or to the Telnet session of a Cisco IOS device.

Figure 6-2 *ACL Filtering*

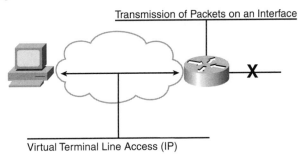

Transmission of Packets on an Interface

Virtual Terminal Line Access (IP)

Cisco provides ACLs to permit or deny the following:

■ The crossing of packets to or from specified router interfaces and traffic going through the router

■ Telnet traffic into or out of the router vty ports for router administration

By default, all IP traffic is permitted in and out of all the router interfaces.

When the router discards packets, some protocols return a special packet to notify the sender that the destination is unreachable. For the IP protocol, an ACL discard results in a "Destination unreachable (U.U.U.)" response to a ping and an "Administratively prohibited (!A * !A)" response to a traceroute.

IP ACLs can classify and differentiate traffic. Classification enables you to assign special handling for traffic that is defined in an ACL, such as the following:

■ Identify the type of traffic to be encrypted across a virtual private network (VPN) connection.

■ Identify the routes that are to be redistributed from one routing protocol to another.

■ Use with route filtering to identify which routes are to be included in the routing updates between routers.

■ Use with policy-based routing to identify the type of traffic that is to be routed across a designated link.

■ Use with Network Address Translation (NAT) to identify which addresses are to be translated.

- Use with quality of service (QoS) to identify which packets should be scheduled in a given queue during times of congestion.

Figure 6-3 shows some examples of using ACLs for traffic classification, such as which traffic to encrypt across the VPN, which routes should be redistributed between Open Shortest Path First (OSPF) and Enhanced Interior Gateway Routing Protocol (EIGRP), and which addresses to translate using NAT.

Figure 6-3 *ACLs Identify Traffic*

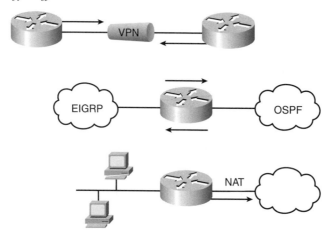

ACL Operation

ACLs express the set of rules that give added control for packets that enter inbound interfaces, packets that relay through the router, and packets that exit outbound interfaces of the router. ACLs do not act on packets that originate from the router. Instead, ACLs are statements that specify conditions of how the router handles the traffic flow through specified interfaces.

ACLs operate in two ways:

- **Inbound ACLs:** Incoming packets are processed before they are routed to an outbound interface. An inbound ACL is efficient because it saves the overhead of routing lookups if the packet will be discarded after it is denied by the filtering tests. If the packet is permitted by the tests, it is processed for routing.

- **Outbound ACLs:** Incoming packets are routed to the outbound interface and then processed through the outbound ACL.

Figure 6-4 shows an example of an outbound ACL.

Figure 6-4   *Outbound ACL Operation*

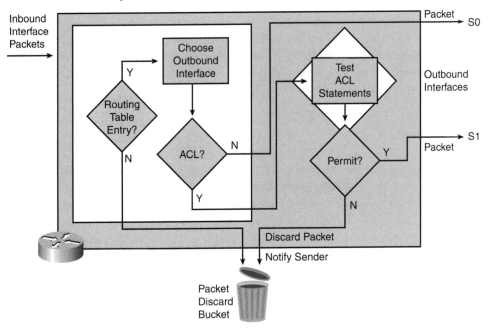

When a packet enters an interface, the router checks the routing table to see if the packet is routable. If the packet is not routable, it is dropped.

Next, the router checks to see whether the destination interface is grouped to an ACL. If the destination interface is not grouped to an ACL, the packet can be sent to the output buffer. Examples of outbound ACL operations are as follows:

- If the outbound interface is S0, which has not been grouped to an outbound ACL, the packet is sent to S0 directly.

- If the outbound interface is S1, which has been grouped to an outbound ACL, the packet is not sent out on S1 until it is tested by the combination of ACL statements that are associated with that interface. Based on the ACL tests, the packet is permitted or denied.

For outbound lists, "to permit" means to send the packet to the output buffer, and "to deny" means to discard the packet.

With an inbound ACL, when a packet enters an interface, the router checks to see whether the source interface is grouped to an ACL. If the source interface is not grouped to an ACL, the router checks the routing table to see if the packet is routable. If the packet is not routable, the router drops the packet. Examples of inbound ACL operations are as follows:

- If the inbound interface is S0, which has not been grouped to an inbound ACL, the packet is processed normally, and the router checks to see whether the packet is routable.

- If the inbound interface is S1, which has been grouped to an inbound ACL, the packet is not processed, and the routing table is not consulted until it is tested by the combination of ACL statements that are associated with that interface. Based on the ACL tests, the packet is permitted or denied.

For inbound lists, "to permit" means to continue to process the packet after receiving it on an inbound interface, and "to deny" means to discard the packet.

ACL statements operate in sequential, logical order. They evaluate packets from the top down, one statement at a time. If a packet header and an ACL statement match, the rest of the statements in the list are skipped, and the packet is permitted or denied as determined by the matched statement. If a packet header does not match an ACL statement, the packet is tested against the next statement in the list. This matching process continues until the end of the list is reached. Figure 6-5 shows the logical flow of statement evaluation.

Figure 6-5 *ACL Evaluation*

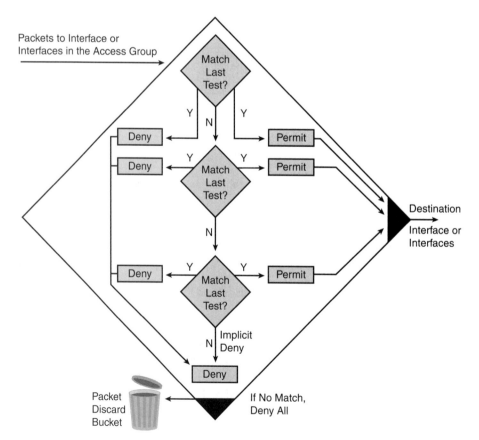

A final implied statement covers all packets for which conditions did not test true. This final test condition matches all other packets and results in a "deny" instruction. Instead of proceeding into or out of an interface, the router drops all of these remaining packets. This final statement is often referred to as the "implicit deny any statement." Because of this statement, an ACL should have at least one permit statement in it; otherwise, the ACL blocks all traffic. This implicit deny all will not show up in the router configuration. In many of the examples in this text, it will be added as a reminder.

You can apply an ACL to multiple interfaces. However, only one ACL can exist per protocol, per direction, and per interface.

Types of ACLs

IPv4 ACLs come in various types. These differing ACLs are used depending on the functionality required. The types of ACLs can be classified as follows:

- **Standard ACLs:** Standard IP ACLs check the source addresses of packets that can be routed. The result either permits or denies the output for an entire protocol suite, based on the source network, subnet, or host IP address.

- **Extended ACLs:** Extended IP ACLs check both the source and destination packet addresses. They can also check for specific protocols, port numbers, and other parameters, which allow administrators more flexibility and control.

You can use two methods to identify standard and extended ACLs:

- Numbered ACLs use a number for identification.

- Named ACLs use a descriptive name or number for identification.

ACL Identification

When you create numbered ACLs, you enter an ACL number as the first argument of the global ACL statement. The test conditions for an ACL vary depending on whether the number identifies a standard or extended ACL.

You can create many ACLs for a protocol. Select a different ACL number for each new ACL within a given protocol. However, you can apply only one ACL per protocol, per direction, and per interface.

Specifying an ACL number from 1 to 99 or 1300 to 1999 instructs the router to accept numbered standard IPv4 ACL statements. Specifying an ACL number from 100 to 199 or 2000 to 2699 instructs the router to accept numbered extended IPv4 ACL statements.

Table 6-1 lists the different ACL number ranges for each protocol.

Table 6-1 *Protocol ACL Numbers*

Protocol	Range
IP	1–99
Extended IP	100–199
Ethernet type code	200–299
Ethernet address	700–799
Transparent bridging (protocol type)	200–299
Transparent bridging (vendor code)	700–799
Extended transparent bridging	1100–1199
DECnet and extended DECnet	300–399
XNS[1]	400–499
Extended XNS	500–599
AppleTalk	600–699
Source-route bridging (protocol type)	200–299
Source-route bridging (vendor code)	700–799
IPX[2]	800–899
Extended IPX	900–999
IPX SAP[3]	1000–1099
Standard Banyan VINES[4]	1–100
Extended Banyan VINES	101–200
Simple Banyan VINES	201–300
Standard IP (expanded)	1300–1999
Extended IP (expanded)	2000–2699

[1] XNS = Xerox Network Services

[2] IPX = Internetwork Packet Exchange

[3] SAP = Service Advertisement Protocol

[4] VINES = Virtual Integrated Network Service

As of Cisco IOS Software Release 12.0, IPv4 ACLs have been expanded. The table shows that standard IPv4 ACLS have been expanded to include the numbers 1300 to 1999, and the extended IPv4 ACLs have been expanded to include the numbers 2000 to 2699.

The named ACL feature enables you to identify IP standard and extended ACLs with an alphanumeric string (name) instead of the numeric representations. Named IP ACLs give you more flexibility in working with the ACL entries.

IP access list entry sequence numbering has several benefits:

- You can edit the order of ACL statements.

- You can remove individual statements from an ACL.

Where additions are placed in an ACL depends on whether you use sequence numbers. There is no support for sequence numbering in software versions earlier than Cisco IOS Software Release 12.3; therefore, all the ACL additions for earlier software versions are placed at the end of the ACL.

IP access list entry sequence numbering is a new edition to Cisco IOS Software that enables you to use sequence numbers to easily add, remove, or reorder statements in an IP ACL. With Cisco IOS Software Release 12.3 and later, additions can be placed anywhere in the ACL based on the sequence number.

Earlier than Cisco IOS Software Release 12.3, only named ACLs enable the removal of individual statements from an ACL using the following command:

```
no {deny ¦ permit} protocol source source-wildcard destination destination-wildcard
```

The *protocol source source-wildcard destination destination-wildcard* parameters match the line you are trying to remove. With numbered ACLs, you would have to remove the whole list and re-create it with the desired statements. With Cisco IOS Software Release 12.3 and later, you can also use the **no** *sequence-number* command to delete a specific access list entry.

Well-designed and well-implemented ACLs add an important security component to your network. Follow these general principles to ensure that the ACLs you create have the intended results:

- Based on the test conditions, choose a standard or extended, numbered, or named ACL.

- Only one ACL per protocol, per direction, and per interface is allowed. Multiple ACLs are permitted per interface, but each must be for a different protocol or different direction.

- Your ACL should be organized to enable processing from the top down. Organize your ACL so that the more specific references to a network or subnet appear before ones that are more general. Place conditions that occur more frequently before conditions that occur less frequently.

- Your ACL contains an implicit deny any statement at the end:

    — Unless you end your ACL with an explicit permit any statement, by default, the ACL denies all traffic that fails to match any of the ACL lines.

    — Every ACL should have at least one permit statement. Otherwise, all traffic is denied.

- You should create the ACL before applying it to an interface. With most versions of Cisco IOS Software, an interface that has an empty ACL applied to it permits all traffic.

- Depending on how you apply the ACL, the ACL filters traffic either going through the router or going to and from the router, such as traffic to or from the vty lines.

- You should typically place extended ACLs as close as possible to the source of the traffic that you want to deny. Because standard ACLs do not specify destination addresses, you must put the standard ACL as close as possible to the destination of the traffic you want to deny so the source can reach intermediary networks.

Additional Types of ACLs

Standard and extended ACLs can become the basis for other types of ACLs that provide additional functionality. These other types of ACLs include the following:

- Dynamic ACLs (lock-and-key)
- Reflexive ACLs
- Time-based ACLs

Dynamic ACLs

Dynamic ACLs depend on Telnet connectivity, authentication (local or remote), and extended ACLs. Lock-and-key configuration starts with the application of an extended ACL to block traffic through the router. Users who want to traverse the router are blocked by the extended ACL until they use Telnet to connect to the router and are authenticated. The Telnet connection is then dropped, and a single-entry dynamic ACL is added to the extended ACL. This permits traffic for a particular period; idle and absolute timeouts are possible. Figure 6-6 shows an example of dynamic access lists.

Figure 6-6 *Dynamic ACL*

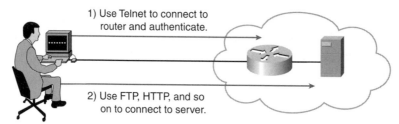

1) Use Telnet to connect to router and authenticate.

2) Use FTP, HTTP, and so on to connect to server.

Some common reasons to use dynamic ACLs are as follows:

■ Use dynamic ACLs when you want a specific remote user or group of remote users to access a host within your network, connecting from their remote hosts via the Internet. Lock-and-key authenticates the user and permits limited access through your firewall router for a host or subnet for a finite period.

■ Use dynamic ACLs when you want a subset of hosts on a local network to access a host on a remote network that is protected by a firewall. With lock-and-key, you can enable access to the remote host only for the desired set of local hosts. Lock-and-key requires the users to authenticate through a TACACS+ server, or other security server, before it allows their hosts to access the remote hosts.

Dynamic ACLs have the following security benefits over standard and static extended ACLs:

■ Use of a challenge mechanism to authenticate individual users

■ Simpler management in large internetworks

■ In many cases, reduction of the amount of router processing that is required for ACLs

■ Reduction of the opportunity for network break-ins by network hackers

■ Creation of dynamic user access through a firewall, without compromising other configured security restrictions

Although the entire configuration for a dynamic ACL is outside the scope of this course, the following example shows the steps that are required to configure a dynamic ACL. The goal of a dynamic ACL is to provide a means for some users on a network to have access through the router without knowing exactly what devices they will be connecting from. This type of list requires the end user to log in to the router from the device to set up a temporary access list to permit the traffic.

The following configuration creates a login name and password for authentication. The idle timeout is set to 10 minutes.

```
RouterX(config)#username test password test
RouterX(config)#username test autocommand access-enable host timeout 10
```

The following configuration enables users to open a Telnet connection to the router that is to be authenticated and blocks all other traffic:

```
RouterX(config)#access-list 101 permit tcp any host 10.1.1.1 eq telnet
RouterX(config)#interface Ethernet0/0
RouterX(config-if)#ip address 10.1.1.1 255.255.255.0
RouterX(config-if)#ip access-group 101 in
```

The following configuration creates the dynamic ACL that will be automatically applied to the existing access-list 101. The absolute timeout is set to 15 minutes.

```
RouterX(config)#access-list 101 dynamic testlist timeout 15 permit ip 10.1.1.0
  0.0.0.255 172.16.1.0 0.0.0.255
```

The following configuration forces users to authenticate when they open a Telnet connection to the router:

```
RouterX(config)#line vty 0 4
RouterX(config-line)#login local
```

After you have done these configurations, when the user at 10.1.1.2 successfully makes a Telnet connection to 10.1.1.1, the dynamic ACL is applied. The connection is then dropped, and the user can access the 172.16.1.x network.

Reflexive ACLs

Reflexive ACLs allow IP packets to be filtered based on upper-layer session information such as TCP port numbers. They are generally used to allow outbound traffic and limit inbound traffic in response to sessions that originate from a network inside the router. Reflexive ACLs contain only temporary entries. These entries are automatically created when a new IP session begins, for example, with an outbound packet, and the entries are automatically removed when the session ends. Reflexive ACLs are not applied directly to an interface but are "nested" in an extended named IP ACL that is applied to the interface.

Reflexive ACLs provide a truer form of session filtering than an extended ACL that uses the **established** parameter. Reflexive ACLs are much harder to spoof because more filter criteria must match before a packet is permitted through; for example, source and destination addresses and port numbers, not just acknowledgment (ACK) and reset (RST) bits, are checked. Figure 6-7 illustrates how the reflexive access list operates.

Figure 6-7 *Reflexive Access Lists*

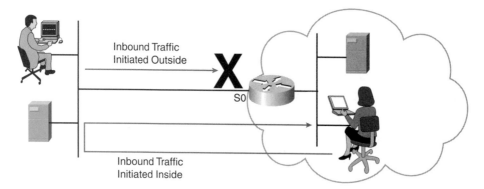

Reflexive ACLs are an important part of securing your network against network hackers and can be included in a firewall defense. Reflexive ACLs provide a level of security against spoofing and certain denial of service (DoS) attacks. Reflexive ACLs are simple to use and, compared to basic ACLs, provide greater control over which packets enter your network.

Although the entire configuration for reflexive ACLs is outside the scope of this course, the following example shows the steps that are required to configure a reflexive ACL. The example is of a reflexive ACL that permits Internet Control Message Protocol (ICMP) outbound and inbound traffic, while it permits only TCP traffic that has initiated from inside. All other traffic is denied.

The following configuration causes the router to keep track of traffic that was initiated from inside:

```
RouterX(config)#ip access-list extended outboundfilters
RouterX(config-ext-nacl)#permit icmp 10.1.1.0 0.0.0.255 172.16.1.0 0.0.0.255
RouterX(config-ext-nacl)#permit tcp 10.1.1.0 0.0.0.255 172.16.1.0 0.0.0.255 reflect
  tcptraffic
```

The next configuration creates an inbound policy that requires the router to check incoming traffic to see whether it was initiated from inside and ties the reflexive ACL part of the outboundfilters ACL, called tcptraffic, to the inboundfilters ACL:

```
RouterX(config)#ip access-list extended inboundfilters
Router(config-ext-nacl)#permit icmp 172.16.1.0 0.0.0.255 10.1.1.0 0.0.0.255 evaluate
  tcptraffic
```

The configuration in Example 6-1 applies to both an inbound and an outbound ACL to the interface.

Example 6-1 *Applying Inbound and Outbound ACLs to an Interface*

```
RouterX(config)#interface Ethernet0/1
RouterX(config-if)#ip address 172.16.1.2 255.255.255.0
RouterX(config-if)#ip access-group inboundfilters in
RouterX(config-if)#ip access-group outboundfilters out
```

Reflexive ACLs can be defined only with extended named IP ACLs. They cannot be defined with numbered or standard named IP ACLs or with other protocol ACLs.

Time-Based ACLs

Time-based ACLs are similar to extended ACLs in function, but they allow for access control based on time. To implement time-based ACLs, you create a time range that defines specific times of the day and week. The time range is identified by a name and then referenced by a function. Therefore, the time restrictions are imposed on the function itself. For example, in Figure 6-8, a user is blocked from transmitting HTTP traffic after 7:00 p.m.

Figure 6-8 *Timed Access Lists*

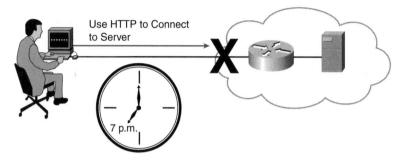

Time-based ACLs have many benefits:

■ The network administrator has more control over permitting or denying a user access to resources. These resources could be an application, identified by an IP address and mask pair and a port number; policy routing; or an on-demand link, identified as interesting traffic to the dialer.

■ Network administrators can set time-based security policies such as the following:

— Perimeter security using the Cisco IOS Firewall feature set or ACLs

— Data confidentiality with Cisco Encryption Technology or IP security (IPsec)

■ Policy-based routing and queuing functions are enhanced.

■ When provider access rates vary by time of day, it is possible to automatically reroute traffic cost effectively.

■ Service providers can dynamically change a committed access rate (CAR) configuration to support the QoS service-level agreements (SLA) that are negotiated for certain times of day.

■ Network administrators can control logging messages. ACL entries can log traffic at certain times of the day but not constantly. Therefore, administrators can simply deny access without analyzing the many logs that are generated during peak hours.

Although the entire configuration for time-based ACLs is outside the scope of this course, the following example shows the steps that are required to configure a time-based ACL. In the example, a Telnet connection is permitted from the inside network to the outside network on Monday, Wednesday, and Friday during business hours.

The following configuration defines the time range to implement the ACL and names it:

```
RouterX(config)#time-range EVERYOTHERDAY
RouterX(config-time-range)#periodic Monday Wednesday Friday 8:00 to 17:00
```

The following configuration applies the time range to the ACL:

```
RouterX(config)#access-list 101 permit tcp 10.1.1.0 0.0.0.255 172.16.1.0 0.0.0.255
   eq telnet time-range EVERYOTHERDAY
```

The following configuration applies the ACL to the interface:

```
RouterX(config)#interface Ethernet0/0
RouterX(config-if)#ip address 10.1.1.1 255.255.255.0
RouterX(config-if)#ip access-group 101 in
```

The time range relies on the router system clock. The router clock can be used, but the feature works best with Network Time Protocol (NTP) synchronization.

ACL Wildcard Masking

Address filtering occurs when you use ACL address wildcard masking to identify how to check or ignore corresponding IP address bits. Wildcard masking for IP address bits uses the numbers 1 and 0 to identify how to treat the corresponding IP address bits, as follows:

■ **Wildcard mask bit 0:** Match the corresponding bit value in the address.

■ **Wildcard mask bit 1:** Do not check (ignore) the corresponding bit value in the address.

> **NOTE** A wildcard mask is sometimes referred to as an *inverse mask*.

By carefully setting wildcard masks, you can permit or deny tests with one ACL statement. You can select a single IP address or many IP addresses. Figure 6-9 illustrates how to check corresponding address bits.

Figure 6-9 *Wildcard Mask*

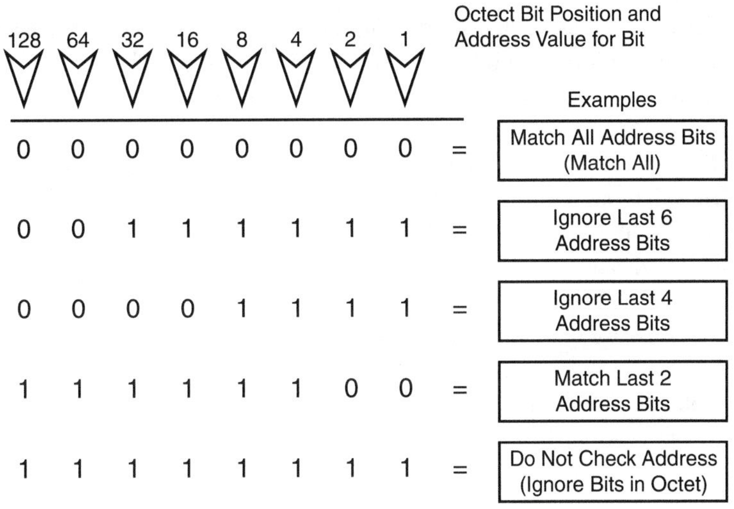

> **NOTE**   Wildcard masking for ACLs operates differently from an IP subnet mask. A "0" in a bit position of the ACL mask indicates that the corresponding bit in the address must be matched. A "1" in a bit position of the ACL mask indicates that the corresponding bit in the address is not interesting and can be ignored.

In Figure 6-10, an administrator wants to test a range of IP subnets that is to be permitted or denied. Assume that the IP address is a Class B address (the first two octets are the network number), with 8 bits of subnetting. (The third octet is for subnets.) The administrator wants to use the IP wildcard masking bits to match subnets 172.30.16.0/24 to 172.30.31.0/24.

Figure 6-10   *Masking a Range of Addresses*

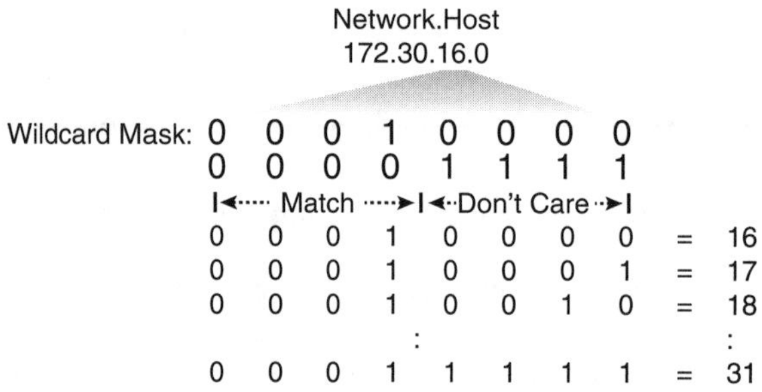

```
                         Network.Host
                          172.30.16.0

Wildcard Mask:  0   0   0   1   0   0   0   0
                0   0   0   0   1   1   1   1
                |◄···· Match ····►|◄·Don't Care·►|
                0   0   0   1   0   0   0   0   =   16
                0   0   0   1   0   0   0   1   =   17
                0   0   0   1   0   0   1   0   =   18
                            :                       :
                0   0   0   1   1   1   1   1   =   31
```

To use one ACL statement to match this range of subnets, use the IP address 172.30.16.0 in the ACL, which is the first subnet to be matched, followed by the required wildcard mask.

The wildcard mask matches the first two octets (172.30) of the IP address using corresponding 0 bits in the first two octets of the wildcard mask.

Because there is no interest in an individual host, the wildcard mask ignores the final octet by using the corresponding 1 bit in the wildcard mask. For example, the final octet of the wildcard mask is 255 in decimal.

In the third octet, where the subnet address occurs, the wildcard mask of decimal 15, or binary 00001111, matches the high-order 4 bits of the IP address. In this case, the wildcard mask matches subnets starting with the 172.30.16.0/24 subnet. For the final (low-end) 4 bits in this octet, the wildcard mask indicates that the bits can be ignored. In these positions, the address value can be binary 0 or binary 1. Thus, the wildcard mask matches subnet 16, 17, 18, and so on up to subnet 31. The wildcard mask does not match other subnets.

In the example, the address 172.30.16.0 with the wildcard mask 0.0.15.255 matches subnets 172.30.16.0/24 to 172.30.31.0/24.

In some cases, you must use more than one ACL statement to match a range of subnets; for example, to match 10.1.4.0/24 to 10.1.8.0/24, use 10.1.4.0 0.0.3.255 and 10.1.8.0 0.0.0.255.

The 0 and 1 bits in an ACL wildcard mask cause the ACL to either match or ignore the corresponding bit in the IP address. Working with decimal representations of binary wildcard mask bits can be tedious. For the most common uses of wildcard masking, you can use abbreviations. These abbreviations reduce how many numbers you are required to enter while configuring address test conditions. Figure 6-11 shows the wildcard masks used to match a specific host or to match all (any) host.

Figure 6-11 *Special Case Wildcard Masks*

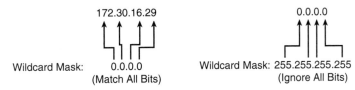

Instead of entering **172.30.16.29 0.0.0.0**, you can use the string **host 172.30.16.29**. Using the abbreviation **host** communicates the same test condition to the Cisco IOS ACL Software.

Instead of entering **0.0.0.0 255.255.255.255**, you can use the word **any** by itself as the keyword. Using the abbreviation **any** communicates the same test condition to the Cisco IOS ACL Software.

Summary of ACL Operations

The following summarizes the key points that were discussed in this section:

- ACLs can be used for IP packet filtering or to identify traffic to assign it special handling.

- ACLs perform top-down processing and can be configured for incoming or outgoing traffic.

- You can create an ACL using a named or numbered ACL. Named or numbered ACLs can be configured as standard or extended ACLs, which determines what they can filter.

- Reflexive, dynamic, and time-based ACLs add more functionality to standard and extended ACLs.

- In a wildcard bit mask, a 0 bit means to match the corresponding address bit, and a 1 bit means to ignore the corresponding address bit.

Configuring ACLs

This section describes the steps to configure named and numbered, standard and extended ACLs. This section also explains how to verify that the ACLs function properly and discusses some common configuration errors to avoid.

Standard IPv4 ACLs, numbered 1 to 99 and 1300 to 1999 or named, filter packets based on a source address and mask, and they permit or deny the entire TCP/IP protocol suite. This standard ACL filtering may not provide the filtering control you require. You may need a more precise way to filter your network traffic. Figure 6-12 illustrates that standard access lists check only the source address in the IPv4 packet header.

Figure 6-12 *Standard IPv4 Access Lists*

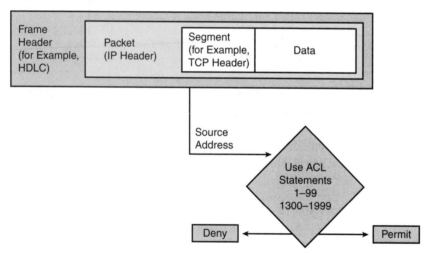

Configuring Numbered Standard IPv4 ACLs

To configure numbered standard IPv4 ACLs on a Cisco router, you must create a standard IPv4 ACL and activate an ACL on an interface. The **access-list** command creates an entry in a standard IPv4 traffic filter list.

The **ip access-group** command links an existing ACL to an interface. Only one ACL per protocol, per direction, and per interface is allowed.

> **NOTE** To remove an IP ACL from an interface, first enter the **no ip access-group** *name/ number* [**in**|**out**]command on the interface; then enter the global **no access-list** *name/number* command to remove the entire ACL.

The following provides an example of the steps that are required to configure and apply a numbered standard ACL on a router:

Step 1   Use the **access-list** global configuration command to create an entry in a standard IPv4 ACL.

RouterX(config)# `access-list 1 permit 172.16.0.0 0.0.255.255`

Enter the global **no access-list** *access-list-number* command to remove the entire ACL. The example statement matches any address that starts with 172.16.x.x. You can use the **remark** option to add a description to your ACL.

Step 2   Use the **interface** configuration command to select an interface to which to apply the ACL.

RouterX(config)# `interface ethernet 1`

After you enter the **interface** command, the command-line interface (CLI) prompt changes from (config)# to (config-if)#.

Step 3   Use the **ip access-group** interface configuration command to activate the existing ACL on an interface.

RouterX(config-if)# `ip access-group 1 out`

To remove an IP ACL from an interface, enter the **no ip access-group** *access-list-number* command on the interface.

This step activates the standard IPv4 ACL 1 on the interface as an outbound filter.

Example: Numbered Standard IPv4 ACL—Permit My Network Only

For the network shown in Figure 6-13, you want to create a list to prevent traffic that is not part of the internal networks (172.16.0.0/16) from traveling out either of the Ethernet interfaces.

Figure 6-13   *Standard ACL Permitting a Specific Network*

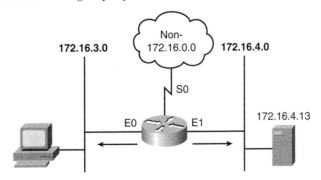

The configuration in Example 6-2 provides a solution for this example.

Example 6-2 *Access List Preventing All Non-172.16.0.0 Traffic*

```
RouterX(config)# access-list 1 permit 172.16.0.0  0.0.255.255
(implicit deny all - not visible in the list)
(access-list 1 deny 0.0.0.0   255.255.255.255)
RouterX(config)# interface ethernet 0
RouterX(config-if)# ip access-group 1 out
RouterX(config)# interface ethernet 1
RouterX(config-if)# ip access-group 1 out
```

Table 6-2 describes the command syntax that is presented in Example 6-2.

Table 6-2 *Numbered Standard IPv4 ACL Example Permitting a Specific Network*

access-list Command Parameters	Description
1	ACL number that indicates that this ACL is a standard list
permit	Indicates that traffic that matches the selected parameters is forwarded
172.16.0.0	IP address that is used with the wildcard mask to identify the source network
0.0.255.255	Wildcard mask; 0s indicate positions that must match, and 1s indicate "don't care" positions
ip access-group 1 out	Links the ACL to the interface as an outbound filter

This ACL allows only traffic from source network 172.16.0.0 to be forwarded out on E0 and E1. Traffic from networks other than 172.16.0.0 is blocked.

Example: Numbered Standard IPv4 ACL—Deny a Specific Host

For the network shown in Figure 6-14, you want to create a list to prevent traffic that originates from host 172.16.4.13 from traveling out Ethernet interface E0.

Figure 6-14 *Standard ACL Denying a Specific Host*

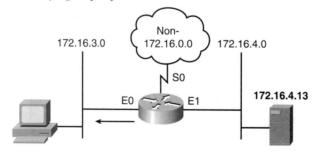

The configuration in Example 6-3 provides a solution for this example.

Example 6-3 *Access List Preventing Traffic Originating from a Specific Host*

```
RouterX(config)# access-list 1 deny 172.16.4.13 0.0.0.0
RouterX(config)# access-list 1 permit 0.0.0.0  255.255.255.255
(implicit deny all)
(access-list 1 deny 0.0.0.0   255.255.255.255)
RouterX(config)# interface ethernet 0
RouterX(config-if)# ip access-group 1 out
```

Table 6-3 describes the command syntax that is presented in Example 6-3.

Table 6-3 *Numbered Standard IPv4 ACL Example Denying a Specific Host*

access-list Command Parameters	Description
1	ACL number that indicates that this ACL is a standard list.
deny	Indicates that traffic that matches the selected parameters is not forwarded.
172.16.4.13	IP address of the source host.
0.0.0.0	A mask that requires the test to match all bits. (This is the default mask.)
permit	Indicates that traffic that matches the selected parameters is forwarded.
0.0.0.0	IP address of the source host; all 0s indicate a placeholder.
255.255.255.255	Wildcard mask; 0s indicate positions that must match, and 1s indicate "don't care" positions. All 1s in the mask indicate that all 32 bits are *not* checked in the source address. In other words, any address will match.

This ACL is designed to block traffic from a specific address, 172.16.4.13, and to allow all other traffic to be forwarded on interface Ethernet 0. The 0.0.0.0 255.255.255.255 IP address and wildcard mask combination permits traffic from any source. This combination can also be written using the keyword **any.**

Example: Numbered Standard IPv4 ACL—Deny a Specific Subnet

In Figure 6-15, the goal is to create a list to prevent traffic that originates from the subnet 172.16.4.0/24 from traveling out Ethernet interface E0.

Figure 6-15   *Standard ACL Denying a Specific Subnet*

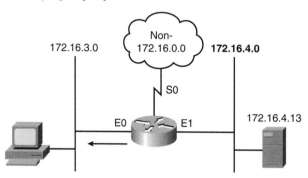

The configuration in Example 6-4 provides a solution for this example.

Example 6-4   *Access List Preventing Traffic Originating from a Specific Subnet*

```
RouterX(config)# access-list 1 deny 172.16.4.0 0.0.0.255
RouterX(config)# access-list 1 permit any
(implicit deny all)
(access-list 1 deny 0.0.0.0   255.255.255.255)
RouterX(config)# interface ethernet 0
RouterX(config-if)# ip access-group 1 out
```

Table 6-4 describes the command syntax that is presented in Example 6-4.

Table 6-4   *Numbered Standard IPv4 ACL Example Denying a Specific Subnet*

access-list Command Parameters	Description
1	ACL number indicating that this ACL is a standard list.
deny	Indicates that traffic that matches the selected parameters is not forwarded.
172.16.4.0	IP address of the source subnet.
0.0.0.255	Wildcard mask; 0s indicate positions that must match, and 1s indicate "don't care" positions. The mask with 0s in the first three octets indicates that those positions must match; the 255 in the last octet indicates a "don't care" condition.
permit	Indicates that traffic that matches the selected parameters is forwarded.
Any	Abbreviation for the IP address of the source. The abbreviation **any** indicates a source address of 0.0.0.0 and a wildcard mask of 255.255.255.255; all source addresses will match.

This ACL is designed to block traffic from a specific subnet, 172.16.4.0, and to allow all other traffic to be forwarded out E0.

Controlling Access to the Router Using ACLs

To control traffic into and out of the router (not through the router), you will protect the router virtual ports. A virtual port is called a *vty*. By default, there are five such virtual terminal lines, numbered vty 0 through vty 4. When configured, Cisco IOS Software images can support more than five vty ports.

Restricting vty access is primarily a technique for increasing network security and defining which addresses are allowed Telnet access to the router EXEC process.

Filtering Telnet traffic is typically considered an extended IP ACL function because it filters a higher-level protocol. Because you are filtering incoming or outgoing Telnet sessions by source addresses and applying the filter using the **access-class** command to the vty lines, you can use standard IP ACL statements to control vty access.

Example 6-5 demonstrates how to limit access to the Telnet process.

Example 6-5   *Access List Preventing Telnet Activity*

```
access-list 12 permit 192.168.1.0 0.0.0.255
(implicit deny any)
!
line vty 0 4
 access-class 12 in
```

In this example, you permit any device on network 192.168.1.0 0.0.0.255 to establish a virtual terminal (Telnet) session with the router. Of course, the user must know the appropriate passwords to enter user mode and privileged mode.

Notice that identical restrictions have been set on every vty line (0 to 4) because you cannot control on which vty line a user will connect. The implicit deny any statement still applies to the ACL when it is used as an access class entry.

Configuring Numbered Extended IPv4 ACLs

For more precise traffic-filtering control, use extended IPv4 ACLs, numbered 100 to 199 and 2000 to 2699 or named, which check for the source and destination IPv4 address. In addition, at the end of the extended ACL statement, you can specify the protocol and optional TCP or User Datagram Protocol (UDP) application to filter more precisely. Figure 6-16 illustrates the IP header fields that can be examined with an extended access list.

Figure 6-16 *Extended IPv4 Access Lists*

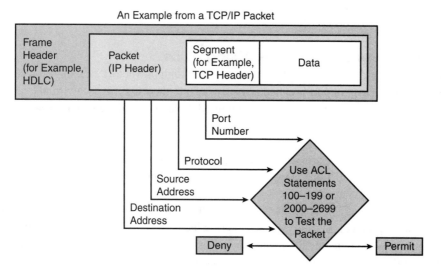

To specify an application, you can configure either the port number or the name of a well-known application. Table 6-5 shows an abbreviated list of some well-known port numbers of the various TCP applications.

Table 6-5 *Well-Known Port Numbers and IP Protocols*

Well-Known Port Number (Decimal)	IP Protocol
20 (TCP)	FTP data
21 (TCP)	FTP control
23 (TCP)	Telnet
25 (TCP)	Simple Mail Transfer Protocol (SMTP)
53 (TCP/UDP)	Domain Name System (DNS)
69 (UDP)	TFTP
80 (TCP)	HTTP

http://www.iani.org/assignments/port-numbers provides a more comprehensive list of well-known port numbers.

To configure numbered extended IPv4 ACLs on a Cisco router, create an extended IPv4 ACL and activate that ACL on an interface. Use the **access-list** command to create an entry to express a condition statement in a complex filter. The full command follows:

```
access-list access-list-number {permit | deny}
    protocol source source-wildcard [operator port]
    destination destination-wildcard [operator port]
    [established] [log]
```

Table 6-6 explains the syntax of the command.

Table 6-6 *Command Parameters for a Numbered Extended ACL*

access-list Command Parameters	Description
access-list-number	Identifies the list using a number in the ranges of 100–199 or 2000–2699.
**permit	deny**	Indicates whether this entry allows or blocks the specified address.
protocol	IP, TCP, UDP, ICMP, GRE[1], or IGRP[2].
source and *destination*	Identifies source and destination IP addresses.
source-wildcard and *destination-wildcard*	Wildcard mask; 0s indicate positions that must match, and 1s indicate "don't care" positions.
operator [*port|app_name*]	The operator can be **lt** (less than), **gt** (greater than), **eq** (equal to), or **neq** (not equal to). The port number referenced can be either the source port or the destination port, depending on where in the ACL the port number is configured. As an alternative to the port number, well-known application names can be used, such as Telnet, FTP, and SMTP.
established	For inbound TCP only. Allows TCP traffic to pass if the packet is a response to an outbound-initiated session. This type of traffic has the acknowledgement (ACK) bits set. (See the Extended ACL with the Established Parameter example.)
log	Sends a logging message to the console.

[1] GRE = generic routing encapsulation

[2] IGRP = Interior Gateway Routing Protocol

The syntax of the **access-list** command that is presented here is representative of the TCP protocol form. Not all parameters and options are given. For the complete syntax of all forms of the command, refer to the appropriate Cisco IOS Software documentation available at Cisco.com.

Extended ACL with the established Parameter

In Example 6-6, the **established** parameter of the extended ACL allows responses to traffic that originate from the mail host, 128.88.1.2, to return inbound on the serial 0 interface. A match occurs if the TCP datagram has the ACK or reset (RST) bits set, which indicates that the packet belongs to an existing connection. Without the **established** parameter in the ACL statement, the mail host could only receive SMTP traffic but not send it.

Example 6-6 *Access List Permitting Responses to an Originating Mail Host*

```
access-list 102 permit tcp any host 128.88.1.2 established
access-list 102 permit tcp any host 128.88.1.2 eq smtp

interface serial 0
 ip access-group 102 in
```

The **ip access-group** command links an existing extended ACL to an interface. Only one ACL per protocol, per direction, and per interface is allowed.

Table 6-7 defines the parameters of the **ip access-group** command.

Table 6-7 *ip access-group Command Parameters*

ip access-group Command Parameters	Description
access-list-number	Indicates the number of the ACL that is to be linked to an interface
**in	out**	Selects whether the ACL is applied as an input or output filter; out is the default

The following list shows the steps that are required to configure and apply an extended ACL on a router:

Step 1   Define an extended IPv4 ACL. Use the **access-list** global configuration command.

RouterX(config)# **access-list 101 deny tcp 172.16.4.0 0.0.0.255 172.16.3.0 0.0.0.255 eq 21**

Use the **show access-lists** command to display the contents of the ACL. In the example, access-list 101 denies TCP traffic from source 172.16.4.0, using the wildcard 0.0.0.255, to destination 172.16.3.0, using the wildcard 0.0.0.255 on port 21 (FTP control port) .

Step 2   Select a desired interface to be configured. Use the **interface** global configuration command.

RouterX(config)# **interface ethernet 0.**

After the **interface** command is entered, the CLI prompt changes from (config)# to (config-if)#.

Step 3   Link the extended IPv4 ACL to an interface. Use the **ip access-group** interface configuration command:

```
RouterX(config-if)# ip access-group 101 in
```

Use the **show ip interfaces** command to verify that an IP ACL is applied to the interface.

Numbered Extended IP ACL: Deny FTP from Subnets

For the network in Figure 6-17, you want to create a list to prevent FTP traffic that originates from the subnet 172.16.4.0/24, going to the 172.16.3.0/24 subnet, from traveling out Ethernet interface E0.

Figure 6-17 *Extended ACL Denying FTP from One Subnet to Another*

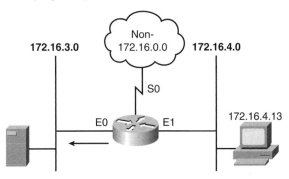

The configuration in Example 6-7 provides a solution for this example.

Example 6-7 *Access List Preventing FTP Traffic from Specific Subnets*

```
RouterX(config)# access-list 101 deny tcp 172.16.4.0 0.0.0.255 172.16.3.0 0.0.0.255 eq 21
RouterX(config)# access-list 101 deny tcp 172.16.4.0 0.0.0.255 172.16.3.0 0.0.0.255 eq 20
RouterX(config)# access-list 101 permit ip any any
(implicit deny all)
(access-list 101 deny ip 0.0.0.0 255.255.255.255 0.0.0.0 255.255.255.255)
RouterX(config)# interface ethernet 0
RouterX(config-if)# ip access-group 101 out
```

Table 6-8 describes the command syntax presented in Example 6-7.

Table 6-8 *Numbered Extended IPv4 ACL Example Denying FTP Between Subnets*

access-list Command Parameters	Description
101	ACL number; indicates an extended IPv4 ACL
deny	Indicates that traffic that matches the selected parameters is not forwarded
tcp	Transport layer protocol
172.16.4.0 0.0.0.255	Source IP address and mask; the first three octets must match but not the last octet
172.16.3.0 0.0.0.255	Destination IP address and mask; the first three octets must match but not the last octet
eq 21	Destination port; specifies the well-known port number for FTP control
eq 20	Destination port; specifies the well-known port number for FTP data
out	Links ACL 101 to interface E0 as an output filter

The deny statements deny FTP traffic from subnet 172.16.4.0 to subnet 172.16.3.0. The permit statement allows all other IP traffic out interface E0.

Numbered Extended ACL: Deny Only Telnet from Subnet

For the network in Figure 6-18, you want to create a list to prevent Telnet traffic that originates from the subnet 172.16.4.0/24 from traveling out Ethernet interface E0.

Figure 6-18 *Extended ACL Denying Telnet from a Given Subnet*

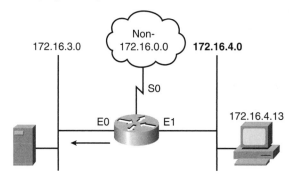

The configuration in Example 6-8 provides a solution for this example.

Example 6-8 *Access List Preventing Telnet Traffic from a Specific Subnet*

```
RouterX(config)# access-list 101 deny tcp 172.16.4.0  0.0.0.255  any eq 23
RouterX(config)# access-list 101 permit ip any any
(implicit deny all)
RouterX(config)# interface ethernet 0
RouterX(config-if)# ip access-group 101 out
```

This example denies Telnet traffic from 172.16.4.0 that is being sent out interface E0. All other IP traffic from any other source to any destination is permitted out E0.

Table 6-9 describes the command syntax that is presented in the example.

Table 6-9 *Numbered Extended IPv4 ACL Example Denying Telnet from a Subnet*

access-list Command Parameters	Description
101	ACL number; indicates an extended IPv4 ACL
deny	Indicates that traffic that matches the selected parameters is not forwarded
tcp	Transport layer protocol
172.16.4.0 0.0.0.255	Source IP address and mask; the first three octets must match but not the last octet
any	Match any destination IP address
eq 23 or eq telnet	Destination port or application; in this example, it specifies the well-known port number for Telnet, which is 23
permit	Indicates that traffic that matches the selected parameters is forwarded
ip	Any IP protocol
any	Keyword matching traffic from any source
any	Keyword matching traffic to any destination
out	Links ACL 101 to interface E0 as an output filter

Configuring Named ACLs

The named ACL feature allows you to identify standard and extended IP ACLs with an alphanumeric string (name) instead of the current numeric representations.

Named IP ACLs allow you to delete individual entries in a specific ACL. If you are using Cisco IOS Release 12.3, you can use sequence numbers to insert statements anywhere in the named

ACL. If you are using a software version earlier than Cisco IOS Release 12.3, you can insert statements only at the bottom of the named ACL.

Because you can delete individual entries with named ACLs, you can modify your ACL without having to delete and then reconfigure the entire ACL. Use named IP ACLs when you want to intuitively identify ACLs.

Creating Named Standard IP ACLs

The following list shows the steps that are required to configure and apply a named standard IP ACL on a router:

Step 1   Define a standard named IPv4 ACL. Use the **ip access-list standard** global configuration command.

```
RouterX(config)# ip access-list standard name
```

Define the list using a unique name. A descriptive name can be helpful when examining the configuration of the router.

Step 2   Enter one of the following commands to establish test parameters:

```
RouterX(config-std-nacl)#[sequence-number] deny {source [source-wildcard]
  ¦ any}
RouterX(config-std-nacl)#[sequence-number] permit {source [source-
  wildcard] ¦ any}
```

In access list configuration mode, specify one or more conditions permitted or denied. This determines whether the packet is passed or dropped. You can also use the sequence number to place the test parameter in a specific location within the list.

Step 3   Exit from named access list configuration mode:

```
RouterX(config-std-nacl)#exit
RouterX(config)#
```

Step 4   Select a desired interface to be configured. Use the **interface** global configuration command:

```
RouterX(config)# interface ethernet 0
```

After you enter the **interface** command, the CLI prompt changes from (config)# to (config-if)#.

Step 5   Link the extended IPv4 ACL to an interface. Use the **ip access-group** interface configuration command:

```
RouterX(config-if)# ip access-group 101 in
```

Use the **show ip interface** command to verify that an IP ACL is applied to the interface.

Creating Named Extended IP ACLs

The steps required to configure and apply a named extended IP ACL on a router are as follows:

Step 1   Define a standard named IPv4 ACL. Use the **ip access-list extended** global configuration command.

```
RouterX(config)# ip access-list extended name
```

Define the list using a unique name. A descriptive name can be helpful when examining the configuration of the router.

Step 2   Enter the following command syntax to establish test parameters:

```
RouterX(config-ext-nacl)# [sequence-number] {deny ¦ permit} protocol source
  source-wildcard destination destination-wildcard [option]
```

In access list configuration mode, specify the conditions allowed or denied. You can use the keyword **any** to abbreviate an address of 0.0.0.0 with a wildcard mask of 255.255.255.255 for the source address, destination address, or both. You can use the keyword **host** to abbreviate a wildcard mask of 0.0.0.0 for the source address or destination address. Place the keyword **host** in front of the address.

Step 3   Exit from named access list configuration mode:

```
RouterX(config-ext-nacl)#exit
RouterX(config)#
```

Step 4   Select a desired interface to be configured. Use the **interface** global configuration command:

```
RouterX(config)# interface ethernet 0
```

After you enter the **interface** command, the CLI prompt changes from (config)# to (config-if)#.

Step 5   Link the extended IPv4 ACL to an interface. Use the **ip access-group** interface configuration command:

```
RouterX(config-if)# ip access-group 101 in
```

Use the **show ip interfaces** command to verify that an IP ACL is applied to the interface.

You can take advantage of the sequence numbers in a named access list to add specific entries within an existing list. In Example 6-9, a new entry is added to a specified location within the access list.

Example 6-9 *Confirming Added Entries to an Existing Access List*

```
RouterX# show ip access-list

Standard IP access list MARKETING
2 permit 10.4.4.2, wildcard bits 0.0.255.255
5 permit 10.0.0.44, wildcard bits 0.0.0.255
10 permit 10.0.0.1, wildcard bits 0.0.0.255
20 permit 10.0.0.2, wildcard bits 0.0.0.255
RouterX(config)# ip access-list standard MARKETING
RouterX(config-std-nacl)# 15 permit 10.5.5.5 0.0.0.255
RouterX# show ip access-list
Standard IP access list MARKETING
2 permit 10.4.4.2, wildcard bits 0.0.255.255
5 permit 10.0.0.44, wildcard bits 0.0.0.255
10 permit 10.0.0.1, wildcard bits 0.0.0.255
15 permit 10.5.5.5, wildcard bits 0.0.0.255
20 permit 10.0.0.2, wildcard bits 0.0.0.255
```

Using the number of a standard access list as the name, you can also use this feature to place an entry in a specific location of a numbered access list. In Example 6-10, a new entry is added to a specified access list.

Example 6-10 *Placing an Entry in a Numbered List Using the Name Function*

```
RouterX# show ip access-list
Standard IP access list 1
2 permit 10.4.4.2, wildcard bits 0.0.255.255
5 permit 10.0.0.44, wildcard bits 0.0.0.255
10 permit 10.0.0.1, wildcard bits 0.0.0.255
20 permit 10.0.0.2, wildcard bits 0.0.0.255
RouterX(config)# ip access-list standard 1
RouterX(config-std-nacl)# 15 permit 10.5.5.5 0.0.0.255
RouterX(config-std-nacl)# end
RouterX# show ip access-list
Standard IP access list 1
2 permit 10.4.4.2, wildcard bits 0.0.255.255
5 permit 10.0.0.44, wildcard bits 0.0.0.255
10 permit 10.0.0.1, wildcard bits 0.0.0.255
15 permit 10.5.5.5, wildcard bits 0.0.0.255
20 permit 10.0.0.2, wildcard bits 0.0.0.255
```

Named Extended ACL: Deny a Single Host from a Given Subnet

For the network shown in Figure 6-19, you want to create a list named "troublemaker" to prevent traffic that originates from the host 172.16.4.13 from traveling out Ethernet interface E0.

Figure 6-19 *Named Extended ACL Denying a Single Host*

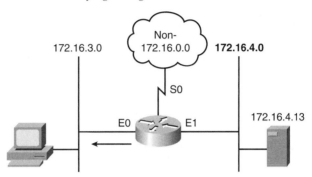

The configuration in Example 6-11 provides a solution for this example.

Example 6-11 *Access List Preventing Traffic from a Specific Host*

```
RouterX(config)#ip access-list standard troublemaker
RouterX(config-std-nacl)#deny host 172.16.4.13
RouterX(config-std-nacl)#permit 172.16.4.0 0.0.0.255
RouterX(config-std-nacl)#interface e0
RouterX(config-if)#ip access-group troublemaker out
```

Table 6-10 describes the command syntax that is presented in Example 6-11.

Table 6-10 *Named Extended IPv4 ACL Example Denying a Single Host*

access-list Command Parameter	Description
standard	Indicates that the named ACL is a standard ACL
troublemaker	Name of the ACL
deny	Indicates that traffic that matches the selected parameters is not forwarded
host 172.16.4.13	Source IP address; "host" indicates a wildcard mask of 0.0.0.0
permit	Indicates that traffic that matches the selected parameters is forwarded
172.16.4.0 0.0.0.255	Source IP address and mask; the first three octets must match but not the last octet
ip access-group troublemaker out	Links ACL "troublemaker" to interface E0 as an output filter

Named Extended ACL—Deny a Telnet from a Subnet

Using Figure 6-19 again, this time you want to create a list named "badgroup" to prevent Telnet traffic that originates from the subnet 172.16.4.0/24 from traveling out Ethernet interface E0.

The configuration in Example 6-12 provides a solution.

Example 6-12 *Access List Preventing Telnet Traffic from a Specific Subnet*

```
RouterX(config)#ip access-list extended badgroup
RouterX(config-ext-nacl)#deny tcp 172.16.4.0 0.0.0.255 any eq 23
RouterX(config-ext-nacl)#permit ip any any
RouterX(config-ext-nacl)#interface e0
RouterX(config-if)#ip access-group badgroup out
```

Table 6-11 describes the command syntax that is presented in the figure.

Table 6-11 *Named Extended IPv4 ACL Example Denying Telnet from a Subnet*

access-list Command Parameter	Description
extended	Indicates that the named ACL is an extended ACL.
badgroup	Name of the ACL.
deny	Indicates that traffic that matches the selected parameters is not forwarded.
tcp	Transport layer protocol.
172.16.4.0 0.0.0.255	Source IP address and mask; the first three octets must match but not the last octet.
any	Match any destination IP address.
eq 23 or eq telnet	Destination port or application name. In this example, it specifies the well-known port number for Telnet, which is 23.
permit	Indicates that traffic that matches the selected parameters is forwarded.
ip	Network layer protocol.
any	Keyword matching traffic to any source and destination.
ip access-group badgroup out	Links ACL "badgroup" to interface E0 as an output filter.

Adding Comments to Named or Numbered ACLs

Comments, also known as *remarks*, are ACL statements that are not processed. They are simple descriptive statements you can use to better understand and troubleshoot either named or numbered ACLs.

Each remark line is limited to 100 characters. The remark can go before or after a permit or deny statement. You should be consistent about where you put the remark so it is clear which remark describes which permit or deny statement. It would be confusing to have some remarks before the associated permit or deny statements and some remarks after the associated statements.

To add a comment to a named IP ACL, use the command **remark** *remark* in access list configuration mode. To add a comment to a numbered IP ACL, use the command **access-list** *access-list-number* **remark** *remark*.

The following is an example of adding a comment to a numbered ACL:

```
access-list 101 remark Permitting_John to Telnet to Server
access-list 101 permit tcp host 10.1.1.2 host 172.16.1.1 eq telnet
```

The following is an example of adding a comment to a named ACL:

```
ip access-list standard PREVENTION
remark Do not allow Jones subnet through
deny 171.69.0.0 0.0.255.255
```

Summary of Configuring ACLs

The following summarizes the key points that were discussed in this section:

- Standard IPv4 ACLs allow you to filter based on source IP address.

- Extended ACLs allow you to filter based on source IP address, destination IP address, protocol, and port number.

- Named ACLs allow you to delete individual statements from an ACL.

Troubleshooting ACLs

When you finish the ACL configuration, use the **show** commands to verify the configuration. Use the **show access-lists** command to display the contents of all ACLs, as demonstrated in Example 6-13. By entering the ACL name or number as an option for this command, you can display a specific ACL. To display only the contents of all IP ACLs, use the **show ip access-list** command.

Example 6-13 *Verifying Access List Configuration*

```
RouterX# show access-lists
Standard IP access list SALES
    10 deny    10.1.1.0, wildcard bits 0.0.0.255
    20 permit 10.3.3.1
    30 permit 10.4.4.1
    40 permit 10.5.5.1
Extended IP access list ENG
```

continues

Example 6-13 *Verifying Access List Configuration (Continued)*

```
10 permit tcp host 10.22.22.1 any eq telnet (25 matches)
20 permit tcp host 10.33.33.1 any eq ftp
30 permit tcp host 10.44.44.1 any eq ftp-data
```

The **show ip interface** command displays IP interface information and indicates whether any IP ACLs are set on the interface. In the **show ip interface e0** command output shown in Example 6-14, IP ACL 1 has been configured on the E0 interface as an inbound ACL. No outbound IP ACL has been configured on the E0 interface.

Example 6-14 *Verifying Access List Configuration on a Specific Interface*

```
RouterX# show ip interface e0
Ethernet0 is up, line protocol is up
  Internet address is 10.1.1.11/24
  Broadcast address is 255.255.255.255
  Address determined by setup command
  MTU is 1500 bytes
  Helper address is not set
  Directed broadcast forwarding is disabled
  Outgoing access list is not set
  Inbound  access list is 1
  Proxy ARP is enabled
  Security level is default
  Split horizon is enabled
  ICMP redirects are always sent
  ICMP unreachables are always sent
  ICMP mask replies are never sent
  IP fast switching is enabled
  IP fast switching on the same interface is disabled
  IP Feature Fast switching turbo vector
  IP multicast fast switching is enabled
  IP multicast distributed fast switching is disabled
  <text ommitted>
```

Take a look at some examples of access list problems. For the following issues, refer to Figure 6-20.

Figure 6-20 *ACL Troubleshooting Reference Network*

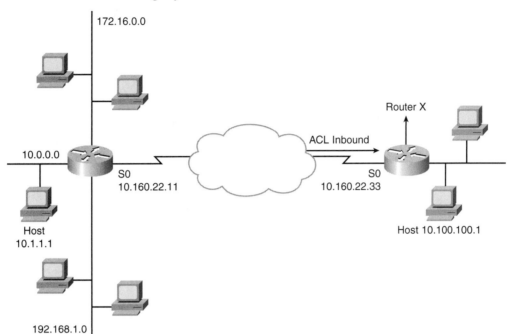

Each of the following problems assumes that an inbound access list is configured to S0 of
RouterX, as shown in Figure 6-20. You will use the **show access-lists** command to determine
information about the access list(s) in place to troubleshoot all these problems.

Problem: Host Connectivity

Host 10.1.1.1 has no connectivity with 10.100.100.1. The following output reveals information
about the access list(s) in place to help determine the possible cause of the problem:

```
RouterX# show access-lists 10
Standard IP access list 10
    10 deny    10.1.1.0, wildcard bits 0.0.0.255
    20 permit 10.1.1.1
    30 permit ip any any
```

The cause of this problem is that Host 10.1.1.1 has no connectivity with 10.100.100.1 because of
the order of the access list 10 rules. Because the router processes ACLs from the top down,
statement 10 would deny host 10.1.1.1, and statement 20 would not be processed. The solution to
this problem is to reverse statements 10 and 20.

The 192.168.1.0 network cannot use TFTP to connect to 10.100.100.1. The following output reveals information about the access list(s) in place to help determine the possible cause of the problem:

```
RouterX# show access-lists 120
Extended IP access list 120
    10 deny tcp 172.16.0.0 0.0.255.255 any eq telnet
    20 deny tcp 192.168.1.0 0.0.0.255 host 10.100.100.1 eq smtp
    30 permit tcp any any
```

The cause of this problem is that the 192.168.1.0 network cannot use TFTP to connect to 10.100.100.1 because TFTP uses the transport protocol UDP. Statement 30 in access list 120 allows all other TCP traffic, and because TFTP uses UDP, it is implicitly denied. The solution to this problem is to correct statement 30; it should be **ip any any**.

The 172.16.0.0 network can use Telnet to connect to 10.100.100.1, but this connection should not be allowed. The following output reveals information about the access list(s) in place to help determine the possible cause of the problem:

```
RouterX# show access-lists 130
Extended IP access list 130
    10 deny tcp any eq telnet any
    20 deny tcp 192.168.1.0 0.0.0.255 host 10.100.100.1 eq smtp
    30 permit ip any any
```

The cause of this problem is that the 172.16.0.0 network can use Telnet to connect to 10.100.100.1 because the Telnet port number in statement 10 of access list 130 is in the wrong position. Statement 10 currently denies any source with a port number that is equal to Telnet trying to establish a connection to any IP address. If you want to deny Telnet inbound on S0, the solution is to deny the destination port number that is equal to Telnet, for example, **deny tcp any any eq telnet**.

Host 10.1.1.1 can use Telnet to connect to 10.100.100.1, but this connection should not be allowed. The following output reveals information about the access list(s) in place to help determine the possible cause of the problem:

```
RouterX# show access-lists 140
Extended IP access list 140
    10 deny tcp host 10.160.22.11 10.100.100.0 0.0.0.255 eq telnet
    20 deny tcp 192.168.1.0 0.0.0.255 host 10.100.100.1 eq smtp
    30 permit ip any any
```

The cause of this problem is that the Host 10.1.1.1 can use Telnet to connect to 10.100.100.1 because there are no rules that deny host 10.1.1.1 or its network as the source. Statement 10 of access list 140 denies the router interface from which traffic would be departing. But as these packets depart the router, they have a source address of 10.1.1.1 and not the address of the router interface. The solution to this problem would be to modify entry 10 so that 10.1.0.0 subnet was denied instead of the address 10.160.22.11.

Problem: Host 10.100.100.1 can use Telnet to connect to 10.1.1.1, but this connection should not be allowed. The following output reveals information about the access list(s) in place to help determine the possible cause of the problem:

```
RouterX# show access-lists 150
Extended IP access list 150
    10 deny tcp host 10.100.100.1 any eq telnet
    20 permit ip any any
```

Access list 150 is applied to interface S0 in the inbound direction.

The cause of this problem is that the Host 10.100.100.1 can use Telnet to connect to 10.1.1.1 because of the direction in which access list 150 is applied to the S0 interface. Statement 10 denies the source address of 10.100.100.1, but that address would only be the source if the traffic were outbound on S0, not inbound. One solution would be to modify the direction in which the list was applied.

Host 10.1.1.1 can connect into RouterX using Telnet, but this connection should not be allowed. The following output reveals information about the access list(s) in place to help determine the possible cause of the problem:

```
RouterX# show access-lists 160
Extended IP access list 160
    10 deny tcp any host 10.160.22.33 eq telnet
    20 permit ip any any
```

The cause of this problem is that the Host 10.1.1.1 can connect into Router B using Telnet because using Telnet to connect *into* the router is different from using Telnet to connect *through* the router to another device. Statement 10 of access list 160 denies Telnet access to the address that is assigned to the S0 interface of Router B. Host 10.1.1.1 can still use Telnet to connect into Router B simply by using a different interface address, such as E0. The solution is recognizing which IOS command to use. When you want to block Telnet traffic into and out of the router, use the **access-class** command to apply access lists to the vty lines.

Summary of Troubleshooting ACLs

The following summarizes the key points that were discussed in this section:

■ An improperly configured access list can prevent legitimate traffic from passing through a router or allow unauthorized traffic to pass through the router.

■ You can use the **show access-lists** command to verify the configuration of an access list on a router.

■ You can use the **show ip interface** command to verify where the access list is applied to an interface and what direction it is applied in.

Chapter Summary

Standard and extended Cisco IOS access control lists (ACL) are used to classify IP packets. The many features of ACLs include security, encryption, policy-based routing, and quality of service (QoS). These features are applied on router and switch interfaces for specific directions (inbound versus outbound).

Numbered ACLs identify the type of ACL that is being created: standard or extended. They also allow administrators more flexibility when they are modifying the ACL entries.

The following list summarizes the key points that were discussed in this chapter:

- ACLs can be used to filter IP packets or identify traffic for special handling.

- ACLs perform top-down processing and can be configured for incoming or outgoing traffic.

- In a wildcard bit mask, 0 means to match the corresponding address bit, and 1 means to ignore the corresponding address bit.

- Standard IPv4 ACLs allow filtering based on source address.

- Extended IPv4 ACLs allow filtering based on source and destination addresses, as well as protocol and port number.

- IP access list entry sequence numbering allows you to delete individual statements from an ACL to add statements anywhere in the ACL.

- The **show access-lists** and **show ip interface** commands are useful for troubleshooting common ACL configuration errors.

Review Questions

Use the questions here to review what you learned in this chapter. The correct answers and the solutions are found in the appendix, "Answers to Chapter Review Questions."

1. What does a Cisco router do with a packet when it matches an ACL permit statement?

   a. Discards the packet

   b. Returns the packet to its originator

   c. Sends the packet to the output buffer

   d. Holds the packet for further processing

2. What does a Cisco router do with a packet when it matches an ACL deny statement?

    a. Discards the packet

    b. Returns the packet to its originator

    c. Sends the packet to the output buffer

    d. Holds the packet for further processing

3. You can apply an ACL to multiple interfaces. How many ACLs per protocol, per direction, and per interface can you apply?

    a. 1

    b. 2

    c. 4

    d. Any number

4. What is the term for the final default statement at the end of every ACL?

    a. Implicit deny any

    b. Implicit deny host

    c. Implicit permit any

    d. Implicit permit host

5. Which statement best describes the difference between standard and extended IPv4 ACLs?

    a. Standard ACLs use the range 100 through 149, whereas extended ACLs use the range 150 through 199.

    b. Standard ACLs filter based on the source and destination addresses, whereas extended ACLs filter based on the source address.

    c. Standard ACLs permit or deny access to a specified well-known port, whereas extended ACLs filter based on the source address and mask.

    d. Standard ACLs permit or deny the entire TCP/IP protocol suite, whereas extended ACLs can choose a specific IP protocol and port number.

6. Which two ranges of numbers can you use to identify IPv4 extended ACLs on a Cisco router? (Choose two.)

    a. 1 to 99

    b. 51 to 151

    c. 100 to 199

    d. 200 to 299

    e. 1300 to 1999

    f. 2000 to 2699

7. ACLs are processed from the top down. Which of the following is a benefit of placing more specific statements and statements that are expected to frequently match at the beginning of an ACL?

   a. Processing overhead is reduced.

   b. ACLs can be used for other routers.

   c. The ACLs are easier to edit.

   d. The less specific tests can be inserted more easily.

8. A system administrator wants to configure an IPv4 standard ACL on a Cisco router to allow packets only from the hosts on subnet 10.1.1.0/24 to enter an interface on a router. Which ACL configuration accomplishes this goal?

   a. **access-list 1 permit 10.1.1.0**

   b. **access-list 1 permit 10.1.1.0 host**

   c. **access-list 99 permit 10.1.1.0 0.0.0.255**

   d. **access-list 100 permit 10.1.1.0 0.0.0.255**

9. Which Cisco IOS command links an extended IPv4 ACL to an interface?

   a. **ip access-list 101 e0**

   b. **access-group 101 e0**

   c. **ip access-group 101 in**

   d. **access-list 101 permit tcp access-list 100 permit 10.1.1.0 0.0.0.255 eq 21**

10. What is the complete command to create an ACL entry that has the following parameters?

   Source IP address is 172.16.0.0

   Source mask is 0.0.255.255

   Permit this entry

   ACL number is 1

   a. **access-list 1 deny 172.16.0.0 0.0.255.255**

   b. **access-list 1 permit 172.16.0.0 0.0.255.255**

   c. **access-list permit 1 172.16.0.0 255.255.0.0**

   d. **access-list 99 permit 172.16.0.0 0.0.255.255**

11. The following is an ACL that is entered on a Cisco router:

```
access-list 135 deny tcp 172.16.16.0 0.0.15.255 172.16.32.0 0.0.15.255 eq telnet
access-list 135 permit ip any any
```

If this ACL is used to control incoming packets on Ethernet 0, which three statements are true? (Choose three.)

   a. Address 172.16.1.1 will be denied Telnet access to address 172.16.37.5.

   b. Address 172.16.31.1 will be permitted FTP access to address 172.16.45.1.

   c. Address 172.16.1.1 will be permitted Telnet access to address 172.16.32.1.

   d. Address 172.16.16.1 will be permitted Telnet access to address 172.16.32.1.

   e. Address 172.16.16.1 will be permitted Telnet access to address 172.16.50.1.

   f. Address 172.16.30.12 will be permitted Telnet access to address 172.16.32.12.

12. Which command applies standard IP ACL filtering to vty lines for an outgoing Telnet session that originates from within a router?

   a. **access-vty 1 out**

   b. **access-class 1 out**

   c. **ip access-list 1 out**

   d. **ip access-group 1 out**

13. Which command is used on a Cisco router to determine if IP ACLs are applied to an Ethernet interface?

   a. **show interfaces**

   b. **show ACL**

   c. **show ip interface**

   d. **show ip access-list**

14. Which command is used to find out if ACL 100 has been configured on a Cisco router?

   a. **show interfaces**

   b. **show ip interface**

   c. **show ip access-list**

   d. **show access-groups**

This chapter includes the following sections:

- Chapter Objectives

- Scaling the Network with NAT and PAT

- Transitioning to IPv6

- Chapter Summary

- Review Questions

CHAPTER 7

Managing Address Spaces with NAT and IPv6

One of the most important drawbacks to IP version 4 (IPv4) is the limited number of unique network addresses; the Internet is running out of address space. Two solutions to this dilemma are Network Address Translation (NAT) and IP version 6 (IPv6).

NAT provides a short-term solution to this problem by translating private IPv4 addresses into globally unique, routable IPv4 addresses. IPv6 is the long-term solution. By increasing the size of an IP address to 128 bits, IPv6 increases the total number of addresses that are available. This chapter discusses both solutions.

Chapter Objectives

Upon completing this chapter, you will be able to describe when to use NAT or Port Address Translation (PAT) on a medium-sized network and configure NAT or PAT on routers. You will also be able to explain IPv6 addressing and configure IPv6 in a Cisco router. This ability includes being able to meet these objectives:

■ Configure and verify static, dynamic, and overloading NAT and identify key **show** and **debug** command parameters that are required for troubleshooting NAT and PAT

■ Explain the format of IPv6 addresses and the components that are required to run IPv6, configure IPv6 capability with RIP, and explain the impact that IPv6 has on network routing

Scaling the Network with NAT and PAT

Two Internet scalability challenges are the depletion of registered IP version 4 (IPv4) address space and scaling in routing. Cisco IOS Network Address Translation (NAT) and Port Address Translation (PAT) are mechanisms for conserving registered IPv4 addresses in large networks and simplifying IPv4 address management tasks. NAT and PAT translate IPv4 addresses within private internal networks to legal IPv4 addresses for transport over public external networks, such as the Internet, without requiring a registered subnet address. Incoming traffic is translated back for delivery within the inside network.

This translation of IPv4 addresses eliminates the need for host renumbering and allows the same IPv4 address range to be used in multiple intranets. This section describes the features that are offered by NAT and PAT and shows you how to configure NAT and PAT on Cisco routers.

Introducing NAT and PAT

NAT operates on a Cisco router and is designed for IPv4 address simplification and conservation. NAT enables private IPv4 internetworks that use nonregistered IPv4 addresses to connect to the Internet. Usually, NAT connects two networks and translates the private (inside local) addresses in the internal network into public addresses (inside global) before packets are forwarded to another network. As part of this functionality, you can configure NAT to advertise only one address for the entire network to the outside world. Advertising only one address effectively hides the internal network from the world, thus providing additional security. Figure 7-1 shows an example of address translation between a private and public network.

Figure 7-1   *Network Address Translation*

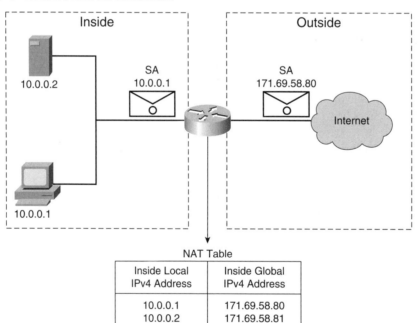

Any device that is between an internal network and the public network—such as a firewall, a router, or a computer—uses NAT, which is defined in RFC 1631.

In NAT terminology, the *inside network* is the set of networks that are subject to translation. The *outside network* refers to all other addresses. Usually these are valid addresses located on the Internet.

Cisco defines the following list of NAT terms:

- **Inside local address:** The IPv4 address that is assigned to a host on the inside network. The inside local address is likely not an IPv4 address assigned by the Network Information Center or service provider.

- **Inside global address:** A legitimate IPv4 address assigned by the NIC or service provider that represents one or more inside local IPv4 addresses to the outside world.

- **Outside local address:** The IPv4 address of an outside host as it appears to the inside network. Not necessarily legitimate, the outside local address is allocated from a routable address space on the inside.

- **Outside global address:** The IPv4 address that is assigned to a host on the outside network by the host owner. The outside global address is allocated from a globally routable address or network space.

NAT has many forms and can work in the following ways:

- **Static NAT:** Maps an unregistered IPv4 address to a registered IPv4 address (one to one). Static NAT is particularly useful when a device must be accessible from outside the network.

- **Dynamic NAT:** Maps an unregistered IPv4 address to a registered IPv4 address from a group of registered IPv4 addresses.

- **NAT overloading:** Maps multiple unregistered IPv4 addresses to a single registered IPv4 address (many to one) by using different ports. Overloading is also known as PAT and is a form of dynamic NAT.

NAT offers these benefits over using public addressing:

- Eliminates the need to readdress all hosts that require external access, saving time and money.

- Conserves addresses through application port-level multiplexing. With NAT, internal hosts can share a single registered IPv4 address for all external communications. In this type of configuration, relatively few external addresses are required to support many internal hosts, thus conserving IPv4 addresses.

- Protects network security. Because private networks do not advertise their addresses or internal topology, they remain reasonably secure when they gain controlled external access in conjunction with NAT.

One of the main features of NAT is PAT, which is also referred to as "overload" in Cisco IOS configuration. PAT allows you to translate multiple internal addresses into a single external address, essentially allowing the internal addresses to share one external address. Figure 7-2 shows an example of Port Address Translation. The following list highlights the operations of PAT:

Figure 7-2 *Port Address Translation*

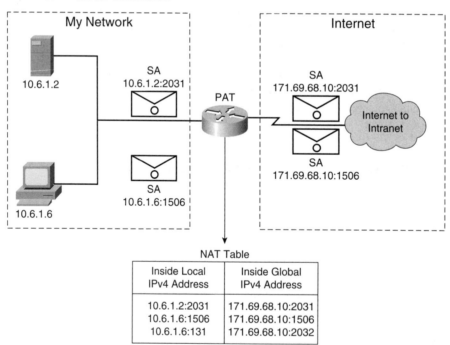

Inside Local IPv4 Address	Inside Global IPv4 Address
10.6.1.2:2031	171.69.68.10:2031
10.6.1.6:1506	171.69.68.10:1506
10.6.1.6:131	171.69.68.10:2032

- PAT uses unique source port numbers on the inside global IPv4 address to distinguish between translations. Because the port number is encoded in 16 bits, the total number of internal sessions that NAT can translate into one external address is, theoretically, as many as 65,536.

■ PAT attempts to preserve the original source port. If the source port is already allocated, PAT attempts to find the first available port number. It starts from the beginning of the appropriate port group, 0 to 511, 512 to 1023, or 1024 to 65535. If PAT does not find an available port from the appropriate port group and if more than one external IPv4 address is configured, PAT moves to the next IPv4 address and tries to allocate the original source port again. PAT continues trying to allocate the original source port until it runs out of available ports and external IPv4 addresses.

Translating Inside Source Addresses

You can translate your own IPv4 addresses into globally unique IPv4 addresses when you are communicating outside your network. You can configure static or dynamic inside source translation.

Figure 7-3 illustrates a router that is translating a source address inside a network into a source address outside the network.

Figure 7-3 *Translating an Address*

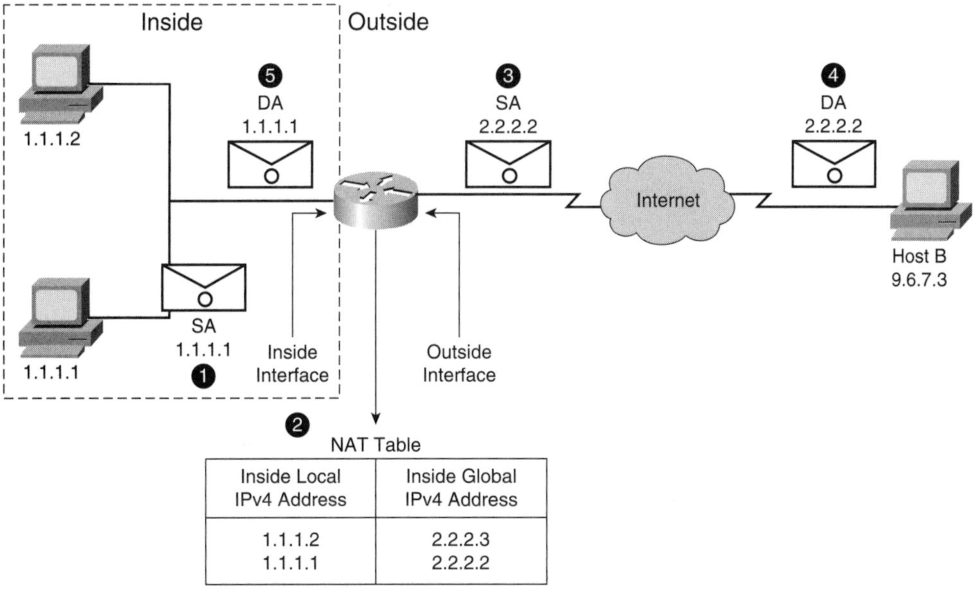

The steps for translating an inside source address are as follows:

Step 1   The user at host 1.1.1.1 opens a connection to host B.

Step 2   The first packet that the router receives from host 1.1.1.1 causes the router to check its NAT table.

- If a static translation entry was configured, the router goes to Step 3.

- If no static translation entry exists, the router determines that the source address 1.1.1.1 (SA 1.1.1.1) must be translated dynamically. The router then selects a legal, global address from the dynamic address pool and creates a translation entry (in the example, 2.2.2.2). This type of entry is called a *simple entry.*

Step 3   The router replaces the inside local source address of host 1.1.1.1 with the translation entry global address and forwards the packet.

Step 4   Host B receives the packet and responds to host 1.1.1.1 by using the inside global IPv4 destination address 2.2.2.2 (DA 2.2.2.2).

Step 5   When the router receives the packet with the inside global IPv4 address, the router performs a NAT table lookup by using the inside global address as a key. The router then translates the address back to the inside local address of host 1.1.1.1 and forwards the packet to host 1.1.1.1. Host 1.1.1.1 receives the packet and continues the conversation. The router performs Steps 2 through 5 for each packet.

The order in which the router processes traffic depends on whether the NAT translation is a global-to-local translation or a local-to-global translation. Table 7-1 illustrates the order in which a router processes traffic, depending on the direction of the translation.

Table 7-1   *Router Processing Order*

Local-to-Global	Global-to-Local
1. Check input access list if using IPsec[1].	1. Check input access list if using IPsec.
2. Perform decryption—for Cisco Encryption Technology or IPsec.	2. Perform decryption—for Cisco Encryption Technology or IPsec.
3. Check inbound access list.	3. Check inbound access list.
4. Check input rate limits.	4. Check input rate limits.
5. Perform input accounting.	5. Perform input accounting.
6. Perform policy routing.	6. Perform NAT outside to inside (global to local translation).
7. Route packet.	7. Perform policy routing.
8. Redirect to web cache.	8. Route packet.
	9. Redirect to web cache.

Table 7-1 *Router Processing Order (Continued)*

Local-to-Global	Global-to-Local
9. Perform NAT inside to outside (local to global translation). 10. Check crypto map and mark for encryption if appropriate. 11. Check outbound access list.	10. Check crypto map and mark for encryption if appropriate. 11. Check outbound access list. 12. Inspect CBAC. 13. Intercept TCP. 14. Perform encryption. 15. Perform queuing.

[1] IPsec = IP security

[2] CBAC = Context-Based Access Control

To configure static inside source address translation on a router, follow these steps:

Step 1 Establish static translation between an inside local address and an inside global address.

```
RouterX(config)# ip nat inside source static local-ip global-ip
```
Enter the **no ip nat inside source static** global command to remove the static source translation.

Step 2 Specify the inside interface.

```
RouterX(config)# interface type number
```
After you enter the **interface** command, the CLI prompt changes from (config)# to (config-if)#.

Step 3 Mark the interface as connected to the inside.

```
RouterX(config-if)# ip nat inside
```
Step 4 Specify the outside interface.

```
RouterX(config-if)# interface type number
```
Step 5 Mark the interface as connected to the outside.

```
RouterX(config-if)# ip nat outside
```
Use the command **show ip nat translations** in EXEC mode to display active translation information, as demonstrated here:

```
RouterX# show ip nat translations
     Pro      Inside global   Inside local   Outside local   Outside global
     - - -         192.168.1.2       10.1.1.2
```

Static NAT Address Mapping

The example shows the use of discrete address mapping with static NAT translations for the network in Figure 7-4. The router translates packets from host 10.1.1.2 to a source address of 192.168.1.2.

Figure 7-4 *Static NAT Address Mapping*

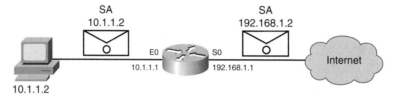

To configure dynamic inside source address translation, follow these steps:

Step 1   Define a pool of global addresses to be allocated as needed.

```
RouterX(config)# ip nat pool name start-ip end-ip {netmask   netmask |
   prefix-length prefix-length}
```

Enter the **no ip nat pool** global command to remove the pool of global addresses.

Step 2   Define a standard access control list (ACL) that permits the addresses that are to be translated.

```
RouterX(config)# access-list access-list-number permit source    [source-
   wildcard]
```

Enter the **no access-list** *access-list-number* global command to remove the ACL.

Step 3   Establish dynamic source translation, specifying the ACL that was defined in the prior step.

```
RouterX(config)# ip nat inside source list access-list-number   pool name
```

Enter the **no ip nat inside source** global command to remove the dynamic source translation.

Step 4   Specify the inside interface.

```
RouterX(config)# interface type number
```

After you enter the **interface** command, the CLI prompt changes from (config)# to (config-if)#.

Step 5   Mark the interface as connected to the inside.

```
RouterX(config-if)# ip nat inside
```

Step 6   Specify the outside interface.

```
RouterX(config-if)# interface type number
```

Step 7   Mark the interface as connected to the outside.

```
RouterX(config-if)# ip nat outside
```

> **CAUTION**   The ACL must permit only those addresses that are to be translated. Remember that there is an implicit **deny any** statement at the end of each ACL. An ACL that is too permissive can lead to unpredictable results. Using **permit any** can result in NAT consuming too many router resources, which can cause network problems.

Use the command **show ip nat translations** in EXEC mode to display active translation information.

Dynamic Address Translation

The example in Figure 7-5 shows how the device translates all source addresses that pass ACL 1, which means a source address from the 192.168.1.0/24 network, into an address from the pool named net-208. The pool contains addresses from 171.69.233.209/28 to 171.69.233.222/28.

Figure 7-5   *Dynamic Address Translation*

```
ip nat pool net-208 171.69.233.209 171.69.233.222 netmask
255.255.255.240
ip nat inside source list 1 pool net-208
!
interface serial 0
 ip address 171.69.232.182 255.255.255.240
 ip nat outside
!
interface ethernet 0
 ip address 192.168.1.94 255.255.255.0
 ip nat inside
!
access-list 1 permit 192.168.1.0 0.0.0.255
```

Host A
192.168.1.100

Host C
10.1.1.1

E0   S0
192.168.1.94   171.69.232.182

Host B
192.168.1.101

Host D
172.16.1.1

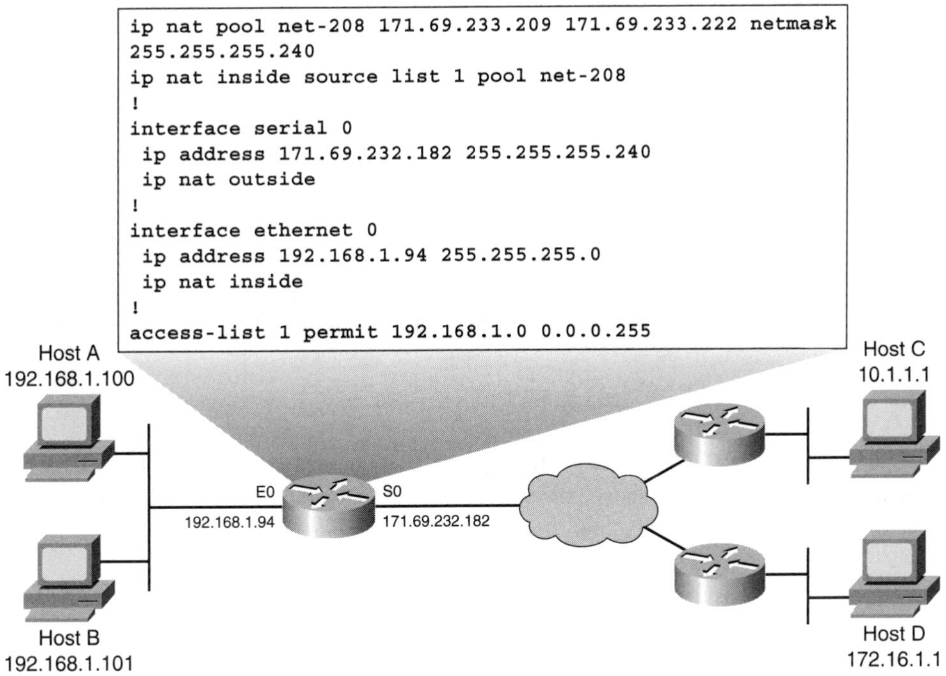

Overloading an Inside Global Address

You can conserve addresses in the inside global address pool by allowing the router to use one inside global address for many inside local addresses. When this overloading is configured, the router maintains enough information from higher-level protocols—for example, TCP or User Datagram Protocol (UDP) port numbers—to translate the inside global address back into the correct inside local address. When multiple inside local addresses map to one inside global address, the TCP or UDP port numbers of each inside host distinguish between the local addresses.

Figure 7-6 illustrates NAT operation when one inside global address represents multiple inside local addresses. The TCP port numbers act as differentiators.

Figure 7-6 *Overloading an Inside Global Address*

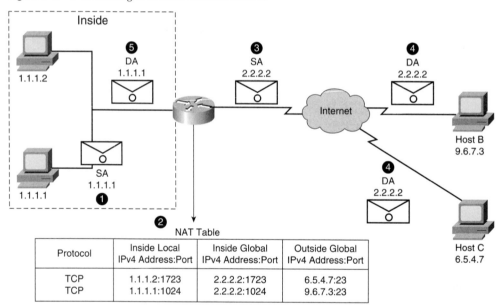

Both host B and host C think they are talking to a single host at address 2.2.2.2. They are actually talking to different hosts; the port number is the differentiator. In fact, many inside hosts could share the inside global IPv4 address by using many port numbers.

The router performs the following process when it overloads inside global addresses:

Step 1 The user at host 1.1.1.1 opens a connection to host B.

Step 2 The first packet that the router receives from host 1.1.1.1 causes the router to check its NAT table.

If no translation entry exists, the router determines that address 1.1.1.1 must be translated and sets up a translation of inside local address 1.1.1.1 into a legal inside global address. If overloading is enabled and another translation is active, the router reuses the inside global address from that translation and saves enough information to be able to translate back. This type of entry is called an *extended entry*.

Step 3 The router replaces the inside local source address 1.1.1.1 with the selected inside global address and forwards the packet.

Step 4 Host B receives the packet and responds to host 1.1.1.1 by using the inside global IPv4 address 2.2.2.2.

Step 5 When the router receives the packet with the inside global IPv4 address, the router performs a NAT table lookup. Using the inside global address and port and outside global address and port as a key, the router translates the address back into the inside local address 1.1.1.1 and forwards the packet to host 1.1.1.1. Host 1.1.1.1 receives the packet and continues the conversation. The router performs Steps 2 through 5 for each packet.

To configure overloading of inside global addresses, follow these steps:

Step 1 Define a standard ACL that permits the addresses that are to be translated.

```
RouterX(config)# access-list access-list-number permit source    [source-
  wildcard]
```

Enter the **no access-list** *access-list-number* global command to remove the ACL.

Step 2 Establish dynamic source translation, specifying the ACL that was defined in the prior step.

```
RouterX(config)# ip nat inside source list access-list-number    interface
  interface overload
```

Enter the **no ip nat inside source** global command to remove the dynamic source translation. The keyword **overload** enables PAT.

Step 3 Specify the inside interface.

```
RouterX(config)# interface type number
RouterX(config-if)# ip nat inside
```

After you enter the **interface** command, the CLI prompt changes from (config)# to (config-if)#.

Step 4 Specify the outside interface.

```
RouterX(config-if)# interface type number
RouterX(config-if)# ip nat outside
```

Use the command **show ip nat translations** in EXEC mode to display active translation information.

The NAT inside-to-outside process comprises this sequence of steps:

Step 1   The incoming packet goes to the route table and the next hop is identified.

Step 2   NAT statements are parsed so that the interface serial 0 IPv4 address can be used in overload mode. PAT creates a source address to use.

Step 3   The router encapsulates the packet and sends it out on interface serial 0.

For the return traffic, the NAT outside-to-inside address translation process works in the following sequence of steps:

Step 1   NAT statements are parsed. The router looks for an existing translation and identifies the appropriate destination address.

Step 2   The packet goes to the route table, and the next-hop interface is determined.

Step 3   The packet is encapsulated and sent out to the local interface.

No internal addresses are visible during this process. As a result, hosts do not have an external public address, which leads to improved security.

By default, dynamic address translations time out from the NAT and PAT translation tables after some period of nonuse. The default timeout periods differ among various protocols. You can reconfigure the default timeouts with the **ip nat translation** command. The syntax for this command is as follows:

```
ip nat translation {timeout | udp-timeout | dns-timeout | tcp-timeout | finrst-timeout |
    icmp-timeout | pptp-timeout | syn-timeout | port-timeout} {seconds | never}
```

Table 7-2 describes the parameters for this command.

Table 7-2   ip nat translation *Parameters*

Parameter	Description
timeout	Specifies that the timeout value applies to dynamic translations except for overload translations. The default is 86,400 seconds (24 hours).
udp-timeout	Specifies the timeout value for the UDP port. The default is 300 seconds (5 minutes).

Table 7-2   ip nat translation *Parameters (Continued)*

Parameter	Description
dns-timeout	Specifies the timeout value for connections to the DNS[1]. The default is 60 seconds.
tcp-timeout	Specifies the timeout value for the TCP port. The default is 86,400 seconds (24 hours).
finrst-timeout	Specifies the timeout value for the Finish and Reset TCP packets, which terminate a connection. The default is 60 seconds.
icmp-timeout	Specifies the timeout value for ICMP[2] flows. The default is 60 seconds.
pptp-timeout	Specifies the timeout value for NAT PPTP[3] flows. The default is 86,400 seconds (24 hours).
syn-timeout	Specifies the timeout value for TCP flows immediately after a synchronous transmission message that consists of digital signals that are sent with precise clocking. The default is 60 seconds.
port-timeout	Specifies that the timeout value applies to the TCP/UDP port.
seconds	Number of seconds after which the specified port translation times out. The default is 0.
never	Specifies that the port translation never times out.

[1] DNS = Domain Name System

[2] ICMP = Internet Control Message Protocol

[3] PPTP = Point-to-Point Tunneling Protocol

Table 7-3 lists commands you can use to clear the entries before they time out.

Table 7-3   clear ip nat translation *Commands*

Command	Description
clear ip nat translation *	Clears all dynamic address translation entries from the NAT translation table.
clear ip nat translation inside *global-ip local-ip* [**outside** *local-ip global-ip*]	Clears a simple dynamic translation entry that contains an inside translation or both an inside and outside translation.
clear ip nat translation outside *local-ip global-ip*	Clears a simple dynamic translation entry containing an outside translation.
clear ip nat translation protocol inside *global-ip global-port local-ip local-port* [**outside** *local-ip local-port global-ip global-port*]	Clears an extended dynamic translation entry (PAT entry).

Resolving Translation Table Issues

When you have IPv4 connectivity problems in a NAT environment, it is often difficult to determine the cause of the problem. Many times NAT is blamed, when in reality there is an underlying problem. When you are trying to determine the cause of an IPv4 connectivity problem, it helps to eliminate NAT as the potential problem. Follow these steps to verify that NAT is operating as expected:

Step 1   Based on the configuration, clearly define what NAT is supposed to achieve. You may determine that the NAT configuration has a problem.

Step 2   Use the **show ip nat translations** command to determine if the correct translations exist in the translation table.

Step 3   Verify whether the translation is occurring by using **show** and **debug** commands.

Step 4   Review in detail what is happening to the translated packet, and verify that routers have the correct routing information for the translated address to move the packet.

If the appropriate translations are not in the translation table, verify the following items:

- There are no inbound ACLs that are denying the packet entry into the NAT router.

- The ACL that is referenced by the NAT command is permitting all necessary networks.

- The NAT pool has enough addresses.

- The router interfaces are appropriately defined as NAT inside or NAT outside.

In a simple network environment, it is useful to monitor NAT statistics with the **show ip nat statistics** command. However, in a more complex NAT environment with several translations taking place, this **show** command is no longer useful. In this case, it may be necessary to run **debug** commands on the router.

The **debug ip nat** command displays information about every packet that is translated by the router, which helps you verify the operation of the NAT feature. The **debug ip nat detailed** command generates a description of each packet that is considered for translation. This command also outputs information about certain errors or exception conditions, such as the failure to allocate a global address. The **debug ip nat detailed** command will generate more overhead than the **debug ip nat** command, but it can provide the detail that you need to troubleshoot the NAT problem.

Example 7-1 demonstrates sample **debug ip nat** output.

Example 7-1 *Displaying Information About Packets Translated by the Router*

```
RouterX# debug ip nat

NAT: s=192.168.1.95->172.31.233.209, d=172.31.2.132 [6825]
NAT: s=172.31.2.132, d=172.31.233.209->192.168.1.95 [21852]
NAT: s=192.168.1.95->172.31.233.209, d=172.31.1.161 [6826]
NAT*: s=172.31.1.161, d=172.31.233.209->192.168.1.95 [23311]
NAT*: s=192.168.1.95->172.31.233.209, d=172.31.1.161 [6827]
NAT*: s=192.168.1.95->172.31.233.209, d=172.31.1.161 [6828]
NAT*: s=172.31.1.161, d=172.31.233.209->192.168.1.95 [23312]
NAT*: s=172.31.1.161, d=172.31.233.209->192.168.1.95 [23313]
```

In Example 7-1, the first two lines show the debugging output that a DNS request and reply produce where the DNS server address is 172.31.2.132. The remaining lines show the debugging output from a Telnet connection from a host on the inside of the network to a host on the outside of the network.

The asterisk (*) next to NAT indicates that the translation is occurring in the fast-switched path. The first packet in a conversation is always process-switched. The remaining packets go through the fast-switched path if a cache entry exists.

The final entry in each line, within brackets ([ ]), provides the identification number of the packet. You can use this information to correlate with other packet traces from protocol analyzers.

Another useful command when verifying the operation of NAT is the **show ip nat statistics** command. This command is shown in Example 7-2.

Example 7-2 **show ip nat** *statistics*

```
RouterX# show ip nat statistics
 Total active translations: 1 (1 static, 0 dynamic; 0 extended)
 Outside interfaces:
 Ethernet0, Serial2
 Inside interfaces:
 Ethernet1
 Hits: 0  Misses: 0
 Expired translations: 0
 Dynamic mappings:
 -- Inside Source
 access-list 7 pool test refcount 0
 pool test: netmask 255.255.255.0
 start 172.16.11.70 end 172.16.11.71
 type generic, total addresses 2, allocated 0 (0%), misses 0
```

Table 7-4 describes the **show ip nat statistics** fields.

Table 7-4   **show ip nat statistics** *Field Descriptions*

Field	Description
Total translations	Number of translations that are active in the system. This number is incremented each time a translation is created and is decremented each time a translation is cleared or times out.
Outside interfaces	List of interfaces that are marked as outside with the **ip nat outside** command.
Inside interfaces	List of interfaces that are marked as inside with the **ip nat inside** command.
Hits	Number of times the software looks up an entry in the translations table and finds an entry.
Misses	Number of times the software looks up a translations table, fails to find an entry, and must try to create one.
Expired translations	Cumulative count of translations that have expired since the router was booted.
Dynamic mappings	Indicates that the information that follows is about dynamic mappings.
Inside source	Indicates that the information that follows is about an inside source translation.
access-list	ACL number that is being used for the translation.
pool	Name of the pool (in this case, test).
refcount	Number of translations that are using this pool.
netmask	IPv4 network mask that is used in the pool.
start	Starting IPv4 address in the pool range.
end	Ending IPv4 address in the pool range.
type	Type of pool. Possible types are generic or rotary.
total addresses	Number of addresses in the pool that are available for translation.
allocated	Number of addresses that are being used.
misses	Number of failed allocations from the pool.

Resolving Issues with Using the Correct Translation Entry

You know from the configuration that the source address (10.10.10.4) should be statically translated to 172.16.6.14. You can use the **show ip nat translation** command to verify that the translation does exist in the translation table, as demonstrated here:

```
RouterX# show ip nat translation
Pro Inside global     Inside local     Outside local      Outside global
--- 172.16.6.14        10.10.10.4       ---                ---
```

Next, ensure that the translation is occurring. You can confirm this in two ways: by running a NAT **debug** command or by monitoring NAT statistics with the **show ip nat statistics** command. Because **debug** commands should always be used as a last resort, start with the **show ip nat statistics** command.

To determine whether the translation is taking place, monitor the hits counter to see if it increases as traffic is sent through the router. The hits counter increments every time a translation in the translation table is used to translate an address. First, clear the statistics and then display them. Next, try to execute a ping through the router and then display the statistics again, as demonstrated in Example 7-3.

Example 7-3 *Verifying That Address Translation Is Occurring*

```
RouterX# clear ip nat statistics
RouterX#
RouterX# show ip nat statistics
 Total active translations: 1 (1 static, 0 dynamic; 0 extended)
 Outside interfaces:
 Ethernet0, Serial2
 Inside interfaces:
 Ethernet1
 Hits: 0  Misses: 0
 Expired translations: 0
 Dynamic mappings:
 -- Inside Source
 access-list 7 pool test refcount 0
 pool test: netmask 255.255.255.0
 start 172.16.11.70 end 172.16.11.71
 type generic, total addresses 2, allocated 0 (0%), misses 0
```

After you ping through the router, the NAT statistics show, as demonstrated in Example 7-4.

Example 7-4 **show ip statistics** *to Verify Translation*

```
RouterX# show ip nat statistics
 Total active translations: 1 (1 static, 0 dynamic; 0 extended)
 Outside interfaces:
 Ethernet0, Serial2
 Inside interfaces:
 Ethernet1
 Hits: 5  Misses: 0
 Expired translations: 0
 Dynamic mappings:
 -- Inside Source
 access-list 7 pool test refcount 0
 pool test: netmask 255.255.255.0
 start 172.16.11.70 end 172.16.11.71
 type generic, total addresses 2, allocated 0 (0%), misses 0
```

You can see from the output of the **show** command that the number of hits incremented by five after the NAT statistics were cleared. In a successful ping, the number of hits should increase by 10. The five ICMP echoes that were sent by the source should be translated, and the five echo reply packets from the destination should be translated, for a total of 10 hits. The five missing hits are most likely due to the echo replies not being translated or not being sent from the destination router.

To determine why the echo reply is not being returned when you issue a ping, check the default gateway of the destination default gateway router for a route back to the translated address, as demonstrated in Example 7-5.

Example 7-5 *Verifying the Default Gateway*

```
RouterY# show ip route
Codes: C - connected, S - static, I - IGRP, R - RIP, M - mobile, B - BGP
       D - EIGRP, EX - EIGRP external, O - OSPF, IA - OSPF inter area
       N1 - OSPF NSSA external type 1, N2 - OSPF NSSA external type 2
       E1 - OSPF external type 1, E2 - OSPF external type 2, E - EGP
       i - IS-IS, L1 - IS-IS level-1, L2 - IS-IS level-2, ia - IS-IS inter are
       * - candidate default, U - per-user static route, o - ODR
       P - periodic downloaded static route

Gateway of last resort is not set

     172.16.0.0/24 is subnetted, 4 subnets
C       172.16.12.0 is directly connected, Serial0.8
C       172.16.9.0 is directly connected, Serial0.5
C       172.16.11.0 is directly connected, Serial0.6
C       172.16.5.0 is directly connected, Ethernet0
```

The routing table of Router B does not have a route for 172.16.6.14, which is the translated address. Therefore, the echo replies in response to the ping fail. Once you add this return route, the ping works.

In Figure 7-7, the network administrator is experiencing the following symptom: Host A (192.168.1.2) cannot ping host B (192.168.2.2).

The next several examples show how to troubleshoot this issue.

To troubleshoot the problem, use the **show ip nat translation** command to see if any translations are currently in the table:

```
RouterA# show ip nat translations
          Pro Inside global    Inside local    Outside local    Outside global
          --- ---              ---              ---              ---
```

Figure 7-7 *NAT Problem Cannot Ping Remote Host*

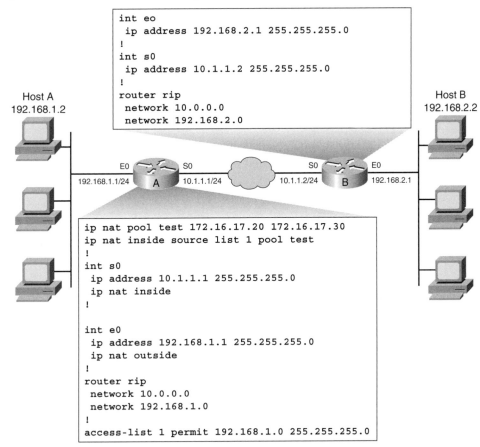

You find that no translations are in the table. This could indicate a problem, or it could mean that no traffic is currently being translated.

Next, you must verify if any translations have ever taken place and identify the interfaces between which translation should be occurring. Use the **show ip nat statistics** command to determine this information, as demonstrated in Example 7-6.

Example 7-6 *Identifying Translations and Interfaces*

```
RouterA# show ip nat statistics
     Total active translations: 0 (0 static, 0 dynamic; 0 extended)
     Outside interfaces:
     Ethernet0
     Inside interfaces:
     Serial0
     Hits: 0   Misses: 0
     ...
```

From the results in Example 7-6, you determine that the NAT counters are at 0, verifying that no translation has occurred. You also find that the router interfaces are incorrectly defined as NAT inside or NAT outside.

After you correctly define the NAT inside and outside interfaces, generate another ping from host A to host B. In the example, the ping still fails. Issue the **show ip nat translations** and **show ip nat statistics** commands again to troubleshoot the problem. In the example, you find that translations are still not occurring.

Next, you should use the **show access-list** command to verify whether the ACL that is referenced by the NAT command is permitting all the necessary networks:

```
RouterA# show access-list

Standard IP access list 1
    10 permit 192.168.1.1, wildcard bits 255.255.255.0
```

From this output, you determine that an incorrect wildcard bit mask has been used in the ACL that defines the addresses to be translated.

After correcting the ACL wildcard bit mask, you generate another ping from host A to host B. The ping still fails. However, when you reissue the **show ip nat translations** and **show ip nat statistics** commands, you find that translations are now occurring:

```
RouterA# show ip nat translations
    Pro   Inside global    Inside local     Outside local    Outside global
    ---   172.16.17.20     192.168.1.2      ---              ---
```

Next, you use the **show ip route** command on Router B to verify the existence of a return route to the translated address.

From the results in Example 7-7, you discover that Router B has no route to the translated network address of 172.16.0.0.

Example 7-7   *Verifying a Return Route to the Translated Address*

```
RouterB# show ip route

Codes: C - connected, S - static, R - RIP, M - mobile, B - BGP

Gateway of last resort is not set

     10.0.0.0/24 is subnetted, 1 subnets
C       10.1.1.0/24 is directly connected, Serial0
     192.168.2.0/24 is subnetted, 1 subnets
R       192.168.2.0/24 is directly connected, Ethernet0
     192.168.1.0/24 is variably subnetted, 3 subnets, 2 masks
R       192.168.1.0/24 [120/1] via 10.1.1.1, 2d19h, Serial0
```

You return to Router A and enter the **show ip protocol** command to determine if Router A is advertising the translated address of 172.16.0.0, as demonstrated in Example 7-8.

Example 7-8   *Verifying Advertisement of a Translated Address*

```
RouterA# show ip protocol
Routing Protocol is "rip"
  Outgoing update filter list for all interfaces is not set
  Incoming update filter list for all interfaces is not set
  Sending updates every 30 seconds, next due in 0 seconds
  Invalid after 180 seconds, hold down 180, flushed after 240
  Redistributing: rip
  Default version control: send version 1, receive any version
  Automatic network summarization is in effect
  Maximum path: 4
  Routing for Networks:
    192.168.0.0
  Routing Information Sources:
    Gateway         Distance      Last Update
  Distance: (default is 120)
```

You find that Router A is advertising 192.168.1.0, which is the network that is being translated, instead of advertising network 172.16.0.0, which is the network to which the addresses are being translated.

So, to fix the original problem where host A (192.168.1.2) could not ping host B (192.168.2.2), you changed the following configurations on Router A:

■ Interface S0 is now the outside interface, rather than the inside interface.

■ Interface E0 is now the inside interface, rather than the outside interface.

■ The wildcard mask now matches any host on the 192.168.1.0 network. Previously, the **access-list 1** command did not match inside local IPv4 address.

■ Router A is now configured to advertise network 172.16.0.0. Previously, Router B did not know how to reach the 172.16.17.0/24 subnet. The configuration is done by creating a loopback interface and modifying the Routing Information Protocol (RIP) network statements.

Summary of Scaling the Network with NAT and PAT

The following summarizes the key points that were discussed in this section.

■ There are three types of NAT: static, dynamic, and overloading (PAT).

- Static NAT is one-to-one address mapping. Dynamic NAT addresses are picked from a pool.

- NAT overloading (PAT) allows you to map many inside addresses to one outside address.

- Use the **show ip nat translation** command to display the translation table and verify that translation has occurred.

- To determine whether a current translation entry is being used, use the **show ip nat statistics** or **clear ip nat statistics** commands to check and clear the hits counter.

- Use the **debug ip nat** command to verify translation of packets.

Transitioning to IPv6

The ability to scale networks for future demands requires a limitless supply of IP addresses and improved mobility. IP version 6 (IPv6) satisfies the increasingly complex requirements of hierarchical addressing that IP version 4 (IPv4) does not provide. IPv6 uses some different address types that make IPv6 more efficient than IPv4. This section describes the different types of addresses that IPv6 uses and how to assign these addresses.

Transitioning to IPv6 from IPv4 deployments can require a variety of techniques, including an auto-configuration function. The transition mechanism you will use depends on the needs of your network. This section describes the different types of transition mechanisms for an IPv6 network.

Reasons for Using IPv6

The IPv4 address space provides approximately 4.3 billion addresses. Of that address space, approximately 3.7 billion addresses are actually assignable; the other addresses are reserved for special purposes such as multicasting, private address space, loopback testing, and research. Based on some industry figures as of January 1, 2007, about 2.407 billion of these available addresses are currently assigned to either end users or Internet service providers (ISPs). That leaves roughly 1.3 billion addresses still available from the IPv4 address space.

An IPv6 address is a 128-bit binary value, which can be displayed as 32 hexadecimal digits, as shown in the figure. It provides $3.4 * 10^{38}$ IP addresses. This version of IP addressing should provide sufficient addresses for future Internet growth needs. Figure 7-8 illustrates the differences between the address space for IPv4 and IPv6.

Figure 7-8   *IPv4 and IPv6*

IPv4:	4 Octets
11000000.10101000.11001001.0111000	
192.168.201.113	
4,294,467,295 IP Addresses	

IPv6:	16 Octets
11010001.11011100.11001001.01110001.11010001.11011100. 11001100.01110001.11010001.11011100.11001001.01110001. 11010001.11011100.11001001.01110001	
A524:72D3:2C80:DD02:0029:EC7A:002B:EA73	
3.4 x 10^{38} IP Addresses	

In addition to its technical and business potential, IPv6 offers a virtually unlimited supply of IP addresses. Because of its generous 128-bit address space, IPv6 generates a virtually unlimited stock of addresses—enough to allocate more than 4.3 billion addresses (the entire IPv4 Internet address space) to every person on the planet.

The Internet will be transformed after IPv6 fully replaces IPv4. Many people within the Internet community have analyzed the issue of IPv4 address exhaustion and published their reports. However, the estimates of when IPv4 address exhaustion will occur vary greatly among the reports. Some predict IPv4 address exhaustion by 2008 or 2009, and others say it will not happen until 2013 or beyond. Nevertheless, IPv4 will not disappear overnight. Rather, it will coexist with and then gradually be replaced by IPv6.

The change from IPv4 to IPv6 has already begun, particularly in Europe, Japan, and the Asia-Pacific region. These areas are exhausting their allotted IPv4 addresses, which makes IPv6 all the more attractive and necessary. Some countries, such as Japan, are aggressively adopting IPv6. Others, such as those in the European Union, are moving toward IPv6, and China is considering building new networks dedicated for IPv6.

As of October 1, 2003, the U.S. Department of Defense mandated that all new equipment purchased be IPv6-capable. In fact, all U.S. government agencies must start using IPv6 across their core networks by 2008, and the agencies are working to meet that deadline. As these examples illustrate, IPv6 enjoys strong momentum.

IPv6 is a powerful enhancement to IPv4. Several features in IPv6 offer functional improvements. What IP developers learned from using IPv4 suggested changes to better suit current and probable network demands:

- **Larger address space:** Larger address space includes several enhancements:

    — Improved global reachability and flexibility

    — The aggregation of prefixes that are announced in routing tables

    — Multihoming to several ISPs

    — Autoconfiguration that can include data link layer addresses in the address space

    — Plug-and-play options

    — Public-to-private readdressing end to end without address translation

    — Simplified mechanisms for address renumbering and modification

- **Simpler header:** A simpler header offers several advantages over IPv4:

    — Better routing efficiency for performance and forwarding-rate scalability

    — No broadcasts and thus no potential threat of broadcast storms

    — No requirement for processing checksums

    — Simpler and more efficient extension header mechanisms

    — Flow labels for per-flow processing with no need to open the transport inner packet to identify the various traffic flows

- **Mobility and security:** Mobility and security help ensure compliance with mobile IP and IPsec standards functionality. Mobility enables people with mobile network devices—many with wireless connectivity—to move around in networks:

    — Mobile IP is an Internet Engineering Task Force (IETF) standard that is available for both IPv4 and IPv6. The standard enables mobile devices to move without breaks in established network connections. Because IPv4 does not automatically provide this kind of mobility, you must add it with additional configurations.

    — In IPv6, mobility is built in, which means that any IPv6 node can use mobility when necessary. The routing headers of IPv6 make mobile IPv6 much more efficient for end nodes than mobile IPv4 is.

— IPsec is the IETF standard for IP network security, available for both IPv4 and IPv6. Although the functionalities are essentially identical in both environments, IPsec is mandatory in the IPv6 protocol. IPsec is enabled on every IPv6 node and is available for use, making the IPv6 Internet more secure. IPsec also requires keys for each party, which implies global key deployment and distribution.

■ **Transition richness:** You can incorporate existing IPv4 capabilities with the added features of IPv6 in several ways:

— First, you can implement a dual-stack method, with both IPv4 and IPv6 configured on the interface of a network device.

— Second, you can use tunneling, which will become more prominent as the adoption of IPv6 grows. A variety of IPv6 over IPv4 tunneling methods exist. Some methods require manual configuration, whereas others are more automatic.

— Third, Cisco IOS Software Release 12.3(2)T and later include Network Address Translation-Protocol Translation (NAT-PT) between IPv6 and IPv4. This translation allows direct communication between hosts that use different versions of the IP protocol.

Understanding IPv6 Addresses

Colons separate entries in a series of 16-bit hexadecimal fields that represent IPv6 addresses. The hexadecimal digits A, B, C, D, E, and F that are represented in IPv6 addresses are not case sensitive.

IPv6 does not require explicit address string notation. Use the following guidelines for IPv6 address string notations:

■ The leading zeros in a field are optional, so 09C0 equals 9C0 and 0000 equals 0.

■ Successive fields of zeros can be represented as :: only once in an address.

■ An unspecified address is written as :: because it contains only zeros.

Using the :: notation greatly reduces the size of most addresses. For example, FF01:0:0:0:0:0:0:1 becomes FF01::1.

NOTE An address parser identifies the number of missing zeros by separating the two parts and entering 0 until the 128 bits are complete. If two :: notations are placed in the address, there is no way to identify the size of each block of zeros.

Broadcasting in IPv4 results in a number of problems. Broadcasting generates a number of interrupts in every computer on the network and, in some cases, triggers malfunctions that can completely halt an entire network. This disastrous network event is known as a *broadcast storm*.

In IPv6, broadcasting does not exist. IPv6 replaces broadcasts with multicasts and anycasts. Multicast enables efficient network operation by using a number of functionally specific multicast groups to send requests to a limited number of computers on the network. The multicast groups prevent most of the problems that are related to broadcast storms in IPv4.

The range of multicast addresses in IPv6 is larger than in IPv4. For the near future, allocation of multicast groups is not being limited.

IPv6 also defines a new type of address called an anycast address. An anycast address identifies a list of devices or nodes; therefore, an anycast address identifies multiple interfaces. Anycast addresses are like a cross between unicast and multicast addresses. These addresses are designed for commonly used services such as DNS. Unicast sends packets to one specific device with one specific address, and multicast sends a packet to every member of a group. Anycast addresses send a packet to any one member of the group of devices with the anycast address assigned.

For efficiency, a packet that is sent to an anycast address is delivered to the closest interface—as defined by the routing protocols in use—that is identified by the anycast address, so anycast can also be thought of as a "one-to-nearest" type of address. Anycast addresses are syntactically indistinguishable from global unicast addresses because anycast addresses are allocated from the global unicast address space.

> **NOTE**   There is little experience with widespread, arbitrary use of Internet anycast addresses, and there are some known complications and hazards when using them in their full generality. Until more experience has been gained and solutions have been agreed upon for those problems, the following restrictions are imposed on IPv6 anycast addresses: (1) An anycast address *must not* be used as the source address of an IPv6 packet. (2) An anycast address *must not* be assigned to an IPv6 host; that is, it may be assigned to an IPv6 router only.

Several basic types of IPv6 unicast addresses exist: global, reserved, private (link-local and site-local), loopback, and unspecified. The sections that follow describe these address types in greater detail.

Global Addresses

The IPv6 global unicast address is the equivalent of the IPv4 global unicast address. A *global unicast address* is an IPv6 address from the global unicast prefix. The structure of global unicast addresses enables the aggregation of routing prefixes, which limits the number of routing table entries in the global routing table. Global unicast addresses that are used on links are aggregated upward through organizations and eventually to the ISPs.

Reserved Addresses

The IETF reserves a portion of the IPv6 address space for various uses, both present and future. Reserved addresses represent 1/256th of the total IPv6 address space. Some of the other types of IPv6 addresses come from this block.

Private Addresses

A block of IPv6 addresses is set aside for private addresses, just as is done in IPv4. These private addresses are local only to a particular link or site; therefore, they are never routed outside of a particular company network. Private addresses have a first octet value of "FE" in hexadecimal notation, with the next hexadecimal digit being a value from 8 to F.

These addresses are further divided into two types, based on their scope.

- Site-local addresses, described further as follows:

    — These are addresses similar to RFC 1918, "Address Allocation for Private Internets," in IPv4 today. The scope of these addresses is an entire site or organization. They allow addressing within an organization without needing to use a public prefix. Routers forward datagrams using site-local addresses within the site, but not outside the site, to the public Internet.

    — In hexadecimal, site-local addresses begin with FE and then C to F for the third hexadecimal digit. So, these addresses begin with FEC, FED, FEE, or FEF.

- Link-local addresses, described further as follows:

    — The concept of link-local scope is new to IPv6. These addresses have a smaller scope than site-local addresses; they refer only to a particular physical link (physical network). Routers do not forward datagrams using link-local addresses, not even within the organization; they are only for local communication on a particular physical network segment.

    — These addresses are used for link communications such as automatic address configuration, neighbor discovery, and router discovery. Many IPv6 routing protocols also use link-local addresses.

Loopback Address

Just as in IPv4, a provision has been made for a special loopback IPv6 address for testing; datagrams sent to this address "loop back" to the sending device. However, IPv6 has just one address, not a whole block, for this function. The loopback address is 0:0:0:0:0:0:0:1, which is normally expressed using zero compression as ::1.

Unspecified Address

In IPv4, an IP address of all zeroes has a special meaning; it refers to the host itself and is used when a device does not know its own address. In IPv6, this concept has been formalized, and the all-zeroes address (0:0:0:0:0:0:0:0) is named the "unspecified" address. It is typically used in the source field of a datagram that is sent by a device that seeks to have its IP address configured. You can apply address compression to this address; because the address is all zeroes, the address becomes just ::.

Global unicast addresses are defined by a global routing prefix, a subnet ID, and an interface ID. The IPv6 unicast address space encompasses the entire IPv6 address range, with the exception of FF00::/8 (1111 1111), which is used for multicast addresses. The current global unicast address that is assigned by the Internet Assigned Numbers Authority (IANA) uses the range of addresses that start with binary value 001 (2000::/3), which is 1/8 of the total IPv6 address space and is the largest block of assigned block addresses.

Addresses with a prefix of 2000::/3 (001) through E000::/3 (111) are required to have 64-bit interface identifiers in the extended universal identifier (EUI)-64 format.

The IANA is allocating the IPv6 address space in the ranges of 2001::/16 to the registries. Figure 7-9 outlines the IPv6 format for a global unicast or anycast address.

Figure 7-9   *IPv6 Address Format*

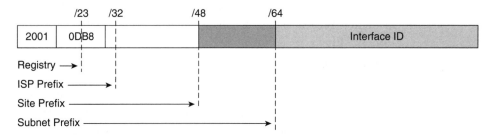

The global unicast address typically consists of a 48-bit global routing prefix and a 16-bit subnet ID. Individual organizations can use a 16-bit subnet field called "Subnet ID" to create their own local addressing hierarchy and to identify subnets. This field allows an organization to use up to 65,535 individual subnets. For more information, refer to RFC 3587, "IPv6 Global Unicast Address Format," which replaces RFC 2374.

IPv6 over Data Link Layers

IPv6 is defined on most of the current data link layer protocols, including the following protocols:

- Ethernet[*]

- PPP[*]

- High-Level Data Link Control (HDLC)[*]

- FDDI

- Token Ring

- Attached Resource Computer network (ARCnet)

- Nonbroadcast multiaccess (NBMA)

- ATM[**]

- Frame Relay[***]

- IEEE 1394

   [*] Cisco supports these data link layers.

   [**] Cisco supports only ATM permanent virtual circuit (PVC), not switched virtual circuit (SVC) or ATM LAN Emulation (LANE).

   [***] Cisco supports only Frame Relay PVC, not SVC.

An RFC describes the behavior of IPv6 in each of these specific data link layers, but Cisco IOS Software does not necessarily support all of them. The data link layer defines how IPv6 interface identifiers are created and how neighbor discovery deals with data link layer address resolution.

Larger address spaces make room for large address allocations to ISPs and organizations. An ISP aggregates all the prefixes of its customers into a single prefix and announces the single prefix to the IPv6 Internet. The increased address space is sufficient to allow organizations to define a single prefix for their entire network. Figure 7-10 shows how this aggregation occurs.

Figure 7-10   *IPv6 Address Aggregation*

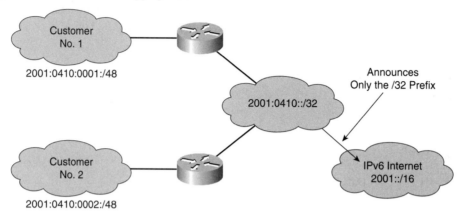

Aggregation of customer prefixes results in an efficient and scalable routing table. Scalable routing is necessary to expand broader adoption of network functions. Scalable routing also improves network bandwidth and functionality for user traffic that connects the various devices and applications.

Internet usage—both now and in the future—can include the following elements:

■   A huge increase in the number of broadband consumers with high-speed connections that are always on

■   Users who spend more time online and are generally willing to spend more money on communications services (such as downloading music) and high-value searchable offerings

■   Home networks with expanded network applications such as wireless VoIP, home surveillance, and advanced services such as real-time video on demand (VoD)

■   Massively scalable games with global participants and media-rich e-learning, providing learners with on-demand remote labs or lab simulations

Assigning IPv6 Addresses

Interface identifiers in IPv6 addresses are used to identify interfaces on a link. They can also be thought of as the "host portion" of an IPv6 address. Interface identifiers are required to be unique on a specific link. Interface identifiers are always 64 bits and can be dynamically derived from a Layer 2 media and encapsulation.

There are several ways to assign an IPv6 address to a device:

■   Static assignment using a manual interface ID

- Static assignment using an EUI-64 interface ID

- Stateless autoconfiguration

- DHCP for IPv6 (DHCPv6)

Manual Interface ID Assignment

One way to statically assign an IPv6 address to a device is to manually assign both the prefix (network) and interface ID (host) portion of the IPv6 address. To configure an IPv6 address on a Cisco router interface and enable IPv6 processing on that interface, use the **ipv6 address** *ipv6-address/prefix-length* command in interface configuration mode.

To enable IPv6 processing on the interface and configure an address based on the directly specified bits, you will use the command demonstrated here:

```
RouterX(config-if) ipv6 address 2001:DB8:2222:7272::72/64
```

EUI-64 Interface ID Assignment

Another way to statically assign an IPv6 address is to configure the prefix (network) portion of the IPv6 address and derive the interface ID (host) portion from the Layer 2 MAC address of the device, which is known as the EUI-64 interface ID.

To configure an IPv6 address for an interface and enable IPv6 processing on the interface using an EUI-64 interface ID in the low order 64 bits of the address (host), use the **ipv6 address** *ipv6-prefix/prefix-length* **eui-64** command in interface configuration mode.

To assign the IPv6 address 2001:0DB8:0:1::/64 to Ethernet interface 0 and use an EUI-64 interface ID in the low order 64 bits of the address, enter the following commands:

```
RouterX(config)# interface ethernet 0
RouterX(config-if)# ipv6 address 2001:0DB8:0:1::/64 eui-64
```

Stateless Autoconfiguration

As the name implies, *autoconfiguration* is a mechanism that automatically configures the IPv6 address of a node. In IPv6, it is assumed that non-PC devices, as well as computer terminals, will be connected to the network. The autoconfiguration mechanism was introduced to enable plug-and-play networking of these devices, to help reduce administration overhead.

DHCPv6 (Stateful)

DHCP for IPv6 enables DHCP servers to pass configuration parameters such as IPv6 network addresses to IPv6 nodes. It offers the capability of automatic allocation of reusable network addresses and additional configuration flexibility. This protocol is a stateful counterpart to IPv6 stateless address autoconfiguration (RFC 2462), and it can be used separately or concurrently with IPv6 stateless address autoconfiguration to obtain configuration parameters.

Use of EUI-64 Format in IPv6 Addresses

The 64-bit interface identifier in an IPv6 address identifies a unique interface on a link. A *link* is a network medium over which network nodes communicate using the link layer. The interface identifier can also be unique over a broader scope. In many cases, an interface identifier is the same as, or is based on, the link-layer (MAC) address of an interface. As in IPv4, a subnet prefix in IPv6 is associated with one link. Figure 7-11 illustrates the IPv6 EUI-64 interface identifier.

Figure 7-11   *IPv6 EUI-64 Interface Identifier*

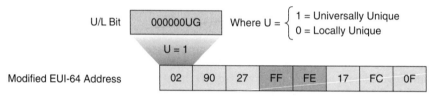

Interface identifiers in global unicast and other IPv6 address types must be 64 bits long and can be constructed in the 64-bit EUI-64 format. The EUI-64 format interface ID is derived from the 48-bit link-layer (MAC) address by inserting the hexadecimal number FFFE between the upper 3 bytes (Organizational Unique Identifier [OUI] field) and the lower 3 bytes (serial number) of the link layer address. To ensure that the chosen address is from a unique Ethernet MAC address, the seventh bit in the high-order byte is set to 1 to indicate the uniqueness of the 48-bit address.

Stateless autoconfiguration is a key feature of IPv6. It enables serverless basic configuration of the nodes and easy renumbering.

Stateless autoconfiguration uses the information in the router advertisement messages to configure the node. The prefix included in the router advertisement is used as the /64 prefix for the node address. The other 64 bits are obtained by the dynamically created interface identifier, which in the case of Ethernet, is the modified EUI-64 format.

Routers periodically send router advertisements. When a node boots up, the node needs its address in the early stage of the boot process. It can be "long" to wait for the next router advertisement to get the information to configure its interfaces. Instead, a node sends a router solicitation message to the routers on the network asking them to reply immediately with a router advertisement so the node can immediately autoconfigure its IPv6 address. All the routers respond with a normal router advertisement message with the all-nodes multicast address as the destination address. Figure 7-12 illustrates stateless autoconfiguration.

Figure 7-12 *Stateless Autoconfiguration*

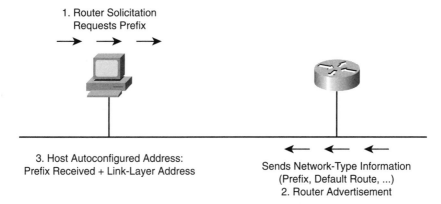

Autoconfiguration enables plug-and-play configuration of an IPv6 device, which allows devices to connect themselves to the network without configuration from an administrator and without servers, such as DHCP servers. This key feature enables deployment of new devices on the Internet, such as cellular phones, wireless devices, home appliances, and home networks.

> **NOTE** Stateless DHCP is a concept, developed in February 2004, that strikes a middle ground between stateless autoconfiguration and the thick-client approach of stateful DHCP. Stateless DHCP for IPv6 is also called "DHCP-lite." See RFC 3736, "Stateless Dynamic Host Configuration Protocol (DHCP) Service for IPv6."

DHCPv6 is an updated version of DHCP for IPv4. It supports the addressing model of IPv6 and benefits from new IPv6 features. DHCPv6 has the following characteristics:

- Enables more control than serverless or stateless autoconfiguration

- Can be employed in an environment that uses only servers and no routers

- Can be used concurrently with stateless autoconfiguration

- Can be used for renumbering

- Can be used for automatic domain name registration of hosts using dynamic DNS

The process for acquiring configuration data for a DHCPv6 client is similar to that in IPv4, with a few exceptions. Initially, the client must detect the presence of routers on the link by using neighbor discovery messages. If at least one router is found, then the client examines the router advertisements to determine if DHCPv6 should be used. If the router advertisements enable the use of DHCPv6 on that link or if no router is found, then the client starts a DHCP solicit phase to find a DHCP server.

DHCPv6 uses multicast for many messages. When the client sends a solicit message, it sends the message to the ALL-DHCP-Agents multicast address with link-local scope. Agents include both servers and relays.

When a DHCP relay forwards a message, it can forward it to the All-DHCP-Servers multicast address with site-local scope. This means that you do not need to configure a relay with all the static addresses of the DHCP servers, as in IPv4. If you want only specific DHCP servers to receive the messages, or if there is a problem forwarding multicast traffic to all the network segments that contain a DHCP server, a relay can contain a static list of DHCP servers.

You can configure different DHCPv6 servers, or the same server with different contexts, to assign addresses based on different polices. For example, you could configure one DHCPv6 server to give global addresses using a more restrictive policy, such as, "do not give addresses to printers." You could then configure another DHCPv6 server, or the same server within a different context, to give site-local addresses using a more liberal policy, such as, "give to anyone."

Routing Considerations with IPv6

IPv6 uses longest-prefix match routing just like IPv4 classless interdomain routing (CIDR) does. Many of the common routing protocols have been modified to handle longer IPv6 addresses and different header structures.

You can use and configure IPv6 static routing in the same way you would with IPv4. There is an IPv6-specific requirement per RFC 2461 that a router must be able to determine the link-local address of each of its neighboring routers to ensure that the target address of a redirect message identifies the neighbor router by its link-local address. This requirement means that using a global unicast address as a next-hop address with IPv6 routing is not recommended.

The Cisco IOS global command to enable IPv6 is **ipv6 unicast-routing**. You must enable IPv6 unicast routing before an IPv6-capable routing protocol, or an IPv6 static route, will work.

Routing Information Protocol next generation (RIPng) (RFC 2080) is a distance vector routing protocol with a limit of 15 hops that uses split horizon and poison reverse to prevent routing loops. RIPng includes the following features:

■ Is based on IPv4 Routing Information Protocol (RIP) version 2 (RIPv2) and is similar to RIPv2

■ Uses IPv6 for transport

■ Includes the IPv6 prefix and next-hop IPv6 address

■ Uses the multicast group FF02::9, the all-RIP-routers multicast group, as the destination address for RIP updates

■ Sends updates on UDP port 521

■ Is supported by Cisco IOS Release 12.2(2)T and later

Strategies for Implementing IPv6

The transition from IPv4 does not require upgrades on all nodes at the same time. Many transition mechanisms enable smooth integration of IPv4 and IPv6. Other mechanisms that allow IPv4 nodes to communicate with IPv6 nodes are available. All of these mechanisms are applied to different situations. Figure 7-13 shows how IPv6 hosts may have to travel across IPv4 networks during this transition.

Figure 7-13   *IPv4-to-IPv6 Transition*

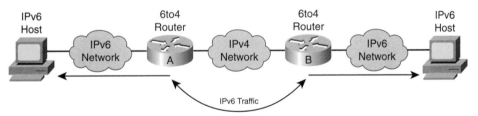

The three most common techniques to transition from IPv4 to IPv6 are as follows:

■ **Dual stack:** Dual stack is an integration method in which a node has implementation and connectivity to both an IPv4 and IPv6 network. As a result, the node and its corresponding routers have two protocol stacks.

■ **Tunneling:** Several tunneling techniques are available:

— **Manual IPv6-over-IPv4 tunneling:** An integration method in which an IPv6 packet is encapsulated within the IPv4 protocol. This method requires dual-stack routers.

— **Dynamic 6to4 tunneling:** A method that automatically establishes the connection of IPv6 islands through an IPv4 network, typically the Internet. The 6to4 tunneling method dynamically applies a valid, unique IPv6 prefix to each IPv6 island, which enables the fast deployment of IPv6 in a corporate network without address retrieval from the ISPs or registries.

— **Intra-Site Automatic Tunnel Addressing Protocol (ISATAP) tunneling:** An automatic overlay tunneling mechanism that uses the underlying IPv4 network as a link layer for IPv6. ISATAP tunnels allow individual IPv4 or IPv6 dual-stack hosts within a site to communicate with other such hosts on a virtual link, creating an IPv6 network using the IPv4 infrastructure.

— **Teredo tunneling:** An IPv6 transition technology that provides host-to-host automatic tunneling instead of gateway tunneling. It is used to pass unicast IPv6 traffic when dual-stacked hosts (hosts that are running both IPv6 and IPv4) are located behind one or multiple IPv4 Network Address Translators.

■ **Proxying and translation (NAT-PT):** A translation mechanism that sits between an IPv6 network and an IPv4 network. The job of the translator is to translate IPv6 packets into IPv4 packets and vice versa.

Dual stack is an integration method in which a node has implementation and connectivity to both an IPv4 and IPv6 network; thus, the node has two stacks, as illustrated in Figure 7-14.

Figure 7-14 *Cisco IOS Dual Stack*

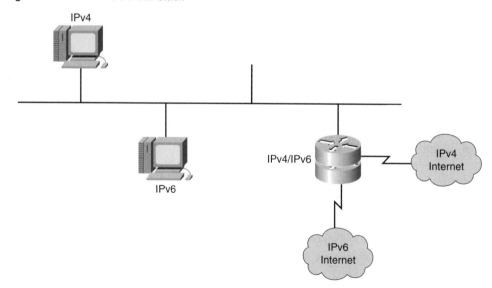

You can accomplish this configuration on the same interface or on multiple interfaces. Features of the dual-stack method are as follows:

- A dual-stack node chooses which stack to use based on the destination address. A dual-stack node should prefer IPv6 when it is available. The dual-stack approach to IPv6 integration, in which nodes have both IPv4 and IPv6 stacks, will be one of the most commonly used integration methods. Old IPv4-only applications continue to work as before. New and modified applications take advantage of both IP layers.

- A new application programming interface (API) is defined to support both IPv4 and IPv6 addresses and DNS requests. This new API replaces the gethostbyname and gethostbyaddr calls. A converted application can use both IPv4 and IPv6. An application can be converted to the new API while still using only IPv4.

- Experience in porting IPv4 applications to IPv6 suggests that, for most applications, there is a minimal change in some localized places inside the source code. This technique is well known and has been applied in the past for other protocol transitions. It enables gradual application upgrades, one by one, to IPv6.

Cisco IOS Software Releases 12.2(2)T and later are IPv6-ready. As soon as you configure basic IPv4 and IPv6 on the interface, the interface is dual-stacked and forwards IPv4 and IPv6 traffic on that interface. Figure 7-15 shows an example of this configuration.

Figure 7-15 *Dual-Stack Configuration*

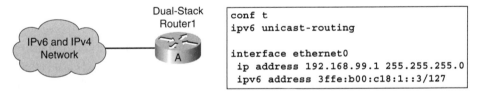

Using IPv6 on a Cisco IOS router requires the global configuration command **ipv6 unicast-routing**. This command enables the forwarding of IPv6 datagrams.

> **NOTE**   You must configure all interfaces that forward IPv6 traffic with an IPv6 address using the interface command **ipv6 address** *IPv6-address* [*/prefix length*].

Tunneling is an integration method in which an IPv6 packet is encapsulated within another protocol, such as IPv4. Figure 7-16 shows how IPv6 tunneling operates.

Figure 7-16 *IPv6 Tunneling*

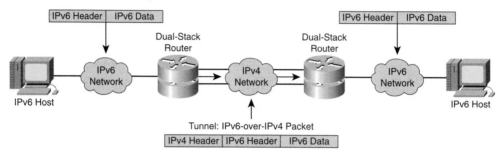

When IPv4 is used to encapsulate the IPv6 packet, a protocol type of 41 is specified in the IPv4 header, and the packet has the following characteristics:

- Includes a 20-byte IPv4 header with no options and an IPv6 header and payload.

- Requires dual-stack routers. This process enables the connection of IPv6 islands without the need to also convert an intermediary network to IPv6. Tunneling presents these two issues:

    — The maximum transmission unit (MTU) is effectively decreased by 20 octets if the IPv4 header does not contain an optional field.

    — A tunneled network is often difficult to troubleshoot. Tunneling is an intermediate integration and transition technique that should not be considered a final solution. A native IPv6 architecture should be the ultimate goal.

In a manually configured tunnel, you configure the IPv4 and IPv6 addresses statically on the routers at each end of the tunnel. These end routers must be dual stacked, and the configuration cannot change dynamically as network and routing needs change. You must also properly set up routing to forward a packet between the two IPv6 networks. Figure 7-17 illustrates the requirements for IPv6 tunnels.

Figure 7-17 *IPv6 Tunnel Requirements*

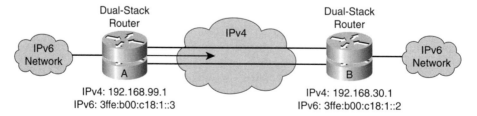

Tunnel endpoints can be unnumbered, but unnumbered endpoints make troubleshooting difficult. The IPv4 practice of saving addresses for tunnel endpoints is no longer an issue for IPv6.

Configuring IPv6

There are two basic steps to activate IPv6 on a router. First you must activate IPv6 traffic forwarding on the router, and then you must configure each interface that requires IPv6.

By default, IPv6 traffic forwarding is disabled on a Cisco router. To activate IPv6 traffic forwarding between interfaces, you must configure the global command **ipv6 unicast-routing**. This command enables the forwarding of unicast IPv6 traffic.

The **ipv6 address** command can configure a global IPv6 address. The link-local address is automatically configured when an address is assigned to the interface. You must specify the entire 128-bit IPv6 address or specify to use the 64-bit prefix by using the **eui-64** option.

You can completely specify the IPv6 address or compute the host identifier (rightmost 64 bits) from the EUI-64 identifier of the interface. In the example shown in Figure 7-18, the IPv6 address of the interface is configured using the EUI-64 format.

Alternatively, you can completely specify the entire IPv6 address to assign an address to a router interface using the **ipv6 address** *ipv6-address/prefix-length* command in interface configuration mode.

> **NOTE**   The configuration of the IPv6 address on an interface automatically configures the link-local address for that interface.

You can perform name resolution from the Cisco IOS Software process in two ways:

- It is possible to define a static name for IPv6 addresses using the command **ipv6 host** *name* [*port*] *ipv6-address1* [*ipv6-address2 . . . ipv6-address4*]. You can define up to four IPv6 addresses for one hostname. The *port* option refers to the Telnet port that should be used for the associated host.

- To specify the DNS server used by the router, use the **ip name-server** *address* command. The *address* can be an IPv4 or IPv6 address. You can specify up to six DNS servers with this command.

Configuring and Verifying RIPng for IPv6

The following paragraph describes the syntax of some commands that are commonly used to configure RIPng. The syntax is similar, if not identical, to their IPv4 counterparts. For

RIPng, instead of using the **network** command to identify which interfaces should run RIPng, you use the command **ipv6 rip** *tag* **enable** in interface configuration mode to enable RIPng on an interface. The *tag* parameter that you use for the **ipv6 rip enable** command must match the *tag* parameter in the **ipv6 router rip** command.

> **NOTE**   Enabling RIP on an interface dynamically creates a "router rip" process if necessary.

Example: RIPng for IPv6 Configuration

Figure 7-18 shows a network of two routers. Router Y is connected to the default network. On both Router X and Router Y, "RT0" is a tag that identifies the RIPng process. RIPng is enabled on the first Ethernet interface of Router Y using the **ipv6 rip RT0 enable** command. Router X shows that RIPng is enabled on both Ethernet interfaces using the **ipv6 rip RT0 enable** command.

Figure 7-18   *RIPng Configuration Example*

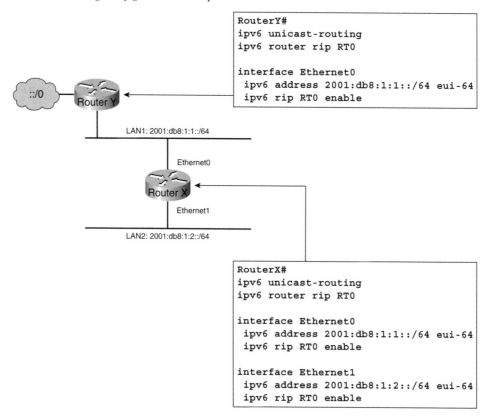

Summary of Transitioning to IPv6

The following summarizes the key points that were discussed in this section:

- IPv6 offers many additional benefits to IPv4, including a larger address space, easier address aggregation, and integrated security.

- The IPv6 address is 128 bits long and is made up of a 48-bit global prefix, a 16-bit subnet ID, and a 64-bit interface identifier.

- There are several ways to assign IPv6 addresses—statically, stateless autoconfiguration, and DHCPv6.

- Cisco supports all the major IPv6 routing protocols—RIPng, OSPFv3, and EIGRP.

- Transitioning from IPv4 to IPv6 requires dual stacks, tunneling, and possibly NAT-PT.

- Use the **ipv6 unicast-routing** command to enable IPv6 and the **ipv6 address** *ipv6-address/prefix-length* command to assign interface addresses and enable an IPv6 routing protocol.

Chapter Summary

To conserve the IPv4 address space, you can use three types of Network Address Translation (NAT): static NAT, dynamic NAT, and Port Address Translation (PAT). Static NAT provides a one-to-one mapping of inside-local to inside-global addresses. With Dynamic NAT, the inside global addresses are automatically picked from a pool. PAT, also known as NAT overloading, allows you to translate many internal addresses into just one or a few inside global addresses.

IPv6 addresses the exhaustion of IP resources and offers an alternative to conserving addresses through the use of NAT. By increasing the size of the IP address to 128 bits, there is ample address space. IP version 4 (IPv4) will not be converted to IP version 6 (IPv6) overnight. Transition techniques, such as dual stacks, IPv6-to-IPv4 tunnels, and NAT-Protocol Translation (NAT-PT), provide options for transitioning from IPv4 and IPv6.

The following summarizes the key points that were discussed in this chapter:

- NAT is a short-term solution to the limited number of unique IP addresses that IPv4 provides. The types of NAT you can configure include static, dynamic, and overloading (PAT).

- IPv6 is a long-term solution to running out of IPv4 addresses. IPv6 increases the size of the IP address to 128 bits and incorporates features such as autoconfiguration, security, and several solutions for transitioning from IPv4 to IPv6.

Review Questions

Use the questions here to review what you learned in this chapter. The correct answers and solutions are found in the appendix, "Answers to Chapter Review Questions."

1. Match each NAT term with its definition.

   ____ 1. Static NAT

   ____ 2. Dynamic NAT

   ____ 3. Inside local

   ____ 4. Inside global

   a. Address that is subject to translation with NAT

   b. Address of an inside host as it appears to the outside network

   c. Maps an unregistered IPv4 address to a registered IPv4 address on a one-to-one basis

   d. Maps an unregistered IPv4 address to a registered IPv4 address from a group of registered IPv4 addresses

2. Which Cisco IOS command would you use to define a pool of global addresses that can be allocated as needed?

   a. **ip nat pool**

   b. **ip nat inside pool**

   c. **ip nat outside pool**

   d. **ip nat inside source static**

3. What does the **ip nat inside source static** command do?

   a. Selects the inside static interface

   b. Marks the interface as connected to the outside

   c. Creates a pool of global addresses that can be allocated as needed

   d. Establishes permanent translation between an inside local address and an inside global address

4. Match each of these commands, which are used to configure NAT overloading, with its function.

      _____ 1. **ip nat inside**

      _____ 2. **ip nat outside**

      _____ 3. **access-list 1 permit 10.1.1.0 0.0.0.255**

      _____ 4. **ip nat inside source list 1 pool nat-pool overload**

      _____ 5. **ip nat pool nat-pool 192.1.1.17 192.1.1.20 netmask 255.255.255.240**

    a. Marks an interface as connected to the inside

    b. Marks an interface as connected to the outside

    c. Defines a pool of inside global addresses that can be allocated as needed

    d. Establishes dynamic port address translation using the defined ACL

    e. Defines a standard ACL that will permit the addresses that are to be translated

5. Which command clears a specific extended dynamic translation entry from the NAT translation table?

    a. **clear ip nat translation ***

    b. **clear ip nat translation inside**

    c. **clear ip nat translation outside**

    d. **clear ip nat translation protocol inside**

6. The output of which command displays the active translations for a NAT translation table?

    a. **show ip nat statistics**

    b. **show ip nat translations**

    c. **clear ip nat translation ***

    d. **clear ip nat translation outside**

7. You are troubleshooting a NAT connectivity problem on a Cisco router. You determine that the appropriate translation is not installed in the translation table. Which three actions should you take? (Choose three.)

    a. Determine whether the NAT pool has enough addresses.

    b. Run **debug ip nat detailed** to determine the source of the problem.

    c. Use the **show ip route** command to verify that the selected route exists.

    d. Verify that the router interfaces are appropriately defined as NAT inside or NAT outside.

    e. Verify that the ACL that is referenced by the NAT command is permitting all necessary inside local IPv4 addresses.

8. The output of which command provides information about certain errors or exceptional conditions, such as the failure to allocate a global address?

    a. **debug ip nat**

    b. **debug ip nat detailed**

    c. **show ip nat statistics**

    d. **show ip nat translations**

9. Which advantage does IPv4 have over IPv6?

    a. Larger address space

    b. Shorter header

    c. Simpler header

    d. Support for IPsec on every link

10. Why is NAT not a requirement for IPv6?

    a. NAT is not available with IPv6.

    b. IPv6 addresses do not have a private address space.

    c. IPv6 allows all users in an enterprise to have a global address.

    d. Hexadecimal addresses cannot be translated.

11. How does IPv6 enable smaller routing tables in Internet routers?

    a. By defining aggregation points in the address space

    b. By using a new routing protocol

    c. With autoconfiguration

    d. By using site local addresses

12. How can you condense consecutive sets of zeros in an IPv6 address?

    a. By using the ::: symbol

    b. By eliminating leading zeros

    c. By replacing four consecutive zeros with a single zero

    d. By using the :: symbol

13. Which type of IPv6 address is a global unicast address that is assigned to more than one interface?

    a. Anycast

    b. Unicast

    c. Multicast

    d. Broadcast

14. Which address type from IPv4 was eliminated in IPv6?

    a. Unicast

    b. Multicast

    c. Broadcast

    d. Everycast

15. Which statement is true about the EUI-64 address format of the system ID for stateless autoconfiguration that is used by Cisco?

    a. It is the MAC address plus the Site-Level Aggregator.

    b. It is the MAC address plus the ISO OUI.

    c. It expands the 48-bit MAC address to 64 bits by inserting FFFE into the middle 16 bits.

    d. It does not follow IEEE standards for uniqueness of the address.

    e. It is only used by Cisco.

16. Which term means that an IPv6 router is involved in providing an IPv6 address to a requesting host?

   a. Autoaddressing

   b. Link local

   c. IPv6 NAT

   d. Standard stateless autoconfiguration

   e. DHCP autoconfiguration

17. Which two of the following options are *not* IPv6 routing protocols? (Choose two.)

   a. IGRP6

   b. OSPFv3

   c. EIGRP for IPv6

   d. RIPng

   e. ODR

   f. MP-BGP4

18. What are the two most common IPv4-to-IPv6 transition techniques? (Choose two.)

   a. IPv6 NAT

   b. Dual stack

   c. 6to4 tunnels

   d. IPv6 mobile

19. Which command is the global command that enables IPv6 or dual stack in a Cisco router?

   a. **ipv6 routing**

   b. **ipv6 unicast-routing**

   c. **ipv6 address**

   d. **ipv6 dual stack**

20. Which two statements regarding dual stack are true? (Choose two.)

   a.   A new API replaces gethostbyname and gethostbyaddr calls.

   b.   Tunneling is automatic.

   c.   Dual stack prefers IPv4 over IPv6.

   d.   You cannot use IPv4 while converting to IPv6.

   e.   The stack to use is chosen based on the destination address.

This chapter includes the following sections:

- Chapter Objectives

- Introducing VPN Solutions

- Establishing a Point-to-Point WAN Connection with PPP

- Establishing a WAN Connection with Frame Relay

- Troubleshooting Frame Relay WANs

- Chapter Summary

- Review Questions

Extending the Network into the WAN

WANs are most often charge-for-service networks, providing the means for users to access resources across a wide geographic area. Some services are considered Layer 2 connections between your remote locations, typically provided by a telephone company (telco) over its WAN switches. Some of these technologies include a serial point-to-point (leased line) connection and Frame Relay connections.

Other connections leverage the Internet infrastructure, a Layer 3 alternative, to interconnect the remote locations of an organization. To provide security across the public Internet, you can implement a virtual private network (VPN) solution.

This chapter introduces the components of a VPN solution for WAN connectivity, explains how to configure a PPP connection, and describes Frame Relay operation, configuration, and troubleshooting.

Chapter Objectives

Upon completing this chapter, you will be able to identify and implement the appropriate WAN technology based on network requirements. This ability includes being able to meet these objectives:

- Describe the uses of VPNs for site-to-site and remote-user access

- Connect to a service provider over a network and describe the operation and configuration of PPP

- Connect to a service provider over a network and describe the operation and the basic configuration of Frame Relay

- Identify an approach for troubleshooting common Frame Relay problems and offer solutions

Introducing VPN Solutions

Cisco VPN solutions provide an Internet-based WAN infrastructure for connecting branch offices, home offices, business partner sites, and remote telecommuters to all or portions of a company network. With cost-effective, high-bandwidth Internet connectivity that is secured by encrypted VPN tunnels, you can reduce WAN bandwidth costs while increasing connectivity speeds.

By integrating advanced network intelligence and routing, Cisco VPNs reliably transport complex mission-critical traffic, such as voice and client-server applications, without compromising communications quality or security.

VPNs and Their Benefits

A VPN is an encrypted connection between private networks over a public network such as the Internet. The *V* stands for *virtual,* and the *N* stands for *network*. The information from a private network is securely transported over a public network, the Internet, to form a virtual network. The *P* stands for *private*. To remain private, the traffic is encrypted to keep the data confidential. Instead of using a dedicated Layer 2 connection such as a leased line, a VPN uses IPsec to form virtual connections that are routed through the Internet from the private network of the company to the remote site or employee host. Figure 8-1 shows some examples of using VPNs to connect different types of remote sites.

Figure 8-1   *VPN Connectivity*

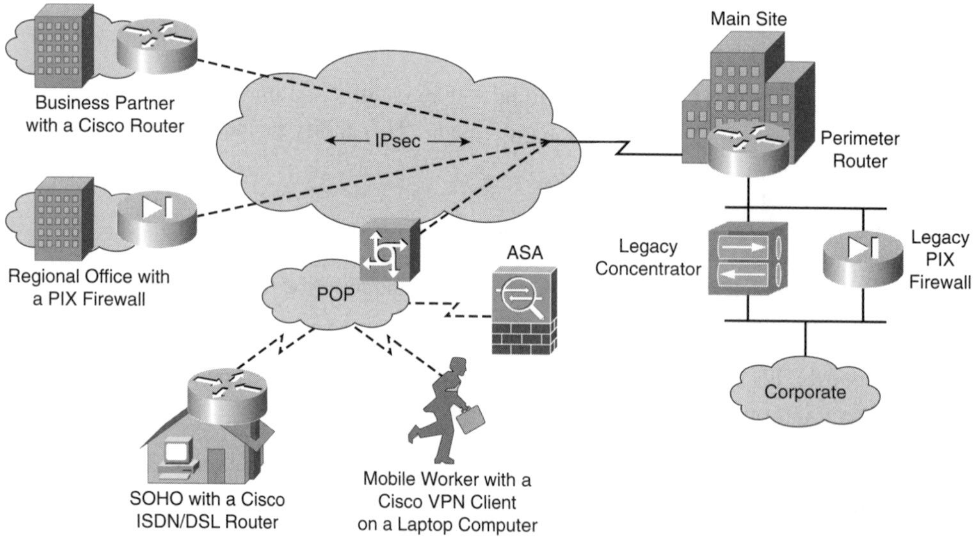

Benefits of VPNs include the following:

■   **Cost savings:** VPNs enable organizations to use cost-effective third-party Internet transport to connect remote offices and remote users to the main corporate site, thus eliminating expensive dedicated WAN links and modem banks. Furthermore, with the advent of cost-effective high-bandwidth technologies, such as DSL, organizations can use VPNs to reduce their connectivity costs while simultaneously increasing remote connection bandwidth.

■   **Security:** VPNs provide the highest level of security by using advanced encryption and authentication protocols that protect data from unauthorized access.

■   **Scalability:** VPNs enable corporations to use the Internet infrastructure within ISPs and devices, which makes it easy to add new users. Therefore, corporations are able to add large amounts of capacity without adding significant infrastructure.

■   **Compatibility with broadband technology:** VPNs allow mobile workers, telecommuters, and people who want to extend their work day to take advantage of high-speed, broadband connectivity, such as DSL and cable, to gain access to their corporate networks, providing workers significant flexibility and efficiency. Furthermore, high-speed broadband connections provide a cost-effective solution for connecting remote offices.

Types of VPNs

There are two types of VPN networks:

■   Site-to-site

■   Remote-access, which includes these two types of VPN solutions:

    — Cisco Easy VPN

    — Cisco IOS IP Security (IPsec)/Secure Socket Layer (SSL) VPN, also known as WebVPN

A site-to-site VPN is an extension of a classic WAN network. Site-to-site VPNs connect entire networks to each other. For example, they can connect a branch office network to a company headquarters network. In the past, a leased line or Frame Relay connection was required to connect sites, but because most corporations now have Internet access, these connections can be replaced with site-to-site VPNs. Figure 8-2 shows an example of a site-to-site VPN.

Figure 8-2 *Site-to-Site VPN*

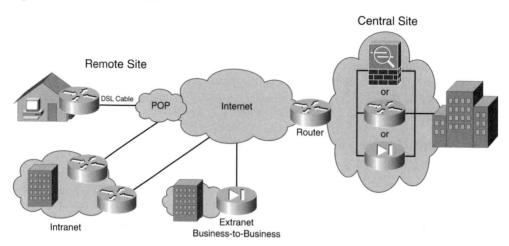

In a site-to-site VPN, hosts do not have Cisco VPN Client software; they send and receive normal TCP/IP traffic through a VPN "gateway," which could be a router, firewall, Cisco VPN Concentrator, or Cisco ASA 5500 Series adaptive security appliance. The VPN gateway is responsible for encapsulating and encrypting outbound traffic for all the traffic from a particular site and sending it through a VPN tunnel over the Internet to a peer VPN gateway at the target site. Upon receipt, the peer VPN gateway strips the headers, decrypts the content, and relays the packet toward the target host inside its private network.

Remote access is an evolution of circuit-switching networks, such as plain old telephone service (POTS) or ISDN. Remote-access VPNs can support the needs of telecommuters, mobile users, and extranet consumer-to-business traffic. Remote-access VPNs connect individual hosts that must access their company network securely over the Internet. Figure 8-3 shows an example of a remote-access VPN.

In the past, corporations supported remote users by using dial-in networks and ISDN. With the advent of VPNs, a mobile user simply needs access to the Internet to communicate with the central office. In the case of telecommuters, their Internet connectivity is typically a broadband, DSL, or cable connection.

In a remote-access VPN, each host typically has Cisco VPN Client software. Whenever the host tries to send traffic, the Cisco VPN Client software encapsulates and encrypts that traffic before sending it over the Internet to the VPN gateway at the edge of the target network. Upon receipt, the VPN gateway behaves as it does for site-to-site VPNs.

Figure 8-3 *Remote-Access VPN*

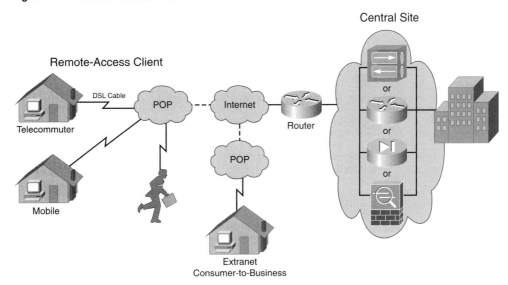

When you are deploying VPNs for teleworkers and small branch offices, the ease of deployment is increasingly important. Cisco Easy VPN makes it easier than ever to deploy VPNs as part of a small, medium, or large enterprise network that has Cisco products. Cisco Easy VPN is a cost-effective solution that is ideal for remote offices that have little information technology support.

There are two components of Cisco Easy VPN:

■ **Cisco Easy VPN Server:** The server can be a dedicated VPN gateway such as a Cisco VPN Concentrator, a Cisco PIX Firewall, a Cisco ASA adaptive security appliance, or a Cisco IOS router with the firewall feature set. A VPN gateway that uses Cisco Easy VPN Server software can terminate VPN tunnels that are initiated by mobile and remote workers that run Cisco VPN Client software on PCs. A VPN gateway can also terminate VPN tunnels from remote devices that act as Cisco Easy VPN remote nodes in site-to-site VPNs.

■ **Cisco Easy VPN Remote Clients:** Cisco Easy VPN Remote Clients enables Cisco IOS routers, PIX Firewalls, Cisco ASA adaptive security appliances, and Cisco VPN Hardware Clients to receive security policies from a Cisco Easy VPN Server, minimizing VPN configuration requirements at the remote location. Cisco Easy VPN allows the VPN parameters, such as internal IP addresses, internal subnet masks, DHCP server addresses, Microsoft Windows Internet Name Service (WINS) server addresses, and split-tunneling flags (to allow local Internet access while connected to the VPN), to be pushed from the Cisco Easy VPN Server to the remote device.

Figure 8-4 shows how Cisco Easy VPN components provide the framework for VPN connectivity to remote sites.

Figure 8-4   *Cisco Easy VPN*

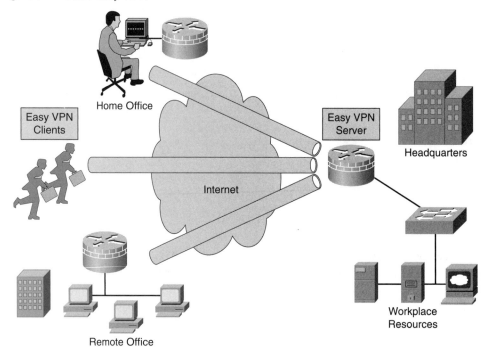

Benefits

The following are benefits of Cisco Easy VPN:

- Centrally stored configurations allow dynamic configuration of end-user policy and require less manual configuration.

- The local VPN configuration is independent of the remote peer IP address. This feature allows the provider to change equipment and network configurations as needed, with little or no reconfiguration of the end-user equipment.

- Cisco Easy VPN provides centralized security policy management.

- Cisco Easy VPN enables large-scale deployments with rapid user provisioning.

- Cisco Easy VPN removes the need for end users to install and configure Cisco Easy VPN Remote software on their PCs.

Restrictions

Implementing Cisco Easy VPN might not be appropriate for all networks because of restrictions. The following restrictions apply to Cisco Easy VPN:

■ No manual Network Address Translation (NAT) or Port Address Translation (PAT) configuration is allowed.

— Cisco Easy VPN Remote automatically creates the appropriate NAT or PAT configuration for the VPN tunnel.

■ Only one destination peer is supported.

— Cisco Easy VPN Remote supports the configuration of only one destination peer and tunnel connection.

— If an application requires the creation of multiple VPN tunnels, you must manually configure the IPsec VPN and NAT and PAT parameters on both the remote client and server.

■ Cisco Easy VPN requires destination servers.

— Cisco Easy VPN Remote requires that the destination peer be a Cisco Easy VPN remote-access server.

■ Digital certificates are not supported.

— Authentication is supported using pre-shared keys (PSK).

— Extended Authentication (XAUTH) can also be used in addition to PSKs to provide user-level authentication in addition to device-level authentication.

■ Only Internet Security Association and Key Management Protocol (ISAKMP) policy group 2 is supported on IPsec servers.

— Cisco VPN Client and server support only ISAKMP policies that use group 2 (1024-bit Diffie-Hellman [DH]) Internet Key Exchange (IKE) negotiation.

■ Some transform sets are not supported.

— The Cisco Easy VPN Remote feature does not support transform sets that provide encryption without authentication (ESP-DES and ESP-3DES) or transform sets that provide authentication without encryption (ESP-NULL, ESP-SHA-HMAC, and ESP-NULL ESP-MD5-HMAC).

— Cisco VPN Client and server do not support Authentication Header (AH) authentication but do support Encapsulating Security Payload (ESP).

IPsec SSL VPN (WebVPN)

Cisco IOS IPsec/SSL–based VPN, also known as WebVPN, is an emerging technology that provides remote-access connectivity from almost any Internet-enabled location using a web browser and its native SSL encryption. WebVPN provides the flexibility to support secure access for all users, regardless of the endpoint host from which they establish a connection. If application access requirements are modest, WebVPN does not require a software client to be preinstalled on the endpoint host. This ability enables companies to extend their secure enterprise networks to any authorized user by providing remote-access connectivity to corporate resources from any Internet-enabled location. Figure 8-5 shows how an SSL VPN tunnel can be built through the Internet using a web browser.

Figure 8-5 *IPsec SSL VPN (WebVPN)*

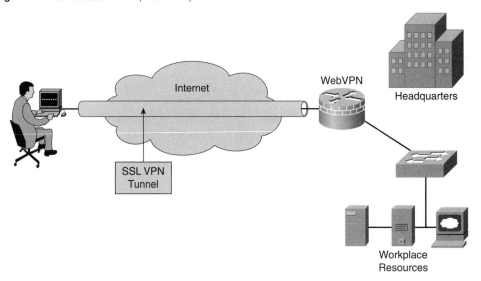

WebVPN currently delivers two modes of SSL VPN access: clientless and thin client. WebVPNs allow users to access web pages and services, including the ability to access files, send and receive e-mail, and run TCP-based applications, without IPsec VPN Client software. WebVPNs are appropriate for user populations that require per-application or per-server access control, or access from nonenterprise-owned desktops.

In many cases, IPsec and WebVPN are complementary because they solve different problems. This complementary approach allows a single device to address all remote-access user requirements.

Benefits

The primary benefit of WebVPN is that it is compatible with Dynamic Multipoint VPNs (DMVPN), Cisco IOS Firewalls, IPsec, intrusion prevention systems (IPS), Cisco Easy VPN, and NAT.

Restrictions

As with other VPN software, some restrictions also exist with IPsec SSL VPN (WebVPN). The primary restriction of WebVPN is that it is currently supported only in software. The router CPU processes the WebVPN connections. The on-board VPN acceleration that is available in integrated services routers accelerates only IPsec connections.

Components of VPNs

Cisco provides a suite of VPN-optimized routers. Cisco IOS Software that is running on Cisco routers combines rich VPN services with industry-leading routing, thereby delivering a comprehensive solution. The Cisco VPN software adds strong security through encryption and authentication. These Cisco VPN–enabled routers provide high performance for site-to-site, intranet, and extranet VPN solutions. Figure 8-6 shows how routers can be used to provide VPN solutions.

Figure 8-6   *VPN on Cisco IOS Routers*

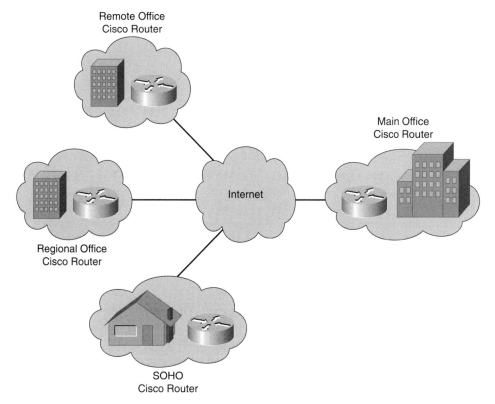

For VPN services, Cisco ASA 5500 Series adaptive security appliances offer flexible technologies that deliver tailored solutions to suit remote-access and site-to-site connectivity requirements. ASA 5500 Series adaptive security appliances provide easy-to-manage IPsec remote access and network-aware site-to-site VPN connectivity, enabling businesses to create secure connections across public networks to mobile users, remote sites, and business partners. Figure 8-7 shows how Cisco ASAs can be used to provide VPN solutions.

Figure 8-7   *VPN on Cisco Adaptive Security Appliances*

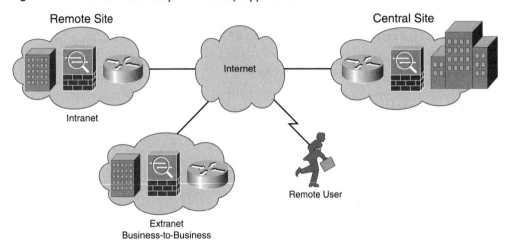

The ASA 5500 Series offers both IPsec and SSL VPN on a single platform, eliminating the need to provide parallel solutions. In addition to VPN services, the ASA 5500 Series offers application inspection firewall and intrusion prevention services.

Cisco remote-access VPNs are able to use three IPsec clients: the Certicom IPsec client, the Cisco VPN Software Client, and the Cisco VPN 3002 Hardware Client. Details are as follows:

■   **Certicom client:** A wireless client that is loaded onto wireless personal digital assistants (PDA) running the Palm or Microsoft Windows Mobile operating systems. Certicom wireless client software allows companies to extend critical enterprise applications, such as e-mail and customer relationship management (CRM) tools, to mobile professionals by enabling handheld devices to connect to corporate VPN gateways for secure wireless access.

- **Cisco VPN 3002 Hardware Client (legacy equipment):** A network appliance that is used to connect small office, home office (SOHO) LANs to the VPN. The device comes in either a single-port or eight-port switch version. The VPN 3002 Hardware Client replaces traditional Cisco VPN Client applications on individual SOHO computers.

- **Cisco VPN Software Client:** Software that is loaded on an individual's PC or laptop. The Cisco VPN Client allows organizations to establish end-to-end, encrypted VPN tunnels for secure connectivity for mobile employees or teleworkers. The Cisco Easy VPN feature allows the Cisco VPN Client to receive security policies from the central site VPN device (Cisco Easy VPN Server) when a VPN tunnel connection is made, minimizing configuration requirements at the remote location.

Figure 8-8 shows an example of the three clients used to connect to a Cisco VPN solution.

Figure 8-8   *VPN Clients*

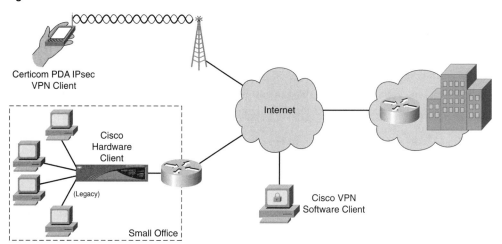

Introducing IPsec

IPsec acts at the network layer, protecting and authenticating IP packets between participating IPsec devices (peers). IPsec is not bound to any specific encryption, authentication, or security algorithms or keying technology. IPsec is a framework of open standards. Figure 8-9 shows how IPsec can be used with different customers and devices to connect.

Figure 8-9   *IPsec Flexibility*

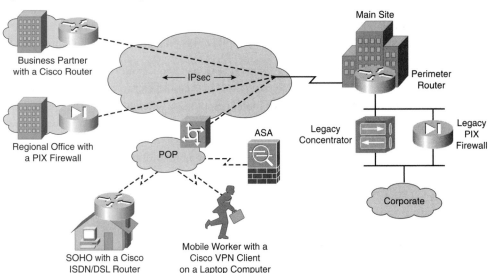

By not binding IPsec to specific algorithms, IPsec allows newer and better algorithms to be implemented without patching the existing IPsec standards. IPsec provides data confidentiality, data integrity, and origin authentication between participating peers at the IP layer. IPsec secures a path between a pair of gateways, a pair of hosts, or a gateway and host.

IPsec security services provide the following four critical functions:

■ **Confidentiality (encryption):** The sender can encrypt the packets before transmitting them across a network. By doing so, no one can eavesdrop on the communication. If the communication is intercepted, it cannot be read.

■ **Data integrity:** The receiver can verify that the data was transmitted through the Internet without being changed. IPsec ensures data integrity by using checksums (also known as a hash value or message digest), a simple redundancy check.

■ **Authentication:** Authentication ensures that the connection is made with the desired communication partner. The receiver can authenticate the source of the packet, guaranteeing and certifying the source of the information.

■ **Antireplay protection:** Antireplay protection verifies that each packet is unique and not duplicated. IPsec packets are protected by comparing the sequence number of the received packets with a sliding window on the destination host or security gateway. A packet that has a sequence number that is before the sliding window is considered either late or a duplicate packet. Late and duplicate packets are dropped.

Plain-text data that is transported over the public Internet can be intercepted and read. To keep the data private, you should encrypt the data. By digitally scrambling the data, it is rendered unreadable. Figure 8-10 shows how the data is encrypted as it passes across the public Internet.

Figure 8-10 *Data Encryption*

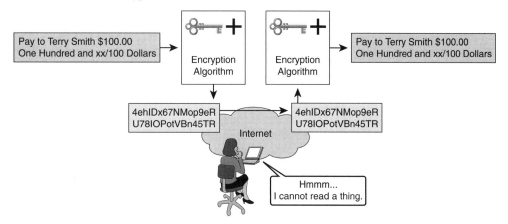

For encryption to work, both the sender and the receiver must know the rules that are used to transform the original message into its coded form. Rules are based on an algorithm and a key. An algorithm is a mathematical function that combines a message, text, digits, or all three with a string of digits called a key. The output is an unreadable cipher string. Decryption is extremely difficult or impossible without the correct key.

In Figure 8-10, someone wants to send a financial document across the Internet. At the local end, the document is combined with a key and run through an encryption algorithm. The output is undecipherable cipher text. The cipher text is then sent through the Internet. At the remote end, the message is recombined with a key and sent back through the encryption algorithm. The output is the original financial document.

The degree of security depends on the length of the key of the encryption algorithm. The time that it takes to process all the possibilities is a function of the computing power of the computer. Therefore, the shorter the key, the easier it is to break. Figure 8-11 shows the role of the key in the process.

Figure 8-11 *Encryption Key*

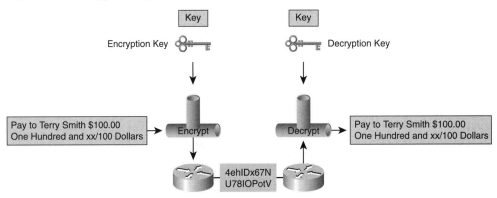

Encryption algorithms such as DES and 3DES require a symmetric shared secret key to perform encryption and decryption. You can use e-mail, courier, or overnight express to send the shared secret keys to the administrators of the devices. But the easiest key exchange method is a public key exchange method between the encrypting and decrypting devices. The DH key agreement is a public key exchange method that provides a way for two peers to establish a shared secret key, which only they know, even though they are communicating over an insecure channel. Figure 8-12 shows that the shared keys need to be established securely over an open network.

Figure 8-12 *Encryption Keys Must Be Established*

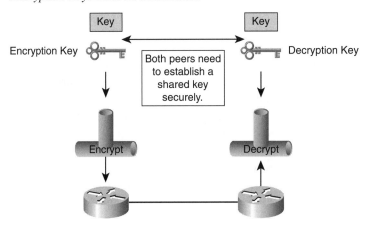

Some of the encryption algorithms and the length of keys they use are as follows:

■ **Data Encryption Standard (DES) algorithm:** DES was developed by IBM. DES uses a 56-bit key, ensuring high-performance encryption. DES is a symmetric key cryptosystem.

- **Triple DES (3DES) algorithm:** The 3DES algorithm is a variant of the 56-bit DES. 3DES operates similarly to DES, in that data is broken into 64-bit blocks. 3DES then processes each block three times, each time with an independent 56-bit key. 3DES provides significant encryption strength over 56-bit DES. DES is a symmetric key cryptosystem.

- **Advanced Encryption Standard (AES):** The National Institute of Standards and Technology (NIST) has recently adopted AES to replace the existing DES encryption in cryptographic devices. AES provides stronger security than DES and is computationally more efficient than 3DES. AES offers three different key lengths: 128-, 192-, and 256-bit keys.

- **Rivest, Shamir, and Adleman (RSA):** RSA is an asymmetrical key cryptosystem. It uses a key length of 512, 768, 1024, or larger. IPsec does not use RSA for data encryption. IKE only uses RSA encryption during the peer authentication phase.

VPN data is transported over the public Internet. Potentially, this data could be intercepted and modified. To guard against this problem, you can use a data integrity algorithm. A data integrity algorithm adds a hash to the message. A hash guarantees the integrity of the original message. If the transmitted hash matches the received hash, the message has not been tampered with. However, if no match exists, the message was altered.

In Figure 8-13, someone is trying to send Terry Smith a check for $100. At the remote end, Alex Jones is trying to cash the check for $1000. As the check progressed through the Internet, it was altered. Both the recipient and dollar amounts were changed. In this case, if a data integrity algorithm were used, the hashes would not match, and the transaction would no longer be valid.

Figure 8-13   *Guarding Against Data Modifications*

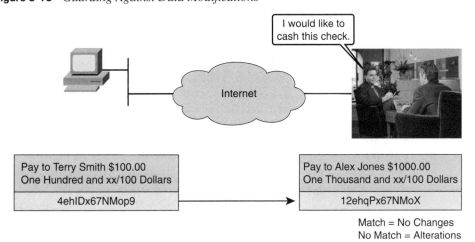

Keyed Hash-based Message Authentication Code (HMAC) is a data integrity algorithm that guarantees the integrity of the message. At the local end, the message and a shared secret key are sent through a hash algorithm, which produces a hash value. The message and hash are sent over the network.

The two common HMAC algorithms are as follows:

■ **HMAC-message digest algorithm 5 (MD5):** Uses a 128-bit shared secret key. The variable-length message and 128-bit shared secret key are combined and run through the HMAC-MD5 hash algorithm. The output is a 128-bit hash. The hash is appended to the original message and forwarded to the remote end.

■ **HMAC-Secure Hash Algorithm 1 (SHA-1):** HMAC-SHA-1 uses a 160-bit secret key. The variable-length message and the 160-bit shared secret key are combined and run through the HMAC-SHA-1 hash algorithm. The output is a 160-bit hash. The hash is appended to the original message and forwarded to the remote end.

When conducting business long distance, it is necessary to know who is at the other end of the phone, e-mail, or fax. The same is true of VPN networks. The device on the other end of the VPN tunnel must be authenticated before the communication path is considered secure. This is illustrated in Figure 8-14.

Figure 8-14 *Peer Authentication*

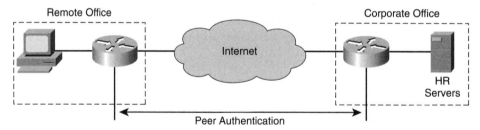

The two peer authentication methods are as follows:

■ **PSKs:** A secret key value that is entered into each peer manually and is used to authenticate the peer. At each end, the PSK is combined with other information to form the authentication key.

■ **RSA signatures:** Use the exchange of digital certificates to authenticate the peers. The local device derives a hash and encrypts it with its private key. The encrypted hash (digital signature) is attached to the message and forwarded to the remote end. At the remote end, the encrypted hash is decrypted using the public key of the local end. If the decrypted hash matches the recomputed hash, the signature is genuine.

IPsec Protocol Framework

IPsec is a framework of open standards. IPsec spells out the messaging to secure the communications but relies on existing algorithms. There are two main IPsec framework protocols, Authentication Header (AH) and Encapsulating Security Payload (ESP). Details are as follows:

- **AH:** AH is the appropriate protocol to use when confidentiality is not required or permitted. It provides data authentication and integrity for IP packets passed between two systems. It is a means of verifying that any message passed from Router A to Router B has not been modified during transit. It verifies that the origin of the data was either Router A or Router B. AH does not provide data confidentiality (encryption) of packets. All text is transported in the clear. Used alone, the AH protocol provides weak protection. Consequently, the AH protocol is used with the ESP protocol to provide data encryption and tamper-aware security features.

- **ESP:** A security protocol that can be used to provide confidentiality (encryption) and authentication. ESP provides confidentiality by performing encryption on the IP packet. IP packet encryption conceals the data payload and the identities of the ultimate source and destination. ESP provides authentication for the inner IP packet and ESP header. Authentication provides data origin authentication and data integrity. Although both encryption and authentication are optional in ESP, at a minimum, one of them must be selected.

IPsec is a framework of open standards that spells out the rules for secure communications. IPsec, in turn, relies on existing algorithms to implement the encryption, authentication, and key exchange. Figure 8-15 shows how the different components of security fit into the IPsec framework, along with the choices of algorithms.

Some of the standard algorithms that IPsec uses are as follows:

- **DES:** Encrypts and decrypts packet data

- **3DES:** Provides significant encryption strength over 56-bit DES

- **AES:** Provides stronger encryption, depending on the key length used, and faster throughput

- **MD5:** Authenticates packet data, using a 128-bit shared secret key

- **SHA-1:** Authenticates packet data, using a 160-bit shared secret key

- **DH (Diffie-Helman):** Allows two parties to establish a shared secret key used by encryption and hash algorithms, for example, DES and MD5, over an insecure communications channel

Figure 8-15 *IPsec Framework Components*

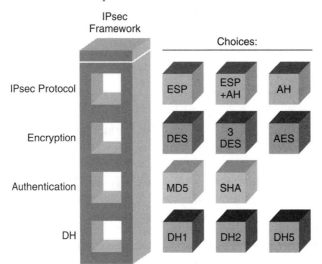

In Figure 8-15, four IPsec framework squares are to be filled in. When you configure an IPsec gateway to provide security services, you must first choose an IPsec protocol. The choices are ESP or ESP with AH. The second square is an encryption algorithm. Choose the encryption algorithm that is appropriate for the desired level of security: DES, 3DES, or AES. The third square is authentication. Choose an authentication algorithm to provide data integrity: MD5 or SHA. The last square is the DH algorithm group. Choose which group to use: DH1, DH2, or DH5. IPsec provides the framework, and the administrator chooses the algorithms that are used to implement the security services within that framework.

Summary of Introducing VPN Solutions

The following summarizes the key points that were discussed in the previous sections:

- Organizations implement VPNs because they are less expensive, more secure, and easier to scale than traditional WANs.

- Site-to-site VPNs secure traffic between intranet and extranet peers. Remote-access VPNs secure communications from the traveling telecommuter to the central office.

- VPNs can be implemented with a variety of different Cisco devices—Cisco IOS routers, ASA 5500 Series adaptive security appliances, and Cisco VPN Client software.

- IPsec is the framework that combines security protocols and provides VPNs with data confidentiality, integrity, and authentication.

- AH and ESP are the two main IPsec framework protocols.

Establishing a Point-to-Point WAN Connection with PPP

Wide-area networking services are typically leased from a service provider. Some WAN services operate as Layer 2 connections between your remote locations and are typically provided by a telephone company (telco) provider over its WAN switches.

PPP emerged as an encapsulation protocol for transporting IP traffic over point-to-point (leased line) serial connections. This section describes the operation, configuration, and verification of PPP.

Understanding WAN Encapsulations

On each WAN connection, data is encapsulated into frames before it crosses the WAN link. To ensure that the correct protocol is used, you must configure the appropriate Layer 2 encapsulation type. The choice of Layer 2 protocol depends on the WAN technology and the communicating equipment. Figure 8-16 highlights some of the choices for connecting to the WAN.

Figure 8-16 *WAN Choices*

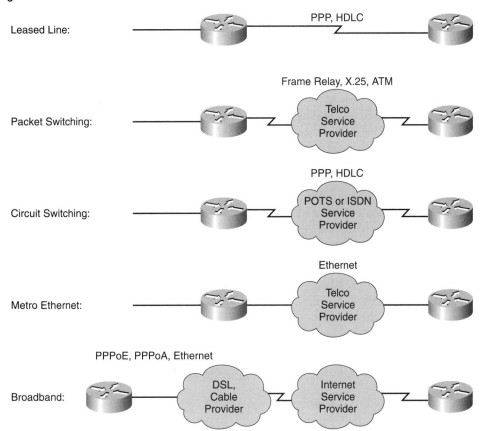

The following are typical WAN protocols:

■ **High-Level Data Link Control (HDLC):** The Cisco default encapsulation type on point-to-point connections, dedicated links, and circuit-switched connections. You typically use HDLC when two Cisco devices are communicating across a point-to-point connection. HDLC is a bit-oriented synchronous data link layer protocol.

■ **PPP:** Provides router-to-router and host-to-network connections over synchronous and asynchronous circuits. PPP was designed to work with several network layer protocols, including IP. PPP also has built-in security mechanisms, such as Password Authentication Protocol (PAP) and Challenge Handshake Authentication Protocol (CHAP).

■ **Frame Relay:** A successor to X.25. This protocol is an industry-standard, switched data link layer protocol that handles multiple virtual circuits (VC). Frame Relay is streamlined to eliminate some of the time-consuming processes, such as error correction and flow control, that were employed in X.25 to compensate for older, less reliable communication links.

■ **ATM:** This protocol is the international standard for cell relay in which multiple service types, such as voice, video, and data, are conveyed in fixed-length (53-byte) cells. ATM, a cell-switched technology, uses fixed-length cells, which allow processing to occur in hardware, thereby reducing transit delays. ATM is designed to take advantage of high-speed transmission media such as T3, E3, and SONET.

■ **Broadband:** Broadband in data communications typically refers to data transmission where multiple pieces of data are sent simultaneously to increase the effective rate of transmission, regardless of the actual data rate. In network engineering, this term refers to transmission methods where two or more signals share a medium, such as the following technologies:

— **DSL-PPP over Ethernet (PPPoE) and PPP over ATM (PPPoA):** A family of technologies that provide digital data transmission over the wires of a local telephone network. Typically, the download speed of consumer DSL services ranges from 256 to 24,000 kbps, depending on DSL technology, line conditions, and the service level that has been implemented. DSL implementations often use PPPoE or PPPoA. Both implementations offer standard PPP features such as authentication, encryption, and compression. PPPoE is a network protocol for encapsulating PPP frames in Ethernet frames. PPPoA is a network protocol for encapsulating PPP frames in ATM adaptation layer 5 (AAL5).

— **Cable-Ethernet:** A cable modem is a type of modem that provides access to a data signal sent over the cable television infrastructure. Cable modems are primarily used to deliver broadband Internet access, taking advantage of unused bandwidth on a cable television network. The bandwidth of business cable modem services typically ranges from 3 Mbps up to 30 Mbps or more. Current cable modem systems use the Ethernet frame format for data transmission over upstream and downstream data channels. Each of the downstream data channels and the associated upstream data channels on a cable network form an extended Ethernet WAN.

- **Metro Ethernet:** The emergence of Metro Ethernet as a viable method of providing both point-to-point and multipoint services has been driven by an abundance of new fiber deployment to business areas. Enterprise customers with years of Ethernet experience in the campus have developed such a comfort level and confidence with Ethernet that they are now asking their service providers for Ethernet as an access option. Ethernet might be the most scalable transport technology ever developed. Starting at 10 Mbps, it has now evolved to 10 Gbps, with plans for 40 Gbps. Several prominent methods exist for transporting Ethernet over Metro networks, including these key solution approaches:

  — Delivering Ethernet services over dark fiber

  — Delivering Ethernet services over SONET/Synchronous Digital Hierarchy (SDH) networks

  — Delivering Ethernet services that use Resilient Packet Ring (RPR) technology

Overview of PPP

Developers designed PPP to make the connection for point-to-point links. PPP, described in RFC 1661, encapsulates network layer protocol information over point-to-point links. RFC 1661 is updated by RFC 2153, "PPP Vendor Extensions."

You can configure PPP on the following types of physical interfaces:

- **Asynchronous serial:** Plain old telephone service (POTS) dialup

- **Synchronous serial:** ISDN or point-to-point leased lines

The Link Control Protocol (LCP) portion of PPP is used to negotiate and set up control options on the WAN data link. PPP offers a rich set of services. These services are options in LCP and are primarily used for negotiation and checking frames to implement the point-to-point controls that an administrator specifies for a connection.

With its higher-level functions, PPP can carry packets from several network layer protocols by using network control protocols (NCP) . The NCPs include functional fields that contain standardized codes to indicate the network layer protocol type that is encapsulated in the PPP frame.

Figure 8-17 shows how NCP and LCP provide these functions for PPP.

Figure 8-17   *PPP Components*

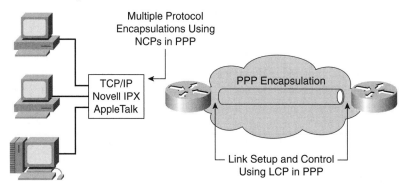

Three phases of a PPP session establishment are described in the following list:

1. Link establishment phase

    In this phase, each PPP device sends LCP packets to configure and test the data link. LCP packets contain a configuration option field that allows devices to negotiate the use of options, such as the maximum receive unit, compression of certain PPP fields, and the link authentication protocol. If a configuration option is not included in an LCP packet, the default value for that configuration option is assumed.

2. Authentication phase (optional)

    After the link has been established and the authentication protocol has been decided on, the peer goes through the authentication phase. Authentication, if used, takes place *before* the network layer protocol phase is begun.

    PPP supports two authentication protocols: PAP and CHAP. Both of these protocols are discussed in RFC 1334, "PPP Authentication Protocols." However, RFC 1994, "PPP Challenge Handshake Authentication Protocol (CHAP)," renders RFC 1334 obsolete.

3.   Network layer protocol phase

In this phase, the PPP devices send NCP packets to choose and configure one or more network layer protocols, such as IP. After each of the chosen network layer protocols is configured, datagrams from each network layer protocol can be sent over the link.

PAP is a two-way handshake that provides a simple method for a remote node to establish its identity. PAP is performed only upon initial link establishment.

After the PPP link establishment phase is complete, the remote node repeatedly sends a username and password pair to the router until authentication is acknowledged or the connection is terminated. Figure 8-18 shows an example of a PAP authentication.

Figure 8-18   *PAP Authentication*

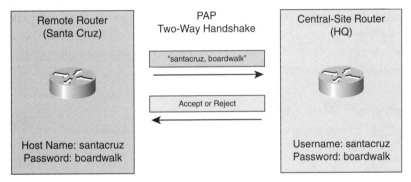

PAP is not a strong authentication protocol. Passwords are sent across the link in plain text, which can be fine in environments that use token-type passwords that change with each authentication, but are not secure in most environments. Also there is no protection from playback or repeated trial-and-error attacks; the remote node is in control of the frequency and timing of the login attempts.

CHAP, which uses a three-way handshake, occurs at the startup of a link and periodically thereafter to verify the identity of the remote node using a three-way handshake.

After the PPP link establishment phase is complete, the local router sends a challenge message to the remote node. The remote node responds with a value that is calculated using a one-way hash function, typically message digest algorithm 5 (MD5), based on the password and challenge message. The local router checks the response against its own calculation of the expected hash value. If the values match, the authentication is acknowledged. Otherwise, the connection is terminated immediately. Figure 8-19 provides an example of CHAP authentication.

Figure 8-19   *CHAP Authentication*

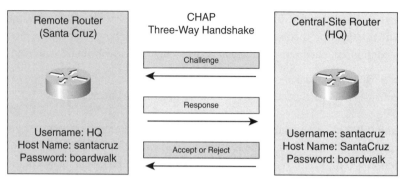

CHAP provides protection against playback attack using a variable challenge value that is unique and unpredictable. Because the challenge is unique and random, the resulting hash value will also be unique and random. The use of repeated challenges is intended to limit exposure to any single attack. The local router or a third-party authentication server is in control of the frequency and timing of the challenges.

Configuring and Verifying PPP

To enable PPP encapsulation with PAP or CHAP authentication on an interface, complete the following checklist:

■   Enable PPP encapsulation as the Layer 2 protocol of an interface.

■   (Optional) Enable PPP authentication by performing these steps:

Step 1   Configure the router host name to identify itself.

Step 2   Configure the username and password to authenticate the PPP peer.

Step 3   Choose the authentication technique to use on the PPP link: PAP or CHAP.

To enable PPP encapsulation, use the **encapsulation ppp** command in interface configuration mode.

To configure PPP authentication, the interface must be configured for PPP encapsulation. Follow these steps to enable PAP or CHAP authentication.

Step 1   Verify that each router has a host name assigned to it. To assign a host name, enter the **hostname** *name* command in global configuration mode. This name must match the username that is expected by the authenticating router at the other end of the link.

Step 2   On each router, define the username and password to expect from the remote router with the **username** *name* **password** *password* global configuration command.

Table 8-1 describes the **username** command parameters.

Table 8-1   username *Parameters*

Parameter	Description
name	This is the host name of the remote router. Note that the host name is case sensitive.
password	On Cisco routers, the password must be the same for both routers. In Cisco IOS Software prior to Release 11.2, this password was an encrypted, secret password. As of Release 11.2, the password is a plain-text password and is not encrypted. To encrypt passwords on your Cisco IOS router, use the **service password-encryption** command while in global configuration mode.

Add a username entry for each remote system that the local router communicates with and that requires authentication. Note that the remote device must have a corresponding username entry for the local router with a matching password.

Step 3   Configure PPP authentication with the **ppp authentication {chap | chap pap | pap chap | pap}** interface configuration command.

If you configure **ppp authentication chap** on an interface, all incoming PPP sessions on that interface are authenticated using CHAP. Likewise, if you configure **ppp authentication pap**, all incoming PPP sessions on that interface are authenticated using PAP.

If you configure **ppp authentication chap pap**, the router attempts to authenticate all incoming PPP sessions using CHAP. If the remote device does not support CHAP, the router tries to authenticate the PPP session using PAP. If the remote device does not support either CHAP or PAP, the authentication fails, and the PPP session is dropped.

If you configure **ppp authentication pap chap**, the router attempts to authenticate all incoming PPP sessions using PAP. If the remote device does not support PAP, the router tries to authenticate the PPP session using CHAP. If the remote device does not support either protocol, the authentication fails and the PPP session is dropped.

NOTE   If you enable both methods, the first method that you specify is requested during link negotiation. If the peer suggests using the second method or refuses the first method, the second method is tried.

Example: PPP and CHAP Configuration

Figure 8-20 shows an example of CHAP configuration on two routers. In this example, a two-way challenge occurs. The hostname on one router must match the username that the other router has configured. The passwords must also match.

Figure 8-20   *PPP & CHAP Configuration Example*

```
hostname RouterX                        hostname RouterY
username RouterY password someone       username RouterX password someone
!                                       !
int serial 0                            int serial 0
 ip address 10.0.1.1 255.255.255.0       ip address 10.0.1.2 255.255.255.0
 encapsulation ppp                       encapsulation ppp
 ppp authentication chap                 ppp authentication chap
```

Example: Verifying PPP Encapsulation Configuration

Use the **show interface** command to verify proper configuration. Example 8-1 shows that PPP encapsulation has been configured and LCP has established a connection, as indicated by "LCP Open" in the command output.

Example 8-1   *Verifying PPP Encapsulation with the* **show interface** *Command*

```
RouterX# show interface s0
Serial0 is up, line protocol is up
  Hardware is HD64570
  Internet address is 10.140.1.2/24
  MTU 1500 bytes, BW 1544 Kbit, DLY 20000 usec, rely 255/255, load 1/255
  Encapsulation PPP, loopback not set, keepalive set (10 sec)
  LCP Open
  Open: IPCP, CDPCP
  Last input 00:00:05, output 00:00:05, output hang never
  Last clearing of "show interface" counters never
  Queueing strategy: fifo
  Output queue 0/40, 0 drops; input queue 0/75, 0 drops
  5 minute input rate 0 bits/sec, 0 packets/sec
  5 minute output rate 0 bits/sec, 0 packets/sec
     38021 packets input, 5656110 bytes, 0 no buffer
     Received 23488 broadcasts, 0 runts, 0 giants, 0 throttles
     0 input errors, 0 CRC, 0 frame, 0 overrun, 0 ignored, 0 abort
     38097 packets output, 2135697 bytes, 0 underruns
     0 output errors, 0 collisions, 6045 interface resets
```

Example 8-1 *Verifying PPP Encapsulation with the* **show interface** *Command (Continued)*

```
0 output buffer failures, 0 output buffers swapped out
482 carrier transitions
DCD=up  DSR=up  DTR=up  RTS=up  CTS=up
```

Example: Verifying PPP Authentication

Example 8-2 illustrates the router output that occurs during CHAP authentication. Because two-way authentication is configured, that is, each router authenticates the other, messages appear that reflect both the authenticating process and the process of being authenticated. Use the **debug ppp authentication** command to display the exchange sequence as it occurs.

Example 8-2 *Verifying Authentication with the* **debug ppp authentication** *Command*

```
RouterX# debug ppp authentication
4d20h: %LINK-3-UPDOWN: Interface Serial0, changed state to up
4d20h: Se0 PPP: Treating connection as a dedicated line
4d20h: Se0 PPP: Phase is AUTHENTICATING, by both
4d20h: Se0 CHAP: O CHALLENGE id 2 len 28 from "left"
4d20h: Se0 CHAP: I CHALLENGE id 3 len 28 from "right"
4d20h: Se0 CHAP: O RESPONSE id 3 len 28 from "left"
4d20h: Se0 CHAP: I RESPONSE id 2 len 28 from "right"
4d20h: Se0 CHAP: O SUCCESS id 2 len 4
4d20h: Se0 CHAP: I SUCCESS id 3 len 4
4d20h: %LINEPROTO-5-UPDOWN: Line protocol on Interface Serial0, changed
```

To determine whether the router is performing one-way or two-way CHAP authentication, look for the following message in the **debug ppp authentication** output, which indicates that the routers are performing two-way authentication:

```
Se0 PPP: Phase is AUTHENTICATING, by both
```

Either one of the following messages indicates that the routers are performing one-way authentication:

```
Se0 PPP: Phase is AUTHENTICATING, by the peer
Se0 PPP: Phase is AUTHENTICATING, by this end
```

The following output highlights output for a two-way PAP authentication:

```
! Two way authentication:
Se0 PPP: Phase is AUTHENTICATING, by both
! Outgoing authentication request:
Se0 PAP: O AUTH-REQ id 4 len 18 from "RouterX"
! Incoming authentication request:
Se0 PAP: I AUTH-REQ id 1 len 18 from "RouterY"
! Authenticating incoming:
Se0 PAP: Authenticating peer RouterY
! Outgoing acknowledgement:
Se0 PAP: O AUTH-ACK id 1 len 5
! Incoming acknowledgement:
Se0 PAP: I AUTH-ACK id 4 len 5
```

To determine whether the router is performing CHAP or PAP authentication, look for the following lines in the **debug ppp authentication** command output:

- Look for CHAP in the AUTHENTICATING phase, as shown in this example:

```
*Mar  7 21:16:29.468: BR0:1 PPP: Phase is AUTHENTICATING, by this end
*Mar  7 21:16:29.468: BR0:1 CHAP: O CHALLENGE id 5 len 33 from "maui-soho-03"
```

- Look for PAP in the AUTHENTICATING phase, as shown in this example:

```
*Mar  7 21:24:11.980: BR0:1 PPP: Phase is AUTHENTICATING, by both
*Mar  7 21:24:12.084: BR0:1 PAP: I AUTH-REQ id 1 len 23 from "maui-soho-01"
```

The most common output from the **debug ppp negotiation** command is described as follows:

- **Timestamp:** Millisecond timestamps are useful.

- **Interface and Interface number:** This field is useful when debugging multiple connections or when the connection transitions through several interfaces.

- **Type of PPP message:** This field indicates whether the line is a general PPP, LCP, CHAP, PAP, or IP Control Protocol (IPCP) message.

- **Direction of the message:** An "I" indicates an incoming packet, and an "O" indicates an outgoing packet. This field can be used to determine whether the message was generated or received by the router.

- **Message:** This field includes the particular transaction under negotiation.

- **ID:** This field is used to match and coordinate request messages to the appropriate response messages. You can use the ID field to associate a response with an incoming message.

- **Length:** The length field defines the length of the information field. This field is not important for general troubleshooting.

The last four fields might not appear in all the PPP messages, depending on the purpose of the message.

Summary of Establishing a Point-to-Point WAN Connection with PPP

The following summarizes the key points that were discussed in the previous sections:

- PPP is a common Layer 2 protocol for the WAN. Two components of PPP exist: LCP negotiates the connection and NCP encapsulates traffic.

- You can configure PPP to use PAP or CHAP. PAP sends everything in plain text. CHAP uses an MD5 hash.

- Common PPP verification commands include **show interface** to verify PPP encapsulation and **debug ppp negotiation** to verify the LCP handshake.

Establishing a WAN Connection with Frame Relay

Frame Relay is a high-performance WAN protocol that was standardized by the ITU-T and is widely used in the United States. This section describes Frame Relay operation, configuration, and troubleshooting.

Understanding Frame Relay

Frame Relay is a connection-oriented data-link technology that is streamlined to provide high performance and efficiency. For error protection, it relies on upper-layer protocols and dependable fiber and digital networks.

Frame Relay defines the interconnection process between the router and the local access switching equipment of the service provider. It does *not* define how the data is transmitted within the Frame Relay service provider cloud. Figure 8-21 shows that Frame Relay operates between the router and the frame relay switch.

Figure 8-21 *Frame Relay*

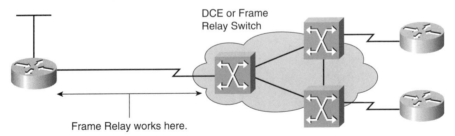

Devices attached to a Frame Relay WAN fall into the following two categories:

- **Data terminal equipment (DTE):** Generally considered to be the terminating equipment for a specific network. DTE devices are typically located on the customer premises and can be owned by the customer. Examples of DTE devices are Frame Relay Access Devices (FRAD), routers, and bridges.

- **Data communications equipment (DCE):** Carrier-owned internetworking devices. The purpose of DCE devices is to provide clocking and switching services in a network and to transmit data through the WAN. In most cases, the switches in a WAN are Frame Relay switches.

Frame Relay provides a means for statistically multiplexing many logical data conversations, referred to as virtual circuits (VC), over a single physical transmission link by assigning connection identifiers to each pair of DTE devices. The service provider switching equipment constructs a switching table that maps the connection identifier to outbound ports. When a frame is received, the switching device analyzes the connection identifier and delivers the frame to the associated outbound port. The complete path to the destination is established prior to the transmission of the first frame. Figure 8-22 illustrates a Frame Relay connection and identifies the many components within Frame Relay.

Figure 8-22 *Frame Relay Components*

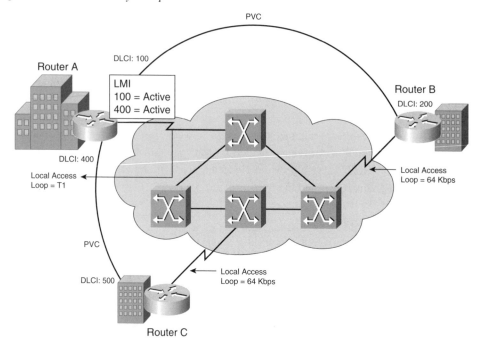

The following terms are used frequently in Frame Relay discussions and can be the same or slightly different from the terms your Frame Relay service provider uses:

■ **Local access rate:** Clock speed (port speed) of the connection (local loop) to the Frame Relay cloud. The local access rate is the rate at which data travels into or out of the network, regardless of other settings.

■ **Virtual circuit (VC):** Logical circuit, uniquely identified by a data-link connection identifier (DLCI), that is created to ensure bidirectional communication from one DTE device to another. A number of VCs can be multiplexed into a single physical circuit for transmission across the network. This capability can often reduce the complexity of the equipment and network that are required to connect multiple DTE devices. A VC can pass through any number of intermediate DCE devices (Frame Relay switches). A VC can be either a permanent virtual circuit (PVC) or a switched virtual circuit (SVC).

- **Permanent virtual circuit (PVC):** Provides permanently established connections that are used for frequent and consistent data transfers between DTE devices across the Frame Relay network. Communication across a PVC does not require the call setup and call teardown that is used with an SVC.

- **Switched virtual circuit (SVC):** Provides temporary connections that are used in situations that require only sporadic data transfer between DTE devices across the Frame Relay network. SVCs are dynamically established on demand and are torn down when transmission is complete.

> **NOTE**   With ANSI T1.617 and ITU-T Q.933 (Layer 3) and Q.922 (Layer 2), Frame Relay now supports SVCs. Cisco IOS Release 11.2 or later supports Frame Relay SVCs. This book does not cover information on configuring Frame Relay SVCs.

- **Data-link connection identifier (DLCI):** Contains a 10-bit number in the address field of the Frame Relay frame header that identifies the VC. DLCIs have local significance because the identifier references the point between the local router and the local Frame Relay switch to which the DLCI is connected. Therefore, devices at opposite ends of a connection can use different DLCI values to refer to the same virtual connection.

- **Committed information rate (CIR):** Specifies the maximum average data rate that the network undertakes to deliver under normal conditions. When subscribing to a Frame Relay service, you specify the local access rate, for example, 56 kbps or T1. Typically, you are also asked to specify a CIR for each DLCI. If you send information faster than the CIR on a given DLCI, the network flags some frames with a discard eligible (DE) bit. The network does its best to deliver all packets but discards any DE packets first if congestion occurs. Many inexpensive Frame Relay services are based on a CIR of 0. A CIR of 0 means that every frame is a DE frame, and the network throws any frame away when it needs to. The DE bit is within the address field of the Frame Relay frame header.

- **Inverse Address Resolution Protocol (ARP):** A method of dynamically associating the network layer address of the remote router with a local DLCI. Inverse ARP allows a router to automatically discover the network address of the remote DTE device that is associated with a VC.

- **Local Management Interface (LMI):** A signaling standard between the router (DTE device) and the local Frame Relay switch (DCE device) that is responsible for managing the connection and maintaining status between the router and the Frame Relay switch.

- **Forward explicit congestion notification (FECN):** A bit in the address field of the Frame Relay frame header. The FECN mechanism is initiated when a DTE device sends Frame Relay frames into the network. If the network is congested, DCE devices (Frame Relay switches) set the FECN bit value of the frames to 1. When these frames reach the destination DTE device, the address field with the FECN bit set indicates that these frames experienced congestion in the path from source to destination. The DTE device can relay this information to a higher-layer protocol for processing. Depending on the implementation, flow control might be initiated or the indication might be ignored.

- **Backward explicit congestion notification (BECN):** A bit in the address field of the Frame Relay frame header. DCE devices set the value of the BECN bit to 1 in frames that travel in the opposite direction of frames that have their FECN bit set. Setting BECN bits to 1 informs the receiving DTE device that a particular path through the network is congested. The DTE device can then relay this information to a higher-layer protocol for processing. Depending on the implementation, flow control might be initiated or the indication might be ignored.

Example: Frame Relay Terminology—DLCI

As shown in Figure 8-22, Router A has two virtual circuits that are configured on one physical interface. A DLCI of 100 identifies the VC that connects to Router B. A DLCI of 400 identifies the VC that connects to Router C. At the other end, a different DLCI number can be used to identify the VC.

Frame Relay allows you to interconnect your remote sites in a variety of topologies. Figure 8-23 illustrates these topologies.

Figure 8-23 *Frame Relay Topologies*

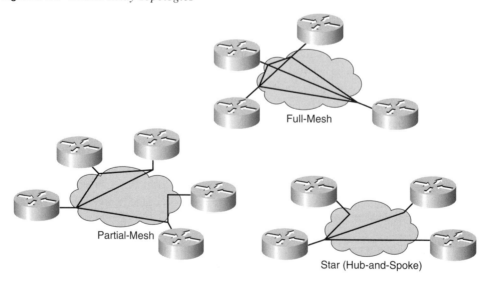

Each topology is further described as follows:

- **Partial-mesh topology:** Not all sites have direct access to all other sites. Depending on the traffic patterns in your network, you might want to have additional PVCs connect to remote sites that have large data traffic requirements.

- **Full-mesh topology:** All routers have VCs to all other destinations. Full-mesh topology, although costly, provides direct connections from each site to all other sites and allows redundancy. When one link goes down, a router can reroute traffic through another site. As the number of nodes in this topology increases, a full-mesh topology can become very expensive. Use the $n\ (n-1)\ /\ 2$ formula to calculate the total number of links that are required to implement a full-mesh topology, where n is the number of nodes. For example, to fully mesh a network of 10 nodes, 45 links are required—10 $(10-1)\ /\ 2$.

- **Star topology:** Remote sites are connected to a central site that generally provides a service or an application. The star topology, also known as a hub-and-spoke configuration, is the most popular Frame Relay network topology. This is the least expensive topology because it requires the least number of PVCs. In the figure, the central router provides a multipoint connection because it typically uses a single interface to interconnect multiple PVCs.

By default, a Frame Relay network provides nonbroadcast multiaccess (NBMA) connectivity between remote sites. An NBMA environment is treated like other broadcast media environments, such as Ethernet, where all the routers are on the same subnet.

However, to reduce cost, NBMA clouds are usually built in a hub-and-spoke topology. With a hub-and-spoke topology, the physical topology does not provide the multiaccess capabilities that Ethernet does, so each router might not have separate PVCs to reach the other remote routers on the same subnet. Split horizon is one of the main issues you encounter when Frame Relay is running multiple PVCs over a single interface.

In any Frame Relay topology, when a single interface must be used to interconnect multiple sites, you can have reachability issues because of the NBMA nature of Frame Relay. The Frame Relay NBMA topology can cause the following two problems:

- **Routing update reachability:** Split horizon updates reduce routing loops by preventing a routing update that is received on an interface from being forwarded out the same interface. In a scenario using a hub-and-spoke Frame Relay topology, a remote router (a spoke router) sends an update to the headquarters router (the hub router) that is connecting multiple PVCs over a single physical interface. The headquarters router then receives the broadcast on its physical interface but cannot forward that routing update through the same interface to other remote (spoke) routers. Split horizon is not a problem if a single PVC exists on a physical interface because this type of connection would be more of a point-to-point connection type.

- **Broadcast replication:** With routers that support multipoint connections over a single interface that terminate many PVCs, the router must replicate broadcast packets, such as routing update broadcasts, on each PVC to the remote routers. These replicated broadcast packets consume bandwidth and cause significant latency variations in user traffic.

The following methods exist to solve the routing update reachability issue:

- To solve the reachability issues brought on by split horizon, turn off split horizon. However, two problems exist with this solution. First, although most network layer protocols, such as IP, do allow you to disable split horizon, not all network layer protocols allow you to do this. Second, disabling split horizon increases the chances of routing loops in your network.

- Use a fully meshed topology; however, this topology increases the cost.

- Use subinterfaces. To enable the forwarding of broadcast routing updates in a hub-and-spoke Frame Relay topology, you can configure the hub router with logically assigned interfaces called subinterfaces, which are logical subdivisions of a physical interface. In split horizon routing environments, routing updates that are received on one subinterface can be sent out another subinterface. In subinterface configuration, each VC can be configured as a point-to-point connection, which allows each subinterface to act like a leased line. When you use a Frame Relay point-to-point subinterface, each subinterface is on its own subnet.

Figure 8-24 shows how to resolve the issues using subinterfaces.

Figure 8-24 *Using Subinterfaces with Frame Relay*

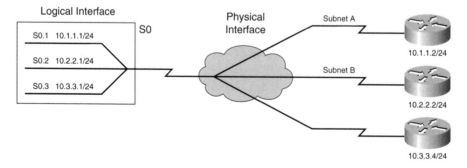

A Frame Relay connection requires that, on a VC, the local DLCI be mapped to a destination network layer address, such as an IP address. Routers can automatically discover their local DLCI from the local Frame Relay switch using the LMI protocol.

On Cisco routers, the local DLCI can be dynamically mapped to the remote router network layer addresses with Inverse ARP. Inverse ARP associates a given DLCI to the next-hop protocol address for a specific connection. Inverse ARP is described in RFC 1293.

Example: Frame Relay Address Mapping

As shown in Figure 8-25, using Inverse ARP, the router on the left can automatically discover the remote router IP address and then map it to the local DLCI. In this case, the local DLCI of 500 is mapped to the 10.1.1.1 IP address. Therefore, when the router must send data to 10.1.1.1, it uses DLCI 500.

Figure 8-25 *Frame Relay Address Mapping*

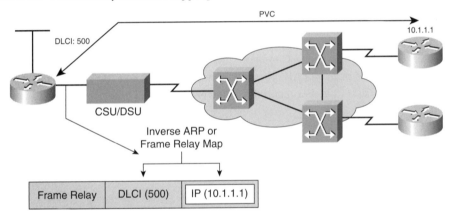

Instead of using Inverse ARP to automatically map the local DLCIs to the remote router network layer addresses, you can manually configure a static Frame Relay map in the map table.

Frame Relay signaling is required between the router and the Frame Relay switch. Figure 8-26 shows how the signaling is used to get information about the different DLCIs.

Figure 8-26 *Frame Relay Signaling*

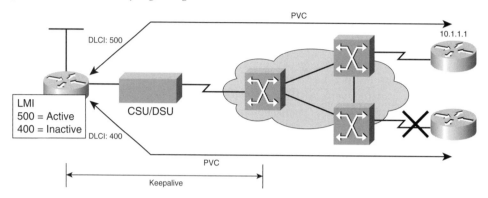

The LMI is a signaling standard between the router and the Frame Relay switch. The LMI is responsible for managing the connection and maintaining the status between the devices.

Although the LMI is configurable, beginning in Cisco IOS Release 11.2, the Cisco router tries to autosense which LMI type the Frame Relay switch is using. The router sends one or more full LMI status requests to the Frame Relay switch. The Frame Relay switch responds with one or more LMI types, and the router configures itself with the last LMI type received. Cisco routers support the following three LMI types:

- **Cisco:** LMI type defined jointly by Cisco, StrataCom, Northern Telecom (Nortel), and Digital Equipment Corporation

- **ANSI:** ANSI T1.617 Annex D

- **Q.933A:** ITU-T Q.933 Annex A

You can also manually configure the appropriate LMI type from the three supported types to ensure proper Frame Relay operation.

When the router receives LMI information, it updates its VC status to one of the following three states:

- **Active:** Indicates that the VC connection is active and that routers can exchange data over the Frame Relay network.

- **Inactive:** Indicates that the local connection to the Frame Relay switch is working, but the remote router connection to the remote Frame Relay switch is not working.

- **Deleted:** Indicates that either no LMI is being received from the Frame Relay switch or that no service exists between the router and local Frame Relay switch.

The following is a summary of how Inverse ARP and LMI signaling work with a Frame Relay connection:

1. Each router connects to the Frame Relay switch through a channel service unit/data service unit (CSU/DSU).

2. When Frame Relay is configured on an interface, the router sends an LMI status inquiry message to the Frame Relay switch. The message notifies the switch of the router status and asks the switch for the connection status of the router VCs.

3. When the Frame Relay switch receives the request, it responds with an LMI status message that includes the local DLCIs of the PVCs to the remote routers to which the local router can send data.

4. For each active DLCI, each router sends an Inverse ARP packet to introduce itself.

    Figure 8-27 illustrates the first four steps of this process.

Figure 8-27   *Stages of Inverse ARP and LMI Operation*

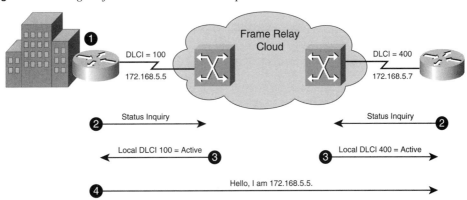

5. When a router receives an Inverse ARP message, it creates a map entry in its Frame Relay map table that includes the local DLCI and the remote router network layer address. Note that the router DLCI is the local DLCI, not the DLCI that the remote router is using. Any of the three connection states can appear in the Frame Relay map table.

    > **NOTE**   If Inverse ARP is not working or the remote router does not support Inverse ARP, you must manually configure static Frame Relay maps, which map the local DLCIs to the remote network layer addresses.

6. Every 60 seconds, routers send Inverse ARP messages on all active DLCIs. Every 10 seconds, the router exchanges LMI information with the switch (keepalives).

7. The router changes the status of each DLCI to active, inactive, or deleted, based on the LMI response from the Frame Relay switch.

Figure 8-28 illustrates Steps 5–7 of this process.

Figure 8-28 *Stages of Inverse ARP and LMI Operation Continued*

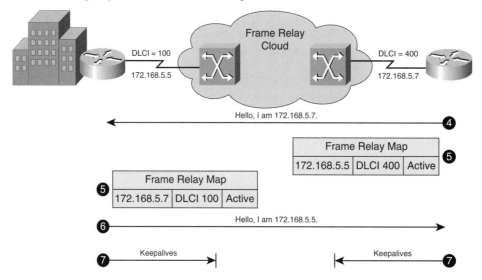

Configuring Frame Relay

A basic Frame Relay configuration assumes that you want to configure Frame Relay on one or more physical interfaces and that the routers support LMI and Inverse ARP.

The following steps are used to configure basic Frame Relay:

Step 1 Select the interface needed for Frame Relay. Use the interface configuration mode.

```
RouterX(config)# interface serial1
```
After the interface configuration is entered, the command-line interface (CLI) prompt changes from (config)# to (config-if)#.

Step 2 Configure a network layer address, for example, an IP address.

```
RouterX(config-if)# ip address 10.16.0.1 255.255.255.0
```

Step 3 Select the Frame Relay encapsulation type that is used to encapsulate end-to-end data traffic. Use the **encapsulation frame-relay** interface configuration command.

```
RouterX(config-if)# encapsulation frame-relay [cisco | ietf]
```

The option **cisco** means that Cisco encapsulation is being used. Use this option if you are connecting to another Cisco router. You do not need to enter the keyword cisco because it is the default encapsulation. The option **ietf** sets the encapsulation method to comply with the Internet Engineering Task Force (IETF) standard (RFC 2427). Select this option if you are connecting to a router from another vendor.

Step 4   Establish LMI connection using the **frame-relay lmi-type** interface configuration command.

```
RouterX(config-if)# frame-relay lmi-type {ansi | cisco | q933a}
```
This command is needed only if you are using Cisco IOS Software Release 11.1 or earlier. With Cisco IOS Software Release 11.2 or later, the LMI type is autosensed and no configuration is needed. The option **cisco** is the default. The LMI type is set on a per-interface basis and is shown in the output of the **show interfaces** EXEC command.

Step 5   Configure the bandwidth for the link using the **bandwidth** [*kilobits*] interface configuration command. For example:

```
RouterX(config-if)# bandwidth 64
```
This command affects routing operations performed by protocols such as Enhanced Interior Gateway Routing Protocol (EIGRP) and Open Shortest Path First (OSPF), as well as other calculations.

Step 6   Enable Inverse ARP if it was disabled on the router. Use the **frame-relay inverse-arp** [*protocol*] [*dlci*] interface configuration command.

The *protocol* parameter indicates the protocol in use. Supported protocols include IP, Internetwork Packet Exchange (IPX), AppleTalk, DECnet, Banyan Virtual Integrated Network Service (VINES), and Xerox Network Services (XNS). The *dlci* parameter indicates the DLCI on the local interface with which you want to exchange Inverse ARP messages. Inverse ARP is on by default and does not appear in the configuration output.

Consider the following configuration, where IP is the protocol, and the DLCI is 16:

```
RouterX(config-if)# frame-relay inverse-arp ip 16
```

When the remote router does not support Inverse ARP, the Frame Relay peers have different Frame Relay encapsulation types. Or when you want to control broadcast and multicast traffic over the PVC, you must statically map the local DLCI to the remote router network layer address. These static Frame Relay map entries are referred to as static maps.

Use the following command to statically map the remote network layer address to the local DLCI:

```
RouterX(config-if)# frame-relay map protocol protocol-address dlci [broadcast]
    [ietf | cisco | payload-compress packet-by-packet]
```

Table 8-2 details the parameters for this command.

Table 8-2   frame-relay map *Command Parameters*

Parameter	Description
protocol	Defines the supported protocol, bridging, or logical link control. The choices include AppleTalk, DECnet, Data-Link Switching (DLSW), IP, IPX, Logical Link Control, type 2 (LLC2), remote source-route bridging (RSRB), Banyan VINES, and XNS.
protocol-address	Defines the network layer address of the destination router interface.
dlci	Defines the local DLCI that is used to connect to the remote protocol address.
broadcast	(Optional) Allows broadcasts and multicasts over the VC. This permits the use of dynamic routing protocols over the VC.
**ietf	cisco**	Enables IETF or Cisco encapsulations.
payload-compress packet-by-packet	(Optional) Enables packet-by-packet payload compression, using the Stacker method. This is a Cisco-proprietary compression method.

You can configure subinterfaces in one of the following two modes:

- **Point-to-point:** A single point-to-point subinterface is used to establish one PVC connection to another physical interface or subinterface on a remote router. In this case, each pair of the point-to-point routers is on its own subnet, and each point-to-point subinterface has a single DLCI. In a point-to-point environment, because each subinterface acts like a point-to-point interface, update traffic is not subject to the split horizon rule.

- **Multipoint:** A single multipoint subinterface is used to establish multiple PVC connections to multiple physical interfaces or subinterfaces on remote routers. In this case, all the participating interfaces are in the same subnet. In this environment, because the subinterface acts like a regular NBMA Frame Relay interface, update traffic is subject to the split horizon rule.

Example: Configuring Frame Relay Point-to-Point Subinterfaces

In Figure 8-29, Router A has two point-to-point subinterfaces. The s0.110 subinterface connects to Router B, and the s0.120 subinterface connects to Router C. Each subinterface is on a different subnet.

Figure 8-29 *Point-to-Point Subinterfaces*

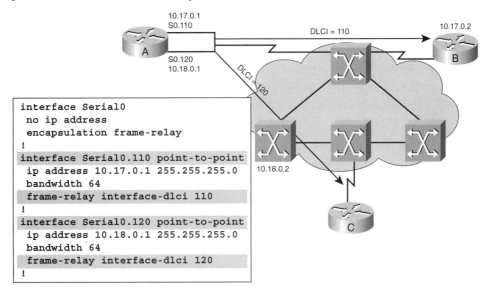

```
interface Serial0
 no ip address
 encapsulation frame-relay
!
interface Serial0.110 point-to-point
 ip address 10.17.0.1 255.255.255.0
 bandwidth 64
 frame-relay interface-dlci 110
!
interface Serial0.120 point-to-point
 ip address 10.18.0.1 255.255.255.0
 bandwidth 64
 frame-relay interface-dlci 120
!
```

Follow these steps to configure subinterfaces on a physical interface:

Step 1 Select the interface upon which you want to create subinterfaces and enter interface configuration mode.

Step 2 Remove any network layer address that is assigned to the physical interface and assign the network layer address to the subinterface.

Step 3 Configure Frame Relay encapsulation.

Step 4 Use the following command to select the subinterface you want to configure and to designate it as a point-to-point subinterface:

```
RouterX(config-if)# interface serial number.subinterface-number point-
     to-point}
```
Table 8-3 describes the options for this command.

Table 8-3 interface serial *Command Parameters*

Parameter	Description
.subinterface-number	Subinterface number in the range 1–4,294,967,293. The interface number that precedes the period (.) must match the physical interface number to which this subinterface belongs.
point-to-point	Select this option if you want each pair of point-to-point routers to have its own subnet.

You are required to enter either the **multipoint** or **point-to-point** parameter; no default is available.

Step 5   If you configured the subinterface as the point-to-point subinterface, you must configure the local DLCI for the subinterface to distinguish it from the physical interface. The command to configure the local DLCI on the subinterface follows:

```
RouterX(config-subif)# frame-relay interface-dlci dlci-number
```

The *dlci-number* parameter defines the local DLCI number that is being linked to the subinterface. No other methods exist to link an LMI-derived DLCI to a subinterface because the LMI does not know about subinterfaces.

Do not use the **frame-relay interface-dlci** command on physical interfaces.

> **NOTE**   If you defined a subinterface for point-to-point communication, you cannot reassign the same subinterface number to use for multipoint communication without first rebooting the router. Instead, use a different subinterface number.

Example: Configuring Frame Relay Multipoint Subinterfaces

In Figure 8-30, all the routers are on the 10.17.0.0/24 subnet. Router A is configured with a multipoint subinterface with three PVCs. The PVC with DLCI 120 is used to connect to Router B, the PVC with DLCI 130 is used to connect to Router C, and the PVC with DLCI 140 is used to connect to Router D.

Figure 8-30   *Frame Relay Multipoint Subinterface*

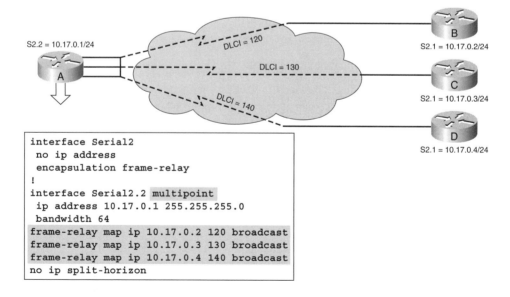

Split horizon is disabled by default on Frame Relay multipoint main interfaces and enabled by default on Frame Relay multipoint subinterfaces. In the figure, which uses a multipoint subinterface, split horizon must be manually disabled at Router A to overcome the split horizon issue.

Follow these steps to configure subinterfaces on a physical interface:

Step 1 Select the interface upon which you want to create subinterfaces and enter interface configuration mode.

Step 2 Remove any network layer address, like the IP address, assigned to the physical interface and assign the network layer address to the subinterface.

Step 3 Configure Frame Relay encapsulation.

Step 4 Use the following command to select the subinterface you want to configure and to designate it as a multipoint subinterface:

```
RouterX(config-if)# interface serial number.subinterface-number
          multipoint
```

Table 8-4 describes the options for this command.

Table 8-4 **interface serial** *Command Parameters*

Parameter	Description
.subinterface-number	Subinterface number in the range 1–4,294,967,293. The interface number that precedes the period (.) must match the physical interface number to which this subinterface belongs.
multipoint	Select this option if you want all routers in the same subnet.

You are required to enter either the **multipoint** or **point-to-point** parameter; no default is available.

Step 5 If you have configured the subinterface as multipoint and Inverse ARP is enabled, you must configure the local DLCI for the subinterface to distinguish it from the physical interface. This configuration is not required for multipoint subinterfaces that are configured with static route maps. The command to configure the local DLCI on the subinterface follows:

```
RouterX(config-subif)# frame-relay interface-dlci dlci-number
```

The *dlci-number* parameter defines the local DLCI number that is being linked to the subinterface. No other methods exist to link an LMI-derived DLCI to a subinterface because the LMI does not know about subinterfaces.

Do not use the **frame-relay interface-dlci** command on physical interfaces.

> **NOTE**   If you defined a subinterface for point-to-point communication, you cannot reassign the same subinterface number to use for multipoint communication without first rebooting the router. Instead, use a different subinterface number.

Verifying Frame Relay

The **show interfaces** command displays information regarding the encapsulation and Layer 1 and Layer 2 status. Verify that the encapsulation is set to Frame Relay.

The command also displays information about the LMI type and the LMI DLCI. The LMI DLCI is not the DLCI that identifies the PVC across which data is passed. That DLCI is shown in the **show frame-relay pvc** command.

The output also displays the Frame Relay DTE or DCE type. Normally, the router will be the DTE. However, a Cisco router can be configured as the Frame Relay switch; in this case, the type will be DCE. Example 8-3 shows the output from this command.

Example 8-3   *Verify Frame Relay Information with the* **show interfaces** *Command*

```
RouterX# show interfaces s0
Serial0 is up, line protocol is up
  Hardware is HD64570
  Internet address is 10.140.1.2/24
  MTU 1500 bytes, BW 1544 Kbit, DLY 20000 usec, rely 255/255, load 1/255
  Encapsulation FRAME-RELAY, loopback not set, keepalive set (10 sec)
  LMI enq sent  19, LMI stat recvd 20, LMI upd recvd 0, DTE LMI up
  LMI enq recvd 0, LMI stat sent  0, LMI upd sent  0
  LMI DLCI 1023  LMI type is CISCO  frame relay DTE
  FR SVC disabled, LAPF state down
  Broadcast queue 0/64, broadcasts sent/dropped 8/0, interface broadcasts 5
  Last input 00:00:02, output 00:00:02, output hang never
  Last clearing of "show interface" counters never
  Queueing strategy: fifo
  Output queue 0/40, 0 drops; input queue 0/75, 0 drops
  <Output omitted>
```

Use the **show frame-relay lmi** command to display LMI traffic statistics. For example, this command shows the number of status messages exchanged between the local router and the local Frame Relay switch. Example 8-4 shows the output of this command.

Example 8-4   *Displaying LMI Traffic Statistics with the* **show frame-relay lmi** *Command*

```
RouterX# show frame-relay lmi

LMI Statistics for interface Serial0 (Frame Relay DTE) LMI TYPE = CISCO
 Invalid Unnumbered info 0 Invalid Prot Disc 0
```

Example 8-4 *Displaying LMI Traffic Statistics with the* **show frame-relay lmi**
Command (Continued)

```
Invalid dummy Call Ref 0 Invalid Msg Type 0
Invalid Status Message 0 Invalid Lock Shift 0
Invalid Information ID 0 Invalid Report IE Len 0
Invalid Report Request 0 Invalid Keep IE Len 0
Num Status Enq. Sent 113100 Num Status msgs Rcvd
```

Table 8-5 describes a few of the fields in the **show frame-relay lmi** display.

Table 8-5 **show frame-relay lmi** *Fields*

Field	Description
LMI Type	Signaling or LMI specification; options are Cisco, ANSI, or ITU-T
Num Status Enq. Sent	Number of LMI status inquiry messages sent
Num Status Msgs Rcvd	Number of LMI status messages received

Use the **debug frame-relay lmi** command to determine whether the router and the Frame
Relay switch are sending and receiving LMI packets properly. Example 8-5 shows the
output associated with this command.

Example 8-5 *Confirming LMI Packet Traffic Delivery/Receipt with the* **debug frame-relay**
lmi *Command*

```
RouterX# debug frame-relay lmi
Frame Relay LMI debugging is on
Displaying all Frame Relay LMI data
RouterX#
1w2d: Serial0(out): StEnq, myseq 140, yourseen 139, DTE up
1w2d: datagramstart = 0xE008EC, datagramsize = 13
1w2d: FR encap = 0xFCF10309
1w2d: 00 75 01 01 01 03 02 8C 8B
1w2d:
1w2d: Serial0(in): Status, myseq 140
1w2d: RT IE 1, length 1, type 1
1w2d: KA IE 3, length 2, yourseq 140, myseq 140
1w2d: Serial0(out): StEnq, myseq 141, yourseen 140, DTE up
1w2d: datagramstart = 0xE008EC, datagramsize = 13
1w2d: FR encap = 0xFCF10309
1w2d: 00 75 01 01 01 03 02 8D 8C
1w2d:
1w2d: Serial0(in): Status, myseq 142
1w2d: RT IE 1, length 1, type 0
1w2d: KA IE 3, length 2, yourseq 142, myseq 142
1w2d: PVC IE 0x7 , length 0x6 , dlci 100, status 0x2 , bw 0
```

The first four lines describe an LMI exchange. The first line describes the LMI request that the router has sent to the Frame Relay switch. The second line describes the LMI reply that the router has received from the Frame Relay switch. The third and fourth lines describe the response to this request from the switch. This LMI exchange is followed by two similar LMI exchanges. The last six lines consist of a full LMI status message that includes a description of the two PVCs of the router.

Table 8-6 describes the significant fields shown in Example 8-5.

Table 8-6   debug frame-relay lmi *Output Fields*

Field	Description
Serial0(out)	Indicates that the LMI request was sent out on interface Serial 0
StEnq	The command mode of message, which can be one of the following: StEnq: Status inquiry Status: Status reply
myseq 140	Myseq counter, which maps to the CURRENT SEQ counter of the router
yourseen 139	Yourseen counter, which maps to the LAST RCVD SEQ counter of the switch
DTE up	State of the line protocol (up or down) for the DTE (user) port
RT IE 1	Value of the report type (RT) information element (IE)
length 1	Length of the report type information element in bytes
type 1	Report type is RT IE
KA IE 3	Value of the keepalive information element
length 2	Length of the keepalive information element in bytes
yourseq 142	Yourseq counter, which maps to the CURRENT SEQ counter of the switch
myseq 142	Myseq counter, which maps to the CURRENT SEQ counter of the router
PVC IE 0x7	Value of the PVC information element type
length 0x6	Length of the PVC IE in bytes
dlci 100	DLCI value, in decimal, for this PVC

Table 8-6   **debug frame-relay lmi** *Output Fields (Continued)*

Field	Description
status 0x2	Status value; possible values are as follows: **0x00:** Added/inactive **0x02:** Added/active **0x04:** Deleted **0x08:** New/inactive **0x0a:** New/active
bw 0	CIR for the DLCI

The "(out)" output is an LMI status message that is sent by the router. The "(in)" output is a message that is received from the Frame Relay switch.

The "type 0" output indicates a full LMI status message. The "type 1" output indicates an LMI exchange.

The "dlci 100, status 0x2" output means that the status of DLCI 100 is active. The common values of the DLCI status field are as follows:

■ **0x0:** "Added" and "inactive" mean that the switch has this DLCI programmed, but for some reason—for example, the other end of this PVC is down—it is not usable.

■ **0x2:** "Added" and "active" mean that the Frame Relay switch has the DLCI, and everything is operational. You can start sending traffic with this DLCI in the header.

■ **0x4:** "Deleted" means that the Frame Relay switch does not have this DLCI programmed for the router but that it was programmed at some point in the past. This status could also happen because the DLCIs are reversed on the router or because the PVC was deleted by the service provider in the Frame Relay cloud.

Use the **show frame-relay pvc** [**interface** *interface*] [*dlci*] command to display the status of each configured PVC as well as traffic statistics. Example 8-6 shows the output of this command.

Example 8-6 *Displaying PVC Status and Traffic Statistics with the* **show frame-relay pvc** *Command*

```
RouterX# show frame-relay pvc 100

PVC Statistics for interface Serial0 (Frame Relay DTE)

DLCI = 100, DLCI USAGE = LOCAL, PVC STATUS = ACTIVE, INTERFACE = Serial0

  input pkts 28           output pkts 10           in bytes 8398
  out bytes 1198          dropped pkts 0           in FECN pkts 0
  in BECN pkts 0          out FECN pkts 0          out BECN pkts 0
  in DE pkts 0            out DE pkts 0
  out bcast pkts 10       out bcast bytes 1198
  pvc create time 00:03:46, last time pvc status changed 00:03:47
```

Table 8-7 describes the fields of the **show frame-relay pvc** command display.

Table 8-7   **show frame-relay pvc** *Output Fields*

Field	Description
DLCI	One of the DLCI numbers for the PVC.
DLCI USAGE	Lists "SWITCHED" when the router or access server is used as a switch or "LOCAL" when the router or access server is used as a DTE device.
PVC STATUS	Status of the PVC. The DCE device reports the status, and the DTE device receives the status. When you disable the LMI mechanism on the interface by using the **no keepalive** command, the PVC status is STATIC. Otherwise, the PVC status is exchanged using the LMI protocol, as follows: **STATIC:** LMI is disabled on the interface. **ACTIVE:** The PVC is operational and can transmit packets. **INACTIVE:** The PVC is configured but is down. **DELETED:** The PVC is not present (DTE device only), which means that no status is received from the LMI protocol.

Table 8-7 **show frame-relay pvc** *Output Fields (Continued)*

Field	Description
	If the **frame-relay end-to-end keepalive** command is used, the end-to-end keepalive (EEK) status is reported in addition to the LMI status. Two examples follow:
	ACTIVE (EEK UP): The PVC is operational according to LMI and end-to-end keepalives.
	ACTIVE (EEK DOWN): The PVC is operational according to LMI, but end-to-end keepalive has failed.
INTERFACE	Specific subinterface that is associated with this DLCI.
LOCAL PVC STATUS	Status of the PVC that is configured locally on the Network-to-Network Interface (NNI).
NNI PVC STATUS	Status of the PVC that is learned over the NNI link.
input pkts	Number of packets that are received on this PVC.
output pkts	Number of packets that are sent on this PVC.
in bytes	Number of bytes that are received on this PVC.
out bytes	Number of bytes that are sent on this PVC.
dropped pkts	Number of incoming and outgoing packets that are dropped by the router at the Frame Relay level.
in pkts dropped	Number of incoming packets that have been dropped. Incoming packets can be dropped for a number of reasons: Inactive PVC Policing Packets received above DE discard level Dropped fragments Memory allocation failures Configuration problems
out pkts dropped	Number of outgoing packets that have been dropped, including shaping drops and late drops.
out bytes dropped	Number of outgoing bytes that have been dropped.

continues

Table 8-7   **show frame-relay pvc** *Output Fields (Continued)*

Field	Description
late-dropped out pkts	Number of outgoing packets that have been dropped because of a quality of service (QoS) policy, such as VC queuing or Frame Relay traffic shaping. This field is not displayed when the value is 0.
late-dropped out bytes	Number of outgoing bytes dropped because of a QoS policy, such as VC queuing or Frame Relay traffic shaping. This field is not displayed when the value is 0.
in FECN pkts	Number of packets that are received with the FECN bit set.
in BECN pkts	Number of packets that are received with the BECN bit set.
out FECN pkts	Number of packets that are sent with the FECN bit set.
out BECN pkts	Number of packets that are sent with the BECN bit set.
in DE pkts	Number of DE packets that have been received.
out DE pkts	Number of DE packets that have been sent.
out bcast pkts	Number of output broadcast packets.
out bcast bytes	Number of output broadcast bytes.

Use the **show frame-relay map** command to display the current map entries and information about the connections. Example 8-7 shows the output of this command.

Example 8-7   *Displaying Frame Relay Map Entries and Connection Information with the* **show frame-relay map** *Command*

```
RouterX# show frame-relay map
Serial0 (up): ip 10.140.1.1 dlci 100(0x64,0x1840), dynamic,
              broadcast,, status defined, active
RouterX# clear frame-relay-inarp
RouterX# show frame map
RouterX#
```

The following information explains the **show frame-relay map** output that appears in the example:

■   The "100" output is the local DLCI number in decimal.

■   The "0x64" output is the hex conversion of the DLCI number (0x64 = 100 decimal).

■   The "0x1840" output is the value as it would appear "on the wire" because of the way the DLCI bits are spread out in the address field of the Frame Relay frame.

- The "10.140.1.1" output is the remote router IP address (a dynamic entry that is learned through the Inverse ARP process).

- Broadcast and multicast are enabled on the PVC because broadcast is stated in the third line.

- The PVC status is active.

To clear dynamically created Frame Relay maps, which are created using Inverse ARP, use the **clear frame-relay-inarp** privileged EXEC command.

Summary of Establishing a WAN Connection with Frame Relay

The following summarizes the key points that were discussed in the previous sections:

- Frame Relay PVCs are identified with DLCIs, and the status of the PVCs is reported through the LMI protocol.

- Frame Relay point-to-point subinterfaces require a separate subnet for each PVC, and multipoint subinterfaces share a single subnet with Frame Relay peers.

- To display connectivity with the Frame Relay provider, use the **show frame-relay lmi** command. To display connectivity with the Frame Relay peer, use the **show frame-relay pvc** and **show frame-relay map** commands.

Troubleshooting Frame Relay WANs

A Frame Relay network offers a few additional benefits that a leased-line implementation does not offer. But with these benefits comes a bit more complexity. The addition of concepts such as nonbroadcast multiaccess (NBMA), Local Management Interface (LMI), Inverse Address Resolution Protocol (ARP), and Frame Relay maps requires that an administrator have a fundamental knowledge of these concepts to better troubleshoot connectivity issues that can arise.

Components of Troubleshooting Frame Relay

Troubleshooting Frame Relay requires a step-by-step approach that identifies and tests each of the major components. Figure 8-31 outlines this approach in a flowchart.

The major components of Frame Relay troubleshooting are described as follows:

- Troubleshooting a Frame Relay link that is down, which could be a Layer 1 or Layer 2 issue

- Troubleshooting Frame Relay remote router connectivity, which is the connectivity between the Frame Relay peer routers

■ Troubleshooting Frame Relay end-to-end connectivity, which is the connectivity between workstations across a Frame Relay network

Figure 8-31 *Flowchart for Troubleshooting Frame Relay*

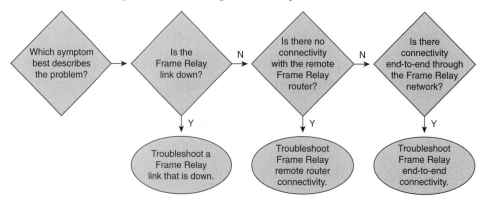

Troubleshooting Frame Relay Connectivity Issues

The first step in troubleshooting Frame Relay connectivity issues is to check the status of the Frame Relay interface. Figure 8-32 gives a flowchart for troubleshooting these issues.

Figure 8-32 *Troubleshooting Connectivity Issues*

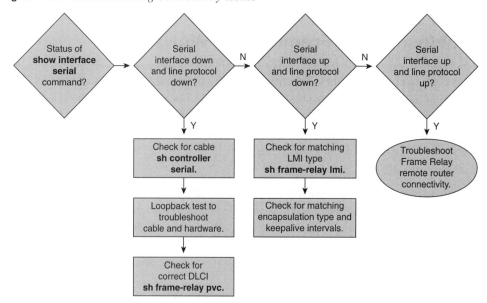

Use the **show interface serial** *number*[/*number*] command to check the status of the Frame Relay interface.

If the output of the **show interface serial** command displays a status of "interface down/line protocol down," this typically indicates a problem at Layer 1, the physical layer. This output means that you have a problem with the cable, CSU/DSU, or the serial line.

First, use the **show controllers serial** [*slot/port*] command to verify that the cable is present and recognized by the router.

Next, you might need to troubleshoot the problem with a loopback test.

Follow these steps to perform a loopback test:

Step 1 Set the serial line encapsulation to High-Level Data Link Control (HDLC) and keepalive to 10 seconds. To do this, use the **encapsulation hdlc** and **keepalive 10** commands in the interface configuration mode of the interface you are troubleshooting.

Step 2 Place the CSU/DSU or modem in local-loop mode. Check the device documentation to determine how to do this. If the line protocol comes up when the CSU/DSU or modem is in local-loop mode, indicated by a "line protocol is up (looped)" message, this suggests that the problem is occurring beyond the local CSU/DSU. If the status line does not change status, a problem could be in the router, connecting cable, CSU/DSU, or modem. In most cases, the problem is with the CSU/DSU or modem.

Step 3 Execute a **ping** command to the IP address of the interface you are troubleshooting while the CSU/DSU or modem is in local-loop mode. No misses should occur. An extended ping that uses a data pattern of 0x0000 is helpful in resolving line problems because a T1 or E1 connection derives clock speed from the data and requires a transition every 8 bits. A data pattern with many 0s helps to determine whether the transitions are appropriately forced on the trunk. A pattern with many 1s is used to appropriately simulate a high 0 load in case a pair of data inverters is in the path. The alternating pattern (0x5555) represents a "typical" data pattern. If your pings fail or if you get cyclic redundancy check (CRC) errors, a bit error rate tester (BERT) with an appropriate analyzer from the telephone company (telco) is needed.

Step 4 When you are finished testing, ensure that you return the encapsulation of the interface to Frame Relay.

An incorrect statically defined DLCI on a subinterface can also cause the status of the subinterface to appear as "down/down," and the PVC status might appear as "deleted." To verify that the correct DLCI number has been configured, use the **show frame-relay pvc** command, as demonstrated in Example 8-8.

Example 8-8   *Verifying DLCI Configuration*

```
RouterX# show frame-relay pvc

PVC Statistics for interface Serial0/0/0 (Frame Relay DTE)

              Active      Inactive      Deleted      Static
  Local         0            0             1            0
  Switched      0            0             0            0
  Unused        0            0             0            0


DLCI = 100, DLCI USAGE = LOCAL, PVC STATUS = DELETED, INTERFACE = Serial0/0/0

  input pkts 9              output pkts 8             in bytes 879
  out bytes 1024            dropped pkts 0            in pkts dropped 0
  out pkts dropped 0        out bytes dropped 0
  in FECN pkts 0            in BECN pkts 0            out FECN pkts 0
  out BECN pkts 0           in DE pkts 0              out DE pkts 0
  out bcast pkts 2          out bcast bytes 138
  5 minute input rate 0 bits/sec, 0 packets/sec
  5 minute output rate 0 bits/sec, 0 packets/sec
pvc create time 00:00:27, last time pvc status changed 00:00:27
```

In the output, the DLCI number shows "100" and reports a status of "deleted." This might indicate that the DLCI you configured was incorrect.

If the output of a **show interface serial** command displays a status of "interface up/line protocol down," this typically indicates a problem at Layer 2, the data link layer. If this is the case, the serial interface might not be receiving the LMI keepalives from the Frame Relay service provider. To verify that LMI messages are being sent and received and to verify that the router LMI type matches the LMI type of the provider, use the **show frame-relay lmi** command, as demonstrated in Example 8-9.

Example 8-9   *Verifying LMI Traffic Delivery/Receipt and LMI Type Matches Between Router and Provider*

```
RouterX# show frame-relay lmi

LMI Statistics for interface Serial0/0/0 (Frame Relay DTE) LMI TYPE = CISCO
  Invalid Unnumbered info 0          Invalid Prot Disc 0
  Invalid dummy Call Ref 0           Invalid Msg Type 0
  Invalid Status Message 0           Invalid Lock Shift 0
  Invalid Information ID 0           Invalid Report IE Len 0
  Invalid Report Request 0           Invalid Keep IE Len 0
```

Example 8-9   *Verifying LMI Traffic Delivery/Receipt and LMI Type Matches Between Router and Provider (Continued)*

```
 Num Status Enq. Sent 236            Num Status msgs Rcvd 31
 Num Update Status Rcvd 0            Num Status Timeouts 206
Last Full Status Req 00:00:38       Last Full Status Rcvd 00:00:38
```

The output shows that 236 LMI status inquiry messages have been sent (Num Status Enq. Sent), 31 LMI status messages have been received (Num Status msgs Rcvd), and the LMI type is set to "Cisco."

For a Frame Relay router to reach a peer router across the Frame Relay network, it must map the IP address of the peer router with the local DLCI it uses to reach that IP address. Figure 8-33 shows the steps involved in troubleshooting remote router connectivity issues.

Figure 8-33   *Troubleshooting Remote Router Connectivity with Frame Relay*

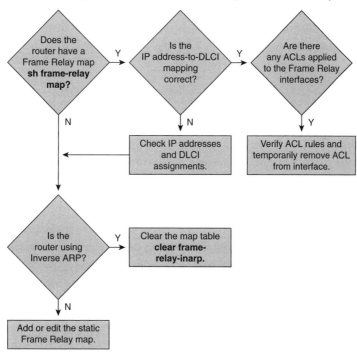

As demonstrated in Example 8-10, the **show frame-relay map** command shows the IP address–to–DLCI mappings and indicates whether the mapping was statically entered or dynamically learned using Inverse ARP.

Example 8-10   *Verifying IP Address–to–DLCI Mappings and Static or Dynamic Configuration*

```
RouterX# show frame-relay map
Serial0/0/0 (up): ip 10.140.1.1 dlci 100(0x64,0x1840), dynamic,
              broadcast,
              CISCO, status defined, active
```

If you have recently changed the address on the remote Frame Relay router interface, you might need to use the **clear frame-relay-inarp** command to clear the Frame Relay map of the local router. This will cause Inverse ARP to dynamically remap the new address with the DLCI.

If the IP address of the peer router does not appear in the Frame Relay mapping table, the remote router might not support Inverse ARP. Try adding the IP address–to–DLCI mapping statically by using the **frame-relay map** *protocol protocol-address dlci* [**broadcast**] command.

Additionally, access control lists (ACL) might be applied to the Frame Relay interfaces that affect connectivity. To verify whether an ACL is applied to an interface, use the **show ip interface** command.

To temporarily remove an ACL from an interface to verify whether it is affecting connectivity, use the **no ip access-group** *acl_num* {**in** | **out**} command in interface configuration mode.

For end-to-end connectivity to exist between two workstations across an active Frame Relay network, general routing requirements must be met. Figure 8-34 shows the troubleshooting steps for verifying end-to-end connectivity.

If you are experiencing end-to-end connectivity problems in your Frame Relay network, check the routing tables to see whether the routers have a route to the destination with which you are having connectivity problems. To check the routing table, use the **show ip route** command, as demonstrated in Example 8-11.

Figure 8-34 *Troubleshooting End-to-End Connectivity with Frame Relay*

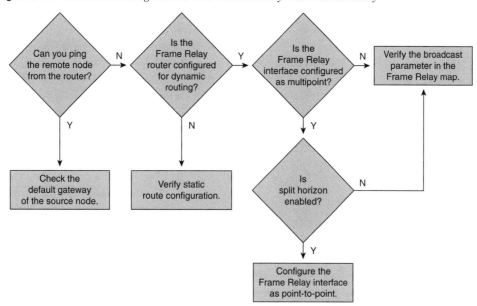

Example 8-11 *Confirming End-to-End Connectivity*

```
RouterX# show ip route
Codes: C - connected, S - static, R - RIP, M - mobile, B - BGP
       D - EIGRP, EX - EIGRP external, O - OSPF, IA - OSPF inter area
       N1 - OSPF NSSA external type 1, N2 - OSPF NSSA external type 2
       E1 - OSPF external type 1, E2 - OSPF external type 2
       i - IS-IS, su - IS-IS summary, L1 - IS-IS level-1, L2 - IS-IS level-2
       ia - IS-IS inter area, * - candidate default, U - per-user static route
       o - ODR, P - periodic downloaded static route

Gateway of last resort is not set

     172.16.0.0/24 is subnetted, 1 subnets
C       172.16.2.0 is directly connected, Loopback1
     10.0.0.0/24 is subnetted, 3 subnets
C       10.23.23.0 is directly connected, Serial0/0/1
C       10.2.2.0 is directly connected, FastEthernet0/0
     192.168.1.0/24 is variably subnetted, 3 subnets, 3 masks
C       192.168.1.64/28 is directly connected, Loopback0
```

If only directly connected routes appear in the routing table, the problem might be that the Frame Relay network is preventing the routing protocol updates from being advertised across it. Because of the NBMA nature of Frame Relay, you must configure the router to pass routing protocol broadcasts or multicasts across the Frame Relay network. With the use of Inverse ARP, this capability is in effect automatically. With a static Frame Relay map, you must explicitly configure the support for broadcast traffic. The **show frame-relay map** command displays whether the broadcast capability is in effect, allowing routing updates to be passed across the Frame Relay network, as demonstrated in Example 8-12.

Example 8-12 *Confirming Broadcast Traffic Capability*

```
RouterX# show frame-relay map
Serial0/0/0 (up): ip 10.140.1.1 dlci 100(0x64,0x1840), dynamic,
            broadcast,
            CISCO, status defined, active
```

Summary of Troubleshooting Frame Relay WANs

The following summarizes the key points that were discussed in the previous sections:

■   There are three aspects of troubleshooting frame relay: troubleshooting the link, troubleshooting the mapping from one router to another, and troubleshooting routing across a Frame Relay network.

■   Use the **show interface serial** and **show frame-relay lmi** commands to verify Layer 1 and Layer 2 link failures. Use the **show frame-relay map** and **show frame-relay pvc** commands to test connectivity between routers.

Chapter Summary

The following summarizes the key points that were discussed in this chapter:

■   Site-to-site VPNs secure traffic between intranet and extranet peers. Remote-access VPNs secure communications from the telecommuter to the central office.

■   PPP can be configured on both asynchronous and synchronous point-to-point links. PPP supports both PAP and CHAP authentication.

■   Frame Relay interfaces can be either point-to-point or multipoint interfaces.

■   To troubleshoot Frame Relay connections, use the **show frame relay lmi**, **show frame relay pvc**, and **show frame relay map** commands.

You have a variety of ways to interconnect users to remote services, and each has its benefits and drawbacks. Traditional Layer 2 WAN technologies, such as leased lines and Frame Relay, are options that are widely used. However, a new trend is to use the public Internet by creating site-to-site and remote-access Virtual Private Networks (VPN) because VPNs are less expensive, more secure, and easier to scale.

Review Questions

Use the questions here to review what you learned in this chapter. The correct answers and solutions are found in the appendix, "Answers to Chapter Review Questions."

1. Which feature does PPP use to encapsulate multiple protocols?

    a. NCP

    b. LCP

    c. IPCP

    d. IPXCP

2. What is the purpose of LCP?

    a. To perform authentication

    b. To negotiate control options

    c. To encapsulate multiple protocols

    d. To specify asynchronous versus synchronous

3. Which packet type is used in the PPP link establishment phase?

    a. LCP

    b. PAP

    c. NCP

    d. CHAP

4. Which of the following statements best describe CHAP? (Choose two.)

    a. CHAP is performed periodically.

    b. CHAP uses a two-way handshake.

    c. CHAP uses a three-way handshake.

    d. CHAP uses a two-way hash function.

    e. CHAP passwords are sent in plain text.

5. With CHAP, how does a remote node respond to a challenge message?

    a. With a hash value

    b. With a return challenge

    c. With a plain-text password

    d. With an encrypted password

6. Which username must be configured on routers for PPP authentication?

   a. One that matches the host name of the local router.

   b. One that matches the host name of the remote router.

   c. One that matches neither host name.

   d. There is no restriction on username.

7. Which output from the **show interface** command indicates that PPP is configured properly?

   a. Encaps = PPP

   b. PPP encapsulation

   c. Encapsulation PPP

   d. Encapsulation HDLC using PPP

8. Match each Frame Relay operation component with its definition.

   _____Local access rate

   _____SVC

   _____CIR

   _____LMI

   _____Inverse ARP

   a. Maximum average data rate

   b. Clock speed of the connection to the Frame Relay cloud

   c. Method of dynamically associating a remote network layer address with a local DLCI

   d. VC that is dynamically established on demand and is torn down when transmission is complete

   e. Signaling standard between the router device and the Frame Relay switch that is responsible for managing the connection and maintaining status between the devices

9. What identifies the logical circuit between the router and the local Frame Relay switch?

   a. A DLCI

   b. An LMI signal

   c. An FECN packet

   d. A BECN packet

10. Match each Frame Relay topology to its description.

   ____Star

   ____Full-mesh

   ____Partial-mesh

   a. All routers have virtual circuits to all other destinations.

   b. Many, but not all, routers have direct access to all other sites.

   c. Remote sites are connected to a central site that generally provides a service or an application.

11. Which characteristic of Frame Relay can cause reachability issues when a single interface is used to interconnect multiple sites?

   a. Intermittent

   b. Point-to-point

   c. Error-correcting

   d. NBMA

12. What is an alternative method to using Inverse ARP to map DLCIs to network layer addresses on a Frame Relay network?

   a. ARP

   b. RARP

   c. DHCP

   d. Static Frame Relay **map** commands

13. Which of the following LMI types does Cisco support? (Choose three.)

   a. DEC

   b. ANSI

   c. Cisco

   d. Q.931

   e. Q.933A

   f. Q.921

14. Which address must be mapped on a Frame Relay VC to the local DLCI?

   a. Port address

   b. Source port address

   c. Network layer address

   d. Data link layer address

15. Which VC status on a Cisco router indicates that the local connection to the Frame Relay switch is working but the remote router connection to the Frame Relay switch is not working?

   a. LMI state

   b. Active state

   c. Deleted state

   d. Inactive state

16. Which of the following are types of VPNs? (Choose two.)

   a. Remote-access

   b. Remote-to-site

   c. Remote-to-remote

   d. Site-to-site

17. Which option is not a benefit of implementing VPNs?

   a. Is cheaper than Layer 2 WANs

   b. Provides scalability

   c. Does not require a telco

   d. Provides security

18. Which is not a component of the IPsec framework?

   a.   ESP

   b.   MD5

   c.   AES

   d.   RSMAC

19. Which component of security ensures that the data has not been tampered with?

   a.   Authentication

   b.   Integrity

   c.   Confidentiality

   d.   Antiplayback

20. Which of the following algorithms are used to check for data integrity? (Choose two.)

   a.   AES

   b.   SHA

   c.   3DES

   d.   MD5

Answers to Chapter Review Questions

Chapter 1

1. D
2. B
3. A
4. A
5. A
6. B
7. C
8. C
9. A
10. __A__ Context-sensitive help

    __C__ Console error messages

    __B__ Command history buffer
11. A
12. __B__ Line

    __D__ Router

    __A__ Interface

    __E__ Controller

    __C__ Subinterface
13. D
14. B
15. C

Chapter 2

1. A

2. D

3. A and E

4. D

5. A

6. B

7. C

8. D

9. C

10. A

11. C

12. D

13. B, C, and E

14. C

15. C

16. A

17. C

18. A

19. A

20. B

21. A

22. D

23. A

24. C

25. D

26. C

27. B

28. C

29. C

30. C

31. B

32. D

Chapter 3

1. B

2. B

3. C

4. B

5. A

6. A

7. B

8. B

9. A

10. A and C

11. D

12. A

13. A and C

14. D

15. C

16. C

17. B

18. C

19. B

20. A

Chapter 4

1. A and C
2. D
3. B
4. A
5. A
6. A
7. B
8. B
9. D

Chapter 5

1. C
2. C
3. D
4. B
5. C
6. C
7. B

Chapter 6

1. C
2. A
3. A
4. A
5. D
6. C and F
7. A
8. C

9. C

10. B

11. B, C, and E

12. B

13. C

14. C

Chapter 7

1.   __C__ 1. Static NAT

     __D__ 2. Dynamic NAT

     __A__ 3. Inside local

     __B__ 4. Inside global

2. A

3. D

4.   __A__ 1. **ip nat inside**

     __B__ 2. **ip nat outside**

     __E__ 3. **access-list 1 permit 10.1.1.0 0.0.0.255**

     __D__ 4. **ip nat inside source list 1 pool nat-pool overload**

     __C__ 5. **ip nat pool nat-pool 192.1.1.17 192.1.1.20 netmask 255.255.255.240**

5. D

6. B

7. A, D, and E

8. B

9. B

10. C

11. A

12. D

13. A

14. C

15. C

16. D

17. A and E

18. B and C

19. B

20. A and E

Chapter 8

1. A

2. B

3. A

4. A and C

5. A

6. B

7. C

8. __B__ Local access rate

   __D__ SVC

   __A__ CIR

   __E__ LMI

   __C__ Inverse ARP

9. A

1. __C__ Star

   __A__ Full-mesh

   __B__ Partial-mesh

2. D

3. D

4. B, C, and E

5. C

6. D

   7. A and D

   8. C

   9. D

   10. B

   11. B and D

Index

J - K - L

W - X - Y - Z

SEARCH THOUSANDS OF BOOKS FROM LEADING PUBLISHERS

Safari® Bookshelf is a searchable electronic reference library for IT professionals that features more than 2,000 titles from technical publishers, including Cisco Press.

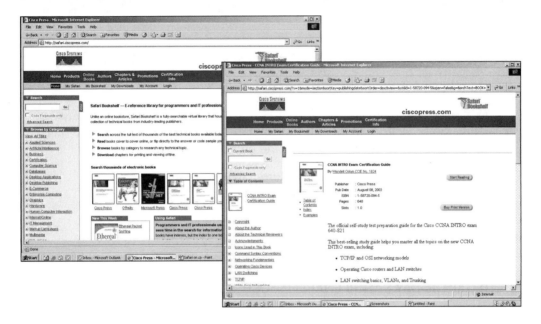

With Safari Bookshelf you can

- **Search** the full text of thousands of technical books, including more than 70 Cisco Press titles from authors such as Wendell Odom, Jeff Doyle, Bill Parkhurst, Sam Halabi, and Karl Solie.

- **Read** the books on My Bookshelf from cover to cover, or just flip to the information you need.

- **Browse** books by category to research any technical topic.

- **Download** chapters for printing and viewing offline.

With a customized library, you'll have access to your books when and where you need them—and all you need is a user name and password.

TRY SAFARI BOOKSHELF FREE FOR 14 DAYS!

You can sign up to get a 10-slot Bookshelf free for the first 14 days.
Visit **http://safari.ciscopress.com** to register.

BOOKS ONLINE

ENABLED

THIS BOOK IS SAFARI ENABLED

INCLUDES FREE 45-DAY ACCESS TO THE ONLINE EDITION

The Safari® Enabled icon on the cover of your favorite technology book means the book is available through Safari Bookshelf. When you buy this book, you get free access to the online edition for 45 days.

Safari Bookshelf is an electronic reference library that lets you easily search thousands of technical books, find code samples, download chapters, and access technical information whenever and wherever you need it.

TO GAIN 45-DAY SAFARI ENABLED ACCESS TO THIS BOOK:

- Go to **http://www.ciscopress.com/safarienabled**

- Complete the brief registration form

- Enter the coupon code found in the front of this book before the "Contents at a Glance" page

If you have difficulty registering on Safari Bookshelf or accessing the online edition, please e-mail customer-service@safaribooksonline.com.